ReCreating Strategy

Praise for the book

Do you worry about organizations becoming slaves to markets? Do you wish that organizations had the nerve to build their own ethos rather than just grubbing for profit? Do you aspire to inspiration rather than perspiration? Why does management practice get in the way of thinking and creativity? Stephen Cummings provides insight and guidance in a book of genuine scholarship and creativity.

John McGee, President of the Strategic Management Society

I thoroughly recommend the book as a way of teaching strategy in a new and invigorating way.

Stewart Clegg, University of Technology, Sydney

Management courses need more of what Stephen is offering. He wants us to go on an 'unlearning curve', one which leads to fresh thinking about strategy and the emerging roles and responsibilities of business and companies. This book not only tells us where we are coming from but, more importantly, it inspires us to think profoundly about where we could go. It's also a very good read.

Josephine Green, Director of Trends and Strategy, Philips

Recreating Strategy provides a challenging examination of the emergence of management. Stephen Cummings is able to provide not only a fresh treatment of strategy and ethics but also to engage with a variety of potential audiences. He provokes and informs in equal measure.

Richard Whipp, Cardiff University

A truly eclectic approach to strategy! Intellectually capturing, the book is great fun to read at the same time. A must for those who want to discuss management beyond styles, fads and fashions.

Hubert Wagner, Qonsult

ReCreating Strategy

Stephen Cummings

SAGE Publications
London • Thousand Oaks • New Delhi

To Denise and Joanna, Noelle and Be

SAGE Publications Ltd
6 Bonhill Street
London EC2A 4PU

SAGE Publications Inc
2455 Teller Road
Thousand Oaks, California 91320

SAGE Publications India Pvt Ltd
32, M-Block Market
Greater Kailash - I
New Delhi 110 048

British Library Cataloguing in Publication data

A catalogue record for this book is available
from the British Library

ISBN 0 7619 7009 6
ISBN 0 7619 7010 X (pbk)

Library of Congress Control Number: 2002108296

Typeset by C&M Digitals (P) Ltd., Chennai, India
Printed and bound in Great Britain by Athenaeum Press, Gateshead

Contents

List of Figures and Table

Figures

Table

Acknowledgements

This book is a synthesis of the ideas of others, more than one of original scholarship. As such its contributors are many. However, one of the key ideas behind its conception was to introduce a range of subject matter to students of strategy and management that would go beyond their conventional ambit, without getting bogged down in an exacting and overly academic style of referencing. To enable this, I chose – with some concern about setting aside academic conventions – not to burden the text with dense citations. While bibliographical notes are provided at the end of the book, I apologize in advance to those who would have preferred a more conventional, scholarly style. My defence is that this book is written not for researchers or scholars of management, but for managers, or students who will one day become, or return to being, managers, with the simple aim of provoking them to think differently about strategy.

While the aforementioned bibliographical notes convey my debt to the words of others, they do not convey the extent to which this book has gained from those I would count more as my friends than as scholars (although they generally fall into both categories). Sophia Lum, John Brocklesby, David Stewart and John Davies, from Victoria University of Wellington. Roger Dunbar from the Stern School of Business in New York. Richard Dunford from the University of Western Sydney. Dominique Bouchet from Odense University in Denmark. Jane Parker, Noelle Donnelly, Francesco Curto, Chantal Rivest, Tom Cooper, Javier Quintanilla, Bitten Hansen, Martin Brigham, Torkild Thanem, Ianna Contardo, Gerrado Patriotta, Manuela Faia-Correia, Carmen and Luis Lages, Paula Jarzabkowski, Bridgette Sullivan-Taylor, Katy Mason, Jonathan Menuhin, Ilan Oshri, Claudia Simoes and the many others with whom I worked toward a doctorate at Warwick Business School. Sheila Frost, Janet Biddle, Ann Evans, Duncan Angwin, Chris Smith, David Wilson, John McGee, Andrew Pettigrew, Simon Collinson, Sue Bridgewater, Scott Dacko, Ian Munro, Gibson Burrell, Robin Wensley, Haridimos Tsoukas and Bob Galliers, whom I have been so fortunate to work with at WBS. All of these people are contributors to *ReCreating Strategy*.

Most of the cases and case boxes described in the book have been developed with the help of students and/or helpful, enthusiastic and open-mined people within the respective organizations described. These people are acknowledged by name in the notes at the end of the relevant cases. I am also indebted to Niki Hastings-McFall for allowing me to use her art on the cover, and to many others, for allowing me to use their images to illustrate many of the ideas that could really only be expressed fully in pictures.

Thanks also to Rosemary Nixon for being so enthusiastic about the initial proposal for this book, to Kiren Shoman and Gladys Calix-Ferguson for continuing in that vein, and to Rachel Burrows, Keith Von Tersch and Verity Wood and everyone else at Sage for seeing what was not an unproblematic book through to production.

Lastly, I would like to thank the many students at Victoria, Warwick, and Vlerick Business School in Belgium, who suffered through, wrestled with and constructively criticised earlier drafts of the material that added up to this book. Their patience and enthusiasm for being not just consumers but producers taught me much about what worked, what did not but could have, and what never would.

Stephen Cummings

Every effort has been made to trace all the copyright holders, but if any have been inadvertantly overlooked the publishers will be pleased to make the necessary arrangement at the first opportunity.

Case Box 1.2: S. Cummings, 'The Organizational Advantages of Double Vision', *Proceedings of the 1992 Anzam Conference*; J. Glancey, 'Beautiful Strangeness', *Guardian*, 4 November 2000.

Figure 2.1: L.R. Farrell, *The Cults of Greek States*, Top, Volume IV, Plate III, p. 331, 1907; Bottom, Volume V, Plate XLIV, p. 264, 1907. Oxford: The Clarendon Press.

Figure 2.2: Top, Munich, Bayr. Staats-Bibl., ms. Lat. 13003, f. 7v; Bottom, Copenhagen, Kongel-Bibl., G1. Kgl. S. 78, f. 8r.

Figure 2.3: O. Lodge, *Pioneers of Science*, Figure 15, p. 29, 1893. London: Richard Clay and Sons.

Figure 2.4: Vienna, Nat-Bibl., ms. 2359, f. 52v.

Figure 2.5: Archives Nationales de France.

Figure 2.6: Bordone, *Isolario*, 1528. Venice.

Figure 2.7: Top, reproduced by kind permission of the Marquess of Tavistock and the Trustees of the Bedford Estate; Bottom, reproduced by kind permission of the National Portrait Gallery, London.

Figure 2.8: J.T. Bonner, *The Ideas of Biology*, Figure 8, p. 68, 1963. London: Eyre & Spohistroode. © J.T. Bonner.

Figure 2.9: D. Diderot, *Encyclopedie*, frontispiece of Volume 1 of the index, c. 1751-80. Paris: Hermann.

Figure 2.10: Top, Leonardo da Vinci, c. 1500, reproduced by gracious permission of Her Majesty the Queen; Bottom, G.A. Borelli, 1680, reproduced by kind permission of the syndics of Cambridge University Library.

Figure 2.12: Photograph reproduced by kind permission of Ian Nolan.

Case Box 2.2: 'Back to Classic Coke', *Financial Times*, 27 March 2000; 'Ice-cold Times for an Icon', *Independent*, 20 January 2000; H. Pearman, 'Curiouser and Curiouser', *The Sunday Times*, 7 February 1999; R. Hutton, 'A Vintage Harvest', *The Sunday Times*, 7 January 2001.

Case Box 3.3: 'The Quest for Quality', *Time*, 27 August 2001.

Figure 4.1: Top, S.P. Robbins, *Organization Theory, third edition*, Figure 1.1, p. 13, 1990. Upper Saddle River, NJ: Pearson Education. Reprinted by permission of Pearson Education Inc.; Bottom, G. Morgan, *Images of Organization*, Figure 3.3, p. 43, 1997. Beverly Hills, CA: Sage.

Figure 4.2: H.G. Wells, J. Huxley and G.P. Wells, *The Science of Life*, Figure 26, p. 51, 1931. London: Cassell.

Figure 4.3: H. Mintzberg, *Structure in Fives: Designing Effective Organizations, second edition*, Figure 1.2, p. 11, 1983. Upper Saddle River, NJ: Pearson Education. Reprinted by permission of Pearson Education Inc. © Henry Mintzberg.

Case Box 4.2: '"Asian Culture" Link in Jet Crashes', *Time*, 19 March 1998; 'Crashes Put Aviation in Spotlight in Asia', *Nando Times*, 16 December 1998; A.C. Merritt and R.L. Helmrich, 'Culture in the Cockpit', *Proceedings of the Eighth International Symposium on Aviation Psychology*, Columbus OH, 2000.

Figure 4.4: Top, photograph by Adrian Sherratt accompanying 'KPMG Chief Proposes Far-reaching Changes' article in *The Times* (21 February 1998) © Adrian Sheratt/Times Newspapers Limited, London.

Case Box 4.4: 'Health Service Damned by Virgin Report', *Scotsman*, 22 July 2000; 'Virgin Team Highlights NHS Shambles', *Guardian*, 22 July 2000; 'How Labour has Blown £1 billion on Consulting Outside "Experts"', *Independent on Sunday*, 28 May 2000; 'Britain Asks Virgin's Branson for Advice of Hospitals; Workers Skeptical', *Financial Post*, 8 May 2000.

Figure 5.1: C.W.L. Hill and G.R. Jones, *Strategic Management: An Integrated Approach, fourth edition*, Figure 2.6, p. 62, 1998. Boston, MA: Houghton Mifflin Company © 1998 by Houghton Mifflin Company. Reprinted with permission.

Case Box 5.2: 'Who's Your Favourite Television Channel', *The Times*, 2 September 1998; '"Channel Filth" Plays the Family Card', *Guardian*, 12 August 2000; 'Channel 5 Boss Demands Explicit Sex on Television', *Independent*, 21 August 2000.

Figure 5.2: A. Campbell, D. Young and M. Devine, *A Sense of Mission*, Figure 1.1, 1993. London: FT Pitman. Ashridge Mission Model used with permission of the authors.

Case Box 5.4: 'Science Body Snubs "Impractical" Ethics Oath', *The Times Higher Education Supplement*, 2 March 2001.

Case Box 5.5: 'Lager Than Life', *Marketing*, 23 April 1998; 'John Smith's in £10m Sales Push', *Marketing*, 9 September 1998; 'Media Case Study: John Smith's', *Marketing*, 23 September 1998; 'Cardboard Cut-out With Cult Status', *Scotsman*, 24 September 1998; 'Live Update', *Campaign*, 25 September 1998; 'Design and Advertising Brave an Uneasy Alliance', *Campaign*, 14 May 1999.

Figure 6.1: H.I. Ansoff, *Business Strategy*, Figure 1, p. 14, 1969. Harmondsworth: Penguin.

Figure 6.2: M.E. Porter, *Competitive Advantage: Creating and Sustaining Superior Performance*, Figure 2.2, p. 37, 1985/1998. New York: Free Press. Reprinted with the permission of the Free Press, a division of Simon & Schuster, Inc. © 1985, 1998 by Michael E. Porter.

Figure 6.3: M.E. Porter, *Competitive Strategy: Techniques for Analyzing Industries and Competitors*, Figure 1.1, p. 4, 1980/1998. New York: Free Press. Reprinted with the permission of the Free Press, a division of Simon & Schuster, Inc. © 1980, 1998 by the Free Press.

Figure 6.4: M.E. Porter, *Competitive Strategy: Techniques for Analyzing Industries and Competitors*, Figure 2.1, p. 39, 1980/1998. New York: Free Press. Reprinted with the permission of the Free Press, a division of Simon & Schuster, Inc. © 1980, 1998 by the Free Press.

Figure 6.5: H.I. Ansoff, *Implanting Strategic Management*, Figure 7.2.4, p. 467, 1984. Englewood Cliffs, NJ: Prentice-Hall.

Figure 6.6: Dilbert cartoon reproduced by permission of Knight Features and United Media © Scott Adams.

Figure 6.7: Maps reproduced with the kind permission of The London Transport Museum.

Case Box: 6.4: 'Women's Sociable Route to Success', *Financial Times*, 24 March 2000.

Case Box 7.1: 'Jersey Beat', *The Times*, 19 May 1988; 'Liverpool Show Way Forward', *The Times*, 21 December 1999; 'Best League Table in the World … Ever!', *The Times*, 1 January 2000; 'Managing to Put the Side Back into Mersey, *Irish Sunday Tribune*, 13 February 2000; 'IMF in Need of New Faith', *Guardian*, 17 April 2000; 'Eco Soundings', *Guardian*, 19 April 2000; 'Bill and Dave Show', *Human Resources*, January/February 1996; 'Cook Sells Britain's New Look Abroad', *The Times*, 23 July 1999.

Figure 7.1: Top, D. Nadler and M. Tushman, 'A Model for Diagnosing Organizational Behavior', *Organizational Dynamics*, Autumn 1980: 35–51; Bottom, R. Beck, 'Bank of America Change Agenda', *The Academy of Management Executive*, February 1987: 33–41, reproduced with the permission of The Academy of Management Executive.

Figure 7.2: J.P. Kotter, 'Why Transformation Efforts Fail', *Harvard Business Review*, March–April 1995: 59–67. Reproduced with the permission of the Harvard Business Review.

Figure 7.4: S. Cummings and J. Brocklesby, 'Toward Demokratia: Myth and the Management of Change in Ancient Athens', *Journal of Organizational Change Management*, 1997, 10 (1): 71–95. © S. Cummings.

Figure 7.5: Special thanks to Matt Hardisty and Stacy Arnold.

Case Box 7.3: D. Thomas, 'Why Pat Must be Saved for the Nation', *Independent*, 28 November 2000.

Case 2: 'The Crisp Wars', *Cara Magazine*, May/June 2000.

Case 3: 'A New Chapter', *Guardian*, 2 December 1999; 'Expansion and the Net Take Toll of Ottakar's', *The Times*, 12 April 2000; 'Site Test', *Doors*, 29 April 2001.

Case 4: 'Critics Can't Stop Swatting the Swoosh', *Footwear News*, 26 May 1997; 'Is it Time to Jump on Nike?', *Fortune*, 26 May 1997; 'Nike's New Sneaker Challenge', *WWD*, 18 September 1997; 'Is Nike No Longer Cool?', *Financial Times*, 20 December 1997; 'I Will Just do it Better, Hope Nike', *Financial Times*, 1 January 1998; 'S&P Downgrades Nike', *WWD*, 18 March 1998; 'Can Nike get Unstuck', *Time*, 30 March 1998; R. Goldman and S. Papson, *Nike Culture*, 1998, London: Sage; 'Shoe Giants are Caught on the Hop', *European*, 5 April 1998; 'Down at Heel: can Nike Change Directon?', *The Sunday Times*, 23 August 1998; 'Nike to Sport a Smaller "Swoosh"', *Financial Times*, 16 September 1998; 'Nike's Plea: Judge us by our Actions', *Financial Times*, 25 January 1999; 'Nike Seeks a Footpath Back to Growth', *Financial Times*, 20 March 1999; 'Nike Takes the Pain in its Stride', *Financial Times*, 15 August 1999; 'Nike Agrees to Show Students its Factories', *Financial Times*, 12 November 1999.

1 Deconstructing History, ReCreating Strategy

It is obvious that invention or discovery takes place by combining ideas. The Latin verb cogito *for 'to think' etymologically means 'to shake together' ... The creative act, by connecting previously unrelated dimensions of experience is an act of liberation – the defeat of habit by originality.*

Arthur Koestler

At the end of the twentieth century a revisionist history caused something of a stir in New Zealand. James Belich argued that the native Maori had won most of their battles against the colonizing British forces. While the evidence present at the time clearly showed this to be the case, when the history of New Zealand was written up in the subsequent decades (by Europeans) the British were described as universally victorious. Over time, the idea that things could have been different became absurd.

The Maori won, Belich argued, not by chance or brute force (they were already vastly outnumbered by British troops at the outset of the Wars), nor did they win because of British incompetence, as some of the writers of the time, more in tune with the actual results, suggested. They won through strategies that combined their local traditions and local knowledge with elements borrowed from modern European technologies; strategies that were designed and *ad hoc*; strategies that were coordinated to suit their unique strengths and weaknesses. However, this was not strategy as the British had been brought up to understand it. It did not appear to be based on a hierarchical chain of command, it was not meticulously planned and handed down from the 'men at the top', and it was not based on established military 'best practice'. European writers were subsequently disdainful. 'No strategical knowledge was shewn by the Maori.' 'The Maori displayed the military weaknesses generally associated with savage races ... he fought under no definite strategical plan and without unity of command.' 'They lacked enterprise, perseverance in a single line of action, and a knowledge of the broader principles of campaigning.' '[The Maori's courage] was not matched by strategic sense.' And so on. These misconceptions persisted throughout the Wars and became further entrenched as later writers, right up until our own times, referred to these earlier accounts as 'evidence'.

New Zealand's most commonly used high-school history text in the 1980s and 1990s told students that 'throughout the wars the Maoris adopted no co-ordinated strategy.'

Belich went on to suggest that there was much that Europeans could have learnt from these Wars, had they considered the Maori worthy of learning from. For example, a long forgotten fact is the Maori's invention of the artillery bunker and trench warfare, a system developed through the adaptation of traditional forts (*pa*) in response to modern rifles and artillery. Even during the Wars the European commanders did not seem able to take account of what the Maori had created and why they were inflicting so many casualties. In 1860, after another humiliating reverse in which the artillery sergeant described the resistance enabled by the *pa* his company faced as 'a cause of extreme surprise', the British had the opportunity to visit the fortifications. Despite the fact that the *pa's* construction was more or less the same as those visited by the sergeant's predecessors over the past 15 years, he reported that its insides were 'curiously hollowed out.'

As Belich stood upon an old *pa*, overgrown and forgotten but still readily apparent, recreating the battles for a television documentary based on his research, it was hard to believe that the Maori's achievement in this regard had not been acknowledged. And hard not to agree that the European wars of the early twentieth century might have been fought differently, had the British allowed their previously effective habits to be challenged by 'shaking' their and the Maori's traditions together. 'It is true,' Belich concluded, 'that Maori organization was informal and unstructured. But the absence of European forms of organization does not mean that organization *per se* was absent.'

One hundred and fifty years on we find an interesting parallel. In the 1990s, a group of management theorists disagreed with the mainstream view of 'what strategy was'. The mainstream view was that strategy happened 'at the top', over and above operations. It should be a rational *planning* process whereby an organization's strengths are consciously mapped on to projected market needs. However, the 'mavericks' began to wonder as they examined the success of certain Asian companies. Strategy, they argued, was actually about an *emergent* pattern of behaviour, chance and opportunism. After a decade of increasingly fractious debate between those who supported the emergence perspective and those who backed the planning view, strategic management's most powerful voice, Michael Porter, stepped in to sort things out. In a *Harvard Business Review* paper he dismissed the new thinking, arguing that 'Japanese companies rarely have strategies [as they] rarely develop a distinct strategic position, [a concept that was] once the heart of strategy.' (In 2001 Porter went further, claiming in *The Wall Street Journal* that the Japanese companies are just 'bad at strategy'.) Hence, he concluded in his *HBR* article that we were in danger of being mislead and distracted by 'dangerous half-truths' that confuse strategy with other things. We must, Porter stressed, return to 'the heart of strategy.'

Placing these two visions of history side by side today raises some interesting questions for strategy, and the discipline on which it is based, management:

1 If the British vision and ability to learn at the end of the nineteenth century was limited by its being so blinkered as to not recognize anything other than approaches that confirmed its preconceptions, is the same not true of strategy and management as they leave the twentieth?
2 Is the vision of the 'heart of strategy' that Porter uses to dismiss Eastern views any less cultural or contingent than that which informed the British and New Zealand historians one hundred years previously? Eastern approaches may be different, but does that mean that strategy *per se* is absent?
3 If management and strategy are limited in this way, and if these limits are contingent and cultural rather than fundamental, can we be inspired to think strategy differently by deconstructing management's historical preconceptions?

ReCreating Strategy investigates these questions.

How management and strategy may be limited by our view of their history

The limitations of management thinking are not difficult to see, if one looks for them. Despite the fact that management, perhaps more than any other field, is littered with claims of 'revolutionary new theories', most of these, when placed up against earlier management theories, seem incremental at best and obviously the same view with a snappy new title at worst. (Later chapters will outline many examples of this). But what, if anything, might preconceptions of history have to do with this? Some clues may be found by exploring the ideas of Michel Foucault, the most prominent revisionist historian of the past 30 years. Before his death in the 1980s, Foucault's examination of fields like psychology and criminology did much to show how a subject's accepted history can unwittingly limit our ability to see things differently.

Foucault argued that people look to history to sort through things so as to show that the present rests upon profound intentions and immutable necessities, largely because they are troubled by the notion that their conventions might otherwise be perceived as foundationless. In order to ensure our belief in current conventions, historians scour the past for their 'grand origin' and demonstrate how we have built from there to our present state. What historians interpret these origins to be then become the fundamental 'foundation stones' of a subject or a practice. In a circular manner, these foundations make possible a field of knowledge that then sets out to reveal those foundations. This 'truth' of what a field of knowledge is, at base, about, then becomes irrefutable or common knowledge. Hardened into an unalterable form through uncritical repetition it becomes increasingly difficult to challenge or undo.

All practice and knowledge is subsequently related to an understanding of history and all history is largely a series of circular interpretations. The series of interpretations favoured in a society depends upon the cultural conventions, contingencies and problems faced by that society at a particular point in time, rather than things that were actually thought in earlier times. 'In placing current needs at the origin,' Foucault explains, a subject's history 'would convince us of an obscure purpose that sought its realization at the moment it arose.' Subjects that thrive are subsequently those that match current conditions and perceived needs. Thus, the interpretations of history that order our knowledge have been created and imposed by contingent interests, not by the essential nature of things.

So, our historical foundations may have no real objective foundation, but they have real effects in shaping knowledge. The obvious question then is 'If there is nothing positive that knowledge can attach itself to, what sustains our belief in the interpretations that we take as framing our quests for knowledge?' What enables one interpretation of events to prevail over other potential interpretations in the construction of history and knowledge once the conditions that initially encouraged their emergence have passed?

Foucault found the answer to be 'power'. However, this was not power as a possession that one body holds and uses against others. The power that Foucault saw sustaining knowledge was more subtle than that. The power that sustains knowledge is a complex network of relations running between things, a network that generates and then reinforces a particular view through repeating and reduplicating it until it eventually becomes a 'preconception'. By establishing and ordering a subject, by setting out what a particular field of knowledge is about and what it is not, power networks make the development of a 'body of knowledge' possible. However, while this power is positive, producing knowledge out of uncertainty in this sense, it also limits or represses knowledge. As they bring about a focus that enables us to build knowledge or a particular subject of inquiry, relations of power diminish the likelihood of looking in other ways. For example, the moment that the first professional management associations in the 1950s defined management as fundamentally about 'efficiency', 'the division of labour', 'planning', 'directing' and 'controlling', the subject was driven to only consider management in these terms.

Which brings us back to history. Playing an integral part in the power/knowledge network of a field is the history that a subject constructs for itself out of a multiplicity of potentially contributing elements. This historical aspect *produces* by reinforcing the view and boundaries of the subject that make knowledge possible. However, it at once *represses* any other interpretations that could challenge that subject's conventional truths and standing in society. This network may not be consciously developed, but it is played out in a subject's words. For example, textbooks used to educate and initiate students tend to reduplicate events and origins taken to be important so as to nullify, over time, their particularity and cultural contingency, in order to make them seem 'regular' or beyond doubt. This historical common sense with regard to the fundamental heart of subject then becomes useful to people that want to dismiss creative interpretations or approaches.

These theories of how historical preconceptions can limit alternative ideas and creativity may be better understood by relating the example of the subjects of psychology and psychoanalysis and their object 'mental illness'. Foucault argued that they emerged through the coming together of a network of contingencies. The decline of leprosy in Europe in the middle of the last millennium provided a vacancy for social outcasts. The Modern era's move away from traditional forms of governance and discipline required new scientific norms of behaviour to be woven into the fabric of life. This lead to a quest for general classifications – including what was sane and what was insane. The growth of scientific reason encouraged looking for linear-rational cause and effects and the development of Christianity had created a prevailing logic where 'confession' was seen as 'therapeutic'. The coming together of these events led to mental 'abnormality' being seen both as a problem to be solved and one that was solvable. The asylums left empty by the decline of leprosy created an institutional space, or 'laboratory', within which those with 'abnormalities' could be housed, classified and studied toward further refinement of classifications. Eventually the relations between these elements became self-fulfilling and self-sustaining.

However, despite the emergence of objects like mental illness in this non-linear and contingent manner, the history of the subjects that study such objects, like psychology, are generally constituted when a particular group with a particular agenda (for example, to show that their chosen field – such as psychology – is, in actual fact, a worthy science) feel it necessary. Hence the history of a subject generally overlooks the contingencies and presents a linear and evolutionary view of an object that has always existed but which has not been understood as well as it might, showing it to be truly worthy of further investigation. So, when early psychologists drew up their history of their fledgling science the lepers were 'airbrushed out'. But they did incorporate great thinkers like Socrates, St. Augustine and Shakespeare, and looked at how they gradually pieced together the mysteries of madness toward the Modern era's eventual scientific uncovering of the whole 'truth' about it. All this, despite the fact that the likes of Plato and Shakespeare pre-existed most of the conditions that enabled our classification of mental illness, and the fact that the societies in which they lived had very different ways of relating to people whom we would call 'mentally ill'. Different ways whose consideration was made increasingly unlikely by the 'official history' of psychiatry being increasingly taught to new initiates as the fundamental basis that we must build upon: a basis that increasingly went unquestioned by the wider public.

Hence, as Foucault explained, anybody concerned with 'thinking differently instead of just legitimating what is already known' (about psychology or anything else) must question established historical conceptions. Consequently, while this book is primarily concerned with how management could be thought differently, it firstly questions the conventional history of management.

In a nutshell, this history promotes the view that all clever civilizations and all great men have attempted to be more efficient through planning, dividing labour, directing and controlling. Over time our understanding of how best to do this has evolved and gradually progressed toward its present heights. However, *ReCreating Strategy's* deconstruction of this history argues that the creation of management follows a similar pattern to that found by Foucault of psychology. There are two key networks of events, one relating to the formation of the objects of management, the other relating to the formation of the subject.

First, the network of objects that we refer to as management's primary elements emerge in the US in the period around 1900. Here an 'institutional space' was created by the need to make things for a growing economy with an immigrant workforce from diverse backgrounds, who were often unskilled and spoke different languages, but were arriving into a land without the 'encumbrance' of a traditional community's architectural and geographical legacies or craft production values. Factory production as the main mode of manufacture became a possibility and, given communication difficulties and levels of growth, simple and general procedures were seen as necessary. Organizations came to be viewed as machines, and machines were subject to general principles. It should not be a surprise, therefore, that the first management gurus were engineers. They brought to bear a new measure of machine performance that had become popular in the last part of the nineteenth century – 'efficiency', understood as the ratio of inputs over outputs. The laws of efficiency, combined with the prevailing military logic of the time, led to management as we know it and the factory environment provided the 'laboratories' within which 'management principles' could be tested out, categorized and refined.

These new principles quickly spread into other areas of life. At the local level, the productivity gains that could now be shown through their being measured in laboratory-like conditions set off an 'efficiency craze' in the US in the early part of the twentieth century. The concept was quickly applied in all manner of spheres, from sports to religious worship. Theodore Roosevelt even latched on to it as a national slogan in a campaign to encourage Americans to focus on their commonalities rather than the differences. It was self-evident, argued Roosevelt, that all 'Good Americans', whatever their origin, were 'Efficient Americans'. At the global level, management, as the 'science of efficiency', seemed to provide an answer to another of the Modern era's particular quests: the quest for a universal value-neutral end that could be employed to measure all things, but was itself seemingly independent of particular and personal circumstances. In bringing forward 'efficiency' as this universal aim, management seemed to have succeeded where other fledgling sciences, like ethics, had been recently seen to fail.

A second network emerged around the 1950s, again primarily in the US. By this time, management as a practice was well entrenched, but it was still not regarded as a 'serious academic subject'. A network of forces came together to help it to become established. Crucial within this network was the writing of a grand and noble history. This history identified those turn-of-the-century factory engineers as pioneers. However, it also delved further back, showing how all the world's 'great civilizations and men' (the Egyptians, the Greeks, the Romans, Plato, Jesus and so on) had also known and practiced management, albeit in simple terms, and that their 'advances' provided the foundation stones that more scientifically-minded men could build upon and refine.

ReCreating Strategy argues that this history and the conventional view of management that it reinforces are just as culturally biased and historically contingent as those perspectives that Porter and New Zealand historians claimed 'were not strategy'. It is just that the history of the 'heart' of management was first composed in the West by men (and they were all men) who did not recognize how their particular concerns led them to create a self-legitimating history. Indeed, much of the historical 'heart' of management and strategy, particularly that seem to have taken place prior to 1900, is a myth – a modern invention to make prevailing views of the first half of the twentieth century seem more worthy. However, over time this myth became an unquestionably true and thus a largely taken for granted collection of thoughts – a foundation imbued with certain solidity.

The need to deconstruct history and think differently now

Founding mythologies are, in themselves, no bad things with regard to a subject's ability to be creative, if they promote a confidence to try new things that otherwise might not be attempted. However, after having helped produce management as we now understand it, the history-myth of the heart of management and strategy now represses, in two compounding and increasingly worrying ways:

1   The mythology is unidimensional: it refers only to a narrow set of mono-cultural practices. For example, historians might interpret, and we might subsequently be taught, that the Egyptians 'did management' because they appear to have engaged in simple forms of planning, coordinating, directing and controlling in building the pyramids. But no mention is made of the particular spiritual identity that gave the Egyptians' work purpose, or of how their style of management may have been different from ours (and no mention is made of the slavery involved – this is not 'good press'). Apparently these things are not what management is

concerned with and they are certainly not at 'the heart of management'. However, creative leaps spring from the coming together of different traditions, the 'co-agitation or shaking together of already existing but previously unrelated dimensions,' in Arthur Koestler's words. Because management acknowledges only one set of historical influences, and because it only shakes hands with those who have already bought into its logic, it is quite good at efficiently achieving refinements and increments, but not so good at truly creative development (the antithesis of incremental efficiency).

2 Management students have, at best, a cursory knowledge of the history of management. The mainstream of management ceased seeing its history as particularly important almost as soon as management was established as a university subject (how many MBA students think critically about the history of their field?). Because of this lack of critical reflection on its history, management is destined to keep repeating it, and what gets repeated is the same unidimensional set. In George Santayana's famous words: 'Those who cannot remember the past are destined to repeat it.'

This limitation has wider ramifications than ever before, because management now pervades and passes judgment upon so much of how we live. The logic of management could be an even more pervasive and compelling element at the beginning of the twenty-first century than the British Empire was in the nineteenth. Not only businesses, but also schools, hospitals, architects, scientific research organizations and sports teams, subject themselves to analysis by management 'consultants'. Management has become the world's fastest growing tertiary education subject to keep up with the demand. Even traditional overseers like elected governments seem increasingly overseen by management thinking.

Given the extent to which management now permeates the way we judge life, management's limits now potentially undermine our ability to think differently in the twenty-first century in other spheres. We have begun to witness an outpouring of creative works in other applied fields such as medicine, architecture, physics and art through their revisiting different dimensions or styles from their pasts; through their modern developments and technologies shaking hands with other traditions and thus bouncing off in different creative directions. However, the danger is that one of our most unidimensional and least creative applied subjects is now being increasingly employed to monitor and judge the performance of our most creative. This may mean that instead of the multidimensional society necessary to enable creative development to continue, the unidimensional logic of management and strategy could end up overriding other fields in such a way as to limit us to bouncing within the twentieth century's mantra of 'development in the name of efficiency', as the diagram below illustrates.

It is argued here that management has achieved this overriding status not because it is fundamentally progressive, or a truly 'value-neutral' subject as

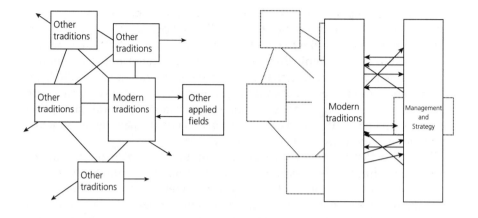

is often thought. Management's status is rather due to its matching the cultural conventions of the Modern era or a way of seeing called 'Modernism'. It appeared to solve a problem that had troubled Westerners in the eighteenth and nineteenth centuries (but which they themselves had created). It fitted a particular mindset that prevailed in the US at the turn of the twentieth century, and the myth of its fundamentality sank deep into the fabric of life in the middle of the same century.

For these reasons, management, as we have come to understand it, is also a very difficult thing to unpick. However, its ingrained nature also makes its unravelling increasingly imperative. Only by understanding that the history of management handed down to us is not the only possible interpretation of events, or the only understanding of what management could be, can we create the 'space' necessary to begin to recreate the subject, question the way it now rules other subjects, and take things in different directions. Deconstructing the history of management, showing its development to be contingent rather than fundamental, is a crucial step toward thinking differently and creatively in the twenty-first century.

An outline of *ReCreating Strategy*

Part One of *ReCreating Strategy*, entitled 'Deconstructing Management', provides a revisionist history. It comprises three chapters. Chapter 2, 'Premodernism, Modernism and Postmodernism', outlines three ways of seeing in order to illustrate that Modernism, which provides the preconditions necessary for seeing management and strategy as we do, is not the only, or necessarily the best, way of conceptualizing development.

Chapter 3 'Deconstructing Management's History', outlines the conventional history of management before seeking to undermine its foundational authority with an alternative or 'counter' history. It investigates how management arose at the end of the nineteenth century as 'the science of efficiency' – a response to a problem created by Modernism's dismissal of Premodern ways of thinking. It then looks at how a 'noble history' was created in the middle of the twentieth century in order to validate management's status as an academic discipline. It concludes by examining how this history has shaped a subject that is, in actual fact, extremely limited. As management can only ever be Modernist (even ancient non-Westerners are seen to have acted along Modernist lines), it is a mono-cultural conception that is not well conceived to inspire creativity, hence its 'new developments' are strikingly similar to the theories they replace.

Chapter 4, 'Management's Historical Limits', illustrates how strategic management thinking has been constrained by its mono-cultural historical conception disabling its ability to take different views seriously. Rather than being challenged or shaken by them, management tends to take different dimensions and adapt them to fit its prevailing logic or habits, thereby limiting creative thinking.

Part I's deconstruction of management provides both bad and good news. The bad news is that management's history has configured the field to disregard difference and cultural and spiritual identity in favour of a Modernist focus on economics, technology, function and efficiency. However, the good news is that because this history was largely constructed according to particular contingencies, it need not serve as a fundamental limit. Hence management, and the view of strategy that grew out of it, may be recreated.

Part II, 'ReCreating Strategy', subsequently seeks to explore how management and strategy may be liberated to think differently by opening up its history to a range of influences wider than just Modernist ones. In so doing, it follows an approach that is similar to that taken in the past two decades by a number of prominent social and scientific commentators who have advocated a re-examination of Premodern thinking as a means of rethinking Modernist assumptions in Postmodern environments. Their work suggests that highlighting how Premodern people may have thought differently and seeing these differences as legitimate alternative ways of seeing, rather than 'misguided' or 'uneducated' or stepping stones to our 'advanced thinking' today, might help us to get beyond current habits and conventions and think originally.

Thus, the ensuing approach in 'ReCreating Strategy' is *re-volutionary*, not in its Modern sense of dismissing the past and being carried forward in a new uniform direction, but in its older paradoxical sense of 'coming back around' while moving forward. And, to continue stretching our understanding of this word, a re-emphasis is also placed on 'volition'. In the light of Part I's discussion, recreating management and strategy requires that analytical and decision-making responsibility is taken back by the individuals who work within an organization's particular contexts and local traditions, rather than being the domain of expert external consultants and academics.

Part II's major 're-volitionary' aspect is its rethinking of the conventional nature and position of *strategy*. The conventional view of management sees us:

- firstly, bringing in a 'best practice' *strategy* from outside and issuing it from top;
- secondly, implementing the necessary *changes* down through the company; and
- thirdly, making sure that operations do not infringe general *ethical* boundaries.

However, *ReCreating Strategy* reworks this and advocates an inside-out approach, whereby individual organizations:

- firstly, focus in on their own unique *ethical* stance or *ethos*;
- secondly, using this to inspire *strategic* differentiation; and
- finally, using this to guide *change* from within.

To borrow Christopher Alexander's philosophy, issued with regard to creating a new approach in architecture, this inside-out rather than outside-in view is all about working with the 'particular grain of a place', about things 'growing out directly from the inner nature of particular groups of people'. Toward this end, Part II is divided into three chapters that seek to rethink the conventional histories of *business ethics, corporate strategy* and *managing change* in order to think them differently. These will be introduced in more detail at the beginning of Part II.

Using *ReCreating Strategy*

ReCreating Strategy is for anybody who wants to *think management, organization and strategy differently*. For students who already have a basic understanding of management and strategy, at the advanced undergraduate, Masters or MBA level, *ReCreating Strategy* offers a perspective that encourages them to question conventions, extend their critical faculties and rethink the future of their field. For managers who want to take more decision-making responsibility in their organizations, this book makes a case and provides a framework for focusing and building upon what they know best: their own particular organization, rather than what external consultants know best: generic best practice. For those in other spheres, like the arts or public service organizations, who find themselves increasingly trammeled by management practices and wonder if this is really the way that progress must be, *ReCreating Strategy* provides a counter-argument.

Providing this counter-argument requires going beyond the material covered in conventional management and strategy texts, material that you may not be particularly well versed in or comfortable with. In order to aid the consequent 'intellectual stretch' required of the reader, each of the chapters incorporate Case Boxes that facilitate reflection on some of the more difficult conception covered in the book by connecting them to concerns that might seem more readily apparent. However, these cases do not make life easy or close things off. Rather, in addition to aiding your understanding, they seek to keep things open by provoking debates (either within yourself or with others) that at once flesh out and cause you to consider further each of the chapter's themes.

Part III, at the end of the book, contains five more in-depth case studies that enable the reader to explore the concepts outlined throughout the book more generally. All of the cases and case boxes are intended as bases of discussion rather than as illustrations of effective or ineffective management.

Part III also comprises a section called 'Source Material and Recommended Further Readings'. This provides further background information as to where you may explore in greater detail the arguments and ideas expressed here. It also includes ideas for those who want to use this book as a teaching text.[1]

But these things will come later. If we are to rethink management, we must first rethink the history of management. It is deconstruction time.

Case Box 1.1   Management's History

To be taken seriously as a 'worthy subject' in a society, a field must meet certain cultural conventions associated with worthiness. In modernity these conventions include clearly defining the particular object or objects that that field is concerned with, the forming of centralized professional associations and becoming an accredited university subject. For management, these things began to come together in the mid-twentieth century in the US.

In 1954, the newly formed American Management Association saw determining the universality of the basic functions of management as one its most important tasks. They found these functions to be planning, organizing (defined to mean the functional division and ordering of labour) and controlling. In the same decade, management sought to become an established university subject and it was thought important that 'The History of Management' be written up.

J.D. Mooney's influential *Onward Industry* had surveyed mankind through the ages and found three universal principles of organization: coordination, scalar hierarchy, and the functional division of labour. While Mooney admitted that ancient people did not speak in the modern terms that he attributed to them (the Greeks, for example, did not have a word that equated to our Modern notion of 'efficiency'), he argued: 'That the great organizers of history applied these principles unconsciously proves only that their technique was inherent in their genius.' Thus, he went on to claim that his principles were universal and, consequently, would hold true in the future as well.

C.S. George's 1968 *History of Management Thought*, is a good representation of the many historical timelines of Management that became popular in this period.

It comprises the following early contributions:

4000 BC	Egyptians	Recognized need for planning, organizing and controlling.
1491	Hebrews	Concepts of organization, scalar principle, exception principle.
1100	Chinese	Recognized need for organization, planning, directing and controlling.
500	Chinese	Principle of specialized recognized.
	Sun Tzu	Recognized need for planning, directing and organizing.
400	Socrates	Enunciation of the universality of management.
	Xenophon	Recognized management as a separate art.
350	Greeks	Scientific method applied.
	Plato	Principle of specialization enunciated.
20 AD	Jesus Christ	Unity of command. Golden rule. Human Relations.

1   Why is a history like that represented by George's timeline important to a subject?
2   How can modern historians like Mooney be sure of what an ancient civilization 'unconsciously recognized'?
3   How are our prevailing understandings of concepts shaped by particular environmental circumstances or cultural beliefs? How and why do these particular views become ingrained? In what ways might the history above limit our understanding?
4   Are Mooney's principles of organization universal? Do they account for network organizations or Internet businesses?
5   How might incorporating other perspectives or dimensions help us to think differently or more creatively?

Case Box 1.2   Drawing Organization

An article in The *Guardian* newspaper on a new book called *Experimental Houses* begins as follows:

> Why don't people live in radical, experimental houses? Answer: Ask a five-year-old child to draw a house. Whether from a rich or poor background, whether born in a council flat in Glasgow or a mock Tudor mansion in Weybridge, the result will almost always be the same. A funny little box-like house with a patched roof, smoking chimney, centrally-placed door, a window on either side downstairs and two windows more or less symmetrically arranged above them.

The same idea can be applied with our perceptions of organization (albeit not to young children – our understanding of 'organization' is seemingly more 'learned' and less 'primal' than 'house').

Pictionary, a board game popular in the 1980s and 90s, is also a good way of illustrating how historical learnings stay with us. The object of the game is to draw things without using words in order to enable your partner or team to guess the word as quickly as possible. Try drawing 'an organization' in such a way that your work colleagues, fellow students, friends or family members can promptly guess what you are trying to express. Despite the fact that we think we live in caring, soft, post-bureaucratic times, the fastest way to get people to think 'an organization' is still to reproduce something like the boxes-and-lines triangular hierarchy.

However, there do seem to be some differences according to different backgrounds. A few years ago, when I had opportunity to be concurrently teaching undergraduate courses in organization studies toward a business degree and ancient history toward an arts degree, I gave out a blank sheet of paper to each student from each class and asked them to draw, without words, 'an organization'. While most from both classes drew organization in terms of the boxes-and-lines triangle without any direct reference to people (not even a stick figure), the percentage for the arts students was significantly less (business students = 49/73 or 67 per cent; arts students 18/33 or 55 per cent). The balance, 24 business students and 15 arts, drew a variety of people interacting or 'flow diagrams'. Some even drew funny little box-like houses.

1   Why do most people still see the boxes-and-lines triangle when thinking organizations?
2   Why do you think the arts students might be less likely to see in terms of the triangle?
3   How might the triangular boxes-and-lines view of what an organization is influence our views of what strategy is? Where, for example, would you say strategy 'happens' on the triangle?
4   How might management and strategy be thought differently if most people drew a house rather than a boxes-and-lines scalar hierarchy to describe an organization?

Sources: This case draws from 'The Organizational Advantages of Double Vision' by Stephen Cummings and 'Beautiful Strangeness' by Jonathan Glancey.

Note

1 For those who would like further guidance as to how to use this book, a dedicated website with tips and ideas is provided at www.sagepub.co.uk.resources/strategy.htm

PART I

DECONSTRUCTING MANAGEMENT

2 Premodernism, Modernism and Postmodernism

By the end of this chapter you should:

1 Be able to distinguish between Premodernism, Modernism and Postmodernism.
2 Be beginning to see how conventional notions of management, organization and strategy are premised upon a Modernist way of seeing.
3 Recognize that Postmodernism does not seek to overthrow or surpass Modern approaches, but rather to combine Premodern and Modern approaches.

This chapter outlines three approaches as the first part of this book's argument that management tends to look with a very narrow frame of reference, despite a history that claims to incorporate a wide range of traditions. In addition to 'Modernism' (the approach from which, it will be argued, management takes its limited points of reference), a style referred to as 'Postmodernism' and the world-view of the Ancient Greek's as representative of 'Premodernism' are outlined. Each is tackled in what might seem an obvious chronological order, but each is best thought of as an approach or way of seeing with regard to how things are 'grounded', 'moved', 'sought', 'timed', 'known' and 'aimed', rather than a historical period. Thus, while Modernism's dominance is after Premodernism, figures like Plato were Modern in their outlook, while Nietzsche, who wrote at the height of Modernism, is Postmodern. However, to dwell on these complexities is to misconstrue the aims of this chapter. It does not attempt to say for certain exactly how all those that might be gathered under each approach always thought, or to show one as a progression on the others. What it seeks to do is to draw a rough outline of the world-view from which management and strategic management would spring, and suggest that there are alternative ways of thinking.

You may wonder what this has to do with management and strategy. Firstly, this chapter takes you a long way 'outside of the box', a necessary step toward illustrating that the conventional views, apparent from Case Boxes 1.1 and 1.2, are particular and historically contingent, rather than universal and fundamental. Secondly, the background it lays out enables the arguments developed in later chapters. However, this chapter should not be viewed as just an academic exercise; the ideas outlined here should also cause you to reflect upon the present and future of management and strategy. For example, debates about Modernism and Postmodernism provide insight into the nature of a world witnessing significant changes in consumption patterns and beliefs. A world increasingly characterized by paradoxes: heterogeneity *and* conformity, passive consumption *with* active customization, localization *and* globalization. At the same time, new trends from 'buying organic' and 'Gaia theory' to 'network organizations' and the 'case study method' of teaching, can be linked to a re-appreciation of Premodern thinking.

I Premodernism

● *Grounding*: the coexistence of *chaos* and *cosmos*

In the beginning, Eurynome rose naked from Chaos, but found nothing substantial to rest her feet on.

Greek foundation myth

The central presupposition in Greek creation myths was that *cosmos* (the general order that can be seen in things) relied upon *chaos* (the 'unseen', 'gap' or 'indeterminate void'). Subsequently, the Greeks appreciated the *co-existence and co-dependence of cosmos and chaos*. The best representation of these forces is the dual characterization of Apollo and Dionysus, a symbolism familiar in most Premodern societies (for example, the Chinese 'yin' and 'yang'). Dionysus and Apollo's 'co-rule' over creation pervaded Greek thought: from Greek tragedy that worked from the premise that even the most ordered life was permeated with uncertainty, ambiguity and fate; to Thucydides' political analysis, where life was a mixture of orderliness and the contingent, unpredictable and indeterminate. Figure 2.1 contrasts their lyre-playing styles. Nietzsche believed that the combination of *cosmos* and *chaos*, the Apollonian propensity to order the world and the unpredictable Dionysian tendency to shatter form and transgress boundaries, enabled the Greeks' many great achievements.

Such thinking was also manifest in Heraclitus' (*c.* 500 BC) description of 'truth'. He defined this as 'taking entities out of their hiddenness and letting them be seen' (an approach that lives on in our word 'dis-cover'). This implied that there were innumerable things that might be known but that *complete certainty of knowledge was never possible*. Many things were 'in light' or formed part of the *cosmos*, while many were unseen. We might each bring things 'out of the *chaos*' during the cycle of our lives, but, at the same time, others would fade into darkness. The unfolding spiral of being meant that while one saw some aspects, one could never see or know everything for certain.

This non-linear view of development led Premoderns to a different understanding of innovation and progress from Moderns. In antiquity it

Figure 2.1   The forms and styles of Apollo and Dionysus

Source: L.R. Farnell, *The Cults of the Greek States*

was believed that collecting, recording and thus *increasing* the *quantity* of remembered skills and styles, arts and sciences was progressive. But by the sixteenth century, and the first stirrings of Modernism, development did not mean the recognition of more styles. On the contrary, by aiming to capture certain, essential or fundamental truths, progress sought to reduce things into the 'one best way', thereby increasing their '*quality*' but *decreasing* their number. As the sixteenth century art historian Vasari claimed when lauding Modern painters, 'it is inherent in the very nature of the arts to progress step by step, from modest beginnings, and finally reach the summit of perfection.'

The Greeks' development of mythology provides a good example of the ancients' different view of innovation. Mythology was dynamic in that new deities, or new stories about old deities, were continuously being 'unconcealed'. However, the new took their place alongside, rather than supplanting, the old. Often old myths would fall into darkness as they lost relevance or popularity, but the Greeks did not actively seek to improve upon or progress beyond traditional beliefs. Their approach was at once innovative *and* conservative, and many contrary deities flourished side by side by a series of expedient compromises. This made for a somewhat 'messy' mythological tapestry. George Elliot's depiction in *Middlemarch* of Casaubon struggling to write a 'Key to All Mythologies' but overwhelmed by material on which he could impose no hierarchical order is illustrative of Modern thinkers' vain attempts to come to grips with a Premodern manner.

This perspective on the co-existence of *cosmos* (the seen and the ordered) and *chaos* (the unseen and indeterminate), on truth as partial and subjective and on progress as quantitative rather than qualitative, meant that both the seen and the unseen were equally real, and that your and other's 'truths' were equally valid. We can see this in the Greek language, where the word *mythos*, for example, could, depending on the context in which it was used, just as easily mean a story or conversation, or unseen things such as something thought or an unspoken word or purpose. This indicates the extent to which the Greeks acknowledged the real influence of both the seen and unseen or heard and unheard on different beings. The word *panic* emerged as Greek shepherds named the spirit that occasionally afflicted their flocks after the god Pan. When the goddess Athena tugs at Achilles and warns him not to strike Agamemnon in the *Illiad*, she may have only been visible to Achilles' truth (and therefore not what Moderns would see as objectively true), but, from a Premodern point of view, she was no less real because of this.

⚡ *Moving*: the analogy of the 'microcosm'

Know thyself.

> *Ancient Athenian proverb.*

The universe was folded in upon itself: the earth echoing the sky, faces seeing themselves reflected in the stars.

> *Michel Foucault*

Figure 2.2 Premodern Microcosms
Sources: Top, Munich, Bayr. Staats–Bibl.; Bottom, Copenhagen, Kongel-Bibl.

Their subjective view of truth led the Greeks to see their individual selves as a reflection of their world. Nature, as a whole, was an intelligent organism and each human reflected this by being like the universe in *microcosm*. Within nature lived different interrelated beings just as a man or woman was made up of different interconnected but distinct elements that required different treatment. People were quite literally 'the measure of all things', and one began one's quest for knowledge by finding certain characteristics within one and then going on to think of nature as similarly possessed. By knowing one's self, one could then look from the inside-out and know the world (Figure 2.2). Hence, the stars were not for the Greeks as they are for us: remote forms that move according to the laws of mechanics and whose composition is chemically determined. They were 'heavenly bodies'. When Premoderns looked up, they saw the bodily vesture of a living being related to a combination of other beings (Figure 2.3).

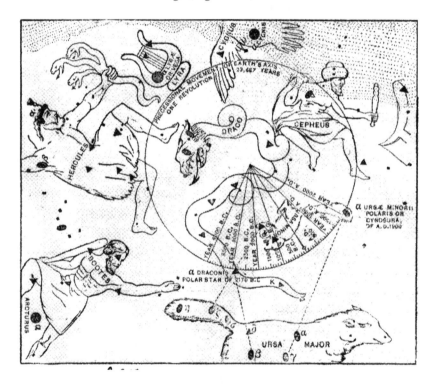

Figure 2.3 A Premodern view of the heavens
Source: O. Lodge, *Pioneers of Science*

In keeping, developments on earth were seen by the Greeks as interconnected to the fates and loyalties experienced by the many 'personable' gods that populated their myths. Viewed through the analogy of themselves, the Greeks conceived of their gods and goddesses as displaying all the human emotions. They were kind and cruel, merciful and merciless, petty and petulant, jealous and interfering. Furthermore, each god had only a limited subjective view of truth and their own 'favourites', special relationships, and spheres of interest that often conflicted with those of others. This made knowledge imperfect, decisions unclear and conflict inevitable. That the gods were not necessarily all-knowing, further reinforced the idea that people could not overcome life's *chaos*. Modern historians claimed that the Greek's 'anthropomorphic system had of course no relation to real religion or morality.' But while the Greek approach did not square with the singular and detached God with whom they were familiar, these historians failed to take account of the way in which the Greeks did not separate the categories of supernatural and the natural, religion and everyday life, the visible and unseen, the determinate and indeterminate, in the way that we tend to.

Movement in space, of a god or any other being, was also conceived in terms of how people saw their own movement. The Greeks generally believed in *teleology*, that all the world's things were animated, like people, by a *unique purpose or **telos*** (a cross between what we might call 'character' and the French might call '*raison d'etre*'). The sun rose over the earth each day because it was fulfilling its *telos*. Thus, all natural motion had a developmental character, in the sense that all bodies naturally moved so as to fulfil their natures, to move toward where it was natural for them to be. Just as the acorn's development into the oak was the proper and obvious transformation of potential into actual, so the fall of a stone or the rising of the sun was the actualization of their potential, the realization of their particular nature. For this reason, Premodern views of matter are now called 'animistic'. *Anima* (a 'personal soul' in Latin) was in all beings in keeping with what were seen as their particular purposes. In the seventeenth century, Thomas Hobbes (1588–1679) could look back and sarcastically remark that it was 'as if stones and metals had a desire, or could discern the place they could be at, as man does.' But Premoderns would not have got the joke. Greek knowledge was heavily dependent upon the personal analogy and the traditions wound up in this to support it and define its 'places for beings'.

👁 *Seeking*: wisdom through connecting to the network of beings

The most important traditional view [of how we know] was that of Aristotle, according to which when we come to know something, the mind becomes one with the object of thought. Of course, this is not to say that they become materially the same thing; rather, that the mind participated in the being of the known object, rather than simply depicting it ... a conception quite different from the [Modernist] representational model.

Charles Taylor

The Modern scientist's access to knowledge is granted by his application of a method that detaches him from the object under investigation. For the Ancients, with the universe a network of interconnected beings pursuing

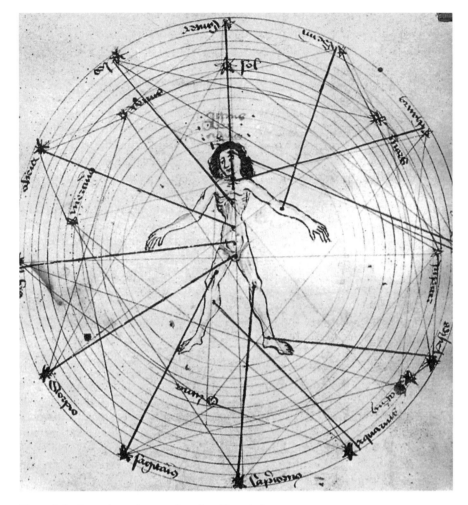

Figure 2.4 Premodern microcosmic webs of knowledge
Source: Vienna, Nat-Bibl.

their own unique purposes, knowing the nature of things was a matter of seeking to develop a *particular relationship or 'sympathy' between oneself and what one was seeking to know*. About linking into the 'similitude' or the similarities between beings.

Thus, the stars, for the Greek's, had the qualities of eyes as both gave out light. Furthermore, as Crollius told it, the constellation of the stars was a matrix of all the plants on earth. Hence, each star was a plant:

> … in spiritual form, which differs from the terrestrial plants in matter alone … the celestial plants and herbs are turned towards the earth and look directly down upon the plants they have procreated, imbuing them with some particular virtue.

Know the plant and one could 'step into' the nature of the star. Know the stars, know the nature of eyes, and so on.

Gradually a matrix of connections emerged. The world here was a vast web of beings. Moderns would separate these out into hierarchical categories: natural and supernatural, terrestrial and celestial, animal, vegetable and mineral, beings and things and so on. But Premoderns saw nature differently, richer and more chaotic, criss-crossed by particular networks of relationships (Figure 2.4).

Similitudes were discerned through the reading of signs on the surface of things. Thus, the affinity between aconite and our eyes would remain in obscurity if there were not some signature on the plant telling us that it is good for diseases of the eye. The sign was legible in aconite seeds: they are tiny dark globes set in skin-like coverings whose appearance is much like that of eyelids covering an eye. The walnut was a microcosm of the human head – so the shell of the fruit cured wounds of the pericranium, while internal head ailments could be prevented by the use of the nut (something which modern scientists have since 'proven', albeit through very different means). Opium sent you to sleep because poppies have a particularly dormant gait, not because it had a corpuscular microstructure that acted on physiological structures in such a way as to cause sleep. Modern scientists criticized Galen's (AD 129–c. 200) anatomical knowledge because it was not based on the dissection of humans. However, Galen, who believed that knowledge could be ascertained by drawing analogies between particular human, animal, plant and mineral 'anatomies', did not see the point of cutting up humans.

Rather than having any detached representational qualities, as it does for us today, language was another living being woven through this tapestry. Due to the fact that words were subject to similitude too, they also contained signs indicating connections. The Greeks wrote from left to right because writing was linked to the movement of the seven planets. The names of beings were lodged within the beings they named: strength was 'written' in the name and body of the lion, regality in the eye of the eagle. Most Premodern societies fancied that numbers had personalities. Odd numbers, for example, had male attributes and evens female.

'Thoughts' could no more be detached from the web of life than language. Hence, there was no separation here between mind and matter, or between subject and object as in Modernism. Humans and their thoughts were just other elements connected via relations of analogy and sympathy. For the ancients, knowledge came as one found one's self connected to the similitudes relevant to their situation. It was as if there was a mass of knowledge elements that one would hope to be able to link with on an as-needed basis. Often wise connections came suddenly, placed by gods who were connected to relevant spheres of interest. Thus, Homer's *Illiad* describes the Trojans as 'remembering flight and forgetting resistance.' It was as if one hoped that the gods would allow them the necessary connections, or at least not conceal them, at the vital moment, as when Automedon is described as having had a god 'put an unprofitable plan into his breast and taken away his excellent understanding.' Or, that when the connection was best not felt, the gods would prevent it, as when Patroclus hoped that the gods would 'preserve him' from Achilles' vindictive feelings. Thus, thoughts were not owned by one's consciousness, but endowed with a personality and energy of their own. Pericles spoke of being 'delivered not from fear but from glory', and of being 'attended by cowardice'. People could have the power of the gods in them, leading to a temporary insanity (which could be either good or bad) that was not ascribed to psychology but to a daemonic agency. In Premodern times, one could speak of madness as 'an Erinys in the brain'; of Achilles sometimes knowing 'lion things'; and Nestor and Agamemnon as sharing thoughts 'friendly to each other'.

Linking many of the themes discussed so far, Demokritos (*c*. 460–370 BC) related that:

> We in reality know nothing firmly but only as it changes in accordance with the condition of the body and of the things which enter it and of the things which resist it … And a man must recognize by this rule that he is removed from reality.

From this perspective one could not 'own' thoughts like a possession or trade in theories. On the one hand, all things were beings and all beings had 'personalities', thus one had to develop their own 'relationships' with them in order to step into their being and know them. On the other hand, because the relations between gods and humans and language and other beings were always unfolding, every situation would be constituted by slightly different relations and no transferable universal theory would be practical. Recognizing this, Premoderns favoured stimulating each person's unique *telos* to connect with knowledge via stories or a 'case-study method'. Perhaps the best-crafted exposition of this approach is that of Plutarch who claimed that we must seek virtuous examples not just to contemplate them but to derive benefit from doing so. He explains further, by analogy, that:

> … a colour is well suited to the eye if its tones stimulate and refresh the vision, and in the same way we ought to apply our intellectual vision to those models which can inspire it to attain its own proper virtue through the sense of delight they arouse.

Such an example is 'no sooner seen,' he continues, 'than it rouses one to action, and yet it does not form his character by mere imitation, but by causing him to reflect on his own particular *telos*.'

⊕ *Timing*: life as a circle

[H]uman affairs form a circle, and there is a circle in all other things that have a natural movement of coming into being and passing away. This is because all things are discriminated by

time, and end and begin as though conforming to a cycle; for
even time itself is thought to be a circle.

Aristotle

History and time for the Greeks were *cyclical,* given that elements would often come around again without forming the same pattern. While things constantly changed and were different than before, they were not qualitatively progressive. Elements, including bits of knowledge, would always be coming and going. In keeping, Herodotus, who described his work as the result of his wanderings and researches from his particular viewpoint (or *'historiai'*) in order to keep some deeds of the past alive in the present, considered his work complete with the revisiting of the character of Cyrus with which he began.

Premoderns consequently saw the *past, present and future as interconnected.* The past and future were very much alive in the present and time could not be separated out into progressive phases. Given the Premodern nature of truth and the web of knowledge relationships, time and history could not follow a linear path toward a unifying end or be connected to qualitatively progressive patterns of overall human development. While Aristotle's *Politics* discussed the causes of revolution and of how one regime yields to another, 'revolution' was used in its Premodern, and now less common, sense of 're-volving', rather than overthrowing and moving forward. Aristotle believed that no regime could satisfy all completely, and that the ensuing dissatisfaction would lead to the development of a different regime as another was concealed in chaos, in an endless cycle.

While Moderns picked out what they saw as the embryonic rational or linear-progressive aspects of Greek thought that would be 'built upon', it was Christianity that first introduced the necessary beliefs to sustain an interest in an objective and linearly progressive history through the concept of the fundamental equality of men and all nations as branches of one humanity under God's master plan. Greek writers were just as attracted to infinity and the indeterminate: that which existed but was not part of present norms, yet could spiral back. This way of seeing was linked to the myth of Hermes, the god of continuous metamorphosis. As Umberto Eco explains:

> In the myth of Hermes we find the negation of the principle of identity, of non-contradiction ... and the causal chains wind back on themselves in spirals: the after precedes the before, the god knows no spatial limits and may, in different shapes, be in different places at the same time.

Moderns would come to see the outlining of the Darwinian evolution of all things and the common processes that underlie this as the fundamental purpose of history writing, but this was not how Premoderns thought.

✳ *Knowing:* many schools of thought

The factors preventing knowledge are many: the obscurity of
the subject, and the shortness of human life ...

Protagoras

Moderns resolved the 'factors preventing knowledge' by agreeing a universal method, dividing the world up and specializing in order to build up the
collective store of *cosmos*: de-personalising knowledge so that intelligence,
accumulated in a life of relations, did not die concealed with individuals.
They, unlike the Greeks, did not assume that knowledge was subjective, that
connections would continuously multiply or that some portions of knowledge would always be in *chaos*. For the Greeks, the spreading, relative and
interpretative nature of things meant that one school of thought would limit
knowledge. Subsequently, *many different and unspecialized schools and philosophies* (now usually referred to collectively as 'Pre-Socratic': that is,'pre proper
Modern philosophy') *existed side by side*, and one could legitimately postulate
many different answers to questions like 'what came first?' Mythology suggested *chaos*. Thales answered *water*; Anaximenes *air*. Parmenides countered
that since plurality and change were 'givens' and no unity could generate a
plurality, there could be no singular primordial element. Empedokles
posited fire, water, earth and air as producing the world through processes
of love and strife or connection and separation; Demokritos, a vast number
of constituent elements. Others named a single divine directive force.

This amounted to what classical historian E.R. Dodds called an 'imperfectly
mapped jungle' of thought. Modern historians would look back on the Greeks
and claim that what needed to be overcome was the existence of many independent schools, each 'infected' with an eager generality. However, this jungle
enabled the development and co-existence of the wide-ranging, and quite
different, views of the West's two most influential thinkers: Plato and Aristotle.

In his *Early Dialogues*, Plato sought the elimination of conflict of meaning
through the convergence of all parties on a single stable view. He depicted
Socrates seeking singular pure definitions through a process of argument,
refutation and counter-argument. Socrates asked questions like 'What is
beauty?' and worked toward the essence of beauty by reasoning against specific beautiful cases. Plato built on this idea in his *Middle Dialogues*, search-
ing for general and un-equivocal bases on which to found knowledge. This
led to Plato's 'Theory of Forms', which evolved from his observation that
common names were used for different examples. Given this, he believed
that there must be a perfect 'beautiful' form that we refer to in giving meaning to calling different things 'beautiful'. Empirical observations would
show that such forms did not exist in the world around us, but they had to
exist, Plato argued, to make our world and language hang together. He
surmised that there must, therefore, be another world that contains these
forms, a 'theory world' of ideal forms. And, given that this was a world other
than that which we inhabit, we could only see it in our 'mind's eye', or

imagination. Imagining, reasoning out and then imposing these forms must then be the starting point for progressive development. Once the ideals are conceived, we can direct our own imperfect world toward them (see below).

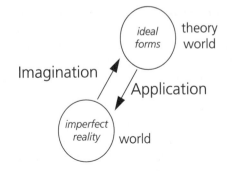

As we shall see, Plato's thinking in this regard is quite orthodox from a Modern scientific point of view. However, it went against the grain of his times. Aristotle's thinking, including his attacks on Plato's idealistic theory world, were far more popular. For Aristotle, every being existed on the surface of everyday life – one could not lift or abstract average or ideal forms out of particular cases. Subsequently, Aristotle argued against applying general theories across a number of examples and for respecting the circumstances of specific cases, claiming that one should 'look for precision just so far as the nature of the subject admits.'

⊙ *Aiming:* **personal *telos* and *ethos***

To ask whether Homer's people are determinists or libertarians is a fantastic anachronism: the question has never occurred to them, and if it were put to them it would be difficult for them to understand what it meant.

E.R. Dodds

A city is composed of different men; similar people cannot bring a city into existence.

Aristotle

For the Premoderns, one's life was directed in many ways at once: by the gods and the particular relationships one had with them, by relationships with other sympathetic beings, by the customs and traditions that shaped these relationships, and by the individual human in question. Even within each human being a number of conflicting relationships played. One could converse with their *thumos* ('the organ of feeling') almost as one person to another, or one could have more than one. Odysseus, for example, 'planned in his *thumos*' to kill the Cyclops immediately, but was restrained by a second voice. It is on this basis that Aristotle describes humans as 'political animals', for they acted not only on instinct or deterministically but also by debating and weighing up the claims of their different interests and influences before making the decisions that contributed to their destiny.

Consequently, the Greeks were *both* libertarians and determinists. They saw their actions as influenced from a number of different competing angles in a manner that Modern psychologists would call 'over-determined'. This allowed them to explain why things did not always work out as anticipated: there was always a *chaos* or gap in knowledge because it was hard to know all the determining forces in play and which would win out until the event. However, this was problematic if one wished to establish linear causal links between actions and consequences. It also made it difficult to believe in a general prescriptive moral code of behaviour, as actions could not be determined in advance of particular circumstances occurring and the interests that converged on these circumstances played themselves out. However, the Greeks saw ethical questions as of great importance and much thought was given to how one could 'carry oneself' in life.

For Aristotle, the responsibility fell to the *prudent individual* who understood that they were operating in an unstable domain, without fundamental norms or overriding laws, and that their success subsequently 'owed more to a good eye than an unshakable knowledge'. The prudent individual must be open to opportunity or inspiration and seek connection to the relevant knowledge and traditions as they became apparent on a case-by-case basis. For example, the Greeks believed that the actions of a skilled physician did not just follow a textbook but were connected to those of a skilled helms-person. Both, given that it was impossible to know with certainty the anger or benevolence of the conditions in advance, had to negotiate a route with the aid of recognizable signs and compared with their experience of analogous situations. And both were obliged to make their way by conjecture based on particular traditions, individual circumstances and opinions in addition to a knowledge of their own character and strengths.

Acknowledging *local traditions and many specific **telos's** rather than general codes* consequently led to a different form of ethics and understanding of correct human action than that with which we are familiar. Aristotle's moral schema involved three elements:

1   An unreflective man.
2   A man-as-he-could-be-if-he-realized-his-*telos*.
3   The principles that would allow him to pass from one to the other.

Telos is the lynchpin here. Once one was aware of their *telos* (an awareness that could only come from self-reflection), what one *is* implied what one's principles at a particular time should be, and thus implied what one *ought* to do. 'Knowing thyself' as opposed to knowing the golden rules or general norms was what was most important, as this would enable one to know the interests, gods, myths, analogous situations and traditions that shaped one. Knowing, or connecting with, these things would help answer what one must do in order to be true to one's network of relationships. This was what one ethically ought to do. On this view, each human must seek to fulfil a different combination of roles and traditions: member of a family, citizen, helmsperson, philosopher, servant of his or her gods and so on. Thus, to be ethical each must discover his or her particular way of acting. Aristotle believed this to be imperative because a healthy community relied upon people having different abilities and priorities and subsequently following different courses.

Premodern ethics was thus more about what we would call *ethos*, individual 'deportment' within a community of relationships, than being universally good or adhering to general norms. About developing a way of carrying oneself in a manner that was consistent enough to contribute to the community and different enough to enable others to recognize you and think you exemplary in your difference. About developing upon your particular constellation of traditions so as to be remembered in a positive light. For the Greeks, ethics were *both* determined *and* existential, *both* individualistic *and* collective.

This schema relied upon subjectivity and the *context* provided by particular customs and traditions, the importance of which was reflected in all aspects of Greek thought. Herodotus considered Cambyses 'mad' for failing to respect traditions other than his own, for not recognizing that 'custom is king of all'. Protagoras showed that any given thing was 'to me such as it appears to me, and is to you such as it appears to you', and Demokritos that everything was 'by convention', meaning 'relative to us' or 'not in virtue of the nature of things in themselves'. Modern science and ethics would seek to overcome the credence paid to such subjectivity.

To summarize, the world seen by Premoderns comprises an irreducible blend of *chaos* and *cosmos*. This way of thinking was informed by the subjective analogy of the individual person and their numerous relations, which they saw as a reflection of a multi-dimensional mesh of gods and goddesses. Seeing the world as an intelligent organism made up of different beings promoted the appreciation that each being had a nature, place and path particular to it. These particular natures were interconnected according to traditional sympathetic relations. Knowledge was thus gained by reading similitudes. However, these connections were always relative, multiple and unfolding so interpretation had to be used and the outcomes of particular actions in advance would always be somewhat uncertain. The plurality of the network of relations encouraged the co-existence of many schools which, because of the connectedness of what Moderns might see as things from disparate categories, did not specialize in particular spheres. Ethically, one sought to become a unique identity while building upon the constellation of one's relations and traditions. One's *ethos* in the present, their aims for the future and their past traditions were all interwoven.

This system privileged a particular approach to knowledge called *metos*, perhaps best translated as 'practical wisdom' or 'effective intelligence'. *Metos* acknowledged a dichotomy between:

- the Apollonian sphere of *being*, of 'the one', the unchanging, of the limited, of the true and definite knowledge; and
- the Dionysian sphere of *becoming*, of 'the multiple', the unstable and the unlimited, of oblique and changeable opinion.

However, it was not that this opposition defined a framework of two exclusive worlds whereby one should impose thinking from one onto the other (as in Plato's *Middle Dialogues*). Rather, *metos* requires *shuttling* between the two spheres. Confronted with a multiple, chaotic reality, the individual who is endowed with *metos* must be just as multiple, mobile and polyvalent. He must keep his intelligence sufficiently wily and supple. His gait 'askew' so that he can be ready to make use of his truths and the truths of others from the sphere of cosmos or being so that he may go in any direction as he operates in the sphere of becoming.

Hence, we see why the multi-dimensional Athena, rather than the necessary but limited Apollo or Dionysus, is described as the wisest of gods. Why the much-admired Odysseus is commonly preceded by the epithet 'resourceful' and lauded as 'expert in *all manners* of contending'. His greatness lay in his 'good eye' picking out and developing the right theory or experience at the right moment so as to determine the best principles for him in the circumstances. This approach relied upon the continued existence of *chaos*. For how could *metos* be practised if not for the gaps in our knowledge and the consequent uncertain collusion, connection and cross-pollination of different circumstances and traditions? Not surprisingly, Plato was at great pains to dismiss *metos*. Aristotle, by contrast, lauded it.

After the coexistence of Plato's and Aristotle's thought in Antiquity, the Middle Ages came to favour an approach termed 'Aristotelianism', a loose coalition of schools based on Aristotle's teachings. Plato's thinking survived in translation in the Arabic world but it had, for the time being, been lost to the West. However, The Renaissance of the sixteenth century saw many Ancient works, in particular Plato's and Pythagoras' (*c.* 550–*c.* 500 BC) writings, brought back from the East. This led to great ferment as thinkers like Machiavelli (1469–1527) and Montaigne (1533–92) once again oscillated between a practically-minded Aristotelianism and a theoretically-minded Platonism. Montaigne's *metos* led him to argue that 'all *grosso-modo* judgements were lax and defective' and that 'irreducible difference' was, paradoxically, the only thing universal about humanity. He also concluded that 'unless some one thing is found of which we are completely certain, we can be certain about nothing.'

In rising to Montaigne's challenge, Modernism would soon upset the co-habitation of *cosmos* and *chaos* that inspired *metos*. The way of seeing that would shape the parameters of management, organization and strategy, as we know them, was on the horizon.

2 Modernism

Modernism is a complex system seeking to assert itself and achieve mastery.

Alain Touraine

'The knowledge, *I think, therefore I am,* is the first and most certain thing that occurs to one who philosophises orderly.' This is René Descartes' rock of certainty, upon which much of how the Modern world approaches things is built. It was well received by a society increasingly ill at ease with the *chaos* and uncertainty accepted in a world-view influenced by the Greeks and provided a successful counter-punch against Montaigne's conclusion. Why was the sixteenth century comfortable with Montaigne while the seventeenth followed Descartes? The general view is that we just got smarter. However, there are other, more contingent, explanations.

Some argue that Protestantism's challenge to Europe's over-arching unifying authority (Catholicism) and the ensuing wars created a desire to find a way whereby divisive pluralism could be laid to rest once and for all – through the development of an overriding, non-spiritual rationality. Others argue that five particular interlocking institutional dimensions that furthered the rise of large nation-states stimulated this desire: *capitalism, industrialization, norms* of behaviour, centralized means of *surveillance* and the *monopoly control of force.*

Nation states mark a break from traditional modes of production and consumption by bringing together the dimensions of *capitalism* and *industrialization* toward the collective implementation of technology in a continuous quest for cost minimization and profit maximization. This promoted continual growth via constant reworking of production processes. Consequently, a capitalist economy is intrinsically unstable and restless. However, for it to function well, it requires a stable environment conducive to long-term investment. The success of a nation-state thus relied upon providing an *underlying order (cosmos)* without overly harnessing capitalism's restless chaotic energy. (Modernism's 'foundation myth' is thus the reverse of the Premodern *cosmos* on an unstable *chaos*). Achieving stable collective growth required other dimensions: the development of objective *norms of behaviour* and corresponding general laws; centralized methods of *surveillance*, to see that these norms were adhered to; and the *monopoly control of force* through the development of national police and judiciary systems that could consistently correct intransigence. These means of co-ordination and control rested on a belief in there being *certain objective foundations* against which particular actions could be measured. In turn such general measurement procedures brought order to property rights, another crucial cog in the wheels of *capitalism*.

However, the *Philosophes* of the eighteenth century 'Enlightenment', or *Modernes* as they were often called, did not see developments as so contingent. For them, the general theories of the seventeenth and eighteenth centuries' great thinkers – Descartes, Galileo, Newton – came about and proved persuasive because they were closer to the truth than what had passed for knowledge before. They saw themselves as adjudicators of a contest between the old world and new knowledge, and they judged the new to be a progression, a sign of contemporary Man's righteous assertion over nature. Combining this with the opposition being fought out in their times between traditional and new forms of production and government enabled this to be seen as 'The Age of Revolutions': the 'Glorious', the 'French', the 'American', the 'Industrial' and the 'Scientific'. And these were very much 'revolutions' in the Modernist sense of the word: the overthrow of the past and leaving it in one's wake. Modernism's key beliefs are thus already revealed:

1   That it is Man's collective aim and destiny to assert himself over or master chaos via the accumulation of an ordered set of general principles that represent the way things certainly work.
2   'Revolution' is key because new discoveries bring us closer to this certain understanding, 'the new' is thus both an advance on the past and 'consigning it to history'.

These beliefs enabled the *Modernes* to make sense of the seventeenth century's new ideas. They saw history as a linear path and themselves as moving on that path, away from a view that accepted an ever-present measure of *chaos* and the corresponding notion of a 'shuttling' *metos*. Man now thought he had the power, if he put his mind to it, to assert *cosmos* over *chaos* so as to enable the development of collective plans for our future direction and gain greater control over things. Intelligence was now about furthering certitude, about, in the words of Francis Bacon, 'enlarging the bounds of Human Empire, to the effecting of all things'.

● *Grounding: cosmos* will conquer *chaos*

Men are taught and wont to attribute stupendous unaccountable effects to sympathy, antipathy and especially to a certain being that they call Nature; for this is represented as a kind of goddess, whose power may be little less than boundless [This] veneration has been a discouraging impediment to the empire of Man over the inferior creatures of God.

Robert Boyle

To measure a quantity one needs a unit. Ideally this unit should [have] universal rather than local significance.

The Making of the Modern World – Milestones of Science and Technology

Premodernism encouraged veneration towards the nature and the opaque networks that sustained and moved its beings. This soft uncertain web was now seen as an impediment to the pediment that had to be laid as a foundation for certain knowledge. Bacon (1561–1626) wrote of commencing 'the whole thing anew upon a better plan … a total reconstruction of sciences, arts, and all human knowledge, raised upon the proper foundations.' Descartes (1596–1650) was 'convinced of the necessity of commencing by establishing a firm and abiding superstructure in the sciences' and set out 'to cast aside the loose earth and sand that I might reach the rock [and] find [this] ground of assurance.' To achieve Modernism's pediment, being had to be depersonalized and de-individualized. 'Surface differences' had to be undermined to reach the common, the underlying and the unvarying. This would require the establishment of a *unitary set of universal foundational categories and units of measure.*

First, things under or behind Man were sorted out. The Aristotelian view had assumed different domains of space, each subject to particular principles dependant on the 'personalities' of the beings involved. All beings on earth were subject to familiar processes of birth and change and decay and all motion was rectilinear and discontinuous, but the perfect bodies of the sun, the stars and the planets moved in steady and smooth circles over the world. Galileo's (1564–1642) identification of blemishes on the sun that moved irregularly and celestial forms that did not seem to be moving in a circular progression threw the Aristotelian system into doubt. His observations and experiments would show space as a singular domain, a *consistent unvarying grid* against which action took place.

Second, a *general set of categories* was being laid out upon this grid. The distinction between animate and inanimate objects, between animal, vegetable and mineral was increasingly common. (In the Greek world-view, all things contained and were moved by a personal *anima* or spirit.) A *progressive scalar hierarchy* was established whereby the mineral and then the vegetable provided the static ground upon which animals, including man, moved.

Third, Descartes found *I think, therefore I am* to be the rock of certainty upon which all knowledge could be founded. The thinking human *mind* was, he reasoned, the one unvarying thing we could be certain of. This bestowed upon Man a privileged status. Because he was the only animal to possess this sort of mind he was at the very top of the animal scale and thus at the top of the hierarchy described above. It also gave *Man's mind an elevated standing*, placing it over and above being and the universal grid against which life or matter was now understood to be ordered. From here, we could build on this foundation toward knowledge of everything else. All other objects below the knowing mind were *matter* (hence the expression 'mind over matter'). The diagram below attempts to pictorially represent this new 'modern' approach.

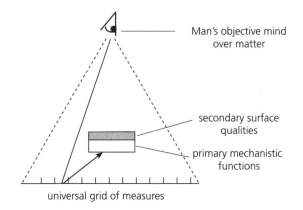

Descartes subsequently moved us beyond the Premodern view of knowing through personal connection. Reason became a detached or 'objective'

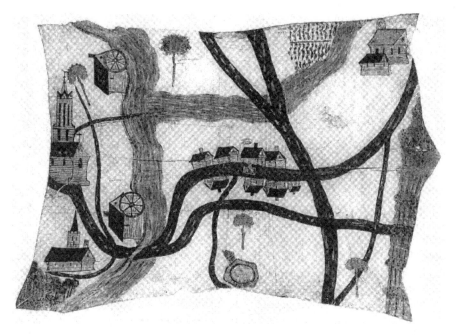

Figure 2.5 The subjectivity of Premodern mapping: Plan des dimes de Champeaux, A fifteenth century map
Source: Archives Nationales de France

activity, humans seen as greater than other beings in that they could think without having their thoughts 'coloured' by particular involvement. From his mind–matter split, Descartes' account of the reality of matter began by distinguishing between *primary* and *secondary* qualities. 'Secondary qualities' were those based on convention and sense data. However, Descartes argued that underneath these lay permanent objective primary qualities and it was here that we should look for knowledge (a quite different perspective from the Ancients' emphasis on interpreting surface signs). Knowledge of underlying primary qualities (or 'self-evident' qualities as Descartes often referred to them) could largely be determined in terms of function or movement across the universal grid. By combining these new ideas it could be said that reality (that is, primary qualities) was pure 'extension' in space. Descartes explained that 'Nothing remains in the idea of a body except that it is something extended in length, breadth and depth; and this something is comprised in our idea of space.' As mind is regarded as 'pure thought', un-extended and separate from the body, so real matter is 'pure extension' devoid of substantial qualities except those measured by objective geometrical or mathematical units.

These new assumptions began to re-order our view of the world. It was as if man could now look down upon life with a spotlight and a big pair of callipers, a change made visible in this period's development of mapping. Premodern maps emphasized the personal rather than the objective qualities of spatial order. They were drawn as if one was standing on the ground, with landmarks depicted in terms of their relative importance to a community at the time of the map's construction, as opposed to their 'actual' size (see the oversized church in Figure 2.5). Modern maps, by contrast, imagined how the world as a globe would look from outside or above. As a result, general mathematical principles could be applied to enable an underlying framework upon which things could be pegged (Figure 2.6). Modern maps became abstract and functional grids for the general codification and control of phenomena in space. Indeed, Elizabethan historian Richard Helgerson argues that Saxton's *Atlas of England and Wales* of 1579 enabled the English to represent and assert a whole new 'visual and conceptual possession of their physical kingdom'.

Man's ability to objectively order space and hence assert himself over his world was also advancing in other spheres. Art historians like Vasari reported the Renaissance's progress with regard to the ability to paint Man and his surrounds with perfect perspective (Byzantine art, for example, was now dismissed as naive, or a step on the way to more truthful expressions, rather than a particular style with different objectives). In the seventeenth century, still-life (*nature morte*) would go further, seeking to isolate, capture the essence of and perfectly represent man's objects. Worth was objectified through centralized monetary systems, while other objectivizing practices emerged in accounting, trade, agricultural production and the setting of standard time.

A *certain depth*, that did not exist within the Premodern web of life had emerged. It marked the beginning of a new hierarchy. The 'Mind of Man' now looked down on all the operations of life with a belief in there being underlying common grids. This new Modern view is made manifest in Elizabethan portraiture, where the presence of maps mastered by Her Majesty became a recurring theme at the end of the sixteenth century. The 'geometry' of *The Armada Portrait*, for example (see Figure 2.7), depicts the Queen with her hand surely on the world and the imperial crown placed over it – the world becoming 'subject' to centralized human knowledge and control.

⚡ *Moving:* like a 'clockwork mechanism'

The universe is not similar to a divine animated being, but similar to a clock.

Johannes Kepler

Kepler added to this view outlined above in a footnote in 1621, writing that 'If you substitute the word "force" for the word "soul" then you have the very principle on which [my] celestial physics is based.' While he had believed that the cause of a planet's motion came from within its internal

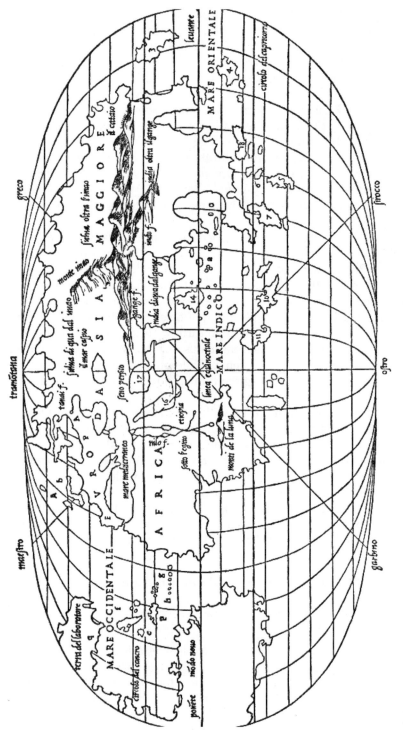

Figure 2.6 The objectivity of modern mapping: A sixteenth century woodcut world map on oval projection

Source: Bordone's *Isolario*

Figure 2.7 The modern gaze: Elizabethan portraiture – The Armada portrait (1588) showing the globe as 'subject' to the monarch and, The 'Ditchley' Portrait (1592) showing the monarch standing over a map of England and Wales.
Sources: Top, The Marquess of Tavistock and the Trustees of the Bedford Estate; Bottom, The National Portrait Gallery, London

soul or particular *telos*, he was now convinced that a *unified external mechanistic force controlled it from without.*

The conception of objective space underneath particular actions was twinned with a reconfiguration of the understanding of movement. The depth provided by universal characteristics and general categories presented a backdrop against which movement or action could be objectively measured, and this action could then be seen to be subject to unifying general principles. As Samuel Edgerton argues in *The Renaissance Rediscovery of the Linear Perspective* that the 'most far-flung places could all be precisely fixed in relation to one another by unchanging co-ordinates [now meant] that their proportionate distance, as well as their directional relationships, would be apparent.'

The Aristotelian animating principle had exasperated Modern thinkers like Bacon. While he could imagine a mechanistic physics that could help enlarge Man's empire, he could not see how teleology could be used to the same effect. But how did one convince others of a new view of movement that, while it might seem more useful to intellectuals, went against everyday experience? Galileo's part in establishing Modernism's objective backdrop has already been mentioned, but while his telescope had enabled him to question many traditional premises, it was not yet so powerful as to provide enough evidence to directly outline an alternative model of movement. He and his supporters required something more to undermine seriously this aspect of the Premodern system. *Plato, mathematics* and *clockwork* would need to be connected together to further develop what Galileo's telescope saw:

1 Reference to *Plato*, whose work was recovered just before Galileo began his quest, legitimated an imaginative and mathematical treatment of the world rather than a traditional empiricism or Aristotelian view. For Plato, the material world was an imperfect realization of an ideal world on which it was patterned. Thus Galileo, a keen reader of Plato, could use this view to argue that one could best understand the material world by imagining it ideally from the vantage-point of the 'mind's eye'.

2 Plato also looked on nature in geometric terms and conceived of the *cosmos* as constructed according to the principles of *mathematics*. Galileo now argued that knowledge ought to be imagined as mathematical in form because nature was mathematical in structure, quoting Plato's dictum that 'the world was God's epistle written to mankind and it was written in mathematical letters.'

3 While abstract mathematical reasoning was difficult for people to grasp, a suitable analogy to explain the geometrics of Galileo's new world-view was now at hand. The development of *clocks* had paralleled advances in the objectification of space. While early clocks were somewhat unreliable and costly, by the late sixteenth century, mechanical clocks telling time according to one constant rhythm that did not vary in length according

to the season or latitude as with the sundial, had become a feature of life. The clock thus provided Galileo a credible and timely analogy that could be used to transmit a challenge to traditional thinking that people could relate to.

Bringing these elements together Galileo could explain that the universe moved like a *clockwork mechanism*, a complex arrangement of parts moving in different directions at different angles and speeds but in unison and regular harmony, according to a universal mathematical logic against a universal space.

Galileo's view began to catch on. If one could infer the movement of the heavens through a mathematical-mechanistic imagination, then, given that space was universal, so it was that the behaviour now attributed to the heavens could be brought down to earth. Perhaps the vegetable, the animal and even Man was like a machine?

Descartes came to argue that 'it is not less natural for a clock, made of the requisite number of wheels, to indicate the hours, than for a tree which has sprung from this or that seed, to produce a particular fruit'; and that the human body must be like 'a machine made by the hand of God'. While one could not sense natural mechanical characteristics, one could employ one's mind's eye to imagine them or look beneath their surface skin to separate them out. This view implied another of Descartes influential Modernist assertions: that complex beings or objects were best tackled by dismantling them and examining and codifying their 'component parts'.

Hobbes, later dubbed 'the father of psychology', wondered what it was that held action in societies together, from whence did or could an underlying order and equilibrium in changing human affairs come? (This was later termed the 'Hobbesian Mystery'). After visiting with Galileo in 1636, he conceived of generalizing the science of mechanics, geometrically deducing human behaviour from the abstract principles of Galileo's science of motion in order to answer this 'mystery'.

The Church gradually took to and reinforced these new mechanistic views. Premoderns believed that the human body was connected to the universe through a series of 'occult' correspondences that had emerged with no overriding logic. But, the mechanical metaphor implied that the world had been built according to some plan, and who else could have planned and built such a magnificent machine but God? This view of *God as an all-knowing, all-overseeing, designer, planner, director and controller* was soon regarded by the Church as far more agreeable than *anima*. Imbuing the natural world with a range of inherent active powers tended to dispense with the explanatory role of a God conceived as the One Almighty. The idea of one all-powerful God as the rational creator and controller of a wondrous artifice that only human vice could upset, promoted Christianity as the monopoly supplier of the supernatural.

Modernism was thus set in motion as mathematically inclined astronomers discovered that their singular God was a mathematician who had employed Platonic principles. From a view of the world from the inside-out and up to the heavens via the analogy of an individual being, the knowing gaze now looked down upon things from the outside-in and conceived of them as operating like clockwork mechanisms.

👁 *Seeking:* objective certainty though representation and categorization

Method consists entirely in the order and disposition of the objects towards which our mental vision must be directed if we would find out any truth.

René Descartes

[N]ow the history of man is merely the continuation of that of animals and plants ... he stands astounded in the face of the enormous way that man has run ... the Modern man who can see all the way! He stands proudly on the pyramid of the world-process; and while he lays the final stone of his knowledge, he seems to cry aloud to listening nature: 'We are at the top, we are at the top!'

Frederich Nietzsche

Modernism would seek to apply three related measures toward formalizing the changes of perspective outlined above and *making knowledge more certain*:

1   To create an *objective universal language* that the separate knowing mind could bring to bear to *represent* 'things' (formerly 'beings').
2   To devise a *'horizontal' set of categorizations* or tables, not unlike the Modern map's grid, upon which different things could be permanently ordered or *classified*.
3   To find the underlying or *essential characteristics* that united the spread of things on the horizontal tables so as to enable a *'vertical' set of categories*.

Now that all matter could be viewed as comprising mechanistic workings expressable in mathematical symbols, mathematics became formally capable of *objectively representing* all things. The seventeenth century thus saw a lively interest in the invention of a unifying mathematical language to replace Latin as the medium of international scholarship. Beyond the belief that such a language was possible, the quest was seen as important because of the lack of clear linear relationships between Latin words and their objects. Greek words like *mythos* could signify so many things because it was understood that their meaning was dependent on the context in which they were used. Latin, although less relativistic than Greek, had similarly developed without rational forethought. Moderns wished for a language built from a clean slate to logically represent objects, a language whose mastery (given that it positively mirrored reality) would provide a certain understanding. In this spirit, Gottfried Leibniz (1646–1716), whose early work included a project to find a rational foundation for Christendom acceptable to both churches and the construction of a calculating machine, developed the *characteristica universalis*: the language used by Newton (1642–1727) to record Modernism's first universal laws.

In addition to language becoming, like Man's mind, regarded as a separate entity capable of objectively representing things, Modernism saw the development of other independent measures. These would enable objective *horizontal grids* or tables upon which different beings could be *classified*. Different 'things' would come to be categorized according to common units of size, function, complexity, life span and so on. While the Premodern system of similitude was messy, hard to graph and always open to fresh possibilities, the Modern system of general comparative order mapped out and fixed things and made the relations between them certain. Linnaeus' (1707–1778) project of discovering the concrete domains of nature, which led to the certain classification of organisms into discrete groups, is a good example of this process. Even humans would be sorted out, measured, categorized and tabled, with general classifications, ideals, averages and norms becoming increasingly important.

Vertical scales would soon be added to this horizontal tabling. In the Age of Revolutions, people became increasingly conscious of change or the discontinuity of the present *vis-á-vis* the past. They wondered at where the characters in their tables had come from and sought to distil the *essential characteristics* that must underlie the different groups they had categorized. A time scale was thus added to tables via the search for internal similarities, similarities that went deeper than the characteristics used in the comparisons that determined the layout of the horizontal grids. In biology, we see the search for essential functions shared by all beings; in linguistics, the root of all languages. This verticality would certainly connect phenomena and express the coherence that underlay the multiplicity of things. It is made manifest in the 'trees' or 'pyramids' that are now a commonplace way of representing life and the linear relations between its different groups: with Man generally perched on top (see Figure 2.8).

Ordering things into general grids, demonstrating their uniform links over time, and recording these things with a universal representative language, encouraged Moderns to see knowledge differently from Premoderns. Knowledge had become both cumulative and progressive and now it did not have to be experienced or connected to. It could be *detached* and then caged, codified, put behind glass and accumulated in the archive. The essential characteristics of things could be melted down into general characteristics and laws and these then transferred without the knower ever having to have a personal connection with the 'object' in question. Learning through stories was now considered a less evolved form: juvenile child's-play.

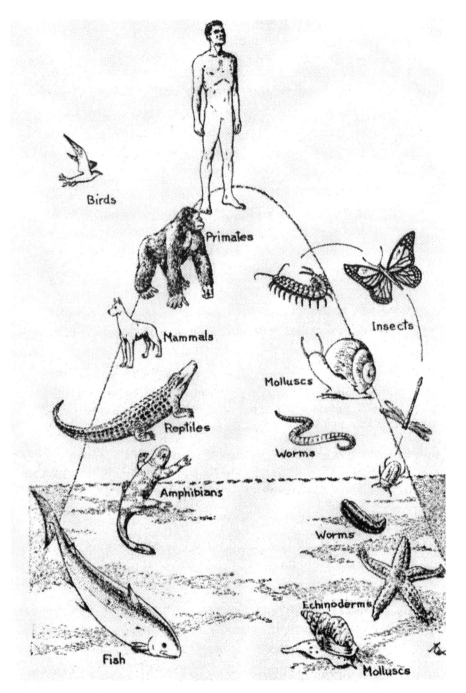

Figure 2.8 The modern biological triangle
Source: J.T. Bonner, *The Ideas of Biology*

⊕ *Timing:* **evolutionary history and being at the 'cutting edge'**

With regard to authority, it shows a feeble mind to grant so much to authors and yet deny time his rights, who is the author of all authors, nay, rather of all authority. For rightly is truth called the daughter of time, not of authority.

Francis Bacon.

[In Modernism i]nfinity is posed as that which has not yet been determined, as that which the will must indefinitely dominate and appropriate. It has to be conquered.

Jean-Francois Lyotard

The notion of time that Bacon refers to was no longer a cycle of past, present and future interwoven. Time, like other units of measure, could be separated from the web of being and reduced to objective regular units. It became *linear, unidirectional and positive*. Time and knowledge were thus cumulative, both quantitatively and qualitatively. Therefore the virtue of being 'new' implied a greater knowledge. The titles of many of the Scientific Revolution's key texts: Kepler's *Astronomia **Nova***, Pascal's *Experiences **Nouvelles** Touchant le Vide*, Boyle's ***New** Experiments* and Bacon's ***New** Organon* indicate the inversion of the Premodern system that had granted past authors intellectual 'authority'. Modernism sees the past as dated and tradition as something that should be overcome, promoting a view whereby being or thinking anew, or at the 'cutting edge', becomes *the* aim. This edge was asserting an advancing mastery, increasing the store of certain objective knowledge and hunting down infinity or *chaos*. To be Modern is to be new, 'over and above' the old.

The processes of modern science and modern art subsequently both promote a *quest for the new*. Modern science sees reason as a process of accumulating and refining toward adding new knowledge upon the collective store. Modern art is said to have begun at the famous *Salon* of 1846, when Baudelaire described the 'advent of the new!' as the imperative that artists must strive for. Manet obliged, and is regarded as the first Modern artist due to his depicting the present, as opposed to mythological or historical stories. Once art represented the present, rather than reflecting traditions, it began to move with the times. It was then a short step to a concern with being at the cutting-edge of these times.

Modern art thus developed a *desire for revolution*. However, in order to distinguish itself from decadence, or change for change's sake, its revolution had to be identified with a course leading toward some sort of collective betterment. To this end, what Modern artists sought was 'the essence of life'. We can thus chart the development of Modern art from the Impressionists to the Cubists to the Abstractionists to Mondrian's primary colours and on to the blank white canvas that supposedly represents everything. All of these 'advances' sought to abstract, reduce, purify and represent the essence of things and to be more *avant-garde* in the attempt.

Progress as a one-way revolutionary development also changed our ideas of what history should be. Descartes had dismissed history as an improper branch of knowledge because it focused on particular stories rather than general causes and themes. If history was to be taken seriously it had to be aligned with the new belief that human nature was universal. It thus became concerned to show 'general progress' rather than just 'wanderings from a particular viewpoint'. As David Hume (1711–76) explained, history's 'chief use' would become:

> ... to discover the constant and universal principles of human nature, by showing men in all varieties of circumstances and situation, and furnishing us with materials from which we may ... become acquainted with the regular springs of human action and behaviour.

On Universal History, written in the same period by French historian/philosopher A.R.J. Turgot, outlines that history in 'the eyes of a true philosopher' must reveal the:

> ... springs and mechanisms of ... the successive advances of the human race, and the elaboration of the causes which have contributed to it ... the human race always remaining the same during these upheavals, like the water during storms, and always proceeding towards its perfection.

As with the Modern categorizations described above, historical similarities would confirm the *horizontal* universality of the human race. Historical differences could then be seen as evidence of groups of people at a different stage of a common process of *vertical* 'human development'. The growing awareness of change over time, combined with the desire to find the common ties that bind, promoted the Modern aim to bring to light the permanent structures and essences that underlay all phenomena. This led to the Modern search for the unifying 'overarching principles' or '*meta-narratives*' (*meta* being Greek for 'over and above'): the general mechanisms by which, or aims toward which, all history's stories moved. Georg Hegel and Charles Darwin developed Modernism's most influential meta-narratives in the nineteenth century.

Hegel (1770–1831) defined history as a purposive process of dialectic change, whereby there is a movement of thesis, anti-thesis and synthesis (or the restoration of equilibrium) toward increasingly higher levels, ultimately aiming at 'absolute knowledge'. Hegel saw each new step signalling the redundancy of those before and identified the historian's task as charting this progression. Aspects that could not be seen as contributing to progression toward the absolute could be dismissed as not particularly relevant. Thus we may understand the mixed reception given the Greeks by Modern historians. What they did not see was Nietzsche's 'brilliant un-unified co-appreciation'. Instead, the Apollonian aspects were categorized as the 'beginnings' of science that would be built upon; the Dionysian aspects and appreciation of *metos* either left aside or listed as evidence of the naiveté that would be overcome by the human race as it progressed.

The idea of historical progress as a common process that connects and effects all aspects of life equally received a great boost from Darwin's (1809–1882) *Origin of Species*. 'All species, here or long gone', wrote Darwin, ultimately 'belong to one biological family [and can therefore be arranged] on the great Tree of Life.' Darwin argued that the species that survived and progressed vertically up the tree were those best suited to their environments. This explained the change of all species, regardless of particular differences. No longer did each species require a special act of divine creation: its particular form could be put down to general causes operating over time.

Whereas early-Modern thinkers like Descartes and Newton had only focused on the workings of God's machine as it came to us fully-formed, Darwin's view encouraged looking back down the linear track of life. Indeed, Darwin's idea was so compelling that his particular employment of 'evolution' eventually changed our conception of the word. No longer would it be seen in its earlier Premodern sense of vegetative growth: an unfolding out from and circling about a centre (like a bud). Modernism would thus come to understand time as an infinite causal chain. Modern man could no longer depend upon definite beginnings any more than he could be comfortable with particular traditional or contextual ends, notions that Aristotelian teleology and Christian providence had provided. Time was now a train, moving through different zones but without hub or terminus. Evolution, or progress, became a straight line with a cutting edge at its forefront.

✸ *Knowing:* **Modern science as the one-best way**

Reason must not be content to follow the leading strings of nature, but must proceed in advance according to unvarying laws, and compel nature to reply to its questions. For accidental observations, made according to no preconceived plan, cannot be united under a necessary law. [Hence] it is only when experiment is directed by rational principles that it can have any real utility. [And it is] to this single idea [that] must the revolution be ascribed, by which, after groping in the dark for so many centuries, natural science was conducted into the path of certain progress.

Immanuel Kant

With time an arrow and knowledge progressive and cumulative, only one 'best way' of thinking could be at the cutting-edge without logical contradiction. Bacon wrote that the mind should not be 'left to take its own course' but should be 'guided at every step; and the business done *as if by machinery.*' The quotation above relates Kant's view of how this mechanical method should be directed and carried out. This 'scientific method' would become Modernism's *one best way of knowing*, a method that is largely 'Newtonian'.

Issac Newton saw his mission as consigning the case-specific approach of the Ancients to history. He claimed that:

... to tell us that every Species of Things is endowed with an occult specifick Quality by with it acts and produces manifest Effects, is to tell us nothing. But to derive two or three general Principles of Motion from Phaenomena, and afterwards to tell us how the Properties and Actions of all corporeal Things follow from those manifest Principles, would be a very great step in Philosophy.

Newton sought to make this great step, discovering the *Modernes'* 'holy grail': universal principles that showed the world and its constituent parts to follow mechanical laws expressible in the universal language of mathematics.

Other laws of force had been developed, but before Newton they were specific (for example, the magnet attracts iron but not copper). Newton's 'Law of Gravitation' proved a power acting upon all things proportional to their quantities of matter. This was universal, applying to planets revolving around the Sun as much as apples falling to Earth. As such, it affirmed Modernism's tenets that space was universal and that all matter comprised the same basic building blocks or essence and was uniformly subject to forces other than *telos*. Newton's Law showed the world to be ordered and determined according to a universal external rationale and, being universal, it encouraged the belief that future actions could be predicted.

Newton summed up his method for arriving at such laws as 'discovering the frame and operations of nature, and reducing them, as far as may be, to general rules or laws – establishing these rules by observations and experiments, and thence deducing the causes and effect of things.' It was based on the 'shape' and assumptions described in the diagram and points below:

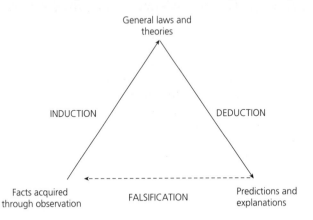

1 Phenomena or 'facts' positively exist unaffected by, and independent of, the human mind.
2 These phenomena follow general laws that govern events.
3 These laws can be grasped and theorized by induction (whereby laws can be *discerned* in the observation of events) combined with deductive reasoning (whereby laws can be *developed* in one's mind).
4 These theoretical laws can then be used to deduce predictions and explanations about the nature of future events.

To these steps, 'falsification', whereby the scientist would seek to refine knowledge by comparing predictions with phenomena and adjusting his laws in light of the difference, would be added and the cycle of refinement toward absolute knowledge would continue. This model of inquiry, in effect formalizing Galileo's combination of empirical observation with Platonic idealism in order to overthrow Aristotle, has held sway in the West since the eighteenth century. One can see how its 'geometry' replicates and fortifies the triangles and assumptions described earlier in this chapter.

Agreement on the best method for gaining knowledge, and the Modern idea that abstract experiment in one domain (for example, calculus, the laboratory) could stand for action in another (for example, life), meant that *knowledge could be centralized* into institutes and outputs aggregated and distributed. Bacon laid out a template for the 'machinery by which this sort of business' could be carried out in his *New Atlantis:* a bureaucratic research institute run by an imperial nation-state. Moves to establish such institutions were soon afoot and many emerged across Europe in the late seventeenth century. The British Royal Society was thus established in 1660 with the aim of bringing together thinkers from different traditions toward 'a Dominion over Things, and not only over one another's Judgments'. It was hoped that the 'subjectivities' of the past would be 'corrected' by the mechanical action of the proper method carried out under the auspices of public 'laboratories'. The medieval schools had employed different styles and thrived on argument, conflict and contentiousness. The 'sickness' of Ancient knowledge practices was seen by the *Modernes* to have at least partly resulted from this bickering about the 'surface details' of their interpretative judgements. The Modern knowledge institute, applying a central gaze, would subject data, or *inputs,* to the same standardized scientific *processes* in order to *output* objectively true laws. Because these were formulated along the same lines, they could then be stacked up and the collective store of knowledge built upon firm foundations, as the following diagram outlines.

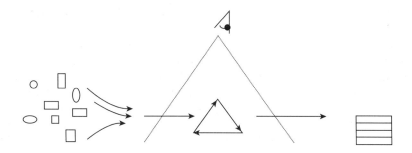

The new Modern centralized academies like The Royal Society and the Academie Français thus took a form uniquely geared to the stable growth of production according to a preconceived plan: bureaucracy. The business of knowledge generation would be properly carried out by an *unvarying*

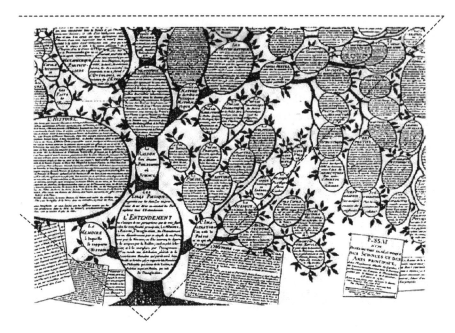

Figure 2.9 The Modern 'Tree of knowledge', the schema underlying Diderot's *Encyclopedie*, with 'Raison' as the central unifying trunk
Source: Frontispiece of Vol. 1 of the index, *Encyclopedie*; only a portion is shown here

input→process→output mechanism whereby the process of taking in data and producing general laws was run like clockwork according to the same general principles to ensure objectivity and the standardization of outputs.

This centralization of academic pursuits went hand in hand with increased academic specialization or the division of labour. Once the general policy as to how one best obtained knowledge was established, scientists did not have to spend time developing and debating approaches and could specialize in particular areas knowing that other areas would be addressed by their peers in a similar fashion. This development is illustrated by the emergence of 'encyclopaedia' in the eighteenth century. Earlier books of knowledge were compiled by 'jacks-of-all-trades'. Modern encyclopaedia recruited dozens of experts as contributors in their respective disciplines. They wrote economically and dispassionately, so as to efficiently publicise only the facts that had been produced. In the Prospectus of the French *Encyclopedie*, Denis Diderot (1713–84) explained that sketching the 'tree of all knowledge' was the 'first crucial step' in the volume's planning. He envisaged the work as truly bringing together the many aspects of knowledge gathered by the Commonwealth (see Figure 2.9). While knowledge now had many branches, sub-branches and leaves, they could all be connected back to one unitary stem: scientific *'raison'*. Having a certain means of gaining knowledge and certain and objective branches and categories meant that everything could now be certainly ordered and classified as *either* one thing *or* another.

Modernism had ordered Premodernism's system of messy webs and subjective connections from top to bottom. The divisionalized and centralized triangle of Diderot's tree is the mirror image of the other triangles pictured in this chapter. Putting the tree up against the grids shown in Figure 2.6 (p. 36) and the triangles shown in Figures 2.7 and 2.8 (p. 37 and p. 42) shows the emerging 'geometry' of Modernism (captured on the right-hand side of the picture under this paragraph). First, one triangle enables the scientist to detach himself from being and gain an objective 'global' viewpoint over and above. Then, horizontal grids enable things to be quartered and objects sorted out and pegged. Then, beneath this, an upside-down triangle shows how different categories or specialisms are connected, at base, by universal or general characteristics or principles that have stood the test of time.

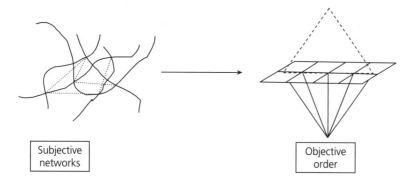

All that was required now was a general aim toward which all of this focussed and ordered energy could be directed.

◉ *Aiming:* efficiency becomes Man's general aim

Newton's [natural philosophy is] chiefly to be valued as it lays a sure foundation for natural religion and moral philosophy.

Colin Maclaurin

While the Modern knowledge institutes that formed in the seventeenth century initially chose to leave human affairs aside, Newton's breakthrough and other discoveries which pointed further toward there being common elements underlying all things soon saw humankind brought into the fold. Finding a correspondence between the now mechanistic underpinnings of nature and that of humans was the next step in Modernism's assertion of control over *chaos*. It was a step that other changes, brought about by the rise of Modernism, had made necessary.

The nation-states of the West had become powerful by developing along capitalist lines. To remain competitive they needed to grow their economies, and this required stability. This stability had previously been ensured by norms supported by particular traditions: religion, culture, *telos*, a sense of community. Modernism's undermining of particular customs in favour of finding general mechanisms now threw these into doubt. Having removed the influence of subjective, tradition-based ends in its quest for general certainties, Modernism required new measures to ensure social stability, to give life an aim and enable progress to be assessed.

Toward this, the development of 'human sciences' would enable objective general norms of behaviour to be identified by transforming the 'human object'. The change can be illustrated by contrasting the figures of Da Vinci and Borrelli (see Figure 2.10). In the sixteenth century, Leonardo reflects an actual life-model, still drawing from Galen's animal analogies. But by the end of the seventeenth century, Borelli saw the body reductively and idealistically as a machine. Da Vinci attributed human action to a spontaneous individual principle from within or the *natura naturans*. By the end of the seventeenth century this concept had disappeared, and the word 'nature' itself had come to mean abstract mechanical properties or *natura naturata*. By the eighteenth century, aesthetes like Camper and von Soemmering claimed that their emphasis on the measurement of human bodily space and proportion was influenced by belief in 'the absence of individuality' as an attribute of beauty.

A *new general object called 'Man'*, comprised of universal functional elements, had emerged. In time, human sciences like physiology and ergonomics would determine Man's smallest actions, outlining ideal forms and de-individualized norms for soldiers' steps, sitting and digestion. All were subjected to detailed analysis and a rigorous classification of bodily inputs, processes and outputs. The generic 'everyman' that emerged (see Figure 2.11), the representation of all of our essential needs and average or ideal functions, would increasingly inform the effective mass-production of goods and services, from chairs to cars to soft drinks.

Man's social relations were similarly analysed. John Locke's (1632–1704) *Treatises on Government* resonated with the objective universals appealed to in other spheres, claiming that all men, first and foremost, are equal. This philosophy was influential in the drafting of the United States' founding documents. *The Declaration of Independence* thus concludes: 'We hold these truths to be self-evident [Franklin having substituted 'self-evident' for Jefferson's original 'sacred']: that all men are created equal.' A view of society where equilibrium would be assured by *underlying essential characteristics and general principles* rather than strong individuals, traditions or spiritual beliefs was emerging. Modern states would govern more certainly by invoking self-evident truths in the way that Descartes had firmly founded Modern philosophy on using underlying self-evidentials.

In the Modern Age these norms and principles would be monitored and upheld by *dispassionate bureaucratic institutions*. Saint-Simon (1760–1825) subsequently saw bureaucracy as the great hope for Man's stability and

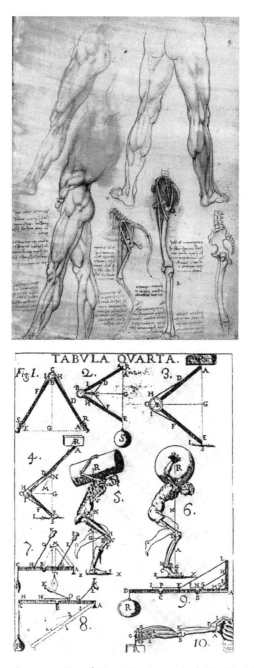

Figure 2.10 The Changing conception of Man I: Top, Leonardo da Vinci (c. 1500); Bottom, Borelli (c. 1700)

Sources: Top, Leonardo da Vinci's 'Comparision of the legs of a horse with that of a man' (c. 1506–7), original held in the Royal Library, Windsor Castle; Bottom, G.A. Borelli's 'De Motu Animalium' (1680)

Ideal sitting

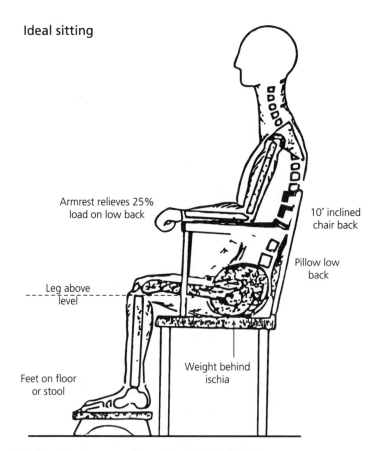

Figure 2.11 The changing conception of Man II: 'Ideal sitting'

progress in the aftermath of the French Revolution. And thus, over the ensuing century, bureaucracy went from being one form of organizing to the ideal, if not the only, form of organization, applicable not only to research academies and the military, but to prisons, police forces, governments and even businesses. The combination of bureaucratic organization and an objective knowledge of Man had a double effect: a knowledge of the categories of normal human behaviour which would then be maintained by bureaucratic institutions or by individuals provided with information about normality by these institutions to keep themselves and their fellows 'in check'.

Premoderns considered themselves individual members of particular traditions that they sought to develop from the inside out. In the Modern world, with all matter made of the same essence and subject to common principles, even society could be broken into constituent units of analysis and *subject to global custom-free laws applied from the outside in*. With particular traditions no longer accepted as guiding action, one thought of oneself in terms of the human race as a whole. One would ask 'Am I a good human?' as opposed to 'Am I a good helmsperson?' or 'Am I being true to myself?'

Institutes of knowledge could now begin to apply themselves to the ethics of Man and how his progress, as a 'race', could be measured – to the possibility of establishing an objective moral code.

Ethical philosopher Henry Sidgwick (1838–1900) duly claimed that a new ethical science would be born by applying 'the same disinterested curiosity to which we chiefly owe the great discoveries of physics.' In keeping, Modern ethical thinkers rejected the Aristotelian view of humans as each having a specific *telos* comprising their many individual roles that implied case-specific ways of acting toward particular ends. Instead, they sought to find the underlying ethical laws behind an individual's different roles, secondary characteristics and traditional circumstances. They sought to disconnect individuality from how a person ought to act.

A number of starts toward the identification of general ends or achievements against which universal progress could be measured were made. Kant arrived at the categorical imperative: 'Act as if the maxim from which you act were to become a general law.' Utilitarians argued that the moral rightness of an action, or progress, was to be judged on the contribution it makes to the increase of general human happiness (or 'greatest good'). The founding-fathers of the United States sought to fill the morality gap left by the removal of *telos* with a mix of a Protestant and Capitalist ethic and a utilitarianism implying that anything that led to financial utility was good. This is characterized in Benjamin Franklin's (1706–90) writings, which declared that: 'Honesty is useful, because it assures credit; so are punctuality, industry, frugality and that is the reason they are virtues.'

But Modern ethical theorists seemed unable to rectify the problem they had opened up by abstaining from particular customs and ends. Despite the apparent dispassionate reasonableness of ends such as the 'greatest good' or the 'greatest use', they were difficult to measure and it was hard to find solid foundational reasons why people should fall in behind them without circularity of argument. Franklin had to circle back to tradition to validate his position. 'If we thus ask, why should "money be made out of men"?', Franklin asserts. 'One only need consult the Bible for the answer: "Seest thou a man diligent in business? He shall stand before kings".' At the same time, Kant and the Utilitarian's moral ends were running aground as it was recognized that people's surface differences often made them act according to their own interests or wish for different general laws. A few decades after his confident boast of a new ethical science, a disappointed Sidgwick wrote that: 'Where we had sought cosmos we found only chaos.'

However, a *de facto* general morality, hinted at in Franklin's words, was taking hold. The capitalist market was coming to be seen as resolving the 'Hobbesian mystery of order' and filling the morality gap that Modernism had created. A new science called 'economics' argued that an underlying social order emerged because of the sum of the free and independent decisions to buy and sell on the market that the price mechanism allows. The market, an 'invisible hand', is thus the source of our underlying order. The objective, fundamental principle or general law that coordinates human behaviour is that every man, whether helmsperson, wood-turner, or parent, acts in terms of economic self-interest. Economic self-interest, once thought of as just a means for achieving particular ends, was discovered to be a general characteristic of the human race and an objective universal end-in-itself.

The founding thesis of this new science, Adam Smith's (1723–90) *Wealth of Nations,* matched Modernism's emerging tenets. Smith used Newton's system as a model. He demonstrated mutual connections between individual cases and thus the underlying dependencies of all economic phenomena. His atoms (or humans), acting according to their universal propensities, were held in equilibrium by the invisible general law of the market, which operates like the invisible hand of gravity. His concept of the market, with its preordained rationality, stood like a Platonic ideal form. Whereas Bernard Mandeville's 1714 *Fable of the Bees* had put forward a view that required the State to maintain 'human vice or passion of luxury for the good of society', Smith's system was a mechanism regulated by a higher, altogether more rational, power. It also replaced Mandeville's key words, 'passion' and 'vice', with dispassionate terms like 'interest' and 'advantage'. Smith's argument that a *laissez-faire* economics was the obvious system of natural liberty and thus the greatest provider of general 'good' suited the emerging Modern way of seeing perfectly. Further, Smith's measure of social progress, the division of labour or specialization toward collective economic achievement, dovetailed neatly into Modernism's triangular-tree way of seeing.

By the end of the nineteenth century, the moralists who had continued the quest for a general law had developed a principle that shared economics' foundation of the self-interested individual. G.E. Moore (1873–1958) had discovered 'emotivism': the view that all moral judgements, for all people in all cultures at all times, are nothing but expressions of preference or feeling. The universal moral foundation is that we all act as separate individuals according to our own detached self-interest. To a large degree, people today now think, talk and act as if emotivism were true, regardless of their theoretical standpoint (this is why psychology came to be given far more credence than ethics as a guide to human action in the twentieth century).

The rise of 'economic man' and 'emotivism' further strengthens the view of bureaucracy as the ideal organizational form, and the implementation of the norms discovered by the human sciences as their main mechanism of control. If we take emotivism to be universally true, owners of capital are justified in believing that workers act in accordance with their short-sighted wants, and thus justified in believing that a measure of external control is necessary to ensure that our collective rational-economic ends are met. Bureaucratic discipline is subsequently not only generally applicable, but also generally necessary. Given Modernism's related belief that Man is, at base, economically self-interested, and thus does not feel any compulsion to do things for others, bureaucracies must apply the laws of motivation, and other psychological and social science, to enable us to get the most out of our human resources.

Even though the scientific norms or ends that are produced via bureaucracies may be questioned, it has become increasingly difficult to question the overarching principle or meta-narrative according to which this Modern system acts. Alasdair MacIntyre terms this principle *'bureaucratic rationality'*: the circular process of achieving *ends* like greater certainty, economic progress and efficiency through the *means* of increasing the efficient production of these things. Consequently, *performative efficiency*, the continual reduction of the ratio inputs/outputs, has become both Modernity's general end and its general means of measuring actions. Subsequently, Modernism's bureaucratic, triangular 'architecture of seeing' informs, and comes to be reinforced by, speaking in terms of the goal of performative efficiency. By the first decades of the twentieth century, this, more than anything else apparent at the time, appeared to provide Man, or the human race, with a certain direction and a measure of progress over and above individual purposes.

Fast forwarding from Elizabeth I's pose in Figure 2.7 (p. 37), we can see that the Modern manner emerging then is still with us today. However, *global* corporations have taken the place of royalty and imperial nation-states as they increasingly span the nations of the world *above local differences* and are taken as indicative of an *underlying universal business culture*. The belief in this underlying fabric enables them to implement general scientific principles of human psychology, motivation and marketing, and direct advances in communications technology that overarch and unite the world's disparate traditions, making our globe an increasingly small and controllable place.

    These corporations are housed in offices of the Modern architectural style, which, drawing from the great technological optimism present in the first decades of the twentieth century, presents Modernism's starkest expressions. Modern architecture seeks to reduce buildings to 'the absolute Platonic, pure minimum evocation', or 'efficient boxes', as indicated in the functional maxims of its gurus (for example, Mies van der Rohe's 'less is more' and Le Corbusier's 'a house is a machine for living in'). On the walls of these towers, Modern abstract art is hung. This cuts under secondary cultural differences, supposedly saying something to everyone from everywhere but nothing that could be claimed to move or offend any. Indeed, by the 1950s, Abstract Impressionists, probably the most common artists within these towers, saw their colours and shapes as the purest means for expressing emotion and sought 'a medium freed of all extraneous conventions to capture the objective essence of the human experience' so as 'to make individual psychology extinct.'

    This extinction of individuality is taken to its logical conclusion by Theodore Levitt in 'The Globalization of Markets', published in the in mid-1980s in *The Harvard Business Review*. Here Levitt famously predicted the progression from multi-national to global corporations in an increasingly homogenized world. Here the 'Model-T Ford' approach of the same standard essential product for all is vindicated as efficiency becomes *the* universal criteria. Levitt explains that multinational corporations have been 'thoughtlessly accommodating' in 'willingly accepting vestigial national differences, not questioning the possibility of their transformation, not recognizing how the world is ready and eager for the benefits of modernity, especially when the price is right.' He went on to claim that this traditional 'accommodating mode to visible national differences [wa]s medieval' or like paying homage to an 'obsolete institution'. And that, by contrast, the Modern corporation of the future will seek to:

> ... constantly drive down prices by standardizing what it sells and how it operates. It treats the world as composed of few standardized markets rather than many customized markets. It actively seeks and vigorously works toward global convergence. Its mission is modernity [hence] the global corporation accepts and adjusts to ... differences only reluctantly, only after relentlessly testing their immutability, after trying various ways to circumvent and reshape them.

3 Postmodernism

Simplifying to the extreme, I define Postmodern as incredulity toward meta-narratives.

Jean-Francois Lyotard

Jean-Francois Lyotard defines the Postmodern in contrast to Modern sociologist Talcott Parsons' view of society as a 'unified totality'. Parsons claimed to have found the answer to Hobbes' mystery of order in 'central value systems' – shared orientations that bound all societies. Hence, for Parsons:

> ... a process or set of conditions either 'contributes' to the maintenance (or development) of the [central value] system or it is 'dysfunctional' in that it detracts from its integration, effectiveness, etc.

For Lyotard, Parson's thinking and the Modernist drive to apply global meta-narratives like 'integration', 'evolutionary progress' and 'efficiency', and seeing things that do not adhere to these unifying aims as dysfunctional, 'does violence to heterogeneity': a heterogeneity that is imperative if we are to continue to be creative beings. *Postmodernism doubts the meta-narratives that Moderns believe must override the particular or the local and speak for all.* It wonders whether efficiency really is more important than diversity. Its seeks to undermine Modernism's hoisting of these meta-narratives above other ways of thinking. However, Postmodernism is realistic enough to realize that the global products that have sprung from Modernist approaches will not go away and is pragmatic enough to see that some good can come from them – if we do not buy into their claims of universality.

We may relate this to Charles Baudelaire's argument that style depends upon one's positioning with respect to *chaos*, change, fragmentation, irrationality and paradox: one 'can contest them or embrace them, try to dominate them or simply swim with them.' Modernism, by this logic, is best defined as seeking to contest and dominate, to ground and build an order that captures, reshapes, channels, directs and controls them. Postmodernism, by contrast, does not view *chaos* or paradox as a predicament to be rectified. It is happy to use Modernism's order and forms while at once embracing the *chaos*. It sees the gaps or *chaos* between things as necessary if one is to swim between and link them in order to create. Postmodernism is subsequently not so much a new age, but a questioning and 'rewiring' of some of the claims of Modernism.

● *Grounding: cosmos* as just a 'necessary appearance'

It remains to be seen whether the ground arrived at is really a ground, that is, whether it provides a foundation; or whether it fails to provide a foundation and is an abyss; or whether the ground is neither one nor the other but presents only a per-haps necessary appearance of foundation.

Martin Heidegger

We are suspended in webs of significance we ourselves have spun.

Clifford Geertz

Postmodernism begins by questioning Modernism's claim to ground itself on objective foundations and the essential elements that underlie different beings – the foundations which make abstract objects like 'Man' and meta-narratives like 'efficiency' possible. One may see why this questioning emerged by examining what happened to our abilities with regard to artistic creativity under Modernism.

Art became Modern as it moved beyond relating past traditions or myths. An avant-garde component emerged that compelled art instead to be at the forefront of the present, to wipe out all vestiges of the past and find an unsullied essential purity underlying all things. Painting subsequently went upwards and onwards until artists found themselves with nothing left to do but to destroy the figure and arrive at the abstract, then the white canvas, the slashed canvas, the charred canvas, and on until there was nothing left to undermine. Modern art consequently painted itself into a corner. By abstracting away from individuality all had eventually come to nothing, to pure sterility. A prominent Modern architect observed that:

> Mies [van de Rohe] based his art on three things: economy, science, technology; of course he was right. It's just that I am bored. We all are bored.

Mies and his peers had reduced art and architecture to a point where it was, in his own words, 'almost nothing'. And after 'almost nothing', the only thing left to do was nothing or produce banal copies of the 'masters' like Mies.

As Modernism's creative quest was thus running out of steam, information technology was bringing more and more plurality into our lives. Developments, from world travel to the Internet, increasingly displayed *different approaches* from around the world in fields from painting to medicine, and highlighted the inability to achieve universal best-views without recourse to anti-progressive censorship. At the same time, an emerging emphasis on consumer wants increased the legitimacy of actively seeking individual or customized products and services, rather passively accepting globally mass-produced 'Model-T Ford' type offerings.

Eventually, creative people who found themselves offered nothing more by Modernism's approach could not resist 'playing' with this plurality. Paradoxically, the unified global culture facilitated by the spread of electronic technologies ultimately began to undermine once-dominant Modernist ideas by enabling individuals to access and juxtapose a myriad of world views for their own individual ends. People began to combine, mix and match or 'channel hop' across different traditional approaches. This is the Postmodern style.

The Postmodern style may be seen in the 'Post-industrial city'. Here, elements of the Premodern city (for example, Athens) with its ancient buildings and cultural and historical landmarks and the Modern (for example, New York) with its gridiron streets and Modern high rises, are mixed together. Los Angeles is a good example. LA houses information technologists and movie stars, squalid slums and gentrified neighbourhoods. It sprawls heterogeneously but lacks an identifiable centre. It comprises mini-cities that refer nostalgically to other geographies (Manhattan, Venice, Westminster) but which in no way represent the original. Greek columns, Chinese dragons and Egyptian pyramids are intermingled with office blocks and giant adverts for Coke and Marlboro. Defined cultural 'spaces' and traditions wash into one another. The work-a-day time-clock world, originally designed to schedule workers so they could uniformly service the machinery of the Industrial Revolution, is changed as global markets and instantaneous communications require, and enable, an increasing number to work 'odd' hours. Living becomes increasingly decentred and interconnected.

But what of 'Hobbes' Mystery'? In the circumstances described above, what is it that stops things from crumbling into total *chaos*? Modernism's answer of 'underlying essences' was running dry. Postmodern thinkers now drew on Ludwig Wittgenstein and Martin Heidegger to theorize how things hung together.

The first paragraph of Wittgenstein's *Philosophical Investigations* is an excerpt from St. Augustine. Wittgenstein claimed that this offers:

> ... a particular picture of the essence of human language: that individual words in language name objects ... Every word has a meaning. This meaning is correlated with the word. It is the object for which the word stands.

Wittgenstein had set his target: the tradition that went back to Plato that words get their meanings by representing essential underlying forms. Due to the acceptance of this particular view, Wittgenstein claimed that we have been led to ask the wrong questions. Specifically:

> ... questions of the essence of language [suggesting that language] is something that lies beneath the surface ... hidden from us. [It thus] comes to look as if we should search for something like a final analysis of our forms of language ... as if there were something hidden in them that had to be brought to light. [W]e feel as if we have to penetrate phenomena.

Heidegger also critiqued the Modern assumption that what is ultimately real is what 'stands under' things. From this, he claimed, springs Modernism's 'spectator attitude' which looks down upon the world and encourages questioning along the lines of 'what *is* this?' or 'what *is* that?', 'what *is* life?' or 'what *is* a culture?', as if these 'things' were solid, stable objects against solid objective units of measure. Heidegger argued that while Descartes' *I think therefore I am*, claimed to put things on a new and firm footing, what it did not determine was 'the meaning of *am*-ness'. It had to abstain from this, claimed Heidegger, because *am*-ing, or being, occurs only as 'unfolding' or 'being-in-life'. It is never an object. By separating things out for analysis in its quest for certainty, Heidegger claimed that Modernism made us forget that 'self and world belong together in the single entity'. We can be the kinds of people we are only by virtue of the practical contexts of worldly involvement in which we exist. Hence, the *am* can only be what unfolds in the web of interactions and traditions that we move through life – there is no external foundation ground beneath or external viewpoint above.

Uncomfortable with paradox, and thus assuming we had an either/or choice between *foundation* or *abyss*, Moderns believed the discovery of un-groundedness to indicate that all was *chaos*. Neither Heidegger nor Wittgenstein saw it thus. For both, we may not be able to determine how the world and words hang together, but we can say that they do, and that they do so by people living and using language. For both, the sources of intelligibility of the world were 'public practices'. What is shared is not a conceptual schema that can be made explicit and justified. Rather, it is *manners* that enable us to 'carry ourselves' in particular publics. And as manners are not a hidden inner mental activity but a socially created public matter, they 'presuppose customs'.

Hence, Wittgenstein saw being as shaped by customs, practices and traditions as conveyed in social interactions through language. Due to the existence of many different unfolding dynamic practices and traditions, there was not one unitary grounding logic, however, but many different *'language games'*, as he termed them, each governed by their own rules. Thus, the same word can have different meanings or uses in different language games. The word 'beauty' only gets its meaning from the particular context of the 'language game' in which it is used, be it a fashion magazine, football match or cookery class. There is no essential 'ideal' underpinning it or measures over and above the context of a particular language game that give 'beauty' its meaning. Indeed, in a humorous context the word 'beauty' could mean 'ugly' or 'really bad'. By the same token, humans comprise many different 'gaming relationships'. While they may have a solid 'character', who they are and how they act will vary according to the game they are in, be it home, work or sports team.

However, things are *imperfectly held together* in this world of different games in a manner that Wittgenstein calls 'family resemblance'. To illustrate, if we take the word 'game' we find that there are many types of things that we call games: professional sports, mind games, games played with children and solitaire games. One might expect that for us to recognize the many different game-things as games, they must all share an essence or a pure form and have qualities that positively distinguish them from those things that are not games. But Wittgenstein claimed that these different 'games' only had a 'family resemblance' in the way that a set of brothers and sisters may share similarities that enable them to be identified as related, without necessarily having a definable essence not shared by other sets of siblings. Understanding the thing referred to by the word 'game' is thus only possible through consideration of the particular context in which it is used.

To express what it means to be Postmodern, Lyotard uses Wittgenstein's notion of the plurality of language games. There is, from a Postmodern perspective, no unified continent of language, only islands ruled by different language games, logical according to their own logic. These games may not have anything in common nor be translated into one another, just as a 'full house' may not be translated into a chess move. However, if we concern ourselves less with establishing the common ground beneath them, we are freer to move in and out of them as our particular concerns see fit. Thus, the heterogeneous web of language games presents the appearance of foundation that prevents all being *chaos*, while enabling people to invent by moving between and combining elements of different games in unusual ways. Development here is more like 'island hopping', as in the right hand figure below, than founding the New World.

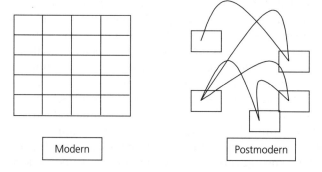

| Modern | Postmodern |

Local games mesh together as people operate across them. This ensures that we act with an *'appearance of ground'*. This 'appearance' allows for the fluidity necessary if people are to be creative, but prevents everything falling into *chaos*. Felix Guattari's book *Chaosmosis* subsequently expresses the

Postmodern condition nicely. His is a vision of a world 'part dipped' in *chaos*, comprising people moving between different games, orders or frameworks while acknowledging that beneath being in particular contexts *no universal ground may exist*.

⚡ *Moving:* the 'rhizome' – global frameworks *and* local networks

We should stop believing in trees. They've made us suffer too much. All of arborescent culture is founded on them, from biology to linguistics. Nothing is beautiful or loving or political aside from underground stems, aerial roots, adventitious growths and rhizomes.

Gilles Deleuze and Felix Guattari

In their book *Mille Platteaux*, Gilles Deleuze and Felix Guattari argue that it 'is odd how the tree has dominated Western reality and all of Western thought, from botany to biology and anatomy ... and all of philosophy.' The tree was well suited to Modernism's development, well suited to depicting categorization so as to determine the one branch to which the object in question belonged, to depicting binary either/or logic. Well suited to showing causal paths and the progression of things across linear time; to illustrating the stem of reason that connects all things and, in mirror image, bureaucratic hierarchies with those at the top (Man or mind) looking down on those below. However, Deleuze and Guattari contend that this tree-like or 'arboreal' view supports the uncritical acceptance of a philosophy that categorizes beings too rigidly, that overlooks difference and that is sedentary or ultimately uncreative.

Lyotard correspondingly concluded *The Postmodern Condition* by arguing that the public in the so-called information age must be given free access to 'the memory and the data banks'. Language games would then be played and connected to with maximum, unchannelled information, so as to be 'non-zero-sum games, and by virtue of that fact discussion would never risk fixating in a position of minimax equilibrium because it had exhausted its stakes'. Knowledge here, in other words, would not be contained in predetermined arboreal categories. Deleuze and Guattari offer an analogy for thinking along such untrammeled lines: the *'rhizome'*, a tangled multidirectional root system that spreads individually and indefinitely across many different 'spaces' or categories.

Unlike a tree that plots points, unifies and fixes a hierarchical order, any point of a rhizome can cut across space and time to connect to another. Rhizomes are thus made up of dynamic multiple lines of connection or alliances, rather than set positions. The tree imposes the sedentary verb 'to be' (as in 'to be this' or 'to be that'), but the fabric of the rhizome is the conjunction 'and ... and ... and ...'. And yet the rhizome does not destroy the tree. Indeed, tree structures may exist and guide action. ('The brain itself is much more a grass than a tree,' Deleuze and Guattari point out, but 'many people have trees [or set frameworks] growing in their heads.) They illustrate the analogy with reference to a musical score that sees a page of conventional ordered Apollonian note-lines, or staves, partially disintergrated, bounced across and linked-up by a wandering Dionysian string.

The shape of the rhizome as simultaneously interconnected across a flat 'strata' maps the Postmodern re-writing of Modernism's relation with the past. Postmodernism recognizes the connection of being across time, the *'inter-mingle' of the many plateaus of past, present and future*. Hence, Postmodernism returns to embrace the past that Modernism sought to overcome, 'recognizing', writes Umberto Eco, 'that the past, since it cannot really be destroyed, because its destruction leads to silence, must be revisited: but revisited with [knowing] irony.' Hence in Eco's novel, *The Name of the Rose*, the plot is developed through reference to past plots, with the action set in motion by a quotation from a discovered manuscript. Eco then set about writing what Vallet said that Mabillon said that Adso said. In talking about the construction of his work, Eco noted his re-appreciation that there are no necessarily new elements, but that one might set about linking elements in inventive ways.

We can return to the post-industrial city to see how people may act 'rhizomatically'. For David Harvey, Jonathan Raban's *Soft City*, an account of London life, is a 'historical marker', a symbol of Postmodernism establishing itself as 'a cultural aesthetic in its own right'. Raban's soft city is 'pliable', Harvey explains, 'a labyrinth, honeycombed with such diverse networks of social interaction oriented to such diverse goals that the encyclopaedia becomes a maniacal scrapbook filled with colorful entries which have no determining, rational or economic scheme.' 'The soft city of illusion, myth, aspiration, nightmare,' writes Raban, 'is as real [as] than the hard city one can locate in maps and statistics.' Thus, he continues:

> For better or worse [the city] invites you to remake it, to consolidate it into a shape you can live in … Decide who you are, and the city will again assume a fixed form around you. Decide what it is, and your own identity will be revealed, like a map fixed by triangulation. Cities … are [thus] plastic by nature. We mould them in our images: they, in their turn, shape us by the resistance they offer when we try and impose our personal form on them. In this sense, it seems to me that living in a city is an art, and we need the vocabulary of art, or style, to describe the peculiar relation between man and material that exists in the continual creative play of urban living.

◉ *Seeking:* creation though nomadology and eclecticism

Discovering no longer means finally reading an essential coherence beneath a disorder.

Michel Foucault

The multiple must be made, *not by always adding a higher dimension, but with the number of dimensions one already has available.*

Gilles Deleuze and Felix Guattari

Questioning the meta-narratives at the level above being and resisting the urge to look for the synthesis underneath, Postmodernism sees the world from the surface, as a rhizome. Here language and 'mind' are intertwined with the customs and practices of being, thereby losing their objective representational ability. Discovery must come from shuttling between things or different language games and drawing connections, the eclectic and pragmatic combination of what unfolds on one's way.

Deleuze and Guttari develop the term *'nomadology'* to express such an approach. They argue that Modernity's unifying system of capitalism promotes paradoxical 'schizoid' *désirants*, or individuals with multiple personalities, thanks to revolutionary desires for the avant-garde and innovation being mingled with opposing desires for repression and conformity. They then attack Freudian psychoanalysis as a mechanism for policing and channelling vagrant desires, thus privileging and reinforcing the dictates of the established order. As a counter-measure, they wish to celebrate this schizoid tendency rather than see it channelled away by promoting a 'nomadism' that encourages people to be multiple, to spread across and pick up different elements in order to *create* and *invent*. Faced with the 'treasure trove' that the information age now places at our fingertips, Lyotard similarly promotes the view that 'eclecticism' must be 'the degree zero of contemporary general culture'. In Postmodernity one is free, he claims, 'to listen to reggae, watch a Western, eat a hamburger for lunch and local cuisine for dinner, wear Paris perfume in Tokyo and retro clothes in Hong Kong.' Free to relate to many identities and be a unique constellation of elements. This eclecticism is now manifest in many spheres.

Architecture

Postmodern architecture recognizes that architecture's scope for innovation had been exhausted by Modernist dictates. By 1970, Robert Venturi was proclaiming that 'less is a bore' (knowingly twisting Mies van der Rohe's dictum 'less is more') and promoting an architecture concerned with the quirks of its users based on a kind of collage – a 'personable' architecture employing the languages of local consumers. Whereas Modernism, believing its calling to be universal, erected the same building everywhere, Postmodernism was free to enjoy contrasting architectural styles from disparate periods of history together with Modern technology. Charles Jencks similarly argues for an architecture that takes its cue from local conditions and their different user-constituencies, that is piecemeal, hybrid and eclectic: an architecture with a 'split personality' that operates at more than one level so

Figure 2.12 Postmodern form: 'Customised trainer' (from Burro)
Source: Photograph Ian Nolan, first appeared in *Guardian Weekend* (15 December 2001)

as to be both new *and* old, elitist *and* popular. Jencks describes Stuttgart's *Staatsgalerie* as exemplary. Here, he explains:

> ... there is not the simple harmony and consistency of either Modernism or Classicism ... instead we are uneasily confronted with the understanding that we live in a complex world where we can't deny either the past and conventional beauty, or the present and current technical and social reality.

The Tate Bankside Gallery in London, a reconfiguration of a 1930's power station, is another good example. Here a distinctive facade remains but the infusion of different materials and technologies has subverted the space within. The architects' philosophy is inscribed at the entry points:

> You cannot always start from scratch. We think this is the challenge of the Tate as a hybrid of tradition, Art Deco and Super-Modernism. Our strategy was to accept the physical power of Banksides' mountain-like brick building ... rather than trying to break or diminish it. This is a kind of *Aikido* strategy: you use your opponent's energy for your own purposes. Instead of fighting it, you take the energy and shape it in a new and unexpected way.

Art

While more difficult to define than Postmodern architecture, Postmodern art is influenced by a questioning of Modernism's drive toward abstraction and a rediscovery of pluralism, irony and paradox. One may point to works like Carlo Maria Mariani's use of Classical sculptural figures to depict illogical paradoxes; Wei Rong's juxtaposition of images of classical and modern

China; Simon Casson's collages of ordered Renaissance forms amid chaos; Cindy Sherman's photographic self-portraits that show a number of 'faces' within one person – how people can at once be *both* multiple *and* unitary (see *www.masters-of-photography.com)*; or Baz Luhrman's movies *Romeo + Juliet* and *Moulin Rouge*. One could even point to the emergence of custom painted trainers – new individualized patterns upon old generic 1970s style canvases – as postmodern forms (see Figure 2.12 and Case Box 2.1)

Literature

Umberto Eco sees Postmodernism as re-writing the Modern distinction between the cutting edge and the popular. Modernists held that the approval of the public was a bad sign: if a novel was popular, this was because it said *nothing new* and only provided what the masses were expecting. By contrast, Postmodern literature seeks to create works that are high *and* low brow, challenging *and* generally enjoyable. The recent success of *The Simpsons* animated television series is likely due to its un-idyllic view of family life (unlike the average 'happy family' television comedies that preceded it), its self-mockery, its knowing references to popular and high culture, and its subsequently being able to straddle mass appeal and critical acclaim.

Music

In music, magazines like *Billboard* now struggle to compile sales charts, organized as they are into objective sedentary categories like 'R&B', 'Rock' and 'Indie'. In a world where artists often create by sampling from across different spheres and styles, it is increasingly difficult to place them into such strict classifications.

In sum, *Postmodern nomadology reworks, and engages in interplay with, Modernist either/or hierarchies*: that *new* is better than *old*, that the *present* is ahead of the *past*, that *progress* is better than *reaction*, that *high culture* is superior to *low culture*, that the *global* must surpass the *local*. Instead of Modernism's cutting edge, where one sought to be ahead of the past, at the benchmark of the present and progressing into the future, Postmoderns see a flat surface, an artist's palette with traditional styles co-existing, waiting to be connected. They create by nomadically weaving a broad repertory of forms.

Case Box 2.1   Postmodern Sneakers

The rise in 'retro' sports shoe styles incorporating modern technology in the 2000s, and the customized pair of Dunlop sneakers (or trainers as they're called in England), shown in Figure 2.12, can be seen as expressions of Postmodernism. While the explosion of technologically advanced sports shoes that took the market by storm in the late 1980s and 1990s can be seen as an expression of Modernist forces. Perhaps then the development of the themes spoken of thus far in this chapter can be described using the analogy of the development of sports shoes?

1   Trace the history of sports shoes. Can you use this story as an analogy to describe the forces that have led to the emergence of modern, and then postmodern, forms?

⊕ *Timing:* history as more than linear and progressive

We can see ... a slow movement of our culture back to a 'centre which could not hold' (to misquote Yeats). The return has various causes, but among the most important is that the value of any work must depend partly on tradition. [A] radical work of quality is [now] likely to have the shock of the old.

Charles Jencks

If the desire to publish of the *new* thinking dismissing tradition was Modernism's marker, then the book titles symbolic of the surfacing of a different world-view are those that claim the *end* of that which sustained and drew upon Modernism. Titles like *The End of the Nation-state, The End of the History of Art, The End of Economic Man* now call into question the vehicles by which Modernity was to claim progress away from particular conventions. Postmodernism subsequently seeks to rewire Modernism's linear conceptions of history, time, direction and progress.

Heidegger and Nietzsche's critique of Modernist history is thus a key Postmodern dimension. Modernist history, Heidegger claimed, believed that every significant element of the past is only a stepping stone toward the present. It is subsequently concerned with the past as an object that no longer exists, which is over and done with or 'dead'. Heidegger, by contrast, argued that we should instead look at the past as still with us, still making its presence felt. From this perspective, future, present and past are interwoven. It followed that history could not be regarded as simply a linear progression and that no meta-narrative existed by which one period could be objectively judged better or worse than what had gone before. Nietzsche similarly hoped that questioning Modernism's assumptions would see 'history placed in the balance again,' allowing 'a thousand secrets of the past,' left in Modernism's wake, 'to crawl out of the shade.' In this respect, Postmodernism is a recovery of things rejected by the Platonic→Cartesian→ Newtonian→Hegelian line of thought, a resurfacing of many of the aspects that Modernism sought to overcome. By combining this view of time and history with its nomadic spirit and rhizomatic form, *Postmodernism is free to connect across many time zones* and activate the 'retro'.

This can now be seen in many fields' reconnections with the past. Political theorists argue that Thucydides' approach to analyzing inter-national conduct, which incorporated national conventions, the individual characters of states-men and the role of rhetoric, should be reanimated as an alternative to the Modern Hobbesian approach that reduces human behaviour to single causes. In ecology, the Modern search for general mechanisms that govern ecosystemic community structure, has been joined by a transdisciplinary 'landscape ecology' and an Aristotelian recognition that there is no objective scale with which to conduct all inquiries. In psychotherapy, authors have begun to see people as contradictory rather than straight-forward beings, and examine the way that Modernity marginalized the study of the soul because it could not objectively quantify and measure its effects. In medi-cine, the complementary combination of traditional and new remedies is a huge growth area. And in physics, developments from Schrodinger's argu-ment for a return to those who worked prior to 'the delimitation of disci-plines in water-tight compartments', to Franz Capra's *The Web of Life, A New Synthesis of Mind and Matter*, signify a shift of emphasis: from 'objects' to the non-grounded relations between beings.

But just as the rhizome incorporates the tree rather than signalling its extinction, the Postmodern incorporates the linear. Gibson Burrell advocates a *spiral view of time* in this respect. Here aspects of the past will resonate in the present and future without things ever being as they were, although we may still observe progress within particular language games, fields or domains.

✺ *Knowing:* **Modern science as just one 'language game' among many**

By an odd fate, the very metaphysicians who think to escape the world of appearances are constrained to live perpetually in allegory. A sorry lot of poets they dim the colours of the ancient fables, and are themselves but gatherers of fables. They produce white mythology.

Jacques Derrida

John Horgan's *The End of Science* argues that science is increasingly unable to make ground-breaking discoveries because of its applying the one method over and over again and the 'theory of diminishing returns'. Just as Modern art was questioned once it led to an increasingly blank canvas, science's dom-inance is increasingly seen to be dimming the lights of other approaches and sterilizing and dulling knowledge. Postmodernism is dubious not so much toward science as an approach, but rather to its dominance over other modes of inquiry, incredulous to one language game being hoisted above others. Hence, Thomas Kuhn, Paul Feyerabend and other scientific historians', rethinking of science's monopoly is another key Postmodern element.

Prompted by a chance reading of Aristotle's *Physics*, Kuhn began to question the textbook view of science's righteous assertion. He concluded that:

> The more carefully [one] stud[ies], say Aristotelian dynamics … the more certain they feel that these once current views of nature were … neither less scientific nor the product of human idiosyncrasy than those current today. If these out-of-date beliefs are to be called myths, then myths can be produced by the same sorts of methods and held for the same sorts of reasons that now lead to scientific knowledge. If, on the other hand they are to be called science, then science has included bodies of belief quite incompatible with the ones we hold today. Given these alternatives, the historian must choose the latter. Out-of-date theories are not in principle unscientific because they have been discarded. That choice, however, makes it difficult to see scientific development as a process of accretion.

Kuhn came to argue that science did not develop rationally through the accumulation of discoveries bringing us ever closer to the 'whole truth'. All theories are based upon particular sets of assumptions and these are shaped by custom, tradition and myth. Kuhn termed these sets 'paradigms'. Once a paradigm is established (by becoming the dominant way of looking at the world and hence dismissing other alternatives), it constrains approaches to knowledge via educational initiation into a disciplinary branch, whereby research becomes a 'strenuous and devoted attempt to force nature into the conceptual boxes supplied by [this] education.'

Feyerabend also sought an approach that acknowledged the inescapable role of particular contexts in formulating knowledge. Modern science, for Feyerabend, was a tradition-bound practice that did not recognize itself so, while criticizing other approaches or traditions on these same grounds. He thus claimed that 'science should be taught as one view among many and not as the one and only road to truth and reality.' His own work found that science knows no 'bare facts'. Indeed, any 'fact' is already viewed in a certain way, and thus ordered by one's particular way of looking. This being so, Feyerabend argued that the progress of knowledge:

> will be as complex, chaotic, full of mistakes, and entertaining as the ideas it contains, and these ideas in turn will be as complex, chaotic, full of mistakes, and entertaining as the minds of those who invented them.

In addition, while Modern science has sought to unite under one paradigm or view, Feyerabend's analysis ironically showed science's greatest discovery to be the result *of particular aims and disparate practices or traditions being linked and combined*: namely Galileo's eclectic interconnection of his own aims, Plato, the clock analogy, and a telescope. Feyerabend was disappointed that development had been so incremental ever since.

This approach is reinforced by Umberto Maturana's biological studies, which suggest that cognition is not about transforming things into representative mirror pictures in the brain, as Cartesian logic would suggest.

Rather, it is a projection of an individual or community's own cognitive structure or mind-set. Given that observation circumscribes all knowledge and we constitute the reality of our observations through language, knowledge is relative to the observer. The observer's ability to receive knowledge is therefore shaped by their previous experiences or the experiences of those who have informed them and the language that their community uses to express things. All of these aspects are culture- and experience-specific. They overlay our general biological make-up with impressions that act like rhizomatic 'waterways', steering our behaviour and inter-actions by 'structurally coupling' us to our environments in particular ways. Consequently, how we receive the world depends on the way our particular cognitive streams emerge. Thus, pure objectivity operating above experience is unattainable and invention can only come from the interaction of different streams.

Illustrating how contexts, reason and particular purpose must always intermingle in each individual to create knowledge despite Modern beliefs to the contrary, Feyerabend invoked the analogy of the relations between an old map and an experienced traveller. Originally, maps were con-structed as images of, and guides to, the nature of reality as traditionally experienced by those who drew them. The traveller uses the map of someone-who-has-gone-before to guide their way, but the map does not tell them what to do – it must be tempered according to their own purposes and its use influenced by their own background of practical experiences. The traveller's action is guided by the interaction between the traditional view embodied in the map, other traditional approaches and the environ-mental context acting upon them in the present and their own personal aims for the future. Feyerabend argued that using reason without paying heed to contextual contingencies (like weather conditions) will soon lead one astray; while reason without the guidance of a particular practical pur-pose cannot lead us anywhere – the map does not tell us where to go. However, at the same time, practice is vastly improved by the structure of a map depicting an order with which to work and the impetus that this provides. Different practices and reason 'maps' (of which science is just one version) must spark off one another for 'creative travel' or invention to take shape.

In the light of Kuhn, Feyerabend and Maturana, scientific commenta-tors like Arthur Koestler and Carl Sagan have recognized 'the death of the spectator' and begun to *question Modern assumptions about the arboreal either/or separation of intellectual branches and categories* and how this works against the creative combination of different logics. In place of this they seek a return to an unspecialized approach whereby the scientist 'includes himself in his science' and where science is made, as Nietzsche argued in *The Gay Science*, a little 'jaunty and ignorant again'. Where thinking is more than just the bureaucratic application of the same procedures in ever-decreasing circles.

⊙ *Aiming:* a return to particular journeys

What matters most is always culture.

Friedrich Nietzsche

*Human beings ... can never create absolutely: all they can do is
choose combinations from a repertory of ideas.*

Claude Levi-Strauss

Lyotard claims that Postmodernism is the result of a 'delegitimation' movement for which Nietzsche's philosophy is a central document. This is largely
because it was Nietzsche who outlined the 'death' of the Rational Universal
God over and above all cultures and the generic Man that belief in Him
inspired. Perhaps this may be more correctly regarded as the death of two
characters, both of which had been given life by the Modern ascendancy of
mind over matter:

1 The death of man as the *subject*, the detached scientist who looks down
   upon things.
2 The death of the *object* 'generic Man', the idea that the human race, a
   species characterized by common elements, is an object subject to the
   scientist's gaze.

This double death leads to Postmodernism's *questioning the essential functions
that the human sciences appeal to,* and, in particular, *Modernism's appeal to self-
evident human characteristics that formed the basis for the universal codes of behaviour* that were to replace particular customs, culture or tradition-based *ethos.*

By the end of the twentieth century, moral historians were recording the
crumbling of the Enlightenment's search for an objective ethics, as it eventually hoisted itself on its own petard in much the same way as Modern art and
architecture ran dry. Alasdair MacIntyre describes the turn of events well in
After Virtue, arguing that in its quest for a global, secular and rational morality in place of Aristotelian particularism, the Modern project created a world
in which an unresolvable tension was inevitable and no moral judgements
actually possible.

MacIntyre explains that Modernism's aims are based on a belief in 'liberal
individualism'. Individuals were to detach themselves from the shackles of
custom and tradition to become the planners, directors and controllers of
their own destinies. However, the problem with this was that it tended to
produce societies that were difficult, or at least inefficient, to control, thus
hindering the development of Man's collective progress. Hence, Modernity
spawned *bureaucracy* as a global form to keep operations progressing
smoothly. Unfortunately, there is no way in which bureaucratic rationality
and liberal individualism can be achieved without one compromising the
other. Thus, MacIntyre concludes that there are now:

... only two modes of social life open to us, one in which the free and arbitrary choices of individuals are sovereign and one in which the bureaucracy is sovereign, precisely so that it may limit the free and arbitrary choice of individuals.

Uncoupling individual morality from the custom-based Aristotelian schema could only lead, argues MacIntyre, to a succession of failed attempts to find an objective moral code and on to the blank canvas of the 'everybody does what they feel' psychology of emotivism. This set of circumstances must then be held in place by an over-arching 'bureaucratic rationality' maintained by managers who claim not to engage in moral questions, preferring to refer decision making back to what are regarded as the objective principle of bureaucratic rationality: 'efficiency'. Hence, the West is left with only a 'simulacra of morality' in MacIntyre's words. This enables us to talk and act as though we have recourse to a framework for resolving moral issues universally and objectively, which we cannot, while at the same time particular moral debates can find no terminus as the appeal to particular circumstances is no longer considered legitimate.

However, Nietzsche prophesised that the nihilistic conclusion of Modernism described above actually offered a way around this predicament. The death of the foundation stones of the human race, and the realization that an objective science of ethics is ill-founded, frees us up to question the 'received opinions' that any history implants, enabling us to 'rewire' our own histories by choosing different combinations and thus 'restyle' ourselves. However, this does not leave us completely free to start from a clean slate, or mean that 'anything goes'. Heidegger's concept of 'throwness' expresses the limit nicely. Here one is thrown toward the future in a direction shaped by historical experience. However, if one recognizes that this is the case and begins to question some of the aspects of the past that are throwing us in this way, we may put something of a rudder in the wash so as to influence our nomadology or travelling to some extent.

This view draws upon a *re-recognition of the role played by culture, practice and stories as things that unite past and future* so as to give the present meaning and provide decision making guidance, and on *a recovery of individual **ethos***. These are aspects that are subjective and must be interpreted, things that Modernism's sought to overcome but could not. Thus, Lyotard reconnects with Aristotle to express the idea that our aims, from a Postmodern perspective, cannot be a matter of conforming to predetermined global schemes. We have no universal models to guide us and must therefore judge 'just so, without criteria. This is, after all, what Aristotle calls prudence.'

To recap, Modernism is an approach that seeks to master or control chaos and uncertainty by asserting an apparatus that looks down on things in the world through the lens of one central or global logic so as to see the general essences, theories or ideals that underlie things. By doing so it believes that we will be able to plan and direct our collective progress. Modernism is therefore an approach that favours commonality, standardization and functional efficiency over difference and diversity.

Postmodernism recognizes no universal language with which to represent all things, no objective global standards, theories, values or products. It claims that diversity is no less important than efficiency and that there must be different schools of thought if we are to create and develop. Postmodernism subsequently advocates a different way of seeing. Lyotard terms this *paralogy*: the *irregular or 'faulty' juxtaposition* of traditions, language games or schools of thought that spawns invention, as opposed to a Modern 'homological' emphasis on the consonance and sameness of relations that promotes incremental refinement. A practice of allowing many logics to grate against one another, as opposed to the repeated implementation of a dominant logic. Postmodernism's view is summed up by Levinas' *End of History*, where what is arrived at 'is not Absolute Logic ... or agreement in the absolute system, but Peace in separation, the Diaspora of absolutes.' Hence Lyotard's Postmodern claim that it is the preservation of 'difference on which the fate of thought depends,' and his interest in developing an approach that acknowledges the 'differ-end' (that is, different ends as opposed to collective meta-narratives).

Harking back to Montaigne, Postmodern sociologist Mike Featherstone paradoxically suggests that the Postmodern thus aims for a 'commonality [that] entails the capacity to recognize differences as legitimate and valid.' Thus, Postmodernism does not suggest an unreflective anarchy – people depend upon their particular community's traditions and frameworks and often, because of information technology, these communities (financial markets, for example) spread across the globe. Postmodernism is consequently not opposed to global realities or approaches *per se*, but about keeping things open enough to allow both Modern and un-Modern, global and local, old and new approaches to compete for attention as individual people and organizations seek to make decisions.

While it may be irrational to Modernists seeking either/or distinctions, Postmoderns see both forces for increased globalization and increased localization paradoxically co-existing in our world. Despite Levitt's assertion that ever-increasing global standardization was both righteous and inevitable, the Postmodern hope is that local identities and differences, partly in response to increasing globalization, will reassert themselves and perhaps even flourish. Indeed, some even contend that Postmodernity will see global companies having to appreciate, accommodate and incorporate regional customs and differences, while smaller companies will increasingly accentuate their connection to local traditions. If this turns out to be so, the Postmodern challenge will be developing the ability to be agile, dextrous and bold enough to recognize these paradoxes and link together global and local concerns for particular purposes. Table 2.1 summarises Postmodernism's key dimensions and 'geometries' alongside those of Modernism and Premodernism.

Table 2.1 Premodern, Modern, Postmodern

	1. Premodern	2. Modern	3. Postmodern
● Grounding	1 *Chaos and cosmos* both necessary and co-dependant. 2 *Ambiguity, uncertainty* and an ever-increasing range of *logics and approaches* is to be expected.	1 *Chaos is a predicament that will be rectified* as we *objectively determine the cosmos.* 2 We can *assert one logic* to assert an ever-increasing measure of *certainty and control.*	1 *The appearance of cosmos* may be *necessary,* but it is *not necessarily objective.* 2 Things are held together by the *imperfect logics of many different language games and traditions.*
ↄ Moving	1 View from *inside-out* in terms of the *microcosm.* 2 Analogies: *individual telos;* the *web of life;* the *multitude* of different gods/goddesses.	1 View from *outside-in,* in the style of a *singular all-controlling God.* 2 Analogies: *clockwork* (or input→process→output mechanism); *hierachical triangle; central-stemmed tree.*	1 A return to the *'surface'* to see in terms of root-structures or *rhizomes.* 2 *Combining* both Modern and Premodern analogies.
? Seeking	1 *Wisdom* through *subjective* connection to sympathetic links between individual beings. 2 *Context* is key.	1 *Certainty* through breaking things into parts, *objective* measurement, generalization, representation, categorization. 2 *Detached reason* is key.	1 *Creation* through *eclectic* "nomadology". 2 *Interplay* of context/reason.
⊕ Timing	1 *Cyclical.* 2 Past, present and future are *interconnected.*	1 *Linear* and evolutionary. 2 Past, present and future *separated out* as steps on common path.	1 *Spiral,* or *linear-cyclical.* 2 Categories of past, present and future can be fruitfully *interlinked.*
✸ Knowing	1 Many cohabiting philosophies.	1 Things can only be either true or false. Hence, there can be only *one* school or best way (e.g., science).	1 Embracing paradox: *both/and* rather than either/or.

Continued

Table 2.1 Continued

	1. Premodern	2. Modern	3. Postmodern
✹ *Knowing [cont.]*	2 Little specialization and many plausible schools of thought.	2 Centralization enables bureaucratic specialization to enhance *the efficient development of general laws.*	2 No one school privileged other others. *Seek to combine* ideas and approaches from many for particular purposes.
⊙ *Aiming*	1 Comparison of context with *particular traditions,* experiences, stories and principles. 2 *Individual telos* and prudence and a *local* sense of *ethos.*	1 *Global laws or codes* based on objective norms administered by bureaucracies. 2 *Bureaucratic rationality/ efficiency becomes universal means and global end.*	1 Generic or global norms and general procedures seen as *limiting difference* and hence creativity. 2 Recovery of *individual ethos* and *local difference* as opposed to just general codes and ends.
Key shapes or 'geometries'			
Overall approach	1 Local view from the inside-out. 2 **Metis:** resourceful *'shuttling'* between orders, forms or approaches through the chaos or gaps in thought.	1 Global view from the outside-in. 2 **Objective scientific reason:** asserts *new best ways,* moves the 'cutting edge' forward and increases the cosmos or general order of things.	1 Local views mixed with global realities. 2 **Paralogy:** 'faulty logic' or the *oscillation between and combination of many logics or categories, including Modern and Premodern.*

Postmodernism sees Modernism's objective view and universal approaches as artificial creations. In doing so, it may look beyond Modern approaches to other forms and styles of thought. 'Knowledge so conceived,' explains Feyerabend:

> ... is [thus] not a series of self-consistent theories that converge towards an ideal view. It is rather an ever-increasing ocean of mutually incompatible alternatives, each single theory [or] myth forcing others into greater articulation and all of them contributing, via this process of competition, to the development of our consciousness. Nothing is ever settled, no view can ever be omitted.

Postmodernism seeks creative invention by 'swimming' this ocean, oscillating between and connecting different theories and myths to develop particular approaches. Simplifying to the extreme, Postmodernism is about individuals, organizations or communities *combining Modern and Premodern, or global and local, ideas, styles and approaches* as they see fit.

CASE BOX 2.2   Cola, Catholicism and Cars

Cola

Coca-Cola's iconic worldwide campaigns, like 'I'd like to buy the world a Coke', 'Always Coca-Cola' and 'You can't beat the Real Thing' represented an age of global standardization and homogenization. However, Coca-Cola's new millennium began with CEO Douglas Daft announcing the abandonment of its worldwide campaigns and global policies. According to Coca-Cola's British head of external affairs, Ian Muir, 'We used to say that we thought globally and acted locally. Now we are thinking locally and acting locally.' Events in Britain provide a good example of why Coca-Cola now feels the need to move this way. Perhaps the most successful soft drink in the UK in recent times has been Tango, a brand spurred on by campaigns determined to connect to the quirkier aspects of British humour (anyone who has seen the ads will recognize that they would not go down well in most other cultures). Coke's global campaigns appear bland and pallid by comparison.

Daft's first move was to send executives out of Atlanta and closer to local customers and give creative leeway to branches to produce their own promotions. On 27 March 2000, Daft, an Australian, outlined his vision for the company:

> Even though our historical strength came from operating as a 'multi-local' business that relied heavily on the insight of our local bottling partners, we knew that we had to centralise control to manage expansion. [Thus], we have been heading in a direction that has served us very well for several decades, generally moving toward consolidation and centralized control. That direction was particularly important when we were 'going global'.
>
> The world, on the other hand, began moving in the 1990s in a different direction ... as globalization accelerated, many national and local leaders understandably sought to ensure sovereignty over their political, economic and cultural identities. As a result the very forces that were making the world more connected and homogeneous were simultaneously triggering a powerful desire for local autonomy and preservation of unique cultural identity.

Consequently, what we learned was that the next big evolutionary step of 'going global' now has to be 'going local'. In other words, we had to rediscover our own multi-local heritage. We must lead a Coca-Cola that not only has the expertise and structures required for success in a globalized economy, but which is also able to act nimbly and with great sensitivity in every local community where our brands are sold.

So, we are placing responsibility and accountability in the hands of our colleagues who are closest to individual sales. We will not abandon the benefits of being global. But if our local colleagues develop a strategy that is the right thing to do locally, then they have the authority and responsibility to make it happen. Our local people are ready to take on their shoulders the authority and accountability that naturally belongs to them.

In our recent past, we succeeded because we understood and appealed to global commonalties. In our future, we'll succeed because we will also understand and appeal to local differences. Think local, act local. The twenty-first century demands nothing less.

Catholicism

The Catholic Church is likely the last millennium's most prominent multi-national corporation. However, in our times it has generally not been regarded as an organization that embraced local differences or promoted divergence from its global doctrines. Perhaps this is why doing the rounds with Kevin, an Irish priest stationed in Kenya, comes as a surprise.

Kevin's parish is based around a large central church and 16 'outstations' that are visited on a rotational basis. Today he is offering mass at three. When asked how long each service will be, he is unable to say for sure; 'it depends on where they take them.' (John, a Kenyan priest who works with Kevin, claims that 'If you talk for too long, or hold them up for just two minutes, the people here will tell you'.) John and Kevin, whose Swahili is good enough to crack intricate and impromptu jokes throughout the service, and the liturgy (also entirely in the local language) provide points of convergence, but there is a lot more going on. A large part of the time is devoted to local song and dance, with troupes of youngsters in 'team uniforms' (each station has its own traditional stripe) particularly prominent. Services end with local leaders reading notices, an important function as this may be the only time that people from the area congregate (indeed, the Church's infrastructure provides the only means for meaningful political opposition here). The result is an eclectic mix of styles that has common themes but varies from station to station. While all this makes the services relatively long, John, who has worked in Ireland, claims that 'people look at their watches a lot less here than in Ireland.'

Michael, an elder at one of the stations, explains the change that has taken place. 'The Church here was declining. I'd go to conferences where the reasons why were discussed, but it was obvious to me – you cannot expect people to get involved in anything unless you accommodate them first. It's good to see how this has now happened. You must accommodate people.' Kevin confirms that it is now the Church's strategy to work with and incorporate local traditions, and people like himself 'on the ground' are now given a great deal of latitude to 'interpret' Church policy and make connections to local traditions.

Kevin's congregation is about to celebrate the opening of an extension to the central church that double its capacity from 800 to 1400. Half the money came from overseas donors and half was raised locally ('we could have got the money more quickly from abroad,' Kevin claims, 'but it was important that people here to really feel that they own it.'). The resulting structure, a large rectangle set onto the existing rectangle to make a 'T' ('If we could build from scratch it would have been good to base it on a circle to reflect the local architecture,' says Kevin), is filled with new iconic paintings by local artists depicting Kenyan people and familiar landscapes. 'You can see how they work when you watch the kids faces,' says Kevin, 'They really light up when they see these. They can relate to them. Unlike the usual Italian blond Jesus pictures.'

Another Kevin, who has travelled from his parish to attend the ceremony, explains what he has learned from working in Africa. 'You have to make what you say relevant to everyday life here, it's no good just lecturing out of a bible, you have to use local everyday examples and get people involved. In Ireland I think sometimes we've lost the ability to relate what we say to people's lives; perhaps it's got stuck in habits of "the way things have always been done".'

However, solutions may not be so simple as just bringing Africa home to Ireland. 'After working in Nigeria I went home and did a service in my parent's village,' Kevin explains. 'It didn't go as long as it would in Nigeria, but it ended up being longer and more involving than what they were used to. My mother was so ashamed that she wouldn't speak to me for days afterwards. Eventually I found out why: People in Ireland put on Sunday dinner before they go to church knowing that the service lasts 45 minutes. There were a lot of burnt dinners that day.'

Cars

'Democracy is the system where everybody gets what nobody wants.'

Anon

The appearance of cars is changing. According to Hugh Pearman, cultural commentator with *The Sunday Times*, 'Manufacturers have been driven to take risks ... to create market niches. Before, everyone wanted their products to look the same. Now, they want them to look distinctive ... Good is bland, bad is good, and suddenly instinct is cooler than logic.' This is culturally significant, claims Pearman, because 'cars dominate our visual surroundings.'

Examples of this distinctiveness are now coming to the fore. Ford may have led the way with its Scorpio ('bugged eyed and strangely proportioned, but you noticed it', says Pearman) and is now 'going back to the future' with its Forty-Nine. Chrysler's new PT Cruiser is described by its makers as 'a love it or hate it car too cool to categorise' (it looks like a 1950s American hotrod). The PT follows on from what Chrysler describes as its 'yestertech' sports cars like the Prowler and Viper, combining retro styling and modern technology (their old-fashioned large-diameter steering wheels housing airbags). Only 41 per cent of the company's focus group members liked the PT (26 per cent hated it, usually more than enough to kill off a prototype). Outside of Britain, Rover's advertising plays upon British heritage (Swedish ads for Rover finish with the line 'welcome back to the future'). Within the UK no reference is made to tradition. Instead, images of non-politically-correct pursuits such as hunting, nudism and boxing are portrayed to convey the idea that not everyone will like the car but those that do will love it. Toyota recently claimed that "Our global strategy used to center on "world cars", which we would modify slightly to accommodate demand in different markets. Today our focus is shifting to models that we develop and manufacture for selected regional markets.'

Why are such examples striking a chord? 'The globalisation of the car industry meant that all cars (and all car ads) came to look much the same everywhere,' Pearman explains. 'The aim of manufacturers was for the greatest number of people to be unoffended by the look of the product. This avoidance of risk was achieved through focus groups, and meant that national and marque differences were ironed out. Weird French cars ceased to be weird, Japanese cars stopped being ugly, the Americans toned down their once incredible styling in the name of international sales.' Handling and performance differences also went the way of stylish eccentricity. The car market, says Pearman, 'became like architecture's dogmatic modern phase.' Homogenisation meant it became impossible to express an individual identity through a new car. 'But now the world's motor magnates are discovering the joys of pluralism. Retro cars, cute baby cars, plug ugly cars, even Modern cars – they're making them all.' Ray Hutton reports from the US that whereas 'Not long ago the world car was the thing, car makers having declared that customer tastes had converged and that the latest designs would be as acceptable in Tamworth as the were in Tuscon or Tokyo. [But] it didn't turn out that way. Buyer's wanted individuality.' Subsequently, says Hutton, all sorts of niche cars are starting to appear and American cars are once more starting to look 'distinctly American.'

The change of emphasis caught some manufacturers on the hop. Citroen, once leaders in quirky French styling, found a few years ago that its new cars resembled last year's Fords and consumers were unsure of Citroen's 'identity'.

These developments have caused many to question the stock traditionally placed on focus groups. Inventor James Dyson believes that you cannot have customers designing products because individual distinctiveness must be a key part of any successful product. 'We have focus groups,' he explains, 'but I take a perverse delight in ignoring them.' Dyson points out that one of the most boring British cars ever made – the Hillman Avenger – emerged from focus groups, whereas the Mini, one of the most memorable, was one man's local vision.

Pearman is unsure whether these shifts have enough substance to make them significant for the long term. Consolidation in the car industry and advances in computerized design have made manufacturers adept at making marques appear different, when they are just the same model with a different skin. The new Beetle is just a Golf (or Seat?) in disguise and the Ka is just a Ford Fiesta with curves. 'Pluralism is all very well,' Pearman concludes, 'but the modern tends to reassert itself over the postmodern.' Which means that the current appreciation of individuality and difference may be 'just another passing phase.'

1   To what extent can conventional approaches to management, strategy or organization theory be related to the style of thinking described in this chapter as 'Modernism'?
2   How would you draw the shape of the organization that Daft appears to want Coca-Cola to become or that the Catholic Church seems to be moving towards? Is it different from the triangular boxes and lines hierarchies that Case Box 1.2 highlighted. Where would strategy come from in your picture?
3   Is Postmodernism 'just another passing phase' or do the examples described here and any others you may think of point to a more significant change?
4   If Postmodernism is more than a 'passing phase', will Modernist perspectives die out?

Source: This case draws on 'Back to Classic Coke', *Financial Times*; 'Ice-cold Times for an Icon', *Independent*; H. Pearman, 'Curiouser and Curiouser', *The Sunday Times*; R. Hutton, 'A Vintage Harvest', *The Sunday Times*. With special thanks to all of those spoken to in Fr. Kevin's parish in Kenya.

3 Deconstructing Management's History

By the end of this chapter you should:

1 Be able to demonstrate that the conventional history of management is based on political expediencies that matched a particular set of cultural conventions.
2 Understand how the 'shape' of the business school and its curriculum reinforces the conventional history of management and what it takes to be the truth.
3 See how the conventional history of management and the shape of business schools both match and reinforce Modernist ways of seeing.
4 Be beginning to see how this 'match' may be limiting our ability to think differently or creatively for the future.
5 Be able to see how things could have worked out otherwise if the history of management had been conceived differently.

This chapter introduces two themes:

1 The conventional history that helped establish management, and subsequently strategy, as the late-twentieth century's most dominant fields is a *particular and contingent* fabrication.
2 This fabrication, through being unquestioningly regarded as fundamental, now *limits* the field's ability to see with anything other than a Modernist approach.

Recognizing this enables us to see that we need not let management's history go unchallenged or dutifully respect it as foundational. *We can rethink* its boundaries in order to regenerate our perspective and think more creatively.

I The conventional (but fabricated) history of management

Having read Chapters 1 and 2 you should be beginning to see how management and strategy tend to view the world in very Modernist terms. What follows is a synopsis of management's conventional history, a history that binds management to Modernism. The quotations are taken from the key historians or the textbooks that draw from them (see this chapter's bibliographical notes for details). The history of management tends to taper off after the 1960s (the so-called 'period of integration' and management's subsequent 'arrival' as a worthy subject) largely because all the major histories were written by the end of this decade. Indeed, the pioneering historians got the story 'down pat' so quickly that no significantly new general history of management has been written since the early 1970s: new editions of these men's classics were considered more than adequate to relate a history that was already fully understood. However, later parts of this chapter will seek to question this history's construction, arguing that it is a contingent fabrication and seeking to counter the assumptions that it promotes.

In the beginning ...

Man has always aimed to be more efficient, but it has taken time to uncover the secrets of how best this might be achieved.

Thus, management's history begins with those clever civilizations like the Egyptians, who recognized the need for planning, organizing (that is, the division of labour) and controlling and the Chinese who recognized the need for organization, planning, directing and controlling, and the principle of specialization. The Greeks also recognized the principle of specialization and applied the scientific method, albeit not to the principle of specialization, while the Romans developed bureaucracies. All of these civilizations, and the Hebrews, were subsequently found by J.D. Mooney to act according to organization's three universal principles, principles that would lead to greater efficiency:

1 Scalar hierachy.

2 The functional division of labour.

3 Coordination.

Management is thus 'as old as human society itself.' Its 'roots go deep, just as do those of such other professions such as theology, law, medicine, and education.'

Key contributions to our knowledge of management were made by individuals like Jethro, who lectured Moses on 'the benefits of delegation and sound organization'; Plato and Socrates who made 'timeless observations about the management of people'; Jesus who applied 'unity of command'

and discovered the need for 'human relations' in management; a number of Italians who developed accounting procedures; and Thomas More who 'called for specialization.'

These ideas were further advanced with the coming of Protestantism: 'As civilization developed, so did more positive feelings about work. Following the teachings of Judeo-Christian philosophers, beliefs in the value of work eventually became a cherished tradition.' This enabled the discoveries that 'Labor is good in itself and that one becomes a better person by virtue of the act of working.' These realizations and the related concept of economic individualism put great stress on the religious and economic advantages of highly specialized work.

The coming of the Scientific Revolution made it inevitable that some hardy pioneers should attempt to provide scientific principles for the management of Man and offered a scientific vehicle upon which the manager could begin to build his discipline. One management history by B.M. Gross, explains the development thus:

> All the ancestors of administrative thought operated on the premise that by the exercise of reason men could devise feasible and *consistent* means for attaining desirable ends. During the great intellectual upsurge of the Enlightenment this premise became an explicit and articulated principle. Copernicus, Galileo and Kepler destroyed the old image of man and his planet as the center of the universe ... By the time of Descartes, Newton, and Locke, rationality had become a widespread article of faith. Both man and universe were seen as behaving in accordance with natural laws. By discovering these laws and acting in accordance with them, man could control his irrational impulses and win true freedom ... Throughout this entire development, superstition, supernaturalism and the dead hand of tradition were persistently countered by sober, skeptical and scientific calculation. If we look closely enough, we can find in the Enlightenment the seed germs of modern administration.

Correspondingly, other historians call the eighteenth century: 'a managerial awakening.'

Building upon the Enlightenment's advance, Adam Smith applied the Newtonian method to economic endeavour so as to see the connection between the division of labour and the progress of civilization. This led to his discovery that 'the division of labour is a universal characteristic of organization'; his applying the 'principle of specialization to manufacturing works'; and his 'foundation of the field of economics' (economics being, of course, the discipline on which management must be based). Smith's discoveries drove the Industrial Revolution and the rise of the factory.

Boulton and Watt are thus doubly important. On the one hand, 'the heart of the Industrial Revolution was really the steam engine.' On the other, their Soho factory was 'an organization in which all of the current and accepted methods of production planning were to be found in embryo.' Hence the importance of Thomas Jefferson. In addition to his constitutional contributions to the formation of the United States America, Jefferson wrote to his friends from France of techniques inspired by Smith's idea. These 'anticipated gunmaker Eli Whitney's whole interchangeable parts idea.' Whitney and his partner, a clockmaker, developed an approach to assembly that 'absorbed Adam Smith's concepts of how to control organizations' in such a way as to anticipate the factory system. Charles Babbage, inventor of calculating engines, then expanded on the virtues of the division of labour, determining that it is 'no less applicable to mental productions than to those in which material bodies are concerned.' Babbage thus recognized that the evolution of management was tied to its increasing connection with the calculating sciences.

In the same era, Robert Owen, who had an 'intuitive grasp of the principles of sound management,' sought a manufacturing principle that would:

> … speedily divest [us] of all the ridiculous and absurd mystery with which it has hitherto enveloped by the ignorance of preceding times. [Hence] all the complicated and counteracting motives for good conduct, which have been multiplied almost to infinity, will be reduced to a single principle of action, which, by its evident operation and sufficiency, shall render this intricate system unnecessary, and ultimately supersede it in all parts of the earth.

Owen was 'far ahead of his time in urging that [we pay] at least as much attention to the welfare of "vital machines" as "inanimate machines" ' and is therefore 'the pioneer of personnel [or "human resource"] management.' 'Living machines,' he informs us:

> … may be easily trained and directed to procure a large increase of pecuniary gain … The economy of living machinery is to keep it neat and clean, treat it with kindness that its mental movements might not experience too much irritating friction.

Alfred Chandler, doyen of management historians, provides us with our best work on the next key period. It the middle of the nineteenth century, the US provided the clean slate upon which the evolution that Smith's brilliant arguments spoke of could progress without the hindrance of the 'dead hand' of tradition. This was when management became a separate and full-time task with the rise of the US railway system. The growth of the railroad across North America enabled companies to become geographically dispersed which, in turn, made the personal surveillance of many business transactions impossible or at least inefficient. These companies had to develop an alternative and this was found in the adoption of military models of administration and bureaucracy (hence, the advances made during the American Civil War are also incorporated into the history of management). The railroads opened up new markets, enabling companies to expand production, improve economies-of-scale and increase efficiency, but this could only be done by employing the same principles as the railroad companies. Thus Chandler claims that 'Modern business enterprise is easily defined … it has two specific characteristics: it contains many distinct operating units and it is managed by a hierarchy of salaried executives.' The figure below is a copy of the one that he used in his masterworks *Strategy and Structure* and *The Visible Hand* to illustrate this form.

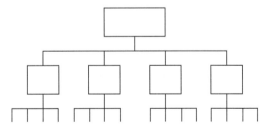

This figure replicates the triangular-hierarchical geometry of Modernism described in Chapter 2. It is a mirror-image of Diderot's 'Tree of Knowledge,' the central disciplining core enabling unified specialization along pre-determined lines. It also reiterates Mooney's universal principles: scalar hierarchy, the division of labour and coordination. The determination of bureaucracy as the general form of organization would enable scientific inquiries to elucidate management's general principles.

Management's scientific foundations

While these roots back into the beginnings of time to show how important management has always been to Man, it is important to recognize that progress was poor until man began to apply modern science. Mooney points out that while some Ancients were clever enough to act according to management principles, they were not so clever as to articulate them. Doing so would enable proper scientific research, the identification of management as a separate discipline, set definitions to be determined, and management knowledge to be accumulated in an ordered fashion. While John Child's history argues that 'Management as a purely technical factor has always been pursued to some degree wherever work activities have been organized,' management begins properly when managers were 'set apart from other employees,' when 'a distinct managerial social stratum' emerged, with the 'foundation of specialized institutes catering for a specifically managerial management.' B.F. Gross points out that, 'although the early political philosophers often discussed aspects of formal organi-zation structure, their thought reveals no clearly-articulated concept of an organization.' Daniel Wren notes that we need not take Premodern man-agement too seriously because its ideas 'were largely localized' seeing as 'there was little or no need to develop a formal body of management thought under … nonindustrialized circumstances.' Further, C.S. George makes it clear that while:

... in these early times, management thought existed, [it did so] only in a somewhat nebulous and unsophisticated state ... the principles were not united in a scheme of management thought, nor is there any evidence of any chronological building of various management techniques upon previous conceived ones.

In sum, H.R. Light's 1966 *The Nature of management* explains that while 'men have always acted in groups', it is only in the:

... last sixty years that serious attempts have been made to deal with the subject of organization analytically and to apply general principles to building up the structure of industrial enterprises. It has only recently been recognized that there is a general ability to manage which can be made the subject of a recognized 'discipline' based on objective research.

As W.J. Duncan makes clear, 'management as a discipline began when people started systematizing it, codifying it, and developing *prescriptions* for how to manage it better.'

Thus, at the turn of the twentieth century, a group of 'pioneers comparable to Galileo,' emerged. With a grasp that was 'scientific rather than intuitive' they recognized the 'gospel of efficiency' and brought the strands of management's ancestry (planning, coordinating, directing, controlling, industrialization, bureaucracy and the division of labour) together so as 'to correlate the growing mass of intuitive ground rules into clearly enunciated principles.' However, in starting 'to apply to administration the methods of scientific observation which had already yielded dramatic and highly applauded results in the physical sciences,' they also recognized, to quote Colonel Lyndall Urwick's *Making of Scientific Management* that:

... the 'antiquated scheme of business principles' ... bore no logical relation to the intellectual standards, the mode of thinking customary in the exact sciences. Yet it was these standards, this mode of thinking, which were the basis of the inventions which had revolutionised its technical processes and were adding incalculably to its productive potential by the decade. On the principle of the 'hair of the dog' they attempted to apply the methods of science to the problems of direction and control.

It is not surprising, therefore, that these management pioneers should be industrial engineers: 'As engineers attempted to make machines more efficient, it was a natural extension of their efforts to work on the human side of the equation.' Most prominent among them were Frederick Taylor, Henri Fayol and Max Weber.

Taylor 'marked the new industrial spirit [with] his substitution of the scientific method [over] records of what has been done or opinion of what can be done.' He described the necessity of a 'great mental revolution' that would focus on 'science, not rule of thumb' and arrived at management's first universal theories, published in 1911 in the *Principles of Scientific Management*. Fayol revolutionized management by conceptualizing it as a separate field applicable to all forms of activity and defined it as a universal set of functions: planning, organizing, directing, coordinating and controlling. He also identified its 14 general principles, the first of which being the division of labour. In 1947, with the publication of *The Theory of Social and Economic Organizations*, Weber consolidated Taylor and Fayol's management theories with his depiction of the matching principles of organization: hierarchization or status differentiation, bureaucratic specialization or the division of labour, centralization, and impersonalized behaviour. 'Management' science was born.

Progress and integration upon grand foundations

Now that the foundation stones of management were set, great currency was attached to advancing the cutting edge of management knowledge. 'New pioneers' like Elton Mayo, Abraham Maslow and Hugo Munsterberg emerged. They discovered that 'man is a human being – even in industry' and focused upon the 'other or human side of work' to that of the engineering pioneers. They did so through the rigorous application of 'more' or 'better science in management' drawing upon advances in the new sciences of psychology and sociology.

If the pioneers brought an engineering outlook to bear and the new pioneers sought to build on this with a psychological perspective, Chester Barnard was a 'pioneer in developing the philosophical groundwork of management,' showing that 'one must begin on the theory of organization with Plato.' Barnard saw traditional mechanistic definitions of organization as overly simplistic and sought to redefine organization as an 'open system of consciously coordinated activities.'

While historians saw Barnard's approach as both a step toward integration in his own day and as an ideal unifying framework for grasping management thought in our times, the period through to the 1940s generally suffered through a lack of integration. The writers listed above 'did recognize and understand the functions of management [but] no unified theory of management was developed.' Because of this, the first half of the twentieth century is inauspiciously termed 'a period of diversity in management thought.' Urwick's *Making of Scientific Management* describes the problem thus:

> Earlier publications have a historical significance in line with the story of the evolution of management itself [because] they represent the oozing out of the spring at source and its first trickling together into the tiny brook. By the 1920s it was growing into a stream, continuous, swelling, broadening. And within ten years – to continue the analogy – it had become necessary to build the reservoir that would contain and marshal the growing flood.

This is how management historians like Mooney and Urwick gain their places on 'management's continuum' in the middle of the twentieth century. Mooney surveyed history to discover the three universal principles underlying all organization: scalar hierarchy, the functional division of labour and coordination. Greatly inspired by Mooney proving the universality of organizing principles, Urwick surveyed the literature in order to 'collect, consolidate, and correlate the principles of management.' These studies led us from the 'period of diversity' toward the period in management characterized as a 'period of integration.'

Herbert Simon's aims during the post-diversity phase of management were much the same as Urwick's. 'We require a serious effort,' said Simon, 'toward the construction of a common language [to] bring together this scattered and diverse body of writing about organizations into a coherent whole.' Most 'Management Continuums' end with Simon, but he is a key contributor to the project that embodies the aims of management beyond his heyday in the 1950s and 60s, a project inspired by the publication of *The Management Theory Jungle* by Harold Koontz in 1961.

Koontz saw that 'no science, now regarded as mature, started out with a complete statement of incontrovertibly valid principles.' Thus, he claimed that while the period of diversity had been a necessary stepping stone, 'any science proceeded, and more than that has been useful, for centuries, on the basis of generalizations.' Koontz argued that management must now take four steps toward maturation:

1   Distilling and testing fundamentals.
2   Defining a body of knowledge (management, he claimed, 'should deal with an area of inquiry that is "manageable" [as] no great advances in knowledge were made so long as man contemplated the whole universe').
3   Clarifying management terms.
4   Making management a specific discipline so that more established branches of knowledge could be identified as its foundation or central stem.

In 1963 Koontz held a conference of the world's most distinguished management practitioners and academics. The conference was called 'Toward a unified theory of management.' Participants concluded that:

> ... within five years – certainly not more than ten years hence – a *general* theory of management will be evolved, stated, and generally accepted in management circles.

Koontz's own suggested strategy toward these aims was to 'encompass and synthesize the diversity of the day' via developing Barnard's open systems

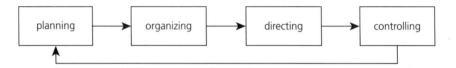

approach which sees managers 'performing the four [Fayolian] functions of planning, organizing, leading and controlling' (generally depicted as above).

Significantly, the sub-field of strategic management was also established during this period. Igor Ansoff, widely regarded as strategy's founding father, sought to build upon the microeconomic theory of the firm (whereby the firm is a mechanism that turns inputs into outputs), which was taken as a foundation stone of management. Ansoff duly outlined three levels of management and organization, which can be seen in the diagram below, reproduced from his 1969 *Business Strategy*.

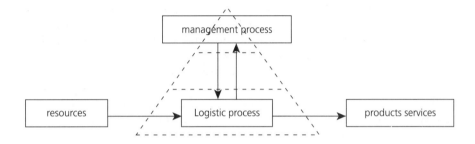

At the bottom is the *operational* level of the firm where the action is divided up. In the middle lies the coordinating stem, the tactical or *administrative* level. And at the top of the hierarchy *strategic* thinking takes place. This is a form that consolidates many of the 'findings' expressed in the history of management (hence, strategic management is to this day defined in text-books as the 'planning, directing, organizing and controlling of a company's strategy-related decisions'). And it is a form that perfectly maps the generic geometry of Modernism described in Chapter 2, thereby making it one of Modernity's most crucial disciplines.

2 A counter-history of management

The smooth, continuous accumulation of knowledge about a universal object called management, related in the history above, is not questioned. But it is a fabrication. It is based on a contingent view that determined per-formative efficiency, a term not invented until the late nineteenth century, to be a universal end, and the triangular-hierarchical organizational form and the Modern scientific method to be the means to this end. It is a particular view of the past in terms of the conditions that prevailed in the first half of the twentieth century. It is a history constituted by men who had particular aims and interests and whose depiction of management's scientific revolu-tion is a myth. Its 'grand origins' rely upon putting words in other's mouths, words that are foreign to their tongues. Subsequently, rather than represent-ing the gradual building of knowledge from past to present, it uses present needs to illuminate the past in order to see only those things that legitimated particular politically expedient practices.

However, this history helped establish management as a truly worthy and truly global field. By mirroring Modernism's overarching geometry it put itself forward as the field that explained how all other fields and institutions should be run. In fact, by defining management as focussed upon late-Modernity's universal evaluative ends (bureaucratic rationality and efficiency), it ensured that management knowledge would come to be regarded as imperative, helping to turn it into the world's fastest growing tertiary subject in a few short decades. This section, Section 2, outlines how this came to pass. Section 3 then investigates how this particular view of management came to be sustained through a self-referential network of bodies including the American Business School, the established curriculum that management students should follow, and the writings of management experts. If these sections investigate the history of management's *productive* effects in helping to establish the field, this chapter's concluding section, Section 4, begins to explore the *repressive* effects brought about by this history's hasty and narrowly-defined construction of the field: how its vision now limits our ability to think differently.

A history founded on particular beliefs

Management as a specific body of knowledge and practice forming the basis of a specialized profession has begin to emerge only in very recent times. Until the science and art of management was thus recognized as a subject in itself there was no foundation on which to build an interest in its history.

Lyndall Urwick and Edward Brech

The conventional history of management religiously reiterates Modernist assumptions. It sees firm foundations as crucial and speaks of an increasing measure of certainty and control through the development of a general logic. It connects to beliefs in a hard-working rational planner/executor God and the analogies of the clockwork, or input→process→output mechanism, and the bureaucratic triangle. It seeks knowledge through detached reason breaking things into parts. It sees progress as linear and cumulative and our present knowledge as an advance on the past. It sees centralized specialization and standardization as the one best approach. And it thus seeks these things in the name of the universal end of efficiency. Its key boundaries – the Enlightenment's development of objective scientific reason, the Age of Revolutions, the turn of the twentieth century and its mechanistic-scientific optimism – are also all key Modernist boundaries. However, is this really the way that all those incorporated into this history were striving to think? Or is it that the people who wrote the history were predisposed to see progress in these terms?

The quotation above, from the introduction of Urwick and Brech's history of management, unwittingly acknowledges something very significant: their history is particular to their time. It was only then that management became considered 'serious enough' to have a history written up. It therefore stands to reason that this history would reflect the particular beliefs of the time. This period, from World War II to the mid-1960s, witnessed the height of Modern art and architecture. It was an age of scientific optimism and functionalist sociology. In the US in particular, the 'Eisenhower Years' were a time associated with emphasizing collective construction, normalization and integration, the building of a new world order over and above divisive differences. This was a good time for management to establish itself as meritorious and those concerned with management took the opportunity with great gusto. In 1954, the newly formed American Management Association (AMA) sought to determine the 'universality of [management's] basic functions.' They found these functions to be 'planning, organizing and executing,' organizing meaning the division of labour, and executing being, by its AMA definition, 'synonymous with controlling.' These functions corresponded to an understanding that management was about improving efficiency.

Within a decade, an extensive study of 'writers, consultants, industrialists and "academicians"' confirmed that these fundamental functions of management were 'true' because most managers accepted them to be so when researchers asked them if they were. Professional associations like the AMA worked with like-minded academics to get schools of business standardized and become normal parts of most US universities. Doctoral programs to train management scholars were set up, along with academic journals. Selznick's 1948 *Foundations of the Theory of Organization* was identified as having laid down the subject's methodological foundations using Barnard's definitions and citing Parsons' structural-functional analysis 'relating contemporary and variable behaviour to a presumptively stable system of needs and mechanisms.'

It should perhaps be no shock, therefore, that what the history of management highlights is related to the specific predilections and the prevailing understandings of progress at this time. Or, in other words, that the signs of the times described above encouraged a history that reflected only Modernist actions as important, rather than telling the story of how things may have been different in the past. A history that was, in other words, biased. This should not be too surprising; those who wrote the history of management were, after all, of a particular type: white males with military, industrial economics or sociology backgrounds. This may explain why one popular history claims 'pre-Protestant' people to be less civilized for not knowing the 'true value of work' and why the current best-selling management history by Daniel Wren diminishes Premodern thinking by noting that it was 'dominated by cultural values that were antibusiness, antiachievement and largely antihuman.'

This dominant mind-set also leads to some fairly questionable assumptions as to the history of management's key boundaries. In 1960, L.A. Appley, Head of the AMA, asked in the foreword to Merrill's *Classics in Management*, 'Should not the professional manager be familiar with the "classic" body of management literature as the theologian is familiar with the Scriptures, the lawyer with Blackstone, the physician with Osler, and the educator with Plato?' Despite referring to ancients like Plato to give the field more kudos, management's 'classics,' the book explains, begin 'with Babbage as exemplified in his essay on the division of labor [and the] application of the scientific method.' Management must have classics, like other fields, but its classics, unlike other fields, begin within Modernity. This seems so obvious at this point in time that historians never feel the need to justify why the educator starts with Greek philosophy while the manager must start with Modern science and the division of labour. Furthermore, those who saw management as becoming more integrated had predetermined that integration was where management should be. Koontz, for example, admitted that his project was 'influenced by the concern that the development of management theory and research was going off in many directions, with confusion [and] interschool rivalries.' He cited Parsons' notion of what social theory should be as what management should be aiming for and the purpose of his quest for unity was 'increasing efficiency, [the] goal of all managers.' The work of the two premier historians of management, Alfred Chandler and Lyndall Urwick, exhibited similarly questionable predilections.

Chandler, it is claimed, 'singlehandedly developed the reference points in business history on which management researchers must rely.' Arguing that 'historians ha[d thus] provided social scientists with little empirical data on which to base generalizations or hypotheses [and had not] formulated many theories or generalizations of their own,' Chandler proposed 'an examination of the way *different* enterprises carried out the *same* activity.' He thus provided what later historians called 'the paradigm for future research.' But it was not so much that Chandler discovered the generality that others were not clever enough to see, as that his education led him to seek commonalities.

Chandler was greatly influenced by Modern economists, his American circumstance, Talcott Parsons (for whom he worked as a graduate student) and Weber's work on bureaucracy. T.K. McCraw's study of Chandler's work subsequently argues that Chandler's education gave him a Parsonian 'preoccupation with rationality,' and the 'absorption of Weber's maxim that bureaucracy represents the institutionalization of rationalism.' Indeed, Chandler came to assume that managers were such rational efficiency seekers that he described them as seeking to 'perfect their techniques' 23 times in *The Visible Hand* (the title a nod to Adam Smith's notion of the market as the 'invisible hand' that solved Hobbes' Mystery).

Chandler subsequently saw the key period in management's history as being around 1850 in the US when the railway companies 'opened up' North America. Their growth enabled companies to become geographically dispersed which, in turn, made the personal surveillance of many business transactions impossible or at least inefficient. These companies had to develop an alternative means of functioning and this was found in the adoption of military models of bureaucracy. At the same time the railroads opened up new markets, enabling companies to expand production and improve economies-of-scale by employing the same bureaucratic principles. As they did so, companies found that many economic transaction costs, for things that would have previously been bought from commission agents on the market, were minimized by their being standardized and carried out under one 'roof.' Chandler showed how the 'visible hand' of organization came into being by *more efficiently* fulfilling the market's ordering functions, thus building upon but surpassing Smith's invisible hand of the market. Management became widespread as it became a necessary function to maximize the efficiency of the structures and technology required for operationalizing such large-scale organizations. Oliver Williamson, for whom, like Chandler, 'efficiency is the main and only systematic factor response,' conversely argued that organizations emerge when markets lapse and become inefficient. But for both of the US's most influential economic or management historians, 'efficiency' is assumed to be the fundamental means and end of organization and management.

While the research agenda in the US is 'cast within Chandler's conceptual framework,' in Britain the 'Chandlerian revolution' has been less marked. The British doyen of management history is Colonel Lyndall Urwick. Particularly influential is his *Making of Scientific Management*, written in the decade after World War II. Urwick described his historical aim as 'to demonstrate that the body of knowledge about management is sufficiently large to make it a more scientific, more unified field than was commonly supposed' via the 'collection, consolidation, and correction of principles of management.' He believed management theorists should 'apply the methods of thought developed by the physical sciences so as to build a store of general principles, arrived at by induction, that can then lift management from the plane of empiricism and tradition.' He claimed organizing to be a process of 'subdividing all the activities necessary to any purpose and arranging them in groups which may be assigned to individuals … in a cold-blooded, detached spirit [like the preparation of an] engineering design.' Urwick's regular co-author, Luther Gulick, summed up the corresponding purpose of management succinctly: 'Whether public or private, the basic "good" is efficiency.'

It is not surprising, then, that Urwick identified management's pioneers as those who first applied the 'discourse of reason to the problems of industrial management, to bring an adequate intelligence to the control of the forces released by a mechanised economy': Taylor and Fayol, in other words. Thus, Urwick wove their thinking to form his history's 'meta-narrative.' Taylor provided Urwick with the archetype of what a management thinker should be: an engineer-scientist; while Fayol's general managerial tasks – forecasting, planning, the division of labour, directing and control – provided a way of categorizing the evolution of this science. Rather than offering an objective value-neutral view of the past, Urwick, who claimed to have been 'profoundly effected' by his first reading of Taylor amid the chaos of Belgian trenches during World War I and who was often described by his peers as a 'Taylor disciple,' effectively wrote the history of his own beliefs.

In the words of R.R. Locke, the writings of the likes of Chandler and Colonel Urwick 'were not histories so much as commentaries on how managerial capitalism came into being.' But what they did pick out of the past neatly matched the prevailing Modernist spirit of their times.

1911: The birth of management science?

Serious thought on organization begins with F.W. Taylor. Management's subsequent writings go back to his bases.

Edward Brech

President Roosevelt, in his address to the Governors at the White House, prophetically remarked that 'The conservation of our national resources is only preliminary to the larger question of national efficiency.'

F.W. Taylor, opening line of The Principles of Scientific Management

Looking in the manner described above, it is not surprising that management's historians should pick out Taylor's *Principles of Scientific Management* as management science's founding document. Even though most believe that his ideas were somewhat simplistic and have subsequently been surpassed, most management texts still begin with and build upon the factory engineer-cum-scientist. However, his 'scientific management,' rather than being the discovery of the foundational attributes of management via proper scientific inquiry that the historians were looking for, actually emerged as the result of the networking together of the interests of three men in a particular culture faced with specific problems. Taylor's nod to Roosevelt at the outset of his thesis may seem a simple demonstration of the importance of the subject matter to follow, but the nature of this 'grand origin' may be better understood through a knowledge of the mutually reinforcing relationships between the President, the engineer and a lawyer named Louis Brandeis.

The politician

Theodore Roosevelt was the most successful politician in what is referred to as the Progressive Movement during what is now called the Progressive Era in US history (1890–1920). The US had grown on the back of a chaotic *laissez-faire* economic approach and the assumption that the country's natural resources were inexhaustible. The Progressive Movement developed in response to the problems that this 'psyche' had caused by the end of the 1800s. Namely, the *ad hoc* and self-serving development of the West by particular business interests and their lobbyists. Looking back on his political career, Roosevelt claimed that 'The relation of the conservation of natural resources to the problems of national efficiency had not yet dawned on the public mind.' It had not dawned because Roosevelt had yet to employ his flair for focusing public opinion upon these particular problems.

Roosevelt's twin platform for the 1901 Presidential Election was the progressive reform of government practices and what he termed 'national conservation.' The momentum granted by his winning this election helped him to push through his 'Reclamation Act,' passed in 1902 to centralize the development of new lands. However, his conservation programme soon ran into formidable obstacles as business lobbyists and Western politicians who saw it as retarding development began to rally against it.

The psyche that had led to the problems that Roosevelt sought to address was well set. US nationality had absorbed the idea of the liberty to do as one wanted, to stake claims and develop things unhindered by traditional customs and central rules. Disavowal of this core belief left one's patriotism open to question. As Haber's excellent study of this period observes, these beliefs 'could not be attacked frontally, they could [only] be outflanked.' At this point in time the new term 'efficiency' provided Roosevelt the best possible means for such a manoeuvre – for promoting centralization and conservation without appearing anti-American.

The development of the word 'efficiency' in the decades either side of 1900 changed the term in such a way that efficient and 'good' came closer to meaning the same thing than in any other period. From the Latin *efficiens* (that which gives rise to something or *produces a particular effect*), efficiency had been used as a personal attribute, to describe an effective being who got a particular thing done. However, in the last quarter of the nineteenth century a concept of mechanical efficiency was developed out of the application of the laws of thermodynamics to the technology of the steam engine. This gradually intermingled with the previous meaning, indicating a *general measure of effectiveness* – the ratio of output relative to energy inputs.

Just as Darwin's thesis had changed our understanding of evolution from an inside-out unfolding to a straight line, the fit of the mechanical engineers' perspective with prevailing beliefs saw their interpretation of efficiency become the common interpretation. Eventually, just as the efficiency of a machine or an individual could be related to the way their parts combined, efficiency came to also signify a relationship between men, or what was termed 'social harmony.' In the space of a few decades, this type of performative efficiency became a term that, through association with machines, had an air of benign objectivity and, through its association with social harmony, a sense of unquestionable 'rightness' not based on any particular interests or beliefs. Efficiency subsequently became a standard measure for evaluating how well things were made rather than a term that described the making of things, any number of things, happen. Roosevelt would take this new universal measure and utilize it as an end in itself.

With his conservation policies running aground, the resourceful Roosevelt changed tack. He began to relate the conservation of natural resources to what he now recognized as 'the problem of national efficiency.' Roosevelt now pitched that 'conservation meant development as much as it does protection' but that the best form of development must be one *that develops the most out of the least*. In this way, Gifford Pinchot, Roosevelt's most able lieutenant, described how both 'government and business [came] to accept conservation in terms of simple efficiency.'

Interpreted in this way, 'conservation as national efficiency' provided a scientific and popular answer to the twentieth century's new problems. It appealed not only to the Progressive reformer's interest in social control or planning but also indicated his patriotism or nationalism. It seemed democratic and liberal but in a nationalistic rather than a 'selfish' sense.

So successful was this tack that by the time of his Seventh Annual Message to Congress, which sought to show that 'the conservation of our natural resources constitute the fundamental problem which underlies almost every other problem of our National life,' Roosevelt was happy to state that conservation was preliminary to the larger question of national efficiency, the line with which Taylor begins *The Principles of Scientific Management*. By 1908, Progressivism, a manifesto that had been difficult to define, had come to mean primarily 'efficiency plus a commitment to collective betterment through the application of the latest advances in science' and leaders in all fields were afraid to be thought of as not Progressive.

The engineer

His quest for conservation reinvigorated, Roosevelt hosted a National Conservation Congress in December 1908. In so doing, the Progressive leadership, keen to associate themselves with the latest and best in expert knowledge, were keen to 'consult' the professions (conveniently helping to spread the blame for any future bad governmental decisions). They particularly looked to engineering, and mechanical engineers were given pride of place at the Congress.

If the Congress had been held 30 years earlier it is doubtful that engineers would have been involved at all: they would not even have been considered a 'profession.' But a Modernist mind-set had recently seen engineering elevated by it now being deemed 'scientific.' This, combined with new sources of recruitment as the scientific association encouraged more boys to take up engineering as a career, and the development of professional associations, saw engineering quickly converted from a trade to a desirable profession. In the early decades of the twentieth century every boy knew the stories of heroic engineers like the Roeblings and the Brooklyn Bridge.

The Association of Mechanical Engineers (ASME) was impressed by Roosevelt and quickly agreed to throw its weight behind his program. The Society's president declared that ASME members must 'direct themselves to the larger interests of humanity' and fall in with conservation. It was not a difficult decision, however. Falling in line with Roosevelt enabled engineers to further encourage patronage for themselves as members of an important profession while supporting a programme whose emphasis on efficiency further elevated the value of their expertise.

One engineer greatly enthused by his profession's developing social significance and political influence was F.W. Taylor. Taylor's greatest technological achievement had been the development of carbon tools that permitted greater precision and a more rapid cutting of steel, and hence the possibility of turning out interchangeable parts. He had also written papers on how men might be similarly arranged to perform work tasks. In 1895 he presented such a paper at an ASME conference. This contained the gist of what would become *The Principles of Scientific Management,* although it was much more overtly moralistic and personalized ('if a man won't do what is right,' Taylor said, 'make him'). Those who heard the paper considered it to be nothing special. Continuing with the themes presented in 1895, Taylor published a book called *Shop Management* in 1903 that achieved a loyal but limited following among a group that was referred to as the 'Taylorites.' In 1910, the ASME shelved a paper submitted by Taylor on the grounds that there was nothing new or interesting in it. As Haber concludes, 'the checkered career of the Taylor system might have been completely disheartening to the Taylorites had it not been for the fullness of response that scientific management found among the Progressive reformers and their public.' A clever lawyer named Louis Brandeis and what became known as The Eastern Rate Case of 1910–11 would stir up this 'fullness.'

The lawyer

In the decade preceding the US's entry into World War I, the high cost of living and persistent price rises were perhaps the most talked about public issues in the US, particularly among middle-class and professional families whose incomes were least responsive to general price changes at this time. This group provided the most vocal segment of the population and 'reform' was on their lips. Their attention was aroused and given a focal point by The Eastern Rate Case.

Action was brought before the Interstate Commerce Commission against the railroad companies' proposed increase in freight rates in the northeastern states. In early hearings, other counsel presented complicated arguments based on a maze of statistics, emphasizing the hardship that an increase would bring to farmers and other shippers, and the railroads responded by justifying their increases in great detail. This line seemed to be leading nowhere and was completely unsuccessful in capturing public opinion (the general conception being that farmers had never had it so good). The dashing Louis Brandeis was brought in to help invigorate the prosecution.

Brandeis, who had come directly from working with Pinchot on Roosevelt's conservation campaign, consulted a friend called Harrington Emerson, a factory consultant and devotee of a little-known technique called 'Taylorism.' Emerson suggested Brandeis contact Taylor and some of his 'disciples.' While he could see the applicability of Taylor's ideas to the case, he found Taylor's advocates a not particularly savvy bunch and was not really surprised that their hero's methods had not caught on. Brandeis, an expert publicist, instantly recognized their lack of popular appeal. Taylor's methods had been called by such names as 'functional management' and 'the Taylor System.' In order to make their case more appealing, and his own case against the railroads more compelling, Brandeis, in an informal meeting with some of Taylor's followers, suggested that they refer to Taylor's work as 'scientific management' and play up the 'efficiency' angle.

Brandeis was well aware that attaching 'scientific' would strengthen Taylor's appeal by suggesting disinterestedness, rigor and a method employing the power of 'natural laws' to enable Man's control. This was, after all, the age where Modernism was at its height, where Walter Lippmann's *Drift and Mastery*, arguing that science ('the only discipline which gives any assurance that from the same set of facts men will come approximately to the same conclusion') was now enabling 'change [to] become a matter of deliberate experiment,' captured the zeitgeist. The phrase 'social science,' used to describe a group of new academic disciplines, had caught the public fancy and the adjective 'scientific' went far in ensuring an interested hearing. Subsequently, 'efficiency' and 'scientific management' became the two catchwords of the popular excitement that followed the case.

Brandeis created this excitement by cutting through the statistics and going on the offensive with a bold and simple claim. Even if the railroads could justify their increases, Brandeis argued that the solutions to everybody's problems lay in introducing 'efficiency' and 'scientific management' into railroading. He promised to show how the railroads could actually save 'a million dollars a day' by doing so. The next day, 10 November 1910, the *New York Times* ran with the headline:

RAILROADS COULD SAVE
$1,000,000 A DAY

Brandeis says Scientific Management
Would Do It – Calls
Rate Increase Unnecessary

As an interested public watched, Brandeis paraded Taylorites like Emerson, Frank Gilbreth and H.L. Gantt as expert witnesses to help argue his case. And, once the public was hooked, Brandeis was not shy of combining their 'science' with a religious fervor, referring to Taylor's scientific management as 'the gospel of hope.'

In 1911, to great public acclaim, Brandeis won.

The engineer

While his followers on the witness stand lauded him, Taylor chose not to appear in person. But this only added to his mystique, fueling the public's desire to know more of this money-saving guru. A bidding war between the US's leading magazines, all desperate to publish his ideas, ensued, with Taylor eventually being swayed by The *American Magazine*'s huge circulation of 340 000, an incredible figure for those times. The *American* published Taylor's work in four parts, describing him in its introductory piece as 'a rare, high type of American, a public servant in the best sense … a man who can show us new ways of commanding our environment.'

These four installments were then collected and published in book form as *The Principles of Scientific Management*. There was nothing very new about the content. Effectively the work that was rejected by the ASME the year before (in itself a continuity of the kernel of the 1895 paper). However, it had a new title and its 'old-fashioned' moralism had been toned down to give it the appearance of a neutral device. Also, the focus on efficiency was now completely overt. Indeed, efficiency is the object of the first five paragraphs of Taylor's 1911 introduction and it appears seven times in the first 264 words. *The Principles* thus hooked into and fed what commentators of the time called 'an efficiency craze,' a 'secular Great Awakening' that hit America like a 'flash flood.' 'Efficiency societies' and magazines devoted to efficiency sprang up (including the popular *Health and Efficiency*). Groups from women's leagues to school boards to Protestant church associations exhorted their constituents to investigate their operations toward becoming more efficient. And Taylor's scientific management now seemed to be the obvious mechanism with which to achieve these sorts of aims. According to Robert Kanigel: 'Suddenly "Taylor", "scientific management" and "efficiency" were household words.'

This outpouring of interest in the newly-developed notion of righteous efficiency also enabled Roosevelt's programme, that had only a few years previously been stymied through being perceived as anti-American, to become ingrained as quintessentially American. The extent to which efficiency had become a feature of America's psyche at this point is illustrated by the histories of efficiency that were subsequently written installing Benjamin Franklin, America's favourite American, as the 'Father of Efficiency.' Efficiency had come so far that Roosevelt now drew on it to give substance to the political issue that inspired his later years: the articulation of a 'New Nationalism.'

The politician

A burst of immigration around the turn of the century had led to increasingly obvious ethnic subcultures and what Roosevelt called 'hyphenated-Americans' (for example, Italian-Americans, Irish-Americans). In this respect, the US at the turn of the twentieth century was a very unusual society. The extent to which the coming together of so many cultures at once seemed completely foreign to commentators from abroad is summed up by startled British writer Israel Zangwill's now famous assertion, issued in 1908, that the US was 'God's Crucible, the great Melting-Pot.' These circumstances gave more power to the principles of scientific management. In a country whose needs are growing at an alarming rate only large-scale production can keep up with demand. In a country with infinite space on which to build, large-scale production facilities are easy to develop. In a land whose workers come from many cultures, speak different languages and have different work traditions, whose previous apprenticeships may not be those required in the 'New World,' standardized and mechanized procedures will be required if the necessary volume is to be produced quickly. Herein lie the reasons why programs like Taylorism would be so timely. Indeed, large portions of *The Principles of Scientific Management* are pseudo transcripts of Taylor in discussion with a 'simple German' called Schmidt (complete with cheesy accents: 'Vell [Mr Taylor], I don't know vat you mean') proving what his system will enable 'such people' to do.

Roosevelt began to turn this unusual set of circumstances into further political capital. He began to speak of there being 'no such thing as a hyphenated-American who is a good American'; of how 'throughout our whole land we must have fundamental common purposes' (one can see why the 'melting-pot' metaphor struck such a chord). Roosevelt appealed 'to all Americans to join in the common effort for the common good,' claiming that 'The prime problem of our nation [now is] to get the right type of good citizenship, and, to get it, we must have progress, and our public men must be genuinely progressive.'

What this all-American 'progressiveness' actually meant was difficult to articulate until performative efficiency became part of the national psyche. Roosevelt began to relate efficiency to his crusade for a New Nationalism, or what he also termed 'Americanization':

> National efficiency ... a necessary result of the principle of conservation widely applied ... will determine our failure and success as a nation. National efficiency has to do, not only with natural resources and with men, but it is equally concerned with institutions. The state must be made efficient [and] the American people are right in demanding that New Nationalism.

By the time that Americanization, as a programme for nation-building, made its first appearance in US politics on the Progressive party platform of 1912, 'efficiency' was one of its foremost catch-cries. Indeed, Progressivism's most famous slogan of this time, '100% Americanism,' was proudly derived from Emerson's phrase, brought to the public's attention during the Eastern Rate Case: '100% Efficiency.' What it was to be "American" and the new passion for efficiency was neatly woven into one.

The aftermath

World War I made efficiency appear common sense internationally. In Britain interest in scientific management boomed, in France Clemenceau ordered that Taylor's principles be applied in military plants, and Taylorism was extremely popular in Russia. However, the efficiency craze soon fizzled out in the US. By 1920, social mores had shifted and the efficiency associations and journals had faded. While Taylor's system retreated from the public domain back to the factory and the use of efficiency in the sense of 'social harmony' declined, the particular nuances of this period had a lasting effect. That 'Americans love efficiency,' Haber concluded, had slipped into the national fabric to the extent that 'serious students of American character have come to see such statements as obvious universal commonplaces.' In addition, this specific moment has now come to be known as the point in time when the universal basis of management was discovered. And management's global spread, and the extent to which America and Americans have been seen as *the* management experts, has seen efficiency, as it was understood at this particular point in time, become a global means of measurement and a general end in itself.

However, it is worth noting that things were certainly not understood this way at the time this view of efficiency emerged. In 1917, when British writer G.H. Seldes reported on the spread of scientific management, he had to indicate the strange sense in which he was using the word efficiency by labelling it 'American Efficiency.' Indeed, just six years earlier a US magazine editorial reporting on the Eastern Rate Case referred to the 'testimony of the "efficiency" witnesses,' similarly demonstrating how unusual this perspective of efficiency was at the time in the US.

In sum, the events that cluster around this period so as to be seen by management historians as a key point of origin are particular, politically contingent responses to one society's problems at a specific point in time. For engineers keen to solidify and advance their status, Roosevelt's conservation initiative offered a programme to which they could not only contribute but which placed them near the top of the tree in terms of determining the future development of society. For politicians in a multi-ethnic state trying to create a unifying programme of reform without an obvious appeal to particular interests, while not appearing to be against established American values, engineering's articulation of efficiency as a universal and objective measure and Taylor's scientific management held great appeal. The Progressives were subsequently able to develop their notion of social control and organization into a programme of planning, directing and controlling that legitimized the role of the politician who sought to centralize government with himself as the overseer on top. In Haber's words:

> The progressive movement is often described as an attempt to revitalize government by the people ... However, alongside [this] was an attempt to keep government somewhat distant. The second tendency was usually explained away as necessary in order to achieve efficiency in the name of scientific management.

The science of efficiency, or scientific management, legitimated a view of democracy that pleased both politicians and engineers and provided a platform that not only placated the general public, it positively excited its most vocal slice. This set of ideas also legitimated the elevation of the professions and expertise controlled by the middle classes and university educated.

Thus, scientific management came into being to accommodate particular interests that believed in the need for an ultimate authority 'on top' to the environment of political democracy in which ultimate authority is believed to lie 'at the bottom.' In other words, it emerged to legitimize Modernism's triangular-hierarchical bureaucratic form. It legitimized the idea that those with 'expertise' should operate above the masses in order to ensure the optimal achievement of the greatest good, as measured by objective universal criteria such as the efficient use of resources, even if this impinged upon individual liberty. It legitimized the particular form that management's first historians saw as their object in the 1950s and 1960s: the universal form of organization that management, for them, was related to.

Scientific management was not, therefore, the discovery that first articulated the universal principles or bases of management, it was a contingent approach that became politically expedient at a particular point in time in a very peculiar society. Beyond this it was neither a new discovery (just a more publicity-conscious continuation of the ideas that Taylor articulated at least 16 years previously), nor was it even scientific. While Taylor fashioned his methods as a science and this attachment gave his system the appearance of the inevitability and objectivity of science and technology, this obscured rather than eliminated his bias. Indeed, in response to a 1912 ASME report on time study that referenced Smith and Babbage but made no mention of Taylor (claiming that his work offered 'nothing new'), Taylor protested that while Babbage was content with the comparison of gross times of actual performance, he broke the job into component parts, tested them (that is, timed different approaches) and re-engineered the job as it should ideally (that is most efficiently) be done. Indeed, Taylor's first principle ('Develop a science for each element of a man's work, which replaces the old rule-of-thumb method'), makes it plain just how subjective he was (that is, he had already judged the outcomes he wanted). There was nothing particularly inductive, objective or scientific about the subsequent development of Taylor's 'laws.' Taylor's ideas were based only upon his specific predilection: that performative efficiency was morally good. That this predilection has come to be regarded as the basis of management is not to say that he was right, only that he was in the right place at the right time.

'Grand foundations' or different individuals and civilizations made to tow the party line?

When we look for recorded administrative thought in a more general sense, we find that in most cases it is part of the rich tapestry of philosophic (or even religious) commentary on man

and his relations to fellowmen, state and society. At times we
find flashes of intellectual lightning that directly illuminate
major aspects of administration.

B.M. Gross

Once the fact that management science began with the likes of Taylor and the arrival of bureaucratic organizations was established, people began to seek out the history of these events so as to provide them with greater gravity. However, as management historian C.S. George points out:

> Ferreting out [this] managerial thought today is no easy task because men, though managers, did not write about or recognise management as such until fairly recent times. The management historian must therefore interpret man's actions in a managerial light. And this selective process makes the whole what it is.

While historians have subsequently incorporated other, older traditions into their story of management, they have been such Modernist 'ferrets' that they have only picked out those instances that correspond with or anticipate Modern practice. In a history of this sort the 'intellectual light' only travels from the present into the past so as to see that which confirms our current 'heights.' Thus 'this selective process that makes the whole what it is' makes management, even in Ancient times, wholly Modern. We may believe that management's principles are universal because its history incorporates all civilizations, but, in actual fact, they still only refer to one way of seeing. Management's history puts Modern words in the mouths of others to further legitimate Modern practices.

Another look at the history in the first section of this chapter reveals how the history of management is one that anticipates the arrival of a particular present. Owen is important because he had an 'intuitive grasp' of personnel management; Boulton and Watt because their factory represented organization 'in embryo'; Whitney because he 'anticipated' the factory system; and Jefferson because he 'anticipated' Whitney (and was a 'first-class American' to boot). Urwick holds up Babbage's 'remarkable achievement' of having said most of what Taylor would later say. George similarly describes Babbage as 'the harbinger of the new scientific management.' The reason for Chandler's discussion of pre-1850 material is shown by the name of his Harvard course on the topic: 'The coming of managerial capitalism.'

Different civilizations

With like-minded hindsight, T. Caplow's *Principles of Organization* developed an organization chart *à la* Chandler and Mooney and found it 'feasible to reconstruct tables of organization for the towns and city states of medieval and early modern times.' He explained that while 'the table of organization seems to be a modern device … the concept it represents is very ancient. A famous example is *Exodus* xviii: 14–22' (A 'management lecture' to Moses that E. Dale's *The Great Organizers* also explains via an organization chart that plots the 'Israelites' restructuring' along the lines suggested by Moses the 'consultant'). George's management continuum referred to Jesus' expert use of human relations and application of the principle of unity of command. Looking in this way, we can see, in the words of one leading textbook, that 'even the Bible refers to management concepts!' Further back, Urwick saw that 'the workshops and markets of Greece and Rome and of earlier civilizations had to be organized, to be managed, *just as are the factories and shops of today.*'

One of the historians' grandest exemplars of management, the Egyptian pyramids, provides a good example of how the 'intellectual lightening' merely confirms particular Modernist beliefs as fundamental. The building of the pyramids is typically discussed because a large group was ordered towards a common goal, labour was broken down, specialized and standardized, and a minimum wage set. Stephen Robbins describes the 'breakthrough' represented by the pyramids thus:

> ... someone had to *plan* what was to be done, *organize* people and materials to do it, lead and *direct* the workers, and impose *controls* to ensure that everything was done as planned.

He goes on to wonder: 'Who told each worker what he or she was supposed to do? Who ensured that there would be enough stones at the site to keep workers busy? The answers to questions such as these is management.'

But to categorize and discuss the building of pyramids only in these Modern terms is to overlook any different meanings. If one stops to think, perhaps the most remarkable thing about the building of the pyramids is *why* they were built? What particular beliefs possessed people to create them? But management, as it was constituted in the twentieth century, does not enter into discussions about particular values or traditions. With such a view, alternative styles that might incorporate, for example, the importance of spiritual beliefs that may have been seen as inseparable from the work itself, cannot be recognized. Indeed, upon reflection, we may be a little disappointed that the Egyptians who offer so much that is different from how we live today on which to ponder, can here only offer us a more simplified version of what we already know: that management is for all people always and only about planning, directing, coordinating and controlling. It is not a particularly rich tapestry.

Mooney's *Onward Industry* blotted out any alternatives in a more universal way: 'Organization in the formal sense means order, and its corollary, an organized and orderly procedure,' said Mooney. 'To find and correlate the formal principles that make this order is [my] aim.' It is no surprise, then, that he should find formal principles of organization and that these should relate to orderly procedures, that they should be:

- scalar hierarchy,
- the functional division of labour; and
- coordination.

While Mooney admitted that the Ancient's did not speak in these Modern terms, even this was used to add power to his argument. 'That the great organizers of history applied these principles unconsciously,' he claimed, 'proves only that their technique was inherent in their genius.'

However, is this really how Premoderns thought? The material presented in Chapter 2 would certainly call the views expressed above into question. Perhaps it is not so much that the Egyptians and Chinese saw things in terms of planning, directing, the division of labour and controlling, as that it suited historians of a field that was attempting to establish itself to find that 'noble' civilizations like these should see management as they saw it?

Different individuals

Not only were whole civilizations' ways of thinking altered from beyond the grave to suit the establishment of management, individuals also had their corpuses reconfigured. In a standard procedure, each chapter of the book *Managing Organizations: New Challenges and Perspectives* by Robbins and Mukerji concludes with 'review questions.' At the end of Chapter 2, 'The Evolution of Management Thought,' one can see how Weber is made a contributor to this evolution in the answer expected of review question 7:

'Describe Weber's ideal organization?'

As the teaching guide makes clear, the 'correct' answer to this is one with 'a clear division of labour, a clearly defined hierarchy, detailed rules and regulations and impersonal relationships.' Management students are expected to know that Weber's 'ideal organization' exhibits bureaucratic principles. In this way Weber can be seen as a founding father of management. But this view can easily be countered.

In addition to the marking of Taylor's work at 1911, some years after its substance was conceived, it is worth noting the year in which Weber is placed on most management time-lines or continuums: 1947. That Weber had been dead by then for 27 years makes 1947 seem an unusual choice, until one recognizes that this was the year that Talcott Parsons' American translation of *The Theory of Social and Economic Organization* appeared. It was only in the 1950s, when scholars in the fledgling subject began systematically to trace the development of management, that they turned to Parsons' recent translation of Weber, mostly in order to legitimate their work. However, in so doing these scholars only grasped specific aspects of Weber.

Weber set his individual projects against the theme that civilizations could be seen in terms of the balance between rationality and magic, a view that resonates with the Apollo/Dionysus analogy (Weber also did not see the problem as choosing one side over the other, but rather how to appreciate both). However, Weber is constantly referred to in management texts with respect to his investigations into bureaucracy as the most rational form of organizing, and not in terms of the other side of this coin that Weber struggled with: the corresponding 'driving out of magic from things.' Weber was sure that bureaucracy was 'always, *from a formal technical point of view*, the most rational type.' But he only believed that this made it the obvious or inevitable form because of the particular value set of his times: that the manifestation of a 'victorious capitalism' resting on 'mechanical foundations' where the '"objective" discharge of business primarily means a discharge of business according to calculable rules and without regard for persons.' For Weber, there were still other forms of organization, and bureaucracy was anything but his ideal. It was one specific mode, exhibiting only a 'purely technical superiority over other forms,' but this was the criterion that Modernity, and hence management historians, brought to the fore.

For those later theorists who read Parson's freshly translated *Theory of Social and Economic Organization* but lacked Weber's broad historical overview (or a knowledge of his earlier works that placed this work in context), bureaucracy defined what organization ideally was, or at least where it started from. By the 1950s, bureaucratic rationality was no longer regarded as a specific way of seeing, but as the truthful objective foundation of organization theory. Correspondingly, ends like efficiency and mechanistic, means like functional subdivision, hierarchy and standardization were not particular culture-bound ways of assessing organization (remember that by this point Mooney had 'proved' this by seeing them in the subconscious of great thinkers from all walks). Weber is thus cast in management as an 'organizational theorist' whose 'expertise' made him able to see the universality of bureaucracy as the rational and hence foundational form of organization. By the 1950s, a technologically optimistic age dismissed, watered-down or did not dwell upon Weber's pessimism with regard to bureaucracy. By the late 1960s, Weber was so distorted that respected theorists could complain that Weber 'went too far in advocating a machine-like organization' and that he paid 'repeated homage to the Taylor system.' He was even criticized for advocating efficiency to too great an extent, despite the fact that the Modern sense of efficiency was a term foreign to Weber's German tongue at the time he wrote.

Others get pulled into the fray and shaped by a later age to add weight to a history of management written after their death on even more tenuous grounds. For example, despite Thomas Edison, 'the great American inventor,' being prominent on his management continuum, all George can find to say about him relates to his study of anti-submarine warfare. Wren incorporates the Declaration of Independence, Benjamin Franklin and a discussion on John Locke's work inspiring the American and French Revolutions into his *Evolution of Management Thought*, although the links are not made obvious. Others note the American Civil War, regarded as a key moment in the making of Modern America, as important to the history of management because it spurred 'considerable study of managerial methods as a means to raising productivity and coping with growing organisational scale and technological complexity.' It would be interesting to know if the key protagonists involved in these events would have actually described things in these Modernist terms.

Case Box 3.1   The Trouble with Chester Barnard's Greek

Management historians regard Chester Barnard as having had 'a more profound impact on the thinking about the complex subject matter of human organization than any other contributor to the continuum of management thought.' His masterpiece, *The Functions of the Executive*, first published in 1938 and reproduced in 1968 to widespread acclaim, is considered the most influential management text after Taylor's *Scientific Management*. *The Functions of the Executive* begins with this quotation from Book XII of Aristotle's *Metaphysics*:

> For the efficiency of an army consists partly in the order and partly in the general; but chiefly in the latter, because he does not depend upon the order, but the order depends upon him.

This reproduction of Aristotle may not seem particularly significant. It is not one of Barnard's famous phrases or a key proposition. However, it 'tees up,' frames and adds weight to the famous phrases to come. The quotation, cast with the authority of Aristotle no less, serves to show how important leadership is to the management of an organization of any sort. In addition, Aristotle's words provide the effective condition within which management is set, the criterion by which the leader or manager will have his worth bestowed: *efficiency*.

This would immediately appear problematic in the light of what has been discussed in this book. The Ancient Greek's did not have a word that equated to our Modern notion of efficiency. How, therefore, is Aristotle attached to management by speaking a language that did not exist when he spoke?

The translation Barnard uses is H. Tredennick's, published in 1935 by *Harvard University Press*, who also published Barnard's work. However, here is the same passage from an earlier translation by Professors Smith and Ross for *Oxford University Press* in 1908:

> We must consider also in which of the two ways the nature of the universe contains the good or the highest good, whether as something separate and by itself, or as the order of the parts. Probably in both ways, as an army does. For the good is found in the order and the leader, and more in the later; for he does not depend on the order but it depends on him.

Barnard's quotation in *The Functions of the Executive* starts part way into Aristotle's passage, turning 'For the efficiency ...' into the beginning of a sentence which is neither in Tredennick or the original Greek (thus, we do not get the sense that Aristotle was using the relations of a general and an army as an analogy to describe how the world contains the highest good – or how the world is given form). However, the word 'efficiency' is used in Tredennick's translation. All of this does not prove that Smith and Ross's translation is better than Tredennick's or that Barnard wrongly appropriated Aristotle to his and his discipline's own ends. It does, however, raise some interesting questions.

1   How is it that by the mid-twentieth century 'efficiency' comes to put in the mouth of one who could not have used it at the beginning of one of management's most influential works?
2   Why have the millions of managers who have read *The Functions of the Executive* not thought to question this? Why does it seem natural to us that efficiency should be, in Aristotle's day and ours, universally, self-evidently, the evaluative criteria of 'good management' and the 'greatest good'?
3   How might this interpretation of the past limit our understanding of management?

---

3   The maintenance of the fabrication

The conventional history of management is based upon the particular aims and influences of those who first wrote it in the middle of the twentieth century. What this history picked out as the subject's main foundation stone, scientific management, is less a new scientific discovery than old ideas cobbled together under a new title which, thanks to a high profile court case, a million dollar promise, a political agenda and a particular cultural situation, found unusual favor in early twentieth-century America. It is a history that puts words in the mouths of other respected civilizations and individuals in order to make its views appear universal.

So why has this fabrication not been questioned or critiqued? Largely because it fitted so well with prevailing Modernist perspectives at the time it was written and because it has been assumed to be self-evident in the decades since, thanks to a contingent self-referential network of forces making it unlikely that anyone with any influence would seek to question it. This network comprises:

1   The particular formation of the American Business School (ABS), a formation that is as contingent as management's history but which perfectly matches it.
2   The generic curriculum of the ABS, which is built around economics.
3   The view that history is not a particularly useful subject within the ABS curriculum (and that, in any case, management students are thought to get ample history from 'root disciplines' like economics whose histories also mirror the history of management's assumptions).
4   The fact that the ABS has been copied as 'best practice' across the globe, meaning there is no authoritative management platform that does not have a vested interested in the current formation.
5   The fact that even academics critical of management do not critique its history.

This network has reproduced and repeated management's historical assumptions to such an extent that they have become an unquestioned element of management's fibre and, as the influence of management has spread, increasingly part of the fibre of life in general.

The formation of the American Business School (or ABS)

The first American Business School was established at the University of Pennsylvania in 1881. The next two schools, at the Universities of Chicago and California, emerged around the turn of the century and a small number of schools followed prior to World War II. However, it would not be until the late 1950s that they would be generally accepted as part of the academic fraternity. To be taken seriously and establish itself, it needed professional associations to give it a central voice and develop a standardized view of what the ABS would be. It then required being seen as legitimate by the existing boards of universities, reflecting back their established procedures and showing how management was a worthy subject and how it fitted into the established tree of knowledge. The following paragraphs show that, true to the prevailing Modernist beliefs of the middle of the twentieth century, the ABS form that emerged from this process would promote a common set of decentralized units, built around the central stem of economics and capped by 'capstone' courses in corporate strategy. In other words, the standardized form of the ABS that came to prevail was one that replicated Modernism's particular triangular-hierarchical vision.

As we have seen, the 1950s, the height of Modernist optimism, provided the climate for the creation of management's grand history. It also provided the climate for the formation of specialized academic journals and professional institutions like the AMA that sought to show that management was a rigorous and socially relevant profession that should be taken seriously. The American Association of Collegiate Schools of Business (AACSB), closely affiliated with the AMA, was also formed at this time. In the late 1950s, the AMA, in partnership with the AACSB, sponsored two studies into the ideal form of a business school: F.C. Pierson's *Education of the American Businessman* sponsored by the Carnegie Foundation, and R.A. Gordon and J. Howell's *Higher Education for Business* funded by Ford. The authors of both reports collaborated closely and came to the same conclusions.

Having identified the main problem to be that management was 'a vague, shifting, rather formless subject in which neither the foundations at the undergraduate level nor the superstructure at the graduate level can be sharply defined,' the tools and solutions that the authors of the 'foundational studies,' as they are now called, were unlikely to have been taken from disciplines with which they were unfamiliar. Hence, it is worth noting that the authors of the reports were trained as economists. Both reports thus offered the view that economics provided the only theoretical framework for the study of management and that the standardization of the ABS curricula must therefore be based on economics. In keeping, they made the following recommendations, recommendations that led to a particularly Modern form:

- First, because 'dozens of minor fields of specialization ha[d] been permitted to develop that never should have been introduced at all,' the reports called for a 'general tightening of standards' and for management to be rationalized and secured upon a clearly defined academic foundational core. Obviously, economics provided the 'only theoretical framework' suitable for this task.

- Second, having prescribed economics as a central stem, the reports turned to consider the proper decentralization of the curricula. The AACSB stated that at least 40 per cent of the total hours required for the bachelor's degree in business must, at the student's discretion, be taken in any subjects other than business and economics. While not questioning this percentage, both reports complained that 'the work that students do in liberal arts subjects appears to have little relation to their studies in business and economics.' Thus, both urged schools to specify which types of course students should take outside of the core by designating particular subject areas as 'relevant.' The model for future curriculum development was thus organized around two generic disciplines in addition to economics: behavioural sciences (psychology and sociology) and applied mathematics.

- Third, having outlined the central core and then having used this to determine a properly ordered range of contributing subjects, the researchers sought to standardize the curricula's super-level or 'sharp end.' They recommended the development of 'capstone courses.' These courses, termed 'business policy' (and later 'corporate strategy'), would 'give students an opportunity to pull together what they have learned in the separate business fields [and] concentrate on integrating what already has been acquired.'

While the perspective of those involved in the preparation of the foundational reports made such a form seem obvious, it will be argued here that the pivotal relationship with economics, and the way of seeing that is reinforced by this, is a specific view based on the subjective understandings and subsequent decisions of key individuals, and a set of circumstances and contingencies particular to the mid-twentieth century.

Economics as the foundational stem

Economics has traditionally provided the only theoretical framework for the study of business. [E]ven today the two fields are so closely related they can hardly be discussed separately.

  F.C. Pierson, Education of the American Businessman.

The recommended ABS form quickly took hold. In 1960, a paper in the *Washington Business Review* promoted schools teaching an eclectic blend of anthropology, biology, ecology, geography, mathematics, philosophy, physics, political science, psychology and sociology (economics was not even mentioned). Two years later, when the 1959 foundational reports had been digested, the relevant contributing disciplines were defined by another paper as only:

> a) the engineering approach, which emphasizes productivity increases through organizational efficiency; b) the human relations approach, incorporating psychological and sociological concerns; c) the economic approach, which emphasizes the development of resource allocation and cost control; and d) the systems approach, with emphasis on models and the use of mathematical techniques.

The increasing uncomfortableness felt in explicitly seeing humans as machines saw engineering and mathematics lose favour, leading to the adoption of a set of three contributing disciplines. Economics, psychology and sociology would serve as the research and literature foundation for all ABS's. But there was a clear pecking order. T. Mosson's history of management education points out that while:

> ... economics, psychology and sociology are all to be found in varying degrees, the high prestige of economics, in academic circles at least, has meant that it has been the dominant discipline.

However, the following paragraphs seek to demonstrate that this perspective is specific to the middle of the twentieth century. When people at Wharton began to think of establishing a business school, economics was not even considered a worthy academic discipline. In the first decades of the twentieth century, when the next schools emerged, economics spoke a language that was seen as of little relevance to business and the majority of economists' disdain for the fledgling subject of management was palpable. Only in the 1950s was economics academically accepted, willing to contribute to business schools, and capable of speaking in terms that managers could relate to. The contingent alliance between economics and management would see ABS's establish themselves, but this is not to say that the formation that grew out of this is, as Pierson stated, 'an obvious and universal foundation.'

From subjective institutionalism to objective neoclassicism

R.R. Locke's comprehensive study of the emergence of business schools after 1940 outlines what had to be done before they could be 'accepted' as being the development of a historical connection between what they taught and an accepted scientific discipline. 'The gap, moreover, was hard to fill,' he claimed:

> ... for it was not a question of finding an existing bridge between theory and practice but of building a bridge between the two. People who established business schools in institutions of higher education quickly learned this lesson for there was, at the outset, no discipline to teach. Science-based management had to be invented.

Such an invention would not have been aided through association with economics in the middle of the nineteenth century because economics itself was still a marginal subject. At this time, most within the field of 'political economy,' as it was then know, were 'Institutionalists.' This school drew from Adam Smith's more historical and humanistic interests and was non-theoretical in orientation, encouraging only descriptions of specific socio-economic contexts. This was clearly not the stuff to gain acceptance from the mainstream scholarship of the day, which consisted of the traditional arts, 'pure' sciences like logic, mathematics and mechanistic physics, and 'empirical' sciences like chemistry and biology. An institutional economics was not a traditional art, nor did it replicate the form of a Modern science.

However, another economics emerged in the later part of the nineteenth century: the 'Neoclassical' school. This took quite a different aspect from Smith, namely the view of Man as detached from family, class, country and custom and thus a self-determining rational being evaluating actions in terms of economic utility. Abstracting economic behaviour away from traditional historical contexts, the Neoclassical school offered a more exacting expression of Smith's general assertion that the pursuit of individual self-interest produces an optimal social 'equilibrium.'

In order to theorize this, Neoclassicists like Walras, Jevons and Pareto borrowed freely from mechanistic physics and its mathematical language. Pareto thus found that the equations that determine equilibrium were not 'new to me, I know them well, they are old friends. They are the equations of rational mechanics. That is why pure economics is a sort of mechanics or akin to mathematics.' While Smith's vision was Newtonian, it was only so in a qualitative sense. Adding mathematics to Smith's thinking in order to rid their universe of purposive human activity, the Neoclassicists created an abstract theoretical model of economic reality. Neoclassical economics subsequently connected to other established disciplines on the tree of knowledge through physics and mathematics. It was accepted as a Modern science. The Institutional school ebbed away.

From Neoclassical economics to nowhere

Economics was considered a worthy academic subject just before the first schools of management were established in the US. Why was it, then, that management and economics did not form the allegiance that would take place after World War II and lead to the establishment of a generic ABS form?

In order to gain acceptance, the Neoclassicists had argued that economics should be a *pure* rather than an empirical science. Indeed, the Neoclassicists abstracted things to the point where behavior was always about utility optimization, to the point where Alfred Marshall could argue that man 'really only produces utilities,' not particular material things. This moved them away from problems of causation and temporal events, with which the empirical sciences were concerned, to problems of building and perfecting general abstract models. But the sort of calculus that sprang from this gave scant guidance to people concerned with doing business. The Neoclassicists wanted to express the mechanism by which the market as a whole worked, something that managers had no direct influence over, and treated organizational operations as a "black box", an unknown or a problem that has already been solved.

Even if Neoclassicists had spoken in terms of the problems facing managers, their general models would have been difficult to apply. Managers had to operate in the practical world without complete knowledge of cause-and-effect or functionality. They were not faced with the perfect solutions or the binary logic that could be either true or false, the things that corresponded with the Neoclassicist's language. At best, they could only hope to think in terms of probabilities of outcomes.

Events in Wharton's first decades demonstrate how this form of economics was unable to provide the bridge that Locke identified as necessary. The early Wharton professors were of two types: either those who, in the words of one disparaging commentator, found 'their curricula material in the business world, not in the universities (in science)' and offered only 'an extended form of business journalism'; or the 'proper academics' who came from other faculties to teach 'traditional subjects.' Among these academics were Neoclassical economists. However, having established themselves as academically legitimate, they were suspicious and skeptical of the practical thrust of Wharton's business programmes, let alone interested in putting much effort into teaching on them. In any case, those 'proper' economists who did deign to teach at the fledgling business schools were roundly criticized for having nothing of relevance to say to their classes. In the 1960s, historians expressed surprise that:

> … even the economists in this group [of traditional academic instructors], whose discipline necessarily called for some acquaintance with business aims and practices, were wont to seek enlightenment more largely by speculative than by [empirical] scientific methods.

Of course, while in the 1960s commentators looking back might be astonished that these economists should be so abstract and unacquainted with business, the leading economists of the day did not see this necessity. This comment, written in 1919 by German educationalist Eugen Schmalenbach, outlines what his contemporaries saw as the natural divide between the two:

> Economics and business [may] handle, to a large extent, the same material but they do not have the same spirit. Economics is a philosophical science with philosophical characteristics. Business is, on the other hand, an applied science. Chemistry [is] closer in spirit to business than is economics.

That economics was the only foundation for business was by no means obvious to thinkers of other ages. Economics would have to take a further turn before the view that shaped the standardized format of the ABS would appear self-evident.

From Neoclassical economics to business economics

Economists' inability to test their hypotheses in the established manner of the empirical sciences (that is, in laboratory conditions) made it contingent for the subject to adapt into a pure science in order to gain access to the club of accepted academic subjects in the nineteenth century. But advances made by the next generation of mathematicians brought mathematical statistics to a point where its workings could be accepted as substitutes for laboratory experiments. Thus, beyond the Modern advance whereby contrived experiments could be taken as representing things in the empirical world, statistical testing would enable Modern thinkers to forgo experiment.

Many economists, tiring of Neoclassical dogma and the consequent lack of applicability of their field preventing them from availing of the professional opportunities available if their theories could be more practical, subsequently found statistics liberating. And the wedding of statistics and economics, 'econometrics,' proved convenient in that probability-based mathematics enabled decisions to be weighed in a manner that seemed to provide advice for business people and leave room for judgment without undermining Neoclassicism's hard-fought principles. However, econometrics was still about numerical data and the inferences that could be made from them. It did not speak a language that managers of the period could relate to. For this to happen, algorithms, rules or routines that could be related to (that is, not expressed in exact mathematical symbols) had to be developed.

Statisticians had applied themselves to making predictions about games of chance from the 1920s. However, with the rising interest in making economics more practically applicable, theorists began to explore the business implications of this thinking with developments like 'game theory,' which sought to show how managers could, under certain assumptions, act in order to achieve a certain minimum gain by following the correct algorithm. By using algebra, matrix theory and probability theory in its calculations, this sort of thinking kept economics connected to its mathematical roots, while bringing it into contact with the realm of electrical engineers working on the linear programming of early computers during World War II using Boolean logic to provide algorithms. While algorithms like these required more information than economics' traditional emphasis on macro costs and revenues, they enabled businesses to define goals in terms of individual optimal quantities of inputs and outputs, and obtain specific directions about how to achieve these goals stated in terms of the various steps available to the firm. Economists of the day recognized that these methods approached the firm more from the viewpoint of engineering than economics, but they went along with it because while it was applied, it did not undermine the economic theories built up during the nineteenth and twentieth centuries. Linear programming was, the economists reasoned, just a special case of marginal analysis and, hence, quite compatible with Neoclassical theory.

By the 1950s, Neoclassical economics, econometrics and engineering had come together in a new field termed 'business economics.' This field provided the bridge necessary to enable management to begin to be taken seriously as an academic subject, an underpinning that granted academic "gravity" *and* supplied methods that its constituents thought applicable.

From business economics to American Business Schools

A history of Columbia University, written in 1954, was subsequently able to put the emerging transformation, from academically unacceptable business schools to their standardized and acceptable face down to the 'evolution of economics':

> A highly interesting and *unforeseen* development which has paralleled the growth of business education in American universities has been the transformation in the science known as economics … Economists are today treading the paths of [empirical rather than pure] science in search of signposts to economic truths, rather than scanning the skies of speculative thought for guides to the interpretation of social action. Business practitioners, business teachers and economic scientists [now] all work in varying degrees with the same data in devising their respective plans and procedures. Rhapsodies on the heroic achievements of 'captains of industry' [have given] way to informative, sober treatises on business and organization and administration. [Thus] schools of business [have come to] form the best available middle ground for a juncture of forces for pursuing these objectives by businessmen and economists.

Other commentators noted that early ABS programs were initially dominated by those economists committed to the proposition that management as a proper discipline could never be or by those who feared that if it did come into being it would sully traditional concepts of economics. However, as ABS 'programs matured,' they wrote, 'and as economists came more and more to grips with the realities of the world, these men began to make many substantial contributions to administrative thought.' 'Economists coming to grips with the real world' meant economics becoming a discipline with academic backing, but which could also offer viable frameworks for managers. 'Programs maturing' meant their becoming standardized. These two things, coinciding in the middle of the twentieth century, bequeathed the form of the ABS and the shape of the management curricula. It did not take long for this particular, contingent alliance to become shrouded in a manner that gave it the air of a universal association. While the 1954 history quoted above would still recognize the 'transformation of economics' as an 'unforeseen development,' and claim that economics had *'often* been defined as the science of business,' by 1959 the ABS's 'foundational' documents, seemingly unaware of this history, would see economics as *always* having providing these schools' *'only* theoretical framework.'

The developments described above were clearly more political expediencies than objective foundations. The ABS formed a juncture for the forces of economists and businessmen in the 1950s that enabled both to gain greater influence in society. Management, like economics, began to attract top students because of its newfound intellectuality, and economics, like management, started to draw greater numbers because of its greater utility. Economists could begin to speak to governments and corporations with the authority granted by an air of practical awareness. Management academics could now speak to corporations and governments with the air of authority granted a science. Management was duly recognized as a serious academic subject and one that people in governments and social organizations believed they needed to know about. But this was not because ABS's finally recognized that economics had always been management's natural foundation and organized themselves accordingly, or because it could be no other way. It was because of management's (or its key players) need to be seen to be founded at a time when economics had gained itself scientific status and was seeking to appear more practically relevant – a set of circumstances quite particular to Western society in the middle of the twentieth century.

The history of management's roots

Out of the melee came a philosopher of astonishing scope. Adam Smith published his Wealth of Nations in 1776, thereby adding a second revolutionary event to that fateful year. A political democracy was born on one side of the ocean; an economic blueprint was unfolded on the other. But while not all of Europe followed America's political lead, after Smith had displayed the first true tableau of modern society, all of the Western world became the world of Adam Smith. [Now] men began to see the world about them with new eyes; they saw how the tasks they did fitted into the whole of society, and saw that society as a whole was proceeding at a majestic pace toward a distant but clearly visible goal.

R.L. Heilbroner and P. Streeten

The institution of management in the 1950s did not require a student to have any knowledge of history. Pierson's study made no mention of history at either an undergraduate or postgraduate level. Gordon and Howell's report recommended 12 hours of either economic or business history, but only in the first two years prior to admission into a business programme. In keeping, nothing in the AACSB's accreditation standards required students to take a course in history. This is partly because, being Modern, management is more concerned with the 'cutting edge'; partly because management theory is thought to be largely ahistorical, and partly because it was thought that all the historical education that students would need could be gleaned from their studies of 'the contributing disciplines.' Serious questioning of the fabrication that is management's historical institution is thus further discouraged by the belief that management stems from economics, sociology and psychology. As they are also framed by a Modernist understanding of the world, their histories reinforce the Modern views and boundaries that management promotes as universal.

Economics

Given the developments described above, management history claims a special bond to the history of economics. In 1959, the first article published in the journal *Business History* congratulates the journal's founders (their 'provenance [being] a guarantee that business-men and their works will be surveyed with the same passionless eyes as political historians turn on statesmen and diplomats, or sociologists on God's creatures in general') and argues that the field must be recognized as an offshoot of economic history. Mosson's review of management education in the 1960s likewise claims that it is greatly 'influenced by the history and the prestige of economics.' The association reinforces management's understanding that it begins properly with the division of labour and its related concepts.

Heilbroner and Streeten's quotation at the head of this section captures the passion that economic historians felt for Smith at the time the history of management was being drafted and the ABS was being established. For twentieth-century historians like Eric Roll, 'Smith was the great starting point for all.' Indeed, Roll reported that:

> There is a surprising unanimity of opinion among historians [that] political economy as a science [i.e., as a serious subject] begins at a time when the foundations of industrial capitalism were already well laid.

The Modern formation of economics consequently provides management's outer limit of 'serious contributions.' However, as in the history of management, economics 'gains weight' by looking beyond Smith and hooking onto the nobility of ancient times. And, as with management, economics' history sees the past only as the anticipation of the Modern present.

Roll's 'pre-history' simply charts the arrival of the foundational 'classics': 'In the three centuries that elapsed between the end of the Middle Ages and the appearance of *Wealth of Nations*, the classical system of political economy was being prepared.' The 'contributions' of the Ancient Greeks are encountered in a similarly Modernist manner. Plato finds a place in economic history 'because one of his central concepts, the division of labour, is of paramount importance in the history of economics.' But it is interesting to wonder by what reckoning the division of labour is discerned to be one of Plato's 'central concepts' as he himself never termed it so.

Descent is also claimed from Aristotle, with particular emphasis being placed on this passage from his *Politics*:

> Of everything which we possess there are two uses: both belong to the thing as such, but not in the same manner, for one is the proper, and the other the improper or secondary use of it. For example, a shoe is used for wear, and is used for exchange; both are uses of the shoe.

In these words, Roll claims that:

> Aristotle laid the foundation of the distinction between use-value and exchange-value [and thus] the foundations of later economic thought ... Although his words are obscure, Aristotle seems to say that the secondary value of an article – as a means of exchange – is not necessarily 'unnatural.'

But Roll addresses this quotation with more than a little wishful thinking. Aristotle was clear that money was barren and that use was far preferable to exchange. For Moderns to see this passage as 'a breakthrough' (because exchange value is not 'necessarily' deemed 'unnatural') and then read this as the 'foundation' of a world view where exchange and the pre-eminence of the market are the tableau against which all human behaviour should be properly understood, is pretty hopeful. Indeed, Aristotle did not possess a 'theory of value' as such, and could not adequately explain the commensurability of products, because, unlike Neoclassical economics (which connects use-value with exchange-value via the concept of utility), he assigned these things to *different* categories, with *different* ends requiring *different* treatments. Antiquity was predominantly governed by a system of use-value and not the market-oriented exchange value that has given rise to the science of economics. Aristotle's finding was that the pursuit of exchange-value must be subject to human ends. Exchange-value does not really deal with particular teleological ends and, as such, Aristotle's inquiries are more ethical and metaphysical than economic in the Modern sense. The Greeks probably could not have contemplated economic thought as the Modern world now conceives it.

In any case, the great economic historian J.A. Shumpeter at once manages to highlight the 'indirect influence' of Greek philosophy on economic thought and minimize its contribution. While he noted Aristotle's 'embryonic' differentiation between use and exchange value, he added that 'this is not only commonplace but common sense, and further than this [Aristotle] did not advance'. Moreover, he terms Aristotle's placing the concept 'happiness' in the center of his social philosophy without giving a utilitarian account of it 'the original sin'. Aristotle's analysis is further found wanting because he 'gave in to the teleological error' and because he went 'hortatory on Virtue and Vice' – subjective, emotive and irrational things. In this manner, the Ancients can be seen as contributing to the history of economics by showing its basis to be a universal human concern, while historians can at once see their views as naive and needing to be overcome by more rational Modern thinkers.

Psychology

The history of psychology provides a similarly Modernist perspective. R. Smith's recent study demonstrates that histories of psychology still point to the 'continuity between powerful symbols of scientific advance and modern psychology.' Beyond the formation of the scientific method providing a point of origin, the crucial period in psychology's history is that from 1870–1920, when advances in the life sciences enabled their research techniques to be applied to human mental problems and psychology became an academic discipline. Prior to this, histories draw links between 'pre-psychology' and selected 'academic classics'. L.S. Hearnshaw's history is typical, including preliminary chapters on the Greeks ('The Sophists were embryo practical psychologists'), Christian theologians and 'significant developments' in the Middle Ages. However, these chapters are only a prelude to the discussion of the 'metamorphosis of psychology ... from speculative philosophy to scientific discipline' in the nineteenth century. Psychology is thus furnished with the authority of science and also with an Ancient wisdom that both adds gravity to the subject and confirms the application of Modern science as an advance.

Sociology

Sociology's history promotes the same boundaries. This view from a typical introductory text is that sociological thought:

> ... has preoccupied thinkers in all periods of history: the philosophers of Ancient Greece and Rome reflected upon the way society operated and/or should operate, and for centuries afterwards social and political theorists and philosophers applied themselves to similar questions. But th[ese] 'philosophical' analyses of society were essentially based on speculation, on dubious and untested assumptions about the motives of human beings in their behaviour, and on undisciplined theorising, and they lacked systematic analysis of the structure and workings of societies ... However, from the 18th century onwards in Western Europe, important

changes took place ... many considerable advances were taking place in scientific discovery with regard to the structure and composition of the physical world surrounding human beings, and with regard to the physical nature and make-up of human beings themselves ... Could such a scientific, 'rational' approach also be applied to the analysis of humans' social worlds, their relationships, experiences and behaviour within it? Scientific and technological advances laid the foundations for the transformation from a predominantly rural, agricultural, 'manual' way of life to an urban, industrial, 'mechanised' pattern of living ... Sociology ... emerged against the background of these intellectual and material changes in the second half of the 19th century.

In this light, it is no surprise to find that sociology's 'founding fathers' are thoroughly Modern (or interpreted as such):

- *Comte*, who stressed the adoption of a scientific method to analyse society so that we might, 'know, predict and control' it (a statement that flows into management texts: for example, 'the purpose of OB is to help you to *explain*, *predict*, and *control* human behaviour');
- *Saint-Simon*, who saw in rationally developed bureaucracies hope for stability and progress in the aftermath of the French Revolution; and
- *Weber*, whose interpretation by Modern historians has already been discussed.

Alain Touraine describes these founding fathers as sharing a belief in the 'gradual obliteration of cultural and social differences in favour of an increasingly broad participation of all in one and the same general model of modernity.'

Sociology, psychology and economics, seen as providing the underlying basis of management, seek to understand the contours of Modernity and are thus framed by the emergence of Modern capitalism and Modern economics. The histories of management's roots only re-double management's historical blinkers and ensure that the intellectual lightning directed at the past can only confirm what we already do in the present.

The lack of an alternative platform

Whatever else can be said about the American collegiate business school, one thing is certain: It is the mechanism for bringing about any change in business education. If innovations are to be made, it will be through the business schools.

L.W. Porter and L.E. McKibbin (their emphasis)

The influence of an American understanding of management on the rest of the world was broached in the discussion on Taylorism meeting certain needs at home and abroad during World War I. However, despite this, Chandler still found fault with Europe's businessmen as they failed to move in the 'appropriate direction' before World War II. A number of studies have examined how The Marshall Plan helped rectify this situation by mobilizing US technology and managerial know-how to rebuild Europe and Asia anew, putting all parties on more or less the same economic path. And beyond the post-War period, the adoption of the ABS form as global 'best practice' enabled a further convergence of management approaches, further diminishing the likelihood that anyone would question its form. Developments in Britain are indicative of how European business schools came to pass.

The British government began to investigate the training of managers needed to aid in reconstruction directly after the War, forming a committee to consider the establishment of a state system of management education. Colonel Urwick was named chair. Urwick was enamoured with the US's pioneering works and was similarly glowing about US management education, a view made explicit in his 1954 study *Management Education in American Business*. Here he noted that 'management development throughout the United States must be predicated on a well designed organization plan,' adding – citing his fellow historian Mooney – that this means 'with basic management responsibilities properly subdivided, classified, grouped, distributed, related and defined.' Urwick's committee subsequently suggested a curriculum for a national management certificate to be taught in night schools and technical colleges with 'background subjects in economics, law and psychology, some "tool" subjects such as accounting; statistical methods; work measurement and incentives; and office organization and methods.'

Despite replicating the emergent ABS form, the 'Urwick Report' is seen as 'a milestone in the development of management studies.' However, historians also note that 'the real … "management education revolution" really started' when the 'Urwick Scheme' was adapted and brought into universities. When this revolutionary decision was taken the consensus among those charged with creating management schools within universities was that they must be based upon 'the best American practice [as] enshrined in the reports of the Ford and Carnegie Foundations.' Whitley's historical review correspondingly saw their development as answering the needs of the 'Chandlerian organization,' reproducing Chandler's triangular-hierarchical organization chart to explain the new skills that British ABS's would seek to provide.

The first postgraduate management programmes were duly established in London and Manchester in the mid-1960s, and a Bachelor's degree in management science began at Warwick University in 1969. Warwick's programme was primarily 'designed to train students in the basic disciplines fundamental to management – economics, quantitative methods and the behavioural sciences.' The Manchester MBA provided instruction in 'accounting, finance, law, economics, psychology, sociology, organization behaviour, and quantitative methods.' LBS's orientation was narrower, with a preoccupation with mathematics that arose from the Principal's belief that 'it was a subject that was as much a necessary part of a manager's education as Latin had once been a gentleman's.' By 1986, Forrester's report into British MBA's found that the 48 programmes that had been established had 'a basic common syllabi' of 'managerial economics, quantitative methods, organizational behaviour, management systems, operational management, marketing, finance, accounting and corporate strategy.'

In keeping with the UK experience, management education throughout Europe in the 1960s and 1970s came to reflect already established American forms. This was thought both a necessity and a good thing, as Mosson's review makes clear:

> The impetus and original model for European management education was the American business school, and the contrast in development and achievement remains a strong incentive to European management teachers. In the United States management education is extensive, widely accepted, firmly institutionalized; above all it is vigorous, self-confident, and successful. In a business society formal education for the higher ranks of business has more scope, more energy, more encouragement. And, in addition, it takes its place as one of the many mechanisms intended to further the democratic ideal.

However, by the end of the 1980s moves were afoot within the US that might have seen the fundamental form of the ABS reconsidered.

In 1988 the AASCB sponsored *Management Education and Development – Drift or Thrust into the 21st Century* (a title reminiscent of Lippmann's *Drift and Mastery*, and one that a Freudian psychologist might make much of). Despite seeking to take a fresh look at the ABS form, it leant on the logic developed in the Ford and Carnegie studies. While the authors noted that schools should pay more attention to business ethics, internationalization and communication in addition to the 'adjacent relevant disciplines' (which they list as 'economics, psychology and the like'), no mention is made of incorporating more history, for example, or anything else very removed from management's established 'contributing stems.'

While *Drift or Thrust* did, more or less, follow the lines of its predecessors, it also highlight two notably new aspects. First, 'in marked contrast to the situation reported in the 1950s,' where there was a recognized need to establish the underlying subject matter of management studies and standardize curricula, it 'found no forceful push for systemic curricula change emanating from business schools themselves.' It seems that by this time norms had become established, a centralized order had been socialized, and management educators were happy with the formula that had seen them become established as recognized members of the academic community.

Second, *Drift or Thrust* commented on ABS doctoral programmes, from whence most developers of management theory now came. It complained that 'new doctorates are emerging who are in many cases unduly specialized and lacking a sufficient appreciation of the complexities of business problems that extend beyond the confines of their own discipline or functional area.' It added that 'this problem is exacerbated by the increasing number of faculty members trained in other disciplines who do not even have the benefit of a business school socialization process.' The upshot is that while we may talk of management theorists being trained with too narrow a *sub-disciplinary* emphasis, it is at once seen as a problem that they are being trained by people from 'unrelated disciplines' (who do not even have the 'benefit of a business school socialization process' that would educate them in 'management's ways'). The form of the *discipline* of management must be respected.

   Drift or Thrust concludes that ABS's are '*the mechanism* for bringing about any innovations' in the production of management knowledge. And the global adoption of the 1950s' US model has indeed made it the only mechanism. But this seems problematic when placed up against *Drift and Thrust's* very last sentences:

> Continuous innovation. In our opinion, if any single element of organization culture ideally should characterize the US business school in the next decade, it should be an ingrained, embedded, and pervasive spirit of innovation. If this occurs, society will be the winner.

Juxtaposed with the earlier quotations from *Drift or Thrust*, the now entrenched and tightly defined nature of what management education should be, and the ideas expressed earlier in this book that innovation and creativity comes from 'different traditions shaking hands,' it is difficult to see how the ABS socialization process that *Drift or Thrust* commends would not work against innovation: 'the single element of organizational culture' that the report claims to value so highly.

   Indeed, another American, but non-AACSB sponsored, survey written at the same time as *Drift or Thrust* concludes with a sobering commentary on what has really been 'ingrained and embedded' within the ABS's bureaucratic knowledge-producing form in the last 50 years:

> As certain as this author is with regard to the above-mentioned need for adaptation and change and the nature of academic governance, he is equally convinced that an alternative model is not likely to arise in the near future. Business schools across the US [now] have long and glorious histories of conservative practices and faculty and administrators have vested interests in the maintenance of past behaviors. One scenario suggests that we may have become victims of our pasts ... Innovation and change may not come in [such] organized, purposeful and systematic procedures.

In the 1990s, the consolidation of what a business school must be enabled a further global push. In the 1997 presidential address to The Academy of Management, Michael Hitt outlined his vision of the future: 'Essentially, management education and research will be globalized.' Despite claims that this would coincide with 'a stronger emphasis on multidisciplinary thinking,' recent developments may work against this prospect. This book was written at a British school entertaining missions from the AACSB toward meeting its US, now global, criteria for accreditation, an accreditation that will keep it, in its own words, at the 'cutting edge' and enable it to be globally ranked against its US counterparts. Indeed, press releases in 1999 claimed that 'The AACSB is well advanced with overseas expansion, planning to assess 12 [further] schools in Japan, Hong Kong, Australia and Europe along similar lines.'

In 1988, the same year as *Drift or Thrust*, a paper by R.R. Locke found that its buying into US pre-eminence had made Britain ignorant of alternative traditions and forms of management education present on the Continent, and that British management education was the lesser for this. The increasing globalization of business schools according to US 'best practice' may mean that alternative local traditions will increasingly be seen as less relevant, further diminishing the likelihood of different approaches challenging this 'one-best way' and inspiring the multidisciplinary thinking and innovation claimed to be so imperative.

The lack of critique

[T]he principal directions in which management thought will develop in the foreseeable future have already been pointed out by the pioneer thinkers who provide the substance of this book ... They present it with vision, with vitality and with an authority that is beyond challenge.

H.F. Merrill

Mooney claimed that his historical principles of organization were universal and would, consequently, hold true in the future as well. While George felt that Mooney's work did not pay enough mind to the 'human side of work,' he admitted that 'subsequent writers [including himself] borrowed freely from Mooney's analysis and have used his concepts as a framework on which to hang more humanistic approaches to the managerial problem.' Indeed, in more recent times, Wren has had no qualms declaring that 'The managerial functions [which he takes to be planning, organizing, leading, controlling] form a convenient framework for a summary discussion of the past *and future.*' It seems that Merrill's quotation above is more than empty rhetoric.

Indeed, there has been little in the way of critique with regard to the authority and vision provided by the history of management. This is partly because of:

1 the singular view of the business school form;
2 the singular view of what a business school should teach;
3 that (1) and (2) pay little attention to history, partly because most assume management principles to be 'timeless' or concerned with the future and being at the 'cutting edge,' and partly because it looks to those fields seen as contributing disciplines (which also put forward histories that are

completely consistent with management's incorporation of Modernism); and

4   that (1), (2) and (3) have become global best practice.

These four self-reinforcing elements make the questioning of the conventional view of management's history and the institutions this promotes less likely, but it does not make such questioning impossible. We could point to other aspects of management for which similar conditions could be true but where academics or practitioners have been highly critical and even brought about changes. However, with regard to the history of management, a fifth element is present. This is a total lack of critique. Nowhere within the normal cycle of the dissemination of knowledge, from (a) academic journals to (b) popular books to (c) teaching texts and on to (d) works that would be critical of the conventional views put forward by the former, does anybody question the historical blinkers described in this chapter.

Thus, through repeating and cross-referencing the initial view of management's history developed in the 1950s and 1960s amongst one another, the academic journals, pop-management literature, textbooks and even the critical management literature made this history appear beyond doubt (see the reinforcing system depicted in the figure below).

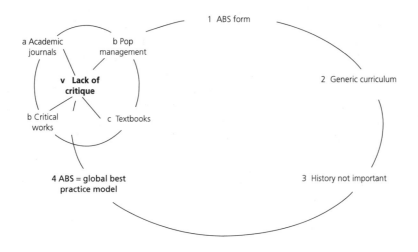

Subsequently, a secondary loop reinforces the primary network that makes up the fabrication described thus far. This loop is described in the paragraphs below.

Academic journals

Given management's general lack of interest in history, academic journals focussed upon management's history are not numerous. But what there is unquestioningly has a heavy Anglo-centric emphasis on the period

1750–1914. *Business History Review* has printed 720 papers in its 41-year history. Of these, three looked prior to the European Renaissance. None looked at the West prior to medieval times. Only one paper out of 1064, on Japanese feudal systems, looked beyond that which led directly to, or is a part of, the Modern Western industrial experience. There are no explicitly marked-out chronological boundaries put before prospective article writers for these journals. Perhaps if there were, they might be questioned, but as things stand, management's historical boundaries are taken for granted – although the one paper on Ancient Japan demonstrates that such boundaries need not apply. In the late 1990s, the *Journal of Management History* was launched with the aim of 'exploring the whole history of management thought,' enabling 'subscriber[s] to judge for [themselves] what contribution the major management theorists have made, and how their ideas have been built on or rejected by subsequent thinkers.' However, who we are steered to see as the 'major management theorists' is apparent in the selection of the journal's first four special issues. These are devoted to 'Taylor,' 'Fayol,' 'Weber' and 'The Engineering Approach to Management.'

Pop managment

Pop management literature reinforces the standard. Peter Drucker, the most authoritative of management gurus, confirms what has become a truism. Citing Chandler, Drucker tells us that 'The roots of the disciplines of management [may] go back [further but] management as a function, management as a distinct work, management as a discipline and area of study – these are all products of this century.' Clutterbuck and Crainer's pop history *Makers of Management* draws extensively on Urwick, Wren and Chandler to present a 'chronology of management thinking' similar in form to George's (see Case Box 1.1). Their chronology draws upon Drucker's 'seven conceptual foundations to the post-war management boom' (the first of which is 'scientific management') as evaluative criteria. And Clutterbuck and Crainer's last entry is 'Peter Drucker's 1986 *The Frontiers of Management.*'

Textbooks

With the history of management subsequently thought to have been 'decided' and of little practical use, students of management will likely only encounter their subjects' history in introductory textbooks. Here the field's history is glossed over by summarizing the accepted history as a stepping stone to the 'subject itself.' Firstly, textbooks demonstrate the worth of the subject that the reader has chosen to study, as in Stephen Robbins' *Management*:

Organized endeavors overseen by people responsible for planning, organizing, leading and controlling activities have existed for thousands of years [this] demonstrate[s] that organizations have been with us for thousands of years and that management has been practiced for an equivalent period.

Secondly, they use history to put current knowledge 'in perspective,' showing how we have progressed from the bases of management, as in G. Dessler's *Organization Theory*:

> An understanding of this [pre-industrial] background is important for putting the classical theories in perspective. [For example,] the highly centralized and mechanistic structures of classical theory had their genesis in the state monopolies of Egypt and the empire of Rome.

However, once this is pointed out, it is made clear that 'it has been only in the past several hundred years that management has undergone systematic investigation, acquired a common body of knowledge, and become a formal discipline for study.' Consequently, textbooks replicate the lines laid down by historians, making it unnecessary for advanced students to read or question them:

> Despite [ancient] accomplishments [their] informal knowledge was, and remains, incomplete. What kind of leadership is best? Should decisions be made by groups or individuals? What tactics are most effective in bringing negotiations to a successful conclusion? Common sense [which the Ancients are seen to have relied on] offers only fragmentary and inaccurate answers to these and many other crucial questions.

After 'the history of management,' textbooks generally move into the 'material of management' by starting with its integration. Robbins and Mukerji's *Managing Organizations* points out that:

> Concern with developing a unifying framework for management only began in earnest in the early 1960s. Like most fields of study, management, in its maturity, has moved towards integration. [The] fact that the most popular current management textbooks follow the process orientation is evidence that the process approach [the line of planning, organizing, leading, controlling] continues to be a viable integrative framework.

Critical works

Even books critical of management's outcomes reinforce or do not question its conventional history. Texts like Thompson and McHugh's *Work Organizations – A Critical Introduction*, the stated aim of which is 'to provide a critical alternative to the standard, often American, texts that still predominate,' does not question the key assumptions at issue here. 'The theory and practice of organization,' it reiterates, 'has developed around bureaucracies, deriving partly from the work of Max Weber, who, at the turn of the century was most responsible for drawing our attention to the significance of large-scale organizations.' Their critical approach follows this lead. The first chapter after their introduction aims to 'locate and explain the formation of the large-scale industrial bureaucracies that have been the primary object of analysis of the subject of organization studies.' The first subsection is entitled 'The rise of the factory system.' This focus on 'large-scale' organization was a criteria that the historian Sidney Pollard used to 'define his terms tightly enough so as to find no significant precedents for management problems prior to 1750.' Thompson and McHugh cite Pollard's History as 'evidence' for their views.

Perhaps the most widely cited critique of management paints a similar picture. Harry Braverman's *Labor and Monopoly Capital's* informs us that the division of labour is the 'earliest innovative principle of the capitalist mode of production' and that it has remained 'the fundamental principle of organization.' Following other historians, Braverman mentions the antecedents of the Pyramids, the Great Wall and the Roman Army, but concludes that the 'management required in such situations remained elementary' and does not dwell on them. Because the 'classical economists were the first to approach the problems of the organization of labor within capitalist relations of production from a theoretical point of view,' Braverman argues that they 'may thus be called the first management experts.' Management's history is processed thus.

4   Why the conventional history of management should be challenged

History repeats itself [because] historians repeat each other.

Philip Guedalla

With every decade it becomes clearer that those who believe in management in the modern sense are inherently in line with the march of events.

Lyndall Urwick and Edward Brech

The history of management is subsequently so 'regular' that it appears to offer little scope for the ambitious historian. Hence, after a flurry of works in the 1960s and early 1970s, no comprehensive new history of management has appeared. Management history had already been effectively dealt with and 'processed.' Having been recorded in this manner, management's historical assumptions are only redoubled as this self-referential network's great works are reproduced. Roll's *A History of Economic Thought* was first published in 1938. The 1992 edition is its fifth incarnation. The re-publication of Barnard's 1938 *Functions of the Executive* in 1968 inspired a new generation to declare his thinking as ahead of its time. Wren's *Evolution of Management*, which was first published in 1972, was into its fourth edition by 1994. Drucker's *Management* was first published in 1974 and reprinted five times before 1991. Robbins' 1996 text (which cites Wren as the basis of its historical appreciation) was first published in 1979. Koontz's textbook *Management* was first published in 1955. It was published for the ninth time in 1988, eight years after Koontz's death, by a previous co-author. This is not to mention the renewed interest in Urwick's work on his death, and the numerous tribute collections recently issued to celebrate Chandler's life work. Chandler's paramount status is further reinforced in the mind of one prominent social historian by 'growing citation of his work beyond the confines of business history [back into] the economics [and] sociology literature.' Subsequently, few have questioned Chandler's fundamental theses.

Management's history seems to have been constructed so quickly and so like-mindedly that the need to revisit the past was quickly closed off. However, it is important to remember that the first historians of management worked with few tangible reference points. Hence their platforms are castles in the air. The pioneering Chandler and Urwick were left to draw on the work of economic historians. And more recent historians legitimated their work through reference to the pioneers who struck out before them, in the process doing little more than embellishing their lines. But, despite being built on air, the quick establishment and reinforcement of the boundaries of what is relevant to the story of management saw the range of management's literature unquestioningly take this history as read.

Of those who have questioned Chandler's vision, perhaps the most vociferous have been M.J. Piore and C.F. Sabel. They contend that crossing from labour-intensive craft manufacture to capital-intensive production was a mistake and advocate moving back toward more flexible, labour-intensive production. However, what is primarily a moral argument has been processed in standard fashion. Piore and Sabel are criticized and dismissed for neglecting to provide any quantitative demonstration that craft production could be economically competitive with bureaucratic production.

The increasing convergence brought about by the loops described above may mean that management and the Modern march of events are increasingly becoming one, as Urwick and Brech claimed, but this is not necessarily a good thing. Indeed, if we see innovation as important, and see any value in the views expressed earlier in this book with regard to creativity being the result of the 'shaking together' of different views, then we must critique the idea that management is but one unitary march. If we are to think differently for the twenty-first century, the conventional history of management must be challenged. We must question the march of events that Urwick and Brech thought inevitable.

Interestingly, given a similar set of circumstances, other fields have begun to question the extent to which their histories have closed off innovative development in their fields. Works from Kuhn's *The Structure of Scientific Revolutions* to Horgan's *The End of Science* have highlighted the cost of a legitimating history determining a one-dimensional view of what is significant in the sciences. Areas as diverse as architecture and medicine now question their prevailing visions of history and progress and the idea that where we are is the pinnacle of human endeavor or the one best way, and are embracing a more eclectic approach that seeks to understand and use rather than marginalize alternative traditions. This line of questioning has now begun to spread into even those fields that management calls its roots. Lowry's *Archaeology of Economic Ideas* argues that the way economics accepts the tenet 'that economic science sprang full-blown in 1776 with Smith's *Wealth of Nations*,' goes against a trend that since the 1970s has seen 'works analysing our ancient debts in areas from physics to city planning, politics, and philosophy to mathematics and the exact sciences.' And R. Smith's *Does the History of Psychology Have a Subject?* sees the implications for his field similarly:

> ... assum[ing] a direct line from the past toward the present, [and] awarding praise for contributions to progress ... contributes to the normative framework of psychological communities. History texts embody, and hence transmit to students, values important to psychologists' sense of worth and identity. In portraying modern psychology as the inevitable or 'natural' outcome of the application of scientific procedures to psychological topics, they give modern psychology its authority. [But] the danger to psychology is that selective history privileges one body of knowledge and practice as 'truth,' reducing the imagination's power to conceptualize alternative truths.

Case Box 3.2 outlines how our ability to conceptualize alternative views is diminished by the conventional history that enabled management to establish its identity and worth in the twentieth century. This theme is developed further in Chapter 4.

We may now recognize management's conventional history as limiting, but could management really be based on anything other than what we see as its foundations today? After 50 years of management so tightly conceived it certainly is difficult for us to think it differently. Perhaps it might have been easier in an environment not so enraptured with the later stages of Modernism? Indeed, a quite different vision of management was put forward by one of the American Civil War's key protagonists. Given that the Civil War was seen as a key stepping stone in the conventional history of management, one might have thought that this would have been paid more attention. But, sadly, it has been largely overlooked. After the War, General Robert E. Lee became president of Washington College (now Washington and Lee University). In 1869 he became interested in forming a business school. His interest along with a proposed curriculum is recorded in the College annals. Lee's curriculum comprised 'ten subject areas, to be studied as equal parts':

1	Mathematics	6	Technology
2	Geometry and drawing	7	Law
3	Book-keeping and penmanship	8	Economy
4	Correspondence and the correct use of the English language	9	History and biography
5	Geography	10	Modern languages.

After this entry a brief note explains that 'General Lee's death in 1870 prevented the fulfillment of his plans.' It is interesting to wonder how management might now be thought differently had Lee's vision come to pass?

Case Box 3.2 Hammered Home

F.W. Taylor's ideas and those of the 1990s' most pervasive new management approach, Michael Hammer's *Business Process Reengineering*, have much in common. Despite Taylor writing at the beginning of the twentieth century and Hammer at the end, it is often hard to see the difference. See if you can guess which of them wrote the statements below (answers are provided at the end of this chapter's biographical notes on p. 334).

1 Tradition counts for nothing. [This approach is] a new beginning. Managers must throw out their old notions about how businesses should be organized and run … the time has come to retire those principles and adopt a new set.

2 The defective systems of management which are in common use [must be substituted for] scientific methods.

3 [This approach] is so much more efficient than the old [ways].

4 [This approach] means doing *more* with less.

5 [This approach] must come from the top of the organization [because] people near the front lines lack … broad perspective … Their expertise is largely confined to the individual functions and departments that they inhabit. They may see very clearly … the narrow problems from which their departments suffer, but it is difficult for them to see a process as a whole.

6 All of the planning which under the old system was done by [people near the front lines], as a result of his personal experience, must of necessity under [this approach] be done by management in accordance with the laws of science. Because even if [he] was well suited to the development and use [of this approach], it would be physically impossible for him to work at his machine and at a desk at the same time.

7 The fundamental principles of [this approach] are applicable to all kinds of human activities … whenever these principles are correctly applied, results must follow which are truly outstanding.

8 [This approach] applies to any organization in which work is performed … [It is] the single best hope for restoring the competitive vigor of American businesses.

9 Fundamentally, [this approach] is about reversing the industrial revolution … We need something entirely different [this approach] is to the next revolution of business what the specialization of labor was to the last.

10 In its essence, [this approach] involves a complete mental revolution.

Both Hammer and Taylor argue for throwing away all that has gone before, because their new ideas are more efficient. Both talk in terms of a hierarchical system of relationships, with those at the top having a better view and thus best placed to make key decisions. Both offer their theory as the new universal 'one best way' (a term first used in a public forum in a magazine article relating Taylor's method in 1911). And both subsequently urge a revolution that will see their ideas save us all. While Hammer states that 'Reengineering rejects the assumptions inherent in Adam Smith's industrial paradigm' and seeks to overcome Smith's taking apart and simplification of work tasks into 'meaninglessly thin slices,' it appears to 'replace' this with the taking apart and simplification of processes. Organizations will no longer be redesigned in terms of efficiency of tasks, but in terms of efficiency of processes. However, the universal criterion of increased efficiency is not questioned.

1 How many of the 10 statements did you correctly associate with the right author?
2 How could it be that a 'dynamic' field such as management could end the twentieth century saying more or less the same things as when that century began?
3 How much use do you think the approaches described above are to those organizations described in Case Box 2.2 (p. 75) as seeking to redefine themselves?
4 If General Lee's vision of the management curriculum had become the conventional view, how might our theories of management now be different?

Case Box 3.3   Who's Thinking Differently?

On 27 August 2001 *Time* magazine ran a special feature based on a three-month international study on quality carried out by dozens of its correspondents. Its cover headline read 'The Quest for Quality: Why Europe's Craftsmen are Still the Best.' The main thrust: after decades of standardization, mass production and globalization, the world is now beginning to 're-value things produced the old, careful way. And Europe, [which] has always been a place where the past and the future happily co-exist, where teens toting the latest cell phones stroll among 2,000 year old Roman ruins … is the center of this new appreciation for excellence.' 'Europe,' *Time* claims, 'is the capital of quality.'

Across 70 pages it ran dozens of case studies on a wide variety of organizations: Irish and Swedish crystal cutters; Scottish Whisky distillers; Belgian jewellers; English car and stove manufacturers; Dutch florists; American-Venetian boat-builders; French patisseries, confectioners, tapestry weavers and beaders; Spanish porcelain producers; Australian-Portuguese wine-makers; French-Italian cobblers; Swiss watchmakers; Danish furniture designers; Czech glassblowers, cosmetics and liqueurs; Hungarian perfumeries; Austrian knitters; Polish woodcarvers; German bakers, brewers and organ-builders; Swedish textile producers; Serbian filigree workers; and Finnish tool makers.

These cases had a number of things in common: their 'bringing forward' of centuries-old local traditions; their recognition that 'in-with-the-new doesn't always have to mean out-with-the-old – good work and modern technology are not mutually exclusive'; 'an intangible value we call individuality'; and the fact that they're 'thriving in the face of globalization.' 'Machines give us precision, volume, economy,' *Time* claimed, 'they have democratized the making of things by putting quality good within the reach of more than just the rich. But the articles whose construction demands the human hand, eye, ear – and, yes – heart, rarely come off a production line.'

Time's conclusion with regard to 'crafting the future' at the end of one of it's longest ever features: 'Artisans can teach the twenty-first century some old tricks.'

1   Why do you think *Time* might promote traditional European 'artisan organizations' as a source of global hope and inspiration at the beginning of the twenty-first century?
2   What sort of 'thinking differently' might these artisan organizations provide?

Source: The case draws on 'The Quest for Quality', *Time*

4 Management's Historical Limits

By the end of this chapter you should:

1 See how management's Modernist history and unreflective desire to be 'new' often means that it unwittingly reproduces the same ideas.
2 Be able to explain how conventional 'organic' views of organization may actually continue to promote Modern mechanistic views and see how this limits our thinking.
3 Be able to explain why culture has conventionally been seen as an 'object' rather than something intrinsic to an organization's being, and how the concept of culture in management continued to promote efficiency and homogeneity as our goals.
4 Be able to explain how and why decentralization and centralization came to be seen as an either/or choice.
5 Understand how the climate created by Modernism has led to the proliferation of external management and strategy experts being called in to advise organizations.

It is simply enough that one perceives modernity for what it was, and to realize that 'yesterday's got nothin'' for me

W.P. Hetrick and H.R. Lozada, editorial for a special issue of The Journal of Organizational Change Management *on 'Postmodern Management'*

Modernism, believing that reality is underpinned by essential functions and laws, that the purpose of knowledge is to increasingly uncover these laws, and that time and knowledge is cumulative and progressive, is obsessed with being at the cutting edge, with revolution and overcoming the past, with finding 'the new' one-best way. However, because Modernism is concerned with establishing order and certainty of method, the new must be produced along predetermined lines (thus bureaucracy becomes Modernism's organizational form *de rigeur* and Modern art and architecture sought to adhere to the central principles of essentialism and functionalism). Because management is historically configured to reflect Modernist beliefs, it is similarly obsessed with the new. This, combined with management's lack of interest in critically reflecting upon its history, has led it to develop in a very limited manner. Its unreflective quest for the next new advance has seen it unwittingly reproduce the same themes. This chapter investigates these unwitting limits in more detail. Its argument suggests that management's development could increasingly go the way of other Modernist forms, further into the production of obvious banal generalizations (at the time of writing "new" management theories included: 'putting people first,' 'empowerment' and 'organizations that do not fully buy into the new technology will die'). It will go this way unless we rethink management's historical limits and begin to accommodate some substantially different approaches.

Nowhere are management's limiting predispositions in this regard better illustrated than with its recent 'processing' of Postmodernism, the perspective that enabled other fields to think their way out of Modernism's ever-decreasing circles. The quotation that began this chapter introduces what the reader of a special issue of a management journal on Postmodern approaches has in store. Postmodernism is defined not as the reinvigoration of different traditions but, in the editors' words, as 'an escape from traditional views'.

Chapter 2 outlined how Postmodernism seeks to rewire aspects of Modernism, questioning its claims that there is 'one best way', that things are underpinned by universal essences, that reality can be objectively represented, and its either/or dichotomies (that the present is separate from and an advance on the past; that the new is distinct from and better than the old). However, management latches on to Postmodernism because it is seen to be the all new one-best way that represents the essence of the new times and because it subsequently dismisses the past. Given that Postmodernism seeks to revive many different traditional approaches so that they can be creatively combined locally toward particular purposes, it is easy to see why management, as it is configured, might struggle with the concept. As we have seen, management only recognizes one way (even the Egyptians are understood to be fledgling Moderns). Thus it will struggle to create anything substantially different, and it will certainly find it hard to be eclectic in the way that other fields are now becoming. But beyond this, management's unreflective predisposition toward the new above all else has seen it 'deal with' Postmodernism in a manner quite different from other applied fields. Consequently, management unwittingly advocates Postmodernism as an anti-pluralistic stance that does not draw from many approaches at all. And when it realizes that nothing substantially new can come from this, it drops it. The paragraphs below explain how this came to pass.

In the late 1980s and early 1990s, Postmodernism was trumpeted in management as 'a new buzzword'; 'not only new but new in entirely new ways'; as about 'ignoring traditional modernist values'; 'an antimodernist programme … that involves the destruction of economic reasoning' and that 'is essentially based on the negation of the modern.' Advocates wrote of how 'Managers must accept that postmodernity is an epochal break from modernity involving the emergence of a new social condition with its own distinct organization principles.' It was thus decided that we needed 'new words for a new age'. These words were provided toward a definition of Post-modernism in relation to Modernism in tables contrasting binary opposite terms. Modernism was associated with the negative *old* approaches and terms and Postmodernism with the *new* words and reality. The two were correspondingly described as 'opposing conceptual positions.' Postmodern-ism in management was thus 'conceptualized in contradistinction to Modernism.'

This privileging of the new over the old, and a so-called Postmodern approach as more realistically capturing the essence of the new reality and hence being 'cutting edge', sees Postmodernism in management turn out to be not particularly pluralistic or paralogical. Despite one paper arguing 'for a non-reducible plurality,' it concluded that a 'positive methodology is mis-guided' in that it 'will never achieve the subtlety, the unpretentiousness required to grasp the natives' point of view.' An ethnographic approach, it claims, is therefore 'far more intellectually legitimate.' Others similarly recommend replacing the 'scientific emphasis on "the single best account" with a multiplicity of constructions,' but finish by 'advocating replacing Modernist assumptions with ones that are more consistent with the advancements of the late twentieth century.' Others still promote a 'revolu-tion' where 'scholars [will] unseat conventional assumptions by offering new forms of theory. The way forward for the Postmodernist requires that the [Modernist] brick wall be demolished.' Modernist approaches were thus destined to 'slip quietly into the archives of obscurity.' Clinging to them could only lead to an:

> ... impoverished state of affairs ... whereby very few new insights are ever gained into the real nature of organization. [T]he task of Postmodern organi-zational analysis is, therefore, precisely to sift through these sedimented layers of abstracted concepts in order to make contact with the implicate organizational reality beyond.

Management must, in other words, heed 'the Postmodern' (sic) call to look beneath surface conventions to find the primary rocks of certainty under-neath. Management had reduced Postmodernism to Modernism.

It was not long before management's critical thinkers, disappointed that this 'revolution' did not seem to be amounting to much that was different, recognized this rhetoric for what it was: the same old song. In 1992, the journal *Organization Studies* published a short note suggesting that Postmodernism was, on reflection, 'nothing new' and should therefore be dismissed:

> Postmodernism [is] nothing more that a new phrase to capture the imagination of the jaded reader. The Modern/Postmodern couplet echoes many of the other dichotomies of control versus commitment, Taylor versus Mayo, formal versus informal, mechanistic versus organic and so on, but adds little that is new. There seems no reason, apart from academic fashion, to introduce [such] a term.

The promised vanquisher of Modernism in management was duly vanquished itself, and academics went out in search of the next revolution. Postmodernism had been processed. In management, because management is bounded by Modernist assumptions, something is either the revolutionary new one-best way or it is quickly left behind in wake of progress, destined to slip quietly into the archives of obscurity.

Part II of this book will put forward a contrary view, that a Postmodern approach to management should not mean revolutionarily opposing and overturning all things Modern. In the meantime, this chapter shows how, in a very real sense, those that were identified as constituting the history of management not only *produce* it, but also *repress* or limit its view of the future. Management, as it is configured, can only see and bounce back simplistic Modernist principles even when it incorporates different things. (Hence recent 'new management directions' include a demonstration of how 'hard-nosed executives are turning to the world of creative talent in a pragmatic effort to improve efficiency' and returning to Douglas McGregor's 1960s work to re-iterate that 'efficient managers tend to be ones who value and trust people'). The underlying preconceptions of management go on without doubt. For this reason management and strategy have been able to create little that is different.

   This chapter picks out four examples of how management's unreflective incorporation of Modernism's backdrop unwittingly confines it:

1   Beyond its 'scientific revolution', management recognized that the mechanistic view of organizations was naive. Organizations, it was claimed, were like organisms – a very different visibility. However, given the Modern limits of the field, management's view of the organism comes highly mechanized. It is a machine in sheep's clothing.
2   In the 1980s, culture gained center stage. But again, rather than promoting a substantially different view, culture was seen through the Modern apparatus of management in a materialist and mechanistic fashion.
3   Believing there to be 'one best way', management spent decades debating whether organizations should be *either* centralized *or* decentralized, rather than exploring the paradox that the existence of one necessitates the other.
4   Finally, this chapter examines how Modernism's promotion of general approaches, and its assumptions that knowledge can be distilled and transferred like a commodity and that the best advice on how to live comes from disinterested, objective experts, has created the hothouse within which management consultants have come to advise us on all aspects of organizational life. A hothouse that increasingly stifles individual difference and creativity.

I   The organization as a mechanical organism

Organization theory was locked into a form of engineering,
pre-occupied with relations between goals, structures, and

efficiency. The idea that organizations are more like organisms
has changed all this.

Gareth Morgan

Gareth Morgan's *Images of Organization* is a groundbreaking and justifiably acclaimed book. It begins by claiming that 'one of the most basic problems of modern management is that the mechanical way of thinking is so ingrained in our everyday conceptions of organization that it is often very difficult to organize in any other way.' Then, as an antidote, it advocates thinking of organizations through alternative images, or in terms of metaphors other than the machine. Morgan's first chapter on a different image is devoted to thinking of organizations as if they were organisms. One might expect that this would encourage us to think differently about particular organizations by thinking of them as different individual beings: by 'developing a sympathy with' or 'connecting to' the experience of such beings as in Premodern times. However, Morgan's organism, representative of management's general view of the organism, is underpinned by Modern, mechanistic assumptions. Subsequently, much that is presented as 'organic' in management should be acknowledged as an extension of mechanistic principles, albeit in kid gloves. The organism metaphor, as it has been developed, has not changed all things mechanical. In many ways it has concealed them, and in so doing, mechanistic principles have been further ingrained.

Nowhere is this more apparent than in the figures in Morgan's organism chapter. There are no pictures of organisms here, only syntheses of ideals and tables of general or essential functions. The first figure Morgan presents is Maslow's 1954 *Hierarchy of Needs.* This is generally depicted as a triangle (see below) moving from base physiological things upward to mind things that Maslow claimed was universal. It is still taught as the basis of human motivation.

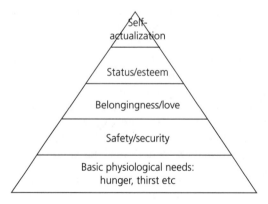

This 'organism' (sic), with its hierarchical and clearly divided 'mind over matter' form, is a replication of the scientific separation of mind and body and the resulting triangular scalar hierarchy of Modernism described in

Chapter 2 (p. 33). It also reproduces Modernist notions of progress as an upward evolutionary process toward a common end that the whole human race is equally subject to. Thus, if anything, the hierarchy's 'technology', which seems objective, benign and neutral (it was based on extensive scientific surveys in the US in the 1950s), discourages acknowledging organic or environmental identity or difference. Many people from Asian backgrounds, for example, accept the framework when it is taught to them, but may later confess to be perplexed by the idea that 'self-actualization' could be more important than 'status' within one's community. A Polynesian student once asked me if the hierarchy suggested that his people were less evolved and thus less likely to be successful, given that they see 'belongingness', particularly with regard to the extended family, as the most important thing.

Following Maslow's hierarchy, Morgan discusses organizations as open systems rather than as closed mechanistic systems (Morgan does not diagram this but one may illustrate the 'new' view with reference to a standard textbook depiction – Figure 4.1, top). The 'advance' that Morgan describes is thus made by adding a feedback loop to the standard input→process→ output view of organizations in a manner similar to that of the 'process approach', whereby a loop was added to the line of 'planning, organizing, directing and controlling' (see Chapter 3, p. 86). This brings us to the second diagram in Morgan's organism chapter. In order to describe how an organization can be seen as a 'set of subsystems', Morgan re-presents the diagram shown here in Figure 4.1 (bottom). It is the same input→process→output mechanism that underpins Modernism, with a fluffy coating. This is the only picture of an 'organism' in Morgan's chapter and one that would have been implausible prior to Modernity. It is an ideal: the mechanistic functional essence of all organisms. The next Figures in Morgan's chapter are a table of generic organic and mechanistic organizational attributes and 'The general form of a matrix organization'.

How did a metaphor that promised to completely change the way we think about organizations come to be so Modern in its continued mechanistic underpinnings? Examining the structure of *Images of Organization* as representative of the field provides some reasons: reasons related to management's treatment of history.

A history of the Modern organism

Morgan begins the first chapter of *Images*, on the machine metaphor, by explaining that the word 'organization' derives:

> … from the Greek *organon*, meaning a tool or instrument. No wonder, therefore that ideas about tasks, goals, aims, and objectives have become such fundamental organizational concepts. For tools and instruments are mechanical devices invented and developed to aid in performing some kind of goal-oriented activity.

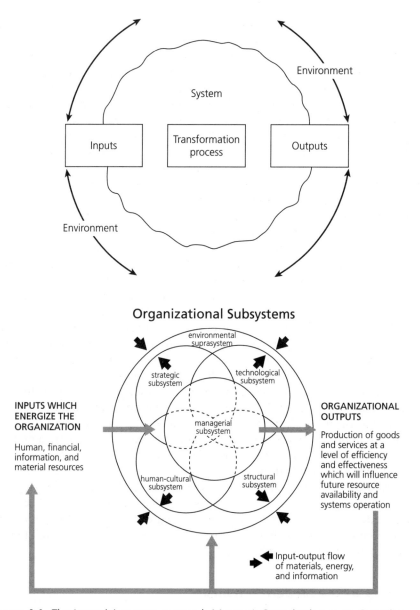

Figure 4.1 The 'organic' systems approach Morgan's Organisation as an Organism
Sources: Top, S.P. Robbins, *Organization Theory, third edition*; Bottom, G. Morgan, *Images of Organization*

Morgan is correct in tracing organization to *organon*. However, his next sentence expands upon this through Modernist eyes. For the Greeks, an *organon* could be much more than 'mechanical devices performing some kind of goal-oriented activity.' In keeping with Ancient Greeks' contextual and relativistic arrangement, the meaning of *organon* was wide-ranging. It could refer to any instrument, method or tool that helped an individual's living, making or performance, any being's form, bodily organs as instruments of sense or faculty, surgical or musical instruments, or war machines. In less relativistic languages, however, its meaning takes on particular emphases. The Latin *organum* came to war machines in particular and mechanical devices in general, and Medieval writers related the word to the church-organ.

However, when the word entered the English language as *organons* in the sixteenth century, a more Greek manner of the word returned. It was used here in two main senses: its primary sense, which the *Oxford English Dictionary* (OED) distinguishes as 'naturalized' ('a bodily organ, especially as an instrument of the soul or the mind'); and a secondary meaning that the OED terms 'alien' ('a system of rules or method of demonstration or investigation'). The earliest uses of *to organise* and *organisation* in English also appear during the Renaissance period, and tend towards the Greek relation to 'natural' bodily meanings (for example, 'to furnish with organs'; 'that [which] is, or has been, endowed with physical life, as an animal or plant body'). The OED lists references of this sort dating from 1413, tapering off during the eighteenth century before disappearing altogether.

Using *to organise* in this sense ceases here because a new variant, which first appeared at the end of the seventeenth century, has, by the end of the eighteenth, emerged to cover the bodily sense of the *organon*. This was the *organism*. Whilst *organisation* is decreasingly related to individual living organic beings or what is within them, we find the rise of a meaning that focuses on a mechanistic and more general concept of 'being organized' from without. Unlike the *organism*, 'being organized' was increasingly associated with applying external rules of coordination, standardization and order toward the newly emerging understanding of performative efficiency.

In the *Oxford Dictionary for the Business World* we find the resonance of the telling split that now exists between the two words once covered by one:

- *organism* equals an 'individual plant or animal' or a 'living being with independent parts'; and
- *organisation* is, somewhat circularly, defined as 'organizing or being organized' or an 'organized body, system or society.'

If one seeks further clarification, one finds that to *organise* is defined as 'to give an orderly structure to'. And *order* is defined as 'tidiness'.

It is this eighteenth-century split that enables us today to take two words that were once one and the same, and use one as an analogy for the other as outlined in *Images*. One might expect that by so doing, by thinking of organizations as if they were organisms, we would recover the 'naturalized' understandings of other civilizations. However, the particularly Modern view of the organism drawn upon by management ingrains mechanistic assumptions as much as it offers a radical alternative. Why? Two main reasons:

- an unwitting Modernist use of language; and
- an unwitting Modernist approach to history.

Firstly, a Modern, mechanistic view of nature, which reached its zenith in the seventeenth and eighteenth centuries (see, for example, Borrelli's view of the human organism in Figure 2.10 on p. 51), initially prevented the need for the development of separate words for the organism and the organization. The organism and the organization could be covered by the *organon* as both were seen as subject to the same mechanistic principles. However, as the idea that all things could be seen as simple machines dimmed (Man and other animals coming to be regarded as different or more evolved from inanimate mechanisms), the possibility of a word like the *organon* that stands for both an individual living being and the application of external, objective, mechanistic principles diminished. This possibility was further diminished in a positivistic age that had little tolerance for the sort of ambiguity of meaning accepted in the Greek system. Hence, the *organism* first appears in the English language in the eighteenth century and becomes increasingly frequent during the nineteenth.

Thus, *organization* and *organism* were now different words. But, because of this background, the organism still carried with it a residue from the time when it was both one with *organization* and mechanistically conceived. The view of the organism was thus not one that could mean many different forms of instrument for particular purposes, nor one whereby every organism has a particular identity or *telos*, as in Premodern times where respecting differences worked against developing syntheses. Rather, it was a Modernist conception shaped by a belief in objective unitary laws governing the universe that all organisms are subject to. Where all organisms, following Descartes, have basic primary qualities and differences are secondary. Where, subsequently, all difference can be looked beyond to find the commonality of the whole species. Where organisms are separate atomic entities characterized by having their parts overseen by a unitary mind. Where they can be seen as made up of separate functions that work according to standardized principles, taking inputs and turning them into outputs via some structured and predictable process. In this sense, the machine lived on as a ghost in the organism into the eighteenth and nineteenth centuries. The diagram below charts the shifts in the meaning of the *organon* from the Greeks co-appreciation of both external mechanical and internal individual meanings to the present day.

The second reason for the mechanism being ingrained in the organization is management's not seeing the history of what went on before Modernity, or beyond the dashed line in the table below. Thus it does not appreciate that the mechanistic background described above is particular rather than universal. It does not think that an organism could be anything other than Modern. And, even those works that have done most to critique management's limits, like Morgan's, interpret the Greek *organon* in Modernist terms. Hence, even works that have been labelled 'Postmodern', like *Images* or

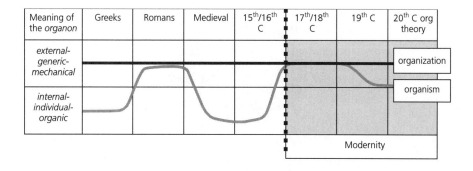

Mary Jo Hatch's *Organization Theory*, take the established history of management as read and work from these foundations. *Images of Organization*, for example, begins its chronologically-ordered list of views of organization with the machine metaphor and the theories of Smith, Babbage, Taylor, Fayol, Urwick, Mooney and Weber (Hatch's classical theorists whose 'ideas form a backdrop to our discussion of the roots of organization,' are Smith, Marx, Taylor, Fayol, Weber and Barnard). *Images* then moves on from this foundation in a manner that sees history as a progressive evolutionary line. Its chapter after the machine chapter begins by claiming that 'We can start this story [of the organism metaphor] with Elton Mayo.' Thus, a linear chronological development is shown from the mechanistic 'pioneers' at the end of the nineteenth century to the 'new pioneers' of the early twentieth.

Mayo, as we have seen, is listed with Münsterberg, Maslow and Barnard as the new pioneers who focused upon the 'other' side of work, 'the human side of the equation' or, to use the words of the *International Encyclopedia of Business and Management*, 'the incorporation of people-related variables into the core of organization theory.' Münsterberg is credited by historians as 'creating the field of industrial psychology with the publication of his text *Psychology and Industrial Efficiency* in 1913,' which described the role that psychologists should play in management *after* having paid tribute to Taylor as the 'brilliant originator of scientific management.' This more human or 'organic' perspective thus 'grew up', according to B.M. Gross:

> ... with the encouragement of the followers of both Taylor, who wanted to design machines and people to fit together, and of Mayo, who felt that psychology was key to understanding the operations of industrial enterprises.

Mayo's thesis in his 1933 *Human Problems of an Industrial Civilization*, is seen by C.S. George as important to management history because it showed that 'logical factors were far less important than emotional factors in determining productive efficiency.'

By viewing history as a cumulative progression and identifying Mayo and his peers as the beginnings of the evolution of the organic perspective,

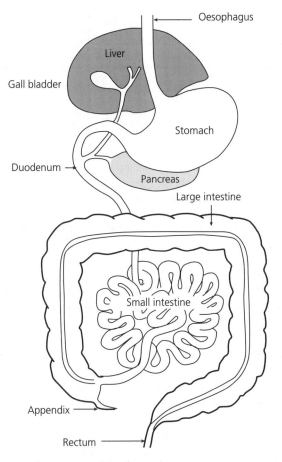
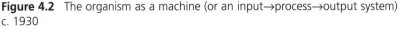

Figure 4.2 The organism as a machine (or an input→process→output system) c. 1930

Source: H.G. Wells, J. Huxley and G.P. Wells, *The Science of Life*

management incorporates the mechanized view of the organism that prevailed into the middle of the twentieth century as foundational. Indeed, one can better understand Figure 4.1 (p. 138) by looking at a popular conception of an organism in the new pioneer's heyday: the 1930s. *The Science of Life* answered the question 'Is a living man fundamentally a machine?' as follows:

> That is a question capable of experimental decision. We can measure the amount of food that a man or an animal consumes over a given period of time, and we can measure the energy yielded during the same period. If we burn an equal weight of similar food in a suitable apparatus and find out how much energy its combustion yields, and if this value is equal to the energy yielded by the experimental subject, then evidently the living-organism so far as its energy output is concerned is really and precisely a combustion engine.

The Science of Life follows this up with an illustrative diagram (see Figure 4.2) which, if placed on its side, is the same input→process→output 'organism' that Morgan reproduced (although Morgan's, being a functional distillation of all organisms rather than just the human organism, looks less like an actual living identity). *The Science of Life* diagram represents the view of the organism that influenced the work of the group known as the 'Harvard Pareto Circle', a group that connected luminaries from across many fields, including Elton Mayo, J.A. Shumpeter, Talcott Parsons and Chester Barnard (see Case Box 3.1 on p. 105). Inspired by Pareto's idea that society should be thought of as 'a system of mutually interacting particles which move from one state of equilibrium to another,' the Circle sought to utilize the ideas of biologists like L.J. Henderson (that we should think of life as a 'physico-chemical mechanism') and Walter Cannon (who was interested in how 'physiological mechanisms' ensured equilibrium in the same manner as a 'governor' maintained an engine's equilibrium) in their own realms.

Consequently, when management 'went organic', the organism was a thing comprised of universal mechanistic-functional elements and processes. The ensuing 'organic perspective' subsequently comes into management only as an overlay of general, synthetic organic functions onto the existing mechanistic foundations. It is this view of the 'organism' that management has built upon, further indoctrinating Modern mechanist views as foundational in the process.

Building on the Modern mechanical organism

Science cannot provide the ultimate answers, but it can provide pertinent questions. And I do not believe that we can formulate even the simplest questions… without the help of the sciences of life. But it must be a true science of life, not the antiquated slot-machine model based on the naively mechanistic world-view of the 19th century. We shall not be able to ask the right questions until we have replaced that rusty idol by a new, broader conception of the living organism.

Arthur Koestler

This ingraining transition from mechanism to organism can also be seen in other key management texts. When March and Simon criticized the pioneers of management's ideas in 1958 for fear that they 'would transform a general-purpose mechanism, such as a person, into a more efficient special-purpose mechanism,' the view that organizations and their 'components' should be viewed mechanistically was carried forward. Man had been naively diag-nosed as the wrong type of machine, but he was still a machine. Simon still described people in organizations as 'decision-making mechanisms' and maintained the line that 'the fundamental criterion of administrative decisions *must be a criterion of efficiency*'.

This continued predisposition is largely because management's underlying foundations are not questioned. While management's early pioneers were seen to be a little naive or limited in their application of the correct sciences to the problem of efficiency, they were thus still built upon. As a leading undergraduate text explains:

> The earliest attempts to study behaviour in organizations came out of the desire of industrial efficiency experts to improve worker productivity. Given this history, it should not be too surprising that the earliest people we now credit for their contributions to OB were actually industrial engineers ... as engineers attempted to make machines more efficient, it was a natural extension of their efforts to work on the human side of the equation.

It was then a further natural extension to apply the human sciences to better manipulate this 'side of the equation'.

Thus, when the field took to Chester Barnard and others' organic/ systemic ideas, the definition of organization that management works with did not change substantially. A focus upon 'the common explicit purpose' and the 'coordinated system of specialized activities for the purposes of achieving common goals (i.e., greater efficiency)', was overlaid upon the mechanistic division of labour basis. Subsequently, Sheldon's mechanistic 1920s definition (which Urwick worked with):

> The process of so combining the work which individuals or groups have to perform with the faculties necessary for the execution that the duties, so formed, provide the best channels for the efficient, systematic, positive and coordinated application of effort.

can be contrasted with Schein's 'more organic' 1960s:

> The rational coordination of the activities of a number of people for the achievement of some common explicit purpose or goal, through division of labour and function, and through a hierarchy of authority and responsibility.

Or contrasted with Robbins' 1980s:

> A formal structure of planned coordination, involving two or more people, in order to achieve a common goal, characterized by authority relationships and the division of labor.

Or, contrasted with the definition that Fineman and Gabriel's study on management textbooks sees as typical in our own times:

> A collection of individuals formed into a coordinated system of specialized activities for the purposes of achieving certain goals over some extended period of time, even though individual membership may change.

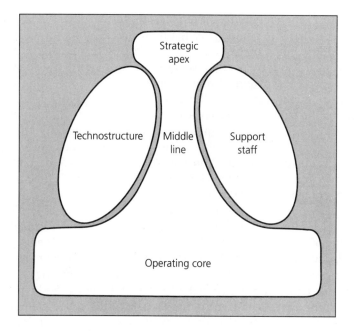

Figure 4.3 Mintzberg's 'organic' organization: The general underlying functions.
Source: Henry Mintzberg, *Structure in Fives: Designing Effective Organizations, second edition*

The traditional Modern triangular visibility of organization with the centralized core enabling a scalar hierarchy to coordinate specialized divisions to operate more efficiently has not really been greatly altered by becoming more 'organic'.

Beyond this, later 'organic thinking' came to be seen as an advance upon the foundational universal mechanistic organizational form (universal because it was the most efficient) on to a contingency perspective whereby one can point to a narrow range of ideal organic forms, one of which will be best (that is, most efficient) for a particular type of environment. Stephen Robbins' review of this literature claimed that 'Henry Mintzberg's work probably gets closest' to a universally agreed-upon framework for classifying organizations in this way. Mintzberg sought to get beyond Modern forms of organizing. He saw all organizations as shaped by specific functions (see Figure 4.3) that combine differently to define five species. On this view, all viable species of organization are based on the underlying genus of a strategic apex where decisions are made, a middle coordinating line and a broad operating base of specialized divisions where the action takes place. Sadly, Mintzberg's forms are just more comfy-looking Modern triangle hierarchies.

In conclusion, it is hard to see how Management's organic turn has taken the mechanistic view of organization and 'changed all this'.

Unfortunately, management's intention to think other than from the ingrained mechanistic perspective is undermined by its unwitting adherence to Modern lines of history. By viewing, with hindsight, the Greek *organon* from a Modern perspective, by taking aboard the idea that the machine view is the origin of management, and by presenting a chronological linear advancement of the field from this point, it incorporates much under the banner of 'organism' that joins it to mechanism. Contrary to Morgan's claim that the 'organic view has fundamentally changed our Modern mechanistic views of organization', management's organism further ingrains the Modern mechanistic model. Shrouded behind an organic covering, it is a model that has, in the process, become more difficult to recognize and hence critique.

One must wonder at the extent to which this approach of implementing somebody else's 'organic' average of what has been 'proven' already diminishes managers' ability to think organization differently for themselves. And wonder also whether a more Premodern sense of connecting or stepping into different individual organic beings to see things through other eyes would not be useful. This is not to say that such connections would be more beneficial than those that are currently more a part of the collective psyche, like the input→process→output mechanism. It is more a wondering whether *both* could be fruitfully combined in a Postmodern manner? Case Box 4.1 explores this idea further.

Case Box 4.1 Mechanisms and 'Leopard-isms' at the SPA

The New Zealand Social Policy Agency (SPA) exists to provide policy advice and was established by combining a number of pre-existing government departments. The NZ Government hoped that the SPA would provide a counterbalance to other advisory agencies, particularly the Treasury, whose advice was perceived by many to be overly driven by 'dry' economic analysts. The organization had been up and running for almost a year before it was decided that more tangible business objectives were required.

Developing these presented certain difficulties. After being subjected to a number of restructurings as the Government increasingly brought in business consultants to review their operations, many of the staff were skeptical with regard to the worth of new initiatives and the value that might come from 'external voices'. In addition, many of the departments had been plucked whole from previous government bodies. Hence, the subcultures within the organization were stronger than the culture of the SPA as a whole, making it likely that people would have a far greater sense of their own local needs and wants as opposed to those of the body corporate.

It was decided that the best first step toward developing useful objectives would be to randomly select people from across the SPA, distribute them into four groups, and then ask each group to think of a non-business metaphor that described what the SPA was like. The groups presented the following four metaphors (two mechanistic, one organic and one something in between): *stationary engine*, *electric generator*, *leopard cub* and *racing yacht*.

The first two group's metaphors were similar, as was their reasoning. They saw the SPA as turning inputs (for example, coal/statistics) into outputs (for example, energy/policy advice) through a series of interrelated processes. The racing yacht group said that the organization was best seen as a collection of individuals each with unique specialist skills who had to work together if the whole was to be greater than the sum of the parts. Additionally, the SPA was an organization that needed a clear strategy, but one that could be quickly adjusted if and when environmental conditions changed. Those who associated the SPA with a leopard said that the organization was like a cub because it was young and needed to find its feet in the 'jungle'. However, like the leopard it 'could not change its spots'. It had to realize that most of its staff had a long history of working in government organizations and it therefore had to be understood that they could not change overnight – certainly not into the sorts of people that many of the previously enlisted consultants had insisted were imperative in the 'new business environment'. The strengths of this history should be recognized rather than swept, wholesale, under the carpet.

The groups were then asked to discuss the achievements that would be necessary for their metaphorical identities to be successful.

The generator/engine groups pointed out the importance of *good quality inputs*, be they coal or statistics, if outputs of a regularly high standard were to be produced. Plus, *regular maintenance* of the parts that made up the organization was crucial.

If the racing yacht was to be successful, two things were thought imperative. While the specialist units needed to maintain their particular skills, ways needed to be found whereby they could develop an *appreciation* of how those skills related to the skills of others. Secondly, systems that enabled the organization to *learn quickly* about environmental changes were required.

Learning was also critical to the leopard cub as it grew. But just as important was a developing *sense of identity*. That it become aware of what it meant to be a leopard – how this made it different from other animals. This developed sense of identity would also help others understand it, what it did and why.

After this exercise, five objectives were developed, which, perhaps not surprisingly, reflected the analogies that had been developed. They are listed below:

i To have secured quality inputs that enable us to provide an excellent policy service (engine/generator).
ii To be an organization that recognizes and continuously maintains and updates [through training and so on] the value of our core assets and puts them to optimal use in providing quality social policy advice (leopard cub and engine/generator).
iii To be an organization which benefits from the synergy between its diverse elements (racing yacht).
iv To become an organization with a 'learning culture' with systems in place to enable the regular questioning of assumptions and methods in light of environmental change (leopard and racing yacht).
v To have a distinct identity that is recognized and respected by clients and stakeholders (leopard cub).

1 What are the advantages of thinking about particular organizations using metaphorical reasoning like this?
2 What insights are added by using organic analogies like the leopard cub, as opposed to synthetic-mechanistic metaphors or the synthetic-organic view promoted by Figure 4.1?

3   Would this exercise have worked out better if the first two groups' mechanistic analogies had been dismissed and they were instructed to come up with organic analogies rather than the stationary engine and electric generator?

The identity of this organization has been disguised.

---

2   The object of culture

Overall economic performance depends on transaction costs, and these mainly reflect the level of trust in the economy. The level of trust depends in turn on culture. An effective culture has a strong moral content. Morality can overcome problems that formal procedures – based on monitoring compliance with contracts – cannot. A strong culture therefore reduces transaction costs and enhances performance – the success of an economy depends on the quality of its culture.

Mark Casson

Culture on the horizon

In the early 1980s, Japan's success began to undermine the Modern Western belief in technology and structure being the only significant variables contributing to economic progress. While America might still boast technological supremacy, Japan was gaining economic supremacy. Authors like Ouchi, Pascale and Athos attributed this to Japanese culture. Pop-management writers soon applied this sort of thinking to particular corporations, drawing correlations between 'excellent' or 'strong' cultures and organizational effectiveness. Their findings seemed to show that the growth could not just be explained by the actions of 'economic man'. Thus a new idea entered management's mainstream, the idea that organizations are like cultures.

Despite this, once culture came to be an important 'object' in management it was viewed from a Modern-economics perspective toward management's foundational aim of increasing efficiency. Not long after the pop gurus brought culture to the fore, more sophisticated surveys began to examine its 'causal links'. In 1983, Wilkins and Ouchi published 'Efficient Cultures: Exploring the Relationship Between Culture and Organizational Performance', presenting a:

> ... view of organizations that will help us link the concept of organizational culture to the economic efficiency of organizations ... A utilitarian view ... essentially a theory of transaction costs, suggest[ting] which governance mode will be most efficient (have the lowest transaction costs) under varying exchange conditions.

This view of culture was solidified in titles like *Bringing Culture to the Bottom Line, Finding the Culture of Productivity* and *The Confucius Connection: From Cultural Roots to Economic Growth*. In this way, rather than challenging the hold of economics and the universal good of efficiency by promoting the importance of difference and particular identities, as one might think an emphasis on culture could do, the new emphasis on culture actually came to reinforce the foundational importance of economic logic and efficiency. Instead of the individual and amorphous nature of culture changing Modern methods of knowing, these methods of knowing shaped the way we understood culture. Management's general end remained the same; 'culture' simply provided an unexplored means for achieving it.

Many early writers on culture warned of treating it as a scientific approach might seek to grasp an object. Pettigrew argued against viewing cultures as static, unified objects and for seeing culture as a loose 'family of concepts' rather than seeking a unifying definition of it. Deal and Kennedy warned of culture being subsumed into: 'the dominant norm of the behavioral sciences [that] emphasizes definitions, operationalization, measurement and quantitative analysis.' Peters and Waterman wrote that we needed 'a different language' to appreciate it. But one did not eventuate. The object of culture was taken into management's Modern apparatus and viewed in a Modern way so as to reinforce the field's established thinking. Management was not comfortable leaving ideas like Peters and Waterman's 'simultaneous loose-tight properties' to hang ungrounded. They had to be broken down, measured, generalized, categorized and causal links determined.

Culture gets mechanized

The first thing to be done, as in any scientific investigation, was to determine a universal definition of 'what culture is'. Thus, organization culture doyen Ed Schein complained that 'the popular use of the concept [culture] ha[d] muddied the waters' with regard to arriving at an agreed objective definition. While he acknowledged that 'culture is a complex phenomenon, and we should not rush to measure things until we better understand what we are measuring,' the underlying assumption was that we must be able to positively determine the object of our inquiries. Schein believed that in this way, and by applying science, the 'real' nature of organizational culture could be 'uncovered' and 'deciphered' and argued that the way forward was 'to study a large number of organizations using these methods to determine the utility of the concept of organization culture and to relate culture variables to other variables, such as strategy, organizational structure and ultimately organizational effectiveness,' which, as we have seen, has become a pseudonym for performative efficiency.

That this predisposition has stuck is evidenced in the textbooks of the 1990s. Such works usually conclude their chapters on culture with a questionnaire that can be used to ascertain a 'type' of a culture that the student is familiar with (for example, Robbins' *Organizational Behaviour* does this before stating: 'Turn to page 718 for scoring directions and key'). Greenberg and Baron's *Behaviour in Organizations* prefaces its questionnaire with the following:

> It is often difficult to recognize the culture of an organization without carefully assessing it. Typically, this is done by administering a questionnaire to large numbers of people working within an organization, and then averaging together all their answers. This simple questionnaire is designed to assess only a single aspect of culture – concern for people. More complex questionnaires would address several different aspects of organizational culture.

Two such 'more complex' approaches are described below.

An article called 'Getting Value From Shared Values' published in *Organizational Dynamics* argued that because 'an organization can turn shared values into competitive advantage … we need to develop values-measurement profiles.' By doing so, the authors suggested that their approach could 'establish implicit control *and* create a sense of belonging by building work environments that manifest shared values.' Toward this aim they begin by asking:

> … why the application of hard science has not put such debates [with regard to the effects of culture] to rest. The answer lies in the abstract nature of the phenomenon. Tangible proof has been elusive as organizational scientists continue to search for reliable and valid measures of values.

The paper claims that 'finding answers' to this means doing as its authors had done, beginning via an empirical approach that focuses on asking 'organizational practitioners' what they think values 'relevant to the modern corporation' are. In this way, they claim that they 'address the concept of shared values more objectively than has been done in the recent past.' The authors duly arrived at 24 value categories (for example, 'Humor', 'Forgiveness', 'Logic', 'Moral integrity') and then were able, via sophisticated statistical processes, to measure and rank the importance accorded to each value in an organization. Organizations could then be placed onto the ensuing general table, decisions could be made as to whether this profile is what they were seeking and, if not, the organization could be re-directed accordingly.

Another article, *The Use of a Corporate Culture Planning Index for Strategic Planning*, similarly 'proposes a method to measure culture'. It does so because 'measuring anything helps us understand it better' (Ed's note: 'anything'?; even Christmas?); and 'closer examination of an organization's culture could assist it to adapt and be more effective.' The authors claim that to 'get to the root of culture, the concealed or unconscious motivation behind outward behaviour must be discovered' and propose 20 measurement categories (for example, 'Goals', 'People', 'Ethics' and so on) for doing this. These can then be scored by participants from 1 to 5, and added and averaged across the sample. The resulting average scores then enable an organization to 'measure its culture against others' and highlight 'weak areas that need improvement'.

The fervor with which researchers attempted to measure culture may be linked to the belief that certain forms of ideal culture correlated with effectiveness or efficiency. This belief may be traced to Blake and Mouton's differentiation between sound cultures that 'stimulated efforts to produce' and unsound cultures where 'beliefs and values bear little relationship to productive achievement or profit seeking' in 1972. Building upon their findings is a long list of papers that have correspondingly shown that 'unsound', 'weak' or 'negative' cultures are composed of disparate *secondary* differences. As the traits of 'good cultures' were sought, 'strong', 'sound', 'powerful' or 'positive' cultures became euphemisms for 'homogenized' or 'unified'. Good cultures were those that were 'cohesive and tight-knit', 'congruent', 'integrated', 'aligned', 'stable' or having a high degree of *primary* commonalities.

While the 'strong culture hypothesis' has now been questioned by some, the association of positive terms with unified homogeneous cultures, and of cultural aspects that do not contribute to efficiency with opposite negative terms (e.g. 'dysfunctional'), continues to influence. The continued use of this language, even by critics of the 'strong culture hypothesis', indicates that:

- finding the cultural type that leads to efficiency is the goal of management with regard to culture;
- there must be sets of superior (or more evolved) cultural traits, sets that best serve all organizations' ends; and
- the continued association with positives ('strong' still sounds better than 'weak') implies that culture must aim for unity, or be the central stem that holds things together, and that good or normal organizations should have a 'single, unitary' stem.

Culture, as Meyerson and Martin's critique points out, was primarily seen by management as an 'integrating mechanism', a predisposition that still resides in our language.

Beyond this primary view, just as the development from the machine to the organism eventually saw a move from one ideal 'species' to a few, so it was with culture. Beyond the binary classification of strong and weak, other researchers developed typologies that suggest a small number of discrete 'species' of culture (for example, 'Clan', 'Academy', 'Baseball Team', 'Club', 'Fortress'). These typologies promote a contingency approach, similar to Mintzberg's five 'organic organizations'. They allow different types of generic strengths and weaknesses to be identified for each 'species' and prospective employees to be asked 'What kind of culture fits you best?' This enables 'good employer–employee matches' to be gained, furthering the aims of increased homogeneity within organizations.

The above predispositions encourage and are encouraged by a view of culture as something that an organization 'has', a separate object, as opposed to something that an organization 'is'. This has promoted the view that culture can be 'engineered', distilled from other 'best practice' companies, bought and injected into an entirely different organization, something that can be brought from the outside-in rather than needing to be grown from the inside-out. These beliefs are manifest in popular titles like *Gaining Control of the Corporate Culture* and *Culture: Software of the Mind*, and Pascale and Athos' and Peters and Austin's descriptions of cultural dimensions like 'ambiguity' and 'enthusiasm' as 'good techniques'.

These ways of seeing and saying culture all rely upon Modernist assumptions. They are carried forward in the name of increasing efficiency and encourage an emphasis on Apollonian integrating dimensions, rather than on difference, particularity, heterogeneity and the individuality of cultures. In Schein's words, 'the concept of culture is most useful if it helps to explain some of the seemingly incomprehensible and irrational aspects of groups and organizations.' Culture subsequently comes to be regarded by management because it may help us explain away or impose order upon *chaos*.

But things could have turned out otherwise. If, for example, Weber's 'founding-father' role had been interpreted differently, culture may have been seen differently by management. One part of Weber's project – the necessity of bureaucracy given a rationalizing culture – is, as Chapter 3 made clear (p. 85), regarded as a key foundation stone of management. But management's historians overlooked other aspects of Weber's thinking, including his concern for culture. Particularly absent from management's memory is Weber's view that any analysis of organizations must be a cultural analysis of culturally diverse practices. Instead, management's focus has been on how differences become eliminated within one overarching cultural frame, theorizing within a relatively restricted set of cultural practices and looking for how organizations can become one in the same toward achieving 'global best practice' or the one-best way.

Case box 4.2   'Best Practice' Pilots?

In the late 1990s people became increasingly concerned about the poor safety record of Asian airlines. Of the five airlines that have had four or more serious crashes in the last decade, four of them are Asian. And researchers identified Korean Airlines as having the world's worst safety record. The airlines with the best records were mostly from Anglo-Saxon English speaking countries like Britain, Australia, Canada, Ireland and, particularly, the US. In 1998 *The Times* ran a story on this research under the headline: *'Asian culture' link in jet crashes.*

However, things may not be as clear as the first cut of the data might suggest. One London-based expert specializing in risk-assessment claimed that 'It is notoriously difficult, even misleading, to try and draw meaningful conclusions from "snapshots" in aviation.' And many commentators are quick to point out that the Japanese, with a similar socio-cultural background to some of the worst performers, have one of the world's best safety records. Despite these warnings, some analysts have begun to look at the extent to which national cultures affect pilot performance by comparing flight data with cultural characteristics.

Research done by Dutch academic Geert Hofstede in the 1970s and 1980s demonstrated that Asian nationals scored higher on dimensions of collectivism, power-distance and uncertainty avoidance than their Western counterparts. Those groups that score 'high' on *collectivism* recognize their interdependent roles and obligations to group consensus, aspects indicative of a 'strong' culture. Those on the 'high' end of the *power-distance* scale expect and accept that power is distributed unequally, accept the necessity of hierarchies and are less likely to challenge authority. Members of 'high' *uncertainty avoidance* cultures prefer rules and set procedures to contain and resolve uncertainty, whereas low uncertainty avoidance cultures tolerate greater ambiguity and prefer more flexibility in responding to situations.

Aviation researchers have identified that total reliance on the autopilot facility is dangerous in potential crash situations, that airline captains can make fatal errors of judgment that can often be corrected by other crew members, and that the speed and decisiveness of decision making is usually vital. A more recent study carried out by psychologists from the University of Texas indicates that 100 per cent of Korean pilots claim to prefer deferring to the autopilot and always used it (the highest percentage of the 12 countries surveyed), and showed greater shame when making a mistake in front of the crew than pilots from other countries.

1 Comparing the aviation and cultural research data related in the last two paragraphs above, can you provide reasons as to why the Asian pilots might be less safe?
2 Do your findings indicate that American and other Anglo-Saxon pilots have an inherent competitive advantage that makes them the industry's 'best-practice' model?
3 People assumed that Maslow's hierarchy was above and beyond subjective difference but it is now accepted that its 'technology', when applied in an organization, can give Anglo-American's an advantage because their behaviour already conforms to it. Are there aspects of the global aviation industry and technologies that surround flying, aspects that we might at first assume to be culturally neutral, that might give Anglo, English-speaking pilots an environmental advantage at the outset?
4 Should Korean Airlines replace all their pilots with pilots from America or other Anglo-Saxon countries? What other strategies would you employ?
5 What are the advantages and disadvantages of seeking to transfer best practice cultures into other organizations?

Sources: The case draws on *www.crashpages.com*; *www.airsafe.com*; '"Asian culture" link in jet crashes', *The Times*; 'Crashes put aviation in spotlight in Asia', *Nando Times*; A.C. Merritt and R.L. Helmrich, 'Culture in the Cockpit', *Proceedings of the Eighth International Symposium on Aviation Psychology*

3 Centralization *or* Decentralization?

Once upon a time it was not relevant to ask managers 'Is your organization centralized or decentralized?' but, rather, 'In what direction is it going this year?' There seemed to be a cyclical process at work.

Colin Carnall

The term *centralized* indicates that the authority to make important decisions lies towards the 'head' of an organization, while conversely *decentralization* implies more autonomy, whereby authority is vested in those further from 'the top'. Much has been written on the relationship between these concepts and most of it has been hindered by Modernist predispositions. In the 1980s and early 1990s, the ideas that history is linear and progressive and that there must, therefore, be one best way of proceeding – *either* decentralization *or* centralization – influenced a raft of works outlining how things were 'moving toward decentralization' as a testament to man's evolution. As Carnall's quotation above indicates, management writers argued that while organizations and their managers were previously stupidly to-ing and fro-ing between centralization and decentralization, the proper implementation of management science would now provide the truth as to which way was best and provide the means whereby managers could assert order over the previous chaos. This section outlines how even a scant appreciation of management writing over the past century would lead to this view being questioned and how a deconstruction of the terms 'centralization' and 'decentralization' would indicate that their development may be anything but linear and either/or.

A history of decentralization

According to the popular literature of the time, a permanent emancipatory movement, away from centralized structures, was taking place in the 1980s. In the US, the world's leading manufacturer and exporter of management knowledge, businesses faced loses in productivity and strong foreign competition in the late 1970s and early 1980s. The answer? Among other things, consultants-cum-authors, headed by Peters and Waterman, wrote that fluid decentralized structures were replacing rigid centralized bureaucracies in the most innovative companies and suggested that such structures would make most companies more competitive.

In countries as far flung as Great Britain and New Zealand, local authors, following in Peter's and Waterman's wake, examined their own excellent companies. Gurus in the UK gushed of 'winning through autonomy' and spoke of a watershed:

> When Fritz Shumacher wrote 'small is beautiful' he was spitting in the wind. Now the wind has turned and even many of the largest companies are scurrying to turn themselves into confederations of small business units.

In New Zealand, leading lights spoke of the need 'to set free the zest and energy that autonomous people discharge when they are really trusted'; and stressed that 'self-determination and self-control enables the organization to build not only its performance but also its complement of people able and willing to accept the responsibilities of the future.' They referred back to their inspiration for legitimation:

> *In Search of Excellence* is full of stories of excellent companies whose route to excellence had included the ruthless excision of a growing head-office cancer of this [centralized control] type.

In turn, these writings were endorsed, and reinforced, by Peters who wrote on their back covers that the British book was 'readable, the data are hard, and the conclusions are unassailable' and that he was 'thrilled' by the New Zealand version.

Other authors saw decentralization as part of a new wave in which 'new political parties, new philosophies, and new management techniques sprung up and explicitly attacked the centralist premises of the previous ruling paradigm.' John Naisbitt subsequently summed up the direction that things were moving in the title of his chapter on the 'megatrend' decentralization: 'Centralization→Decentralization'. This path was re-confirmed and perpetuated by textbooks emphasizing that 'The clear trend today is toward more decentralization.' Probably the 1980s' most thorough study of the relationship between centralization and autonomy suggested that 'beliefs will swing towards decentralization unless this is discredited by a series of disasters.' 'The decentralization of America has transformed our very culture,' wrote Naisbitt:

> Centralized structures are crumbling all across America. But our society is not falling apart. Far from it. The people of this country are rebuilding America from the bottom up into a stronger, more balanced, more diverse society.

These views built upon others that took the issues at stake to be even wider. Centralization came to not only be bad practice but 'anti-Americanization', to use Roosevelt's term. Peter Drucker outlined the contours of the debate thus:

> The importance of the question whether decentralization is absolutely more efficient than centralization does not lie, primarily, in its application to business management. It is actually the question whether a socialist economy can be as efficient economically as a free-enterprise economy.

At the same time an American, but internationally popular, textbook *Understanding Organizational Behaviour* explained why other countries had not yet followed America's lead:

> While Japan has a fairly homogeneous culture that allows more focused and accepted direction from authority, America prides itself on being a melting pot. A

consequence in a society that supports individual rights is that groups and individuals want to be distinct and to have choices that reflect their situations. The trend of decentralization is one response to this diversity.

These associations leave one in little doubt. Centralization is repressive and negative; decentralization is positive, morally good and progressive. Hence, decentralization, according to management in the 1980s and early 1990s, is unquestionably *the* way of the future. Centralization is the way of the past – or evil – and is therefore on the way out, overthrown by this emancipatory decentralization revolution.

However, placing the idea described above in the context of the reported historical development of organizations regarding decentralization and central control over the past 150 years might lead one to question their simplicity. Decentralization, despite extensive re-packaging by pop-management gurus, was not new. In the US, Henry Poor is associated with one of the first proposals endorsing decentralization in the 1850s. Some of his concepts were applied in the construction of the Erie railroad in 1854 and during the American Civil War in the organization of rail transport. However, others, notably Chandler, view these same railroads at the primary models of *centralization* that other large organizations will come to follow.

Fayol stated in 1916 that 'centralization belongs to the natural order of things.' However, in the 1920s, General Motors and du Pont bucked this order and developed the first major decentralization plans for manufacturing concerns, plans upon which other companies then fashioned themselves. According to Chandler, GM's reforms became *the* model and marked the 'real' beginning of a wealth of publications focussing on the merits of decentralization in the US.

By the end of the 1950s almost all the largest firms in the US were reported to have 'embraced decentralization' and theorists wrote that 'the general organizational pattern is one of decentralization.' However, others at once claimed that decentralization was a fad, as a re-centralization was occurring by the early 1960s. Some argued that only functional areas, such as logistic systems and data-processing activities, would become re-centralized, thanks to computer technology, but that overall organizational structures would continue to decentralize. Others claimed that technological advances would allow top management to return to a centralized structure since the information needed for decisions regarding subsidiary operations could be gathered at a moment's notice. Of developments concerning centralization and decentralization in the 20 years since World War II, Simon notes a movement toward decentralization in large US organizations, but cautioned that:

The movement has probably been a sound development, but it does *not* signify that more decentralization is at all times and under all circumstances a good thing. It signifies that at a particular time in history, many American firms ... discovered that they could operate more effectively if they ... decentralized a great deal of decision making ... At the very time this process was taking place there were many crosscurrents of centralization in the same companies.

Beyond this, it was claimed that businesses did continue to decentralize both their functional areas and their supplier–buyer relationships throughout the 1960s and 1970s. However, some studies showed most companies continued to centralize their administrative services – it was not until 1977 that there was a 'decrease in the aggregate of centralization ratios'. Then, of course decentralization stormed onto management's center stage in the 1980s as a new, revolutionary 'megatrend'.

A little awareness of this history might have urged caution with regard to the recent claims made for decentralization. If anything, the nineteenth and twentieth centuries have witnessed a succession of the 'to-ing and fro-ing' that Carnall derides. Moreover, this history shows that many of the *same* developments were interpreted by some researchers as indicating centralizing tendencies and by others as showing the emergence of decentralization. However, perhaps it was just that earlier management theorists were not as insightful, or that society was not yet mature or technologically advanced enough to embrace decentralization properly? Unfortunately, developments in the 1990s would suggest otherwise. While decentralization was the primary direction that most corporations headed in restructuring their operations in the 1980s, the 1990s ushered in yet another turn. A further burst of information technology development, and a realization of decentralization's weaknesses, was credited with enabling another re-centralization within large companies. But, alternatively, and at the same time, a number of writers still continued to argue that 'decentralization on a worldwide scale' was a trend that was still underway.

This brief history seems to indicate that the logic operating with regard to centralization and decentralization is more 'both/and' and characterized by a cycle of interplay than 'either/or' and linearly progressive. An investigation into the etymological nature of the two terms adds weight to this view and helps us think past the limits of management's conventional 'either/or' understanding.

Deconstructing decentralization

In a powerful scene from Spike Lee's movie *Malcolm X*, an underlying racism is 'deconstructed' for Malcolm by a character called Bembry while he is in prison. Bembry does this through juxtaposing the meanings of 'black' and 'white' as reported in a contemporary dictionary in the prison library. This dictionary defines 'black' as:

> Destitute of light, devoid of colour, enveloped on darkness. Hence, utterly dismal of gloomy, as 'the future looked black. Soiled with dirt, foul; sullen, hostile, forbidding – as a black day. Foully or outrageously wicked, as black cruelty. Indicating disgrace, dishonor or culpability. See also *blackmail, blackball, blackguard.'*

'Now look up, "white",' Bembry instructs Malcolm. Malcolm reads the following:

> 'White.' Of the color of pure snow; reflecting all the rays of the spectrum. The opposite of black, hence free from spot or blemish; innocent, pure, without evil intent, harmless. Honest square-dealing, honorable ...

'That's bullshit.' Malcolm eventually exclaims. 'That's a white man's book. Ain't all these books white man's books. What you telling me to study in them for?'

'Because', Bembry explains, 'you got to learn everything the white man says and use it against him. The truth is laying there if you smart. You got to dig it out.'

What Lee is trying to convey here is similar to the 'deconstructive' approach of French philosopher Jacques Derrida. Derrida's starting point is that moral and social beliefs are constructed on the basis of objectively undecidable conceptual oppositions (for example, civilized/barbarian; white/black; decentralized/centralized). Hence, an existential ambivalence and uncertainty pervades our experience. To makes things more certain we structure meaning so that one half of each pair of binary oppositions is *privileged* and the other *marginalized*, and, correspondingly, to give meaning to history by seeing the former as *progressive* and the later as *regressive*. Over time such relationships become ingrained and go unnoticed in our everyday experience until we 'dig them out' and question them. Derridean deconstruction involves two steps toward this:

- First, Derrida seeks to highlight the halves that are marginalized as a consequence of the unquestioned privileging of their opposite (as did Bembry). His aim being to show that 'we are not dealing with the peaceful co-existence, but rather with a violent hierarchy. One of the two terms governs the other or has the upper hand. To deconstruct the opposition, first of all, is to overturn the hierarchy,' or reverse their meanings. Doing this makes those who have unwittingly enjoyed the fruits of privilege (for example, white) know what it might be like to be marginalized.
- Derrida then brings into play a second step: his notion of 'differance'. 'Differance' also builds from an appreciation of writing being based on binary divisions. According to Derrida, there are two ways of thinking about such divisions. One may emphasize the two separate terms, thinking in terms of hierarchized binary oppositions as described above. Alternatively, one can emphasize the actual process of division itself. The later view enables us to see that division is not just an act of separation but is also a way in which terms are connected. In other words, divisions are both separations *and* joins. It is this alternative view, seeing division as the sharing of a 'whole' in a continuous cycle of differentiation or alternation that Derrida wishes to emphasize here.

'Differance' means that no hierarchy can be conceived of as decided as settled as objectively true or progressive.

- Firstly, different communities can view the hierarchy differently (for example, in the *Malcolm X* scene before the one reproduced above Bembry indicates his privileging of black *over* white).
- Secondly, as meanings are shaped by particular customs, and customs change, privilege can change too.
- Thirdly, there is a perpetual double movement *within* each opposition so that the positively valued, or privileged, term (for example, civilized) is defined only by contrast to the negatively valued, or marginalized, second term (for example, barbarian).

The relationship between the apparently opposing terms is therefore one of mutual definition in which the terms 'inhabit' one another to the extent that without one, the other does not exist. The noun 'normal' is a good example. The concept must incorporate the existence of the 'abnormal' in order for it to make any sense, as norms can only be recognized as such through infractions. Consequently, the claim that 'normal' or 'civilized' can be objectively seen as a later development, better, or progressive cannot be supported by appeals to logic. Each 'half' must have always co-existed, must always be co-joined and 'competing' with one another.

It is in this sense that one can understand the thinking behind Derrida's 'differance'. His misspelling of difference is an attempt to capture not only a meaning in terms of the traditional meaning of the word as 'to differ from', but also a meaning 'to defer', as in 'to postpone'. Privileged terms, claims Derrida, not only *differ* from the terms they marginalize, they also *defer* them. Yet the deferred term is only postponed, not cancelled. It always lies in wait for an opportunity, constantly threatening a 'come-back'. Consequently, no term can be conceptualized apart from its 'other'. Far from being something on the way out, a marginalized term is thus always a central feature of the privileged. It can never be overcome and, as such, the tension will be provoked for as long as we use the terms 'un-questioningly'.

The discussion that follows employs an approach in Derrida's or Lee's spirit to question the relationship between centralization and decentralization, juxtaposing definitions and usage of these concepts from the *Comprehensive Oxford English Dictionary*.

It is interesting to note at the outset that the terms did not exist until Modernist triangular-bureaucratic notions of organizing took hold, and then both emerged together in the same period. Beyond this recognition, the juxtaposition below traces a pattern similar to that outlined by Derrida (and similar to many actual corporate decentralization initiatives: see Case Box 4.3 on p. 162). Centralization is seen as a condition that occurs as an evil inherent within the nature of organization.

Centralization ... the concentration of administrative power in the hands of a central authority, to which all inferior departments, local branches etc. are directly responsible. First appearance: **1822** *"Centralization – that ferocious hydra which has preyed upon Europe ..."* **1836** *"The vice of modern legislation centralization as it is called; a word not more strange to our language than the practice is foreign to our ancient habits and feelings."* **1874** *"Business always tends to centralize itself".*

Decentralization ... the weakening of the central authority and distribution of its functions among the branches or local administrative bod ies. First appearance: **1846** *"An irresistible power of decentralization".* **1859** *"What you want is to decentralize your government"* **1872** *"(An) illustration of the dangers of extreme decentralization ..."* **1898** *"The venerable savant, himself a decentralizer"* **1920** *"The struggle between the centralists and the decentralists ..."* **1961** *"The decentralization reform had to be modified".*

Decentralization represents the weakening of centralization's grip, its irresistible power offering the hope of greater freedom. As such, decentralization brings with it a revolutionary fervor and spirit, one which can get out of hand as revolutions, given the energy generation necessary for them to achieve their ends, are prone to do. Thus the irresistible power has a tendency to overrun its instigators' intentions. After winning the 'struggle' against central oppression the dangers of extreme decentralization must be checked, the reform modified. An interesting dynamic is portrayed. The play of meaning between the two terms reveals centralization seen as inherently 'evil' (to be marginalized); decentralization as 'good' (or privileged), offering emancipation from the forces of evil, but naturally going too far – to a point where some measure of centralization will be seen as a 'necessary evil'.

This tension is further highlighted when one goes further into the roots of the words: decentre (incorporating eccentric) and centric (incorporating centred). Here, interestingly, the privilege is reversed. Decentre is marginalized; centred privileged (see below). Combining these two juxtapositions our deconstructive analysis might run as follows. Centralization is understood to suppress natural human desires. Decentralization enables freedom from suppression, but in so doing spills into a decentred or eccentric state. In response we seek to re-centre. A cycle is complete but simultaneously begins again. The pressures for centralization are thus constantly being opposed by beliefs in decentralization. Accepted wisdom and moral beliefs promote separation or delegation; the threat of betrayal to the center at once urges centralization.

Decentre ... To place out of centre, to render eccentric ... **Eccentric** ... Not agreeing with, having little in common. First appearance: **1607** *"His owne ends, which must be often eccentrique to the endes of his Master or State."* **1666** *"My book of Accounts ... is so eccentric to your studies as I thought*

Centric ... Pertaining to the centre. First appearance: **1590** *"The substance of this centric earth."* **1631** *"Some that have deeper digg'd Loves Mine than I, Say, where his centrique happiness doth lie."* **or** Of, pertaining to, or characterized by a centre: **1850** *"Stung to life by centric forces."* **Centered, Centred**...

it unworthy of your acceptance." **or** Misused for: having no centre: **1633** *"Only that is eccentric, which was never made."* **1652** *"Deaths hell deaths Self-out deaths, Vindictive Place! Excentrick Space!"* **or** Regulated by no central Control. a. Of actions, movements, and things in general: Irregular, anomalous, proceeding by no known method, capricious: **1630** *"Finding all eccentrick in our times."* **1972** *"The eccentrick aberration of Charles the Second."*

Placed at the centre or in a central position. **1683** *"They were easie of Access from all Parts; center'd between Spain and Sweden."* **1829** *"A center'd glory-circled memory, Divinest Atlantis."* **or** Fixed on a centre as a point of support or equilibrium; furnished with a centre: **1847** *"Plato is so centred, that he can well spare all his dogmas."* **1850** *"My centred passion cannot move, Nor will it lessen from to-day."* **or** Brought together to a centre, concentrated: **1805** *"There to collect strength, and thence with centred numbers urge the war."*

This analysis presents a picture of the organizational dynamic regarding centralization and decentralization as inherently circular and self-propelling. It will not reach an 'end', nor can we objectively determine the one-best approach, while both terms exist, and one cannot exist without the other. Their's is a paradoxical relationship or tension not unlike that between the likes of Apollo and Dionysus that the Premoderns considered so integral. This suggests that the idea that centralization and decentralized is a matter of either/or and the idea that decentralization will ultimately prevail over centralization is somewhat short-sighted. Once cannot consider decentralization without considering centralization and vice versa. To do so will only lead to over-emphasizing one over the other to such an extent that the violence of reaction and over-reaction is increased.

The above discussion also calls into question a couple of other Modernist assumptions that have pervaded the management literature with regard to decentralization. The first of these is the notion that for each corporation there is an optimal equilibrium of central and decentral that must be arrived at. This dates back to Fayol, who wrote that the problem was 'the finding of the measure that gives the best overall yield.' It was reproduced through the 1960s: 'What are the optimal sizes of the building blocks in the hierarchy? This is the question of centralization and decentralization. What we seek is a golden mean'; and the 1980s: 'somewhere in the spectrum between total bureaucratic inflexibility and institutional anarchy lies the ideal blend.' The second assumption is the belief that the environmental forces external to the relationship between centralization and decentralization (for example, market characteristics, competitive pressures, and availability of materials; size and rate of growth of the organization; top management preferences and the abilities of lower-level managers and so on), determine the 'balance'.

However, if, as Derrida and this analysis suggests, 'differance' is not only outside us or in our environments since we are also 'inhabited' by particular binary contradictions, then there exists no golden mean as the tension will always be in play. The dynamic between the two forces is based upon continual flux and movement, no permanent balance will be reached and any of a linear direction is only true if not viewed within a broader historical context. Moreover, while the movement between centralization and decentralization may be ascribed to causes which can be more readily scrutinized, forces external to the relationship between centralization and decentralization, a deconstruction of the terms highlights forces inherent to the relationship between centralization and autonomy that keeps their cycle ticking over. The cyclical nature of organizational development regarding centralization and decentralization, which was once dismissed as naive, resides *within* the very 'meaning' of decentralization and centralization. It turns out that the idea outlined in the Carnall quotation at the head of this section, that earlier people were a bit dim and that Modern man and his Modern methods can master things, may be more naïve than the view it sought to overthrow.

The dynamic between centralization and decentralization, while being determined by environmental forces, is also inherently binary, inherently cyclical. Consequently, organizational oscillation between the two poles is difficult to plan against and impossible to fully suppress. However, the more that we recognize the oscillatory nature of the phenomena described here and think on the relationship between the two rather than seeking to know which way is best, the more we may avoid the pitfalls that can be associated with adherence to simplistic over-reactions.

While this analysis suggests that clear outcomes or correct balances regarding centralization and autonomy can only ever be precarious and partial, it does not wish to suggest that organizations cannot be moving towards what they believe are better states. Rather, it argues that general trends or solutions will only ever exist in theory and that best practice 'fashions' regarding centralization and decentralization, sold by management consultants, academics and alike, should be viewed for what they are – inherently temporary.

Indeed, it would be interesting to apply this sort of deconstructive analysis to other binary oppositions prevalent within recent management literature. What, for example, might it reveal about the mainstream view that globalization will inevitably overcome and marginalize the local or regional as progress marches on?

Case Box 4.3   Centralization versus Decentralization

Like many organizations over the past two decades, public and private, TELCO bought into the 'decentralization revolution'. In 1988, its annual report described the way in which it had 'adopted a new business philosophy. With the centralized demands of a centralized head office,' it explained, 'the company was slow and unresponsive. [However,] a decentralized organization structure is now being adopted to improve TELCO'S operating performance.'

Their 1989 report reiterated that: 'A bureaucratic organization with centralized control could never function effectively in a competitive marketplace.' And claimed that 'The new organization structure is *now in place*.' The 1990 annual report stuck to the same script but was less gung-ho about the task having been completed: 'The former system of centralized and bureaucratic controls added to overall costs and inhibited the development of a market-reactive business. However, the company is now capable of functioning efficiently in a competitive environment. The restructuring of TELCO is *largely* completed.'

Three years later, TELCO representatives announced that the company was 'reverting back to centralized control'. With hindsight, it was claimed that the rationale for decentralization was that it was simply 'a phase in the company's development', designed to achieve what the head of a prominent union involved in the process called the 'creation of a new culture'.

Whether or not this was in fact the plan, many practicing managers will find the story of a company seemingly on a pendulum, swinging back and forth from centralization to decentralization, very familiar. Interviews with many of TELCO'S senior managers in 1991 and 1992 – the period between the whole-hearted embrace of decentralization and moving back to centralized control – revealed some interesting insights into the process.

The then marketing director explained the logic behind the move in 1988 as follows:

> Essentially we used to be a very bureaucratic organization with everything centrally controlled and directed, and the restructuring concept was to create a much flatter organization with decision making much closer to the customer base and a substantial degree of autonomy in each of the operating companies.

The director of new ventures was more to the point:

> We had a very big problem with what was called Head Office. You couldn't order a rubber [that is, eraser] unless you actually got a bit of paper from Head Office. So, we went through a very deliberate breaking up of Head Office.

TELCO'S corporate office was 'scaled back', or 'emasculated' in the CFO's words. As the GM of accounting explained, 'We had to move very quickly, so the way to do that is to break up the bureaucracy into autonomous responsible divisions.'

The head of one of the newly-autonomous operating companies summed up his own philosophy, and that of the other new power-brokers that had been brought in to shake up the organization, thus: 'Any holding company or any corporate office or any central group should be minimized as much as possible.' However, later on this manager would admit that 'There is not the same degree of performance across the operating companies that we would like ... I guess a lot of this is because we have taken an organization that was totally centralized and said 'we have to be decentralized – quickly'.'

Other managers spoke of the impact of the move to decentralization going too fast, and too far:

- *CFO* 'They wanted to concentrate on getting stuff down close to the customer. But in the process they all started inventing things that actually ended up with entirely different approaches ... I mean it's swung too far ... The operating companies were getting the feeling that they had autonomy in a number of areas, and of course they ran off in a number of different directions ... there is this tendency for people to run off and invent their own bloody systems because they have got their own agendas one way or the other.'
- *Head of corporate strategy* 'The problem with that kind of responsiveness is the anarchy, and I'll give you a piece of day to day responsiveness, you know, when someone has a rush of blood to the head, decides to change the numbering plan in an

area. So whole towns vanish from the toll network. OK. You need that coordinated thing, because we are in a network business.'

- *Director of new ventures* 'As is often the case, we went too far in practical terms by devolving to the regional operating companies too much autonomy. What tended to happen was we saw a breaking up of direction, we heard of some, who were a division of arseholes, going in that direction. Another going in this ...'
- *GM of accounting* 'In fact, you ended up with a whole series of different strategies ... you had one regional unit that believed they were in the customer premises equipment market. Another believed they weren't. And another one that wasn't but believed we should be because of what they perceived to be our corporate image. It all depended on individuals ... you didn't have a common policy.'
- *Head of technology strategy* 'I think there needs to be a lot more standardization of processes, the example I use at the moment, which I really find quite frustrating, is the fact that information systems are purchased and the project managed in a totally different way to other technology contracts.'

The head of corporate strategy summed up the views of most in explaining what went wrong and prefacing why TELCO would now seek to *recentralize*:

> We went from extreme centralization to extreme decentralization very rapidly and because we are a network business, by taking the heart out of the organization like that, a lot of the coordinating mechanisms were broken.

In 1991 new committees were formed to cut across the regional operating companies and empowered to develop common policies in functional areas like human resources, marketing and technology. This was rationalized in the following ways: *GM of accounting*, 'We had to bring back the control aspect that was missing'; *CFO*, 'There clearly needed to be brought back a common approach throughout the organization'; *Director of marketing*, 'I think we had to reduce some of the devolved responsibility.' The committees quickly grew.

By the time the company formally announced it was reverting back to full-blown centralized control, there were murmurings that the early recentralization initiatives were already showing signs of being taken too far. One senior manager was resigned: 'There is a danger that the pendulum will swing back too far as a reaction. Yes. It will happen.' In the CFO's words: 'You just hope that the pendulum doesn't swing too far, [but,] well, it's inevitable, the pendulum swings and then we are up the creek.' He expanded upon this with an example: 'TELCO is becoming strikingly similar to the old organization – run by committees. I mean when the first schedule of the meeting came out, 25 per cent of the nominal working year was taken up with bloody committee meetings. (They are pretty much a waste of time anyway – I tend not to go now).'

'I don't think we have solved the central versus decentral item yet,' said another manager in conclusion. 'We have swung the pendulum from one extreme to the other, we are now on the way back, and we haven't got to a stable end point yet.'

Despite the swings and roundabouts many, perhaps most, of the managers interviewed did reflect that perhaps the notions of centralization and decentralization did not really constitute an 'either/or' choice. The CFO mused that 'It's a paradoxical situation – you provide much more computer ability now to the individual than was ever possible before, but you have to do that within a common framework or else there will be no meaning.' One regional head offered that 'In actual fact, to some degree, all of the tasks we have has a central element and a decentral element in them.' The GM of accounting concluded by saying that 'I have been one of the biggest catalysts in making decentralization happen. But at the end of the day a decentralized environment really didn't make any sense to me, so I began to talk about 'centralized decentralization' – that's my phrase word – and it's not stupid because I can't afford to have, as we have had, 14 computer sites and 14 different configurations, and heaven knows how many sets of accounts.'

Announcements made beyond 1993 would indicate, however, that these voices of paradoxical reason did not prevail.

1   Why is it often the case that companies go 'too far in practical terms in devolving too much autonomy'?
2   Why do you think the GM of accounting felt the need to explain that his phrase 'centralized decentralization' was 'not stupid'?
3   Do managers, and does management in general, take to other popular new trends or buzzwords (for example, 'globalization', 'e-business', 'empowerment', 'innovation') in the same revolutionary way that was often the case with 'decentralization'? Why might this be?

The identity of this organization has been disguised.

---

4   The external expert-consultant and one-best way solutions

In 1981, Alasdair MacIntyre's *After Virtue* identified two characters brought about by our belief in Modernism and, hence, unique to our times: 'the therapist' who dispensed objective advice on how we should behave according to the general laws and norms provided by the human sciences and 'the expert manager' who made decisions to ensure increasing efficiency. Twenty years on, these two have become one, in the form of the increasingly pervasive management consultant bearing best practice solutions.

Expert consultants and their part in management and Modernism's tangled web

The twentieth century has witnessed an increasing emphasis on turning to detached experts to get to know how one generally ought to be and what one ought to do: the scientist, the doctor, the lawyer, the councillor. And, following suit, organizations now increasingly refer to detached and objective expert therapists for the same sort of advice as to what they ought to do. When seeking to know what they should do to be 'more organic', whether they should 'centralize *or* decentralize', or know what 'culture' is the best, most organizations bring in management consultants.

Consequently, over 90 per cent of Britain's top 300 companies now employee outside consultants and an industry that did not exist in 1950 was worth $62 billion and growing at 16 per cent per annum (twice as fast most developed economies) by the end of the last century. In 1994, management consultancies generated $11.4 billion in fees with analysts predicting that this would double by 1999 (in actual fact, the revenue of the top ten consultancies combined, around 80 per cent of the global market, exceeded $34 billion). Andersen's net revenue was $3.5 billion in 1995, $6.5 billion in 1997 and $8.3 billion in 1998, and the newly merged PriceWaterhouse Coopers brought in over $13 billion in 2000. In 1991, Andersen employed 21 000 consultants. In 1998, 53 000. Hence, the handful of troubleshooters who began to go into companies in the early 1960s to tell them how to be 'leaner and less bureaucratic' have themselves become huge global bureaucracies. Consultants were once called only when something out of the ordinary happened. Now, in many companies, the consultants never leave, they just move on to new projects. Companies that call themselves 'meta-consultancies' have emerged specifically to advise other consultancies so that they, in turn, may advise other companies as to how to run their businesses. In the words of one investigative journalist: 'A business, it seems, is no longer a business unless it has someone from the outside telling its managers how it could be run better.'

Given their exponential growth and increasing status it is little wonder that the management consultancies now sit alongside Oxbridge and the Ivy League as the nurseries of the young and upwardly ambitious. Indeed, students from the latter jostle with their peers to get into the former, often attempting to improve their chances by taking an MBA programme in a prestigious business school after their undergraduate degree. Working for one of 'the big five' consultancies has become a plum job, one that then acts as a further training programme and links them on to other positions of corporate power. Subsequently, more and more of the people who 'pull the strings' now come from consultancy backgrounds. For example, McKinsey's alumnus includes the heads of IBM, Levi-Strauss and American Express; France's Bull and the UK's Asda.

The emergence of these links is making it increasingly difficult to distinguish between big business, management consulting, management science, business schools and management gurus within the 'management industry' as it is termed by Micklethwhaite and Wooldridge in *The Witchdoctors: a commentary on the rise of management*. Hence:

- most big companies use the big consultancies;
- most of these companies' executives have MBA's from leading business schools and many used to work for the consultancies;
- most of the world's best-known gurus have worked for the big consultancies, still advise their former employers while running their own consultancies, and are increasingly interviewed in leading management journals such as the *Harvard Business Review*;
- most of the world's leading consultancies now have research academies and provide their corporate clients with their own academic journals which look increasingly like the *Harvard Business Review* (compare the *McKinsey Quarterly* for example);

- most of the 'science' in these journals reports on the knowledge gained through the consultants-academics access to the leading companies;
- many of the most prestigious business schools now run tailor-made MBA programmes for big corporations (including big consultancies);
- these programmes increasingly bring in executives from big companies and consultancies as guest speakers to tell students the latest science. And so on.

This web now spreads out further still. McKinsey's 'old-boy' list also encompasses the head of the Confederation of British Industry, the deputy governor of the Bank of England and leaders of the British Conservative Party. And, although all the major consultancies are US-owned, an industry that was once a US phenomenon has an increasingly global reach: from McKinsey's fastest growing office in India; to a Taiwanese government stuffed with American MBA graduates; to recent moves to replicate the US business school concept across China. While monarchs no longer possess the power or audacity to take the Elizabethan pose that expressed Modernism's new way of thinking, that the heads of management consultancies do indicates that while those in power have changed, Modernist perspectives are still alive and well (compare Figure 2.7 on p. 37 with Figure 4.4).

Indeed, the global status now accorded management consultants as the purveyors of knowledge crucial to the functioning of our society means that the networks described above are now interwoven with the way we think about what is good and right in the world. This pervasiveness can be illustrated by contrasting the reporting of two separate incidents involving Jesus in 1999. In October, British newspapers ran stories on a poster depicting Jesus as a vegetarian sponsored by People for the Ethical Treatment of Animals (PETA). The caption read 'Jesus was a vegetarian. Show respect for God's creatures – follow him.' The Press outlined how experts had been quickly deployed to prove that the poster was 'theologically incorrect' and that it was presently being removed because of protests. Community leaders were quoted as saying that they were 'delighted that this distasteful, unfortunate and inappropriate poster has been halted.' The general tone of the reportage was that the poster was ridiculous and that those who produced it were desperate extremists. In response, all the PETA spokesman could say was that all they were trying to do was build upon the idea that 'Jesus taught us to be compassionate to the vulnerable.'

A month earlier the same newspapers had reported on another new poster, this time developed for a church organization by a group of advertising executives. In an adaptation of Leonardo DaVinci's *The Last Supper*, Jesus was depicted as a trendy management consultant advising his disciples who had been transformed into the CEO's of multinational companies. The poster was titled 'God's Mission Statement for the Millenium.' It was generally seen as a forward step, a sign that the Church was 'moving with the times,' 'updating its image' and 'being progressive'. One Rector involved in the development of the poster explained that 'What we are saying is that if Christ came in the year 2000 he would, strange as it may seem, choose to

Figure 4.4 Global aspirations: The new Queen E? – Top, Chairmen of KPMG and Ernst & Young; Bottom, Advertisement for a recruitment fair for management consultants (2000)

Sources: Top, photograph accompanying 'KPMG Chief Proposes far-reaching changes' article in *The Times* (21 February 1998); Bottom, image from the cover of a brochure titled 'Rekrutierung von Top-Consulting-Nachwuchs in Deutschland, Renaissance Koln Hotel (3–4 July 2000)

sit down with the people who pull the strings.' This seems to make sense, especially seeing as management historians have 'proved' that Jesus was actually one of the first practicing managers. Consequently, the West's most influential spiritual icon of the past 2000 years now sits comfortably with management. Despite the fact that there are no biblical references to Jesus having been either a management consultant or a vegetarian, that Jesus would be a management consultant now makes sense. That he could have vegetarian sympathies appears both absurd and dangerous.

But the almost religious fervour now surrounding management science and the consultant-disciples increasingly brought in to dispense it in what has been termed a 'ones-size-fits-all' fashion, is now beginning to worry some commentators. In the words of Professor Eileen Shapiro, a former McKinsey employee:

> We are now raising a generation of managers who don't know how to take risks and make decisions. I can't think of anything more scary for business.

This is now exacerbated by the fact that many bright young thinkers would rather become consultants than work in traditional industries. Lucy Kellaway, a columnist for the *Financial Times* argues that:

> ... a situation where the brightest and most able young people would much rather become consultants than work for companies that actually make things, is not necessarily a good thing.

These developments are especially scary if one thinks through how consultancies generate knowledge and the reasons that many companies bring in consultancies.

Best practice?

Management consultancies gain much of their kudos through their network of clients: the best consultants have on their books the best-known, the biggest or the most-profitable companies. This is useful in that it gives consultancies access to the stuff of their research. Hence, they, more than anyone else, have the empirical data that enables them to tell other companies what 'the best' are doing; a process that has now been labelled 'benchmarking' or 'best practice'. This is a process that encourages companies to do what the best companies have done, based on the idea that there is one-best way at the cutting edge of progress and that one must be at that cutting edge or be left to drown in the wake. It is a process that seems to be the height of Modernism. 'Best practice' became the twentieth century's last global management buzzword.

Best practice makes sense if an organization is seeking to reduce the cost of its operations – if someone else does exactly the same things cheaper then you might be wise to copy it. But, best practice has increasingly been applied to strategy, despite the fact that one of the most basic tenets of strategy would appear to be that a company's competitive advantage comes from its being different (an idea that will be expanded upon in the following chapters). Going further against this tenet is the fact that as the consultancies themselves engage in best practice, taking on board what their competitors do best, and as the number of consultancies shrinks (the eight biggest consultancies have recently become five through mergers), the knowledge being distributed becomes increasingly similar. 'With everyone basically getting the same information,' one former consultant admitted to The *Guardian* newspaper, companies will soon be 'all doing the same thing so there is no competitive advantage.'

Subsequently, the cutting edge of management and strategy has become a butter-knife – more for spreading than cutting. Horgan's thesis about the end of science (about diminishing returns being the only outcome that can result from everybody using the same approach – see Chapter 2) is now being played out in our leading organizations. Moreover, this normalizing focus on generalizing what others are doing takes managers further away from thinking about the problems unique to their companies. 'You can issue a mission statement, re-engineer, you can total-quality management yourself,' says Shapiro, 'and then you can rightsize. Really, its just your imagination for phrases that limit you in the kind of things you can do to insulate yourself from actually thinking about what [your particular] problem is.'

Why on earth, then, would managers want this sort of advice? Because a manager is less 'accountable' ('accountability' being another management buzzword) and thus less 'stressed-out' (which is not a buzzword but perhaps should be) if they can point out that what they implemented was based on the best advice from the best consultants as to what the world's best companies were doing. 'Management theory has always appealed to the thousands of people who want to get ahead,' claim Micklethwait and Wooldridge, but 'now it has tapped into the market of the millions who are scared of being left behind.' Hence, there is increasing evidence to suggest that many managers bring in consultants to give decisions legitimacy and 'spread the blame'.

All this best practice is great if you want to replicate what has already been done, but, unfortunately, it is also the opposite of creativity. The network described above means that the advice being doled out is becoming increasingly homogenized. And managers in all spheres, given this dynamic, find it increasingly difficult to find the resolution to critique what they are being given. Thus the problem continues to exacerbate. It is hard to see from where substantially new, creative thinking can come from in an environment so conceived.

'Enlightenment,' wrote Immanuel Kant in what is regarded by Modernists and Postmodernists alike as one of the best expressions of where a healthy society should be:

> ... is man's release from his self-incurred immaturity. Immaturity is man's inability to make use of his understanding without direction from another.

Self-incurred is this immaturity when its cause lies not in lack of reason but in lack of resolution.

Ironically, and perhaps tragically, Modernist beliefs have spawned an appreciation of management, and of management's leading advocate and purveyor, the management consultant, at the expense of such enlightenment. If management is, in Drucker's view, 'the most important function in American society,' if other societies are increasingly American, and if being reasonable or rational for a manager increasingly means bringing in consultants to guide decision making, we are perhaps further away from Kant's wish than we have been for quite some time.

Case Box 4.4   Like a Virgin?

At the beginning of the year 2000, consultant's from the Virgin Group, famous for revamping 'maturing' consumer product and service markets like air and rail travel, cola, vodka and banking, were called in by Government ministers to write a report on Britain's hospitals. In an article in *The Sunday Times*, the Secretary for Health, Alan Milburn, described Britain's publicly funded NHS (National Health Service) as 'a 1948 system operating in a twenty-first-century world.' 'That is why,' he explained, 'I have now asked Sir Richard Branson's award-winning Virgin Group to advise us on how hospitals can be made consumer friendly ... It is about transforming the very culture of the NHS to make it a modern consumer service.' Press releases claimed that the Prime Minister, Tony Blair, would use the report to follow up on accusations made by his Health Secretary of the dire 'forces of conservatism' within the NHS and 'lambaste the gross inefficiencies built into the system.'

The consultants visited nine hospitals and several general practitioner's surgeries over a 26-day period and composed a damning report. They wrote of 'over-centralization', 'too much red tape', 'chaotic booking arrangements' and 'poor management'. They concluded that 'the patient is required to fit into the system, rather than the other way around,' and that the 'dead hand of bureaucracy seems to stifle imagination and flair.' However, on the up side, they claimed that 'most [staff] are probably decent people who just need a little leadership and direction.' The actions they believed should be taken to remedy the situation included the sort of ideas that have become commonplace in many organizations, 'empowering workers to be more innovative,' making hospitals more 'consumer friendly' and increasing transparency and accountability. (One recommended means of doing this was to allow patient representatives to go 'behind the scenes' and carry out 'snap inspections'.) There was also talk of 'snack trolleys' and making hospitals 'more fun'.

However, NHS employees were critical of the Virgin report and the Government's handling of it. Doctors felt they were being blamed for poor public perception of the NHS which, they argued, was caused by lack of funding. Stephen Thornton, the chief executive of the NHS Confederation, accepted that declining standards needed to be addressed, but challenged 'the Virgin team to show me what they describe as a suffocating bureaucracy ... Where on earth do they get ridiculous figures that imply there is one administrator to every two clinical staff?' Of all NHS staff, only 3 per cent were managers/administrators, compared to 44 per cent nurses, 8 per cent doctors and 17 per cent clerical, he said, asking 'I wonder how many backup staff it takes Virgin to get one pilot into the air?' In any case, he continued, 'many administrative and clerical staff undertake critical patient-related tasks. It is disingenuous to suggest these people hinder rather than help the treatment of patients.' Peter Hawker, chairman of the British Medical Association's Consultant's Committee, similarly suggested that he was 'all for improving the services to patients but we need real resources, not an exercise in spin [doctoring].'

These criticisms sparked a wider debate about the Blair Government's use of consultants. A survey by the *Independent on Sunday* showed that it had spent almost a billion pounds hiring private consulting firms in its first three years in office. It was revealed that the Department for Education and its agencies spent almost £10 million between 1997 and 1999. In response, Nigel de Gruchy, general secretary of a prominent teaching union, claimed that 'The money could be much better spent. The Government paid Hey McBer consultancies £3 million to come up with criteria for what makes a good teacher. We could have told them that for nothing.'

The Department of Health's spending on consultants in the same period was two and a half times that of Education. According to one source, this could have paid for 2 327 heart bypass operations, 4 421 hip replacements, 737 full cancer treatments and the wages of 1 133 junior doctors. A spokeswoman for the Unison health union said: 'It's an awful amount of money to spend on consultants, particularly if those consultants are at the expense of money going into front-line care. We generally know what the problems are, the difficulty is getting the Government to listen to the people who are on the ground.'

1   Outline the strengths and weaknesses of bringing in external consultants to evaluate an organization like the NHS.
2   Are the employees' criticisms of the Virgin report valid? Can you see any problems with any of the Virgin report's recommendations for the NHS?
3   How else might the Government have gone about gaining insight into the problems that all parties seem to agree need to be addressed within the NHS?

Sources: This case draws on 'Health Service Damned by Virgin Report', the *Scotsman*; 'Virgin Team Highlights NHS Shambles', *Guardian*; 'How Labour has Blown £1 billion on Consulting Outside "Experts"', *Independent on Sunday*; 'Britain Asks Virgin's Branson for Advice of Hospitals: Workers Skeptical', *Financial Post*

5   Concluding Part I: Deconstructing Management

Micklethwait and Wooldridge conclude *The Witchdoctors* by asking why Management is a 'peculiarly faddish discipline, where ideas are grabbed at rather than matured?' Why is it that managers flit from fad to fad? And why do management gurus and consultancies keep tearing up the sacred texts and starting from scratch only to come back with very similar ideas? They conclude that it is largely due to the economics involved. The prevalence of fear and ambition among the consumers of management ideas means that the market is always unstable. The industry thus has a relentless appetite for more fuel – more ideas to process, print, sell and regurgitate. They also point out that 'the success and scope of the industry has also had an effect on the sorts of ideas produced – with such huge vested interests, self-criticism is almost unheard of.'

To these conclusions this deconstruction of management adds the following. Even if the management industry could be more self-critical it would find it difficult to change itself substantially given its historical configuration. Management is a completely Modernist child – this is what made it so successful in the twentieth century. It arose as the science that appeared to address Modernism's desire for a universal value-neutral end and seemed to answer a question that Modernity had been struggling with for some time. After World War II the environment was ripe for establishing the practice of management as a 'serious academic discipline'. Those with a vested interest in seeing such a thing established worked quickly to create the foundations to prop it up. However, in so doing, management's 'hothouse' was so narrow that it contained little difference from which a self-critical standpoint could work or from which the innovative interplay of different ideas and styles could spring. Moreover, these foundations were processed and built upon so quickly that they became part of the unquestionable make-up of the field, a make-up propped up by numerous networks of people that have now established their reputation upon it.

But, being a completely Modernist child comes at a cost. Management, and subsequently strategy, unshakeably brings with it all of Modernism's assumptions without any difference from which these assumptions might be questioned. Thus management, perhaps more than any other field, fundamentally believes in the quest for 'the new', the idea that there is order under *chaos*, that it can discern this order, that it can reduce this into 'one-best ways' that can be applied from the 'outside-in'. And it believes that the best person to advise us on the best ways to act or 'cure abnormalities' are detached objective 'Jesus-like' consultants with lots of experience of averaging out others' excellence and ailments. The beauty, from the management industry's viewpoint, is that none of the subsequent new theories actually work as well as what the Modernist optimists concerned expected they might, thus the quest for a general theory is always beginning anew. Moreover, management and strategy's subsequent lack of focus on history or questioning the past means that it fails to recognize this ever-decreasing circle. This leads to a self-serving and unrelenting cycle of inventing the new, of dismissing the old before unwittingly replacing it with something quite similar, rather than questioning the fundamental beliefs upon which this 'production process' is based.

Part I of *ReCreating Strategy* has outlined how Modernism created an environment ripe for management and strategy as we know them, and how management's subsequently becoming a key player within Modernism created an environment ripe for management consultants selling best practice solutions to become our world's most influential characters at the turn of the twentieth century. However, as this influence now seems to be stifling our ability to think creativity or differently in the twenty-first century, Part II seeks to put forward an alternative. An alternative developed by questioning the unquestioned foundations upon which management and strategy, as we know them, is based and 'regenerating' a different approach by revisiting history.

PART II:

RECREATING STRATEGY

As a group, lemmings may have a rotten image, but no individual lemming has ever received bad press.

Warren Buffet

Five years seems to be the average life cycle of a universal theory of management. As part of management's Modernist process of quickly acclaiming the new and dismissing the old, Total Quality Management (TQM) swept all before it in the late 1980s, only to be dismissed in the mid-1990s. As TQM's star descended, Business Process Re-engineering (or BPR) was on the rise. However, by the end of the 1990s writers saw its rhetoric of obliterating the past and starting afresh with a blank sheet to be just as short sighted as any other 'scorched earth' policy. Of all the buzzwords that vied to take BPR's place at the cutting edge, Best Practice (BP), also known as Benchmarking, prevailed. Best practice formalizes the seemingly intelligent idea that you find out who does something 'best' and then seek to replicate this yourself, thereby benchmarking yourself against the leader and rising, like cream, to the top. But, at the beginning of the twenty-first century there were signs that BP was about to go the way of BPR.

That BP should not be a method of developing an organization's strategy at the end of the twentieth century should have been obvious to anyone who looked back to even the most basic economic or psychological theories. If firms seek to copy others (and are advised by an increasingly small number of consulting firms in the process), then their products and services become increasingly similar. And when that happens the only means of consumers differentiating between competitors is price. Competition is therefore reduced to a price war and, because everyone's costs are similar (because they have sought to replicate BP production practices), everyone's margins decline. (One study has shown that this sort of 'strategic herding' led to a 50 per cent decline in margins in the five years to 1999 among German wireless telecommunications providers). In other words, cream is only a treat worth stretching for when the rest of the bottle is milk. Moreover, everything 'being creamed' is a recipe for stagnation. As managers become more focussed on developing the systems necessary for copying, the less concerned and able they are to promote substantive innovation.

One can further highlight how bereft the application of BP would be by taking some Postmodern liberties with the classic motivation theories of Maslow and Herzberg. If we were to play around a little with Maslow's Hierarchy (see Chapter 4, p. 136), inspired by Deleuze and Guattari to see it more as a grass or a clump of reeds (see Chapter 2, p. 61), we could argue that while our physiological needs may be close knit or common, one important psychological characteristic is the desire to develop an 'identity'. Most of us want to create our own space or *differentiate* ourselves from others by developing a *unique* network of characteristics and associations.

If we add in Herzberg's idea that there are some things that really motivate us to stretch for that little bit extra, and others that are simply 'hygiene factors' – things which we expect and take for granted so that their presence does not act as a motivator but their lack is a demotivator (for example, cleanliness in a restaurant) – we can say that increasingly, in the West at least, the physiological functions of a product or service are hygiene factors. If this is the case then the 'motivators' are increasingly the stuff of identity, such as in the diagram below. (Advertisers at least seem aware of this dynamic – when was the last time that you saw an advertisement that focussed just on the mechanistic functions of a product or service?) This is likely why the big global food brands emerged at the turn of the twentieth century (Coca-Cola, 1886; Heinz Ketchup, 1876; Colgate Toothpaste, 1896; Kellogg's Corn Flakes, 1906), when production technology was available to produce them and there was a population whose corresponding 'physiological needs' were as yet unfulfilled. This analysis might also indicate why most of the big commodity brand producers have, in recent times, had to look for growth in 'less developed' countries as the West is increasingly characterized by what we might call 'common need saturation'.

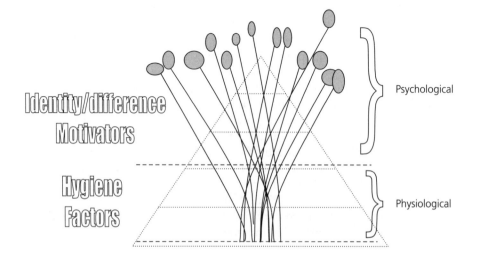

We can see how the shift toward a focus upon identity and difference is emerging at the beginning of the twenty-first century by taking the example of automobiles. In a world were systems that can quickly assimilate and duplicate new technology are more commonplace, differences in things like mechanical reliability and safety become less apparent (see Case Box 2.2). Not so long ago jokes were made about the performance and safety of Skoda and Hyundai cars in this regard. Now it is almost impossible to differentiate them from the more established manufacturers in the categories in which they compete. Hence, these functional aspects have become more hygiene factors than motivators to purchase (in classical strategy parlance we might say that while they are increasingly 'critical success factors' in an industry, they are increasingly less a source of corporate 'competitive advantage'). This leaves the more established manufacturers with two options:

- compete on price (very difficult given their fixed costs); or
- turn to the one thing that they have that cannot be readily copied: 'identity'.

They, like many other organizations in other industries, are increasingly focussing on the latter. Identity, wound up as it is with history, heritage and tradition, is impossible to replicate, whether it be a person's, a car's, a company's or a nation's. Bill Clinton got to the Whitehouse in the early 1990s with the catchphrase 'It's the economy stupid'. However, ten years further on it might be more effective to recognize that it is 'also about identity'.

But if the importance of *unique identities* is so obvious, how did the rise of best practice copy-catting come about? Largely because of the dynamic described at the end of Part I of this book. BP is a tool that makes a lot of sense when applied to reducing the costs of an organization's 'mechanistic operations' or its 'functional technology' – to the hygiene factors. However, the interrelated combination of:

- consultants looking to grow the market for their products; and
- managers feeling the heat of increased 'individual accountability' and out of practice when it came to making independent decisions because of their increasing reliance on consultants,

led to BP being taken to another level.

For managers, modeling their company's performance on its 'best-in-class' competitor is an aim that is easily explained and easy to measure. It sounds 'ambitious' and at the same time 'not too risky'. For the shareholders that managers are seeking to satisfy, BP benchmarking seems like a guarantee of 'soundness'. Hence, thanks to the principle of 'safety in numbers', BP is a wonderful safety net. Indeed, 'no individual lemming has ever received bad press'.

Part I's deconstruction of management contained some bad news and some good news with regard to addressing this situation at the beginning of the twenty-first century. The bad news is that management's historical appreciation of itself has configured it in such a way as to disregard difference or cultural and spiritual identity in favour of a Modernist focus on homogenizing hygiene factors like economics, technology, functionality and efficiency. However, the good news is that because this history was largely constructed according to particular contingencies it need not serve as a fundamental limit. Management may, in other words, be re-created.

Part II of this book seeks to re-create strategy and management by incorporating influences beyond Modernism so as to see past the 'brief memory' inscribed in current practices and 'enable thinking differently', to use Foucault's words. In so doing it follows an approach similar to that recently taken by a number of prominent social and scientific commentators who have advocated a re-examination of Premodern thinking as a means of rethinking Modernist assumptions in Postmodern environments.

Thus the approach taken here is 'revolutionary', but not in its Modern sense of dismissing the past and being carried forward in a new uniform direction. It is revolutionary in an older, paradoxical, sense of 'coming back around' while moving forward. And, to continue stretching our understanding of 'revolution', it seek to reemphasize 'volition'. In the light of Part I's discussion, *ReCreating Strategy* means analytical and decision making-power being *taken back* by the individuals who work in organization's particular contexts under the influence of the local traditions from which identity and difference springs, rather than being the domain of external expert consultants. About individuals and organizations 'having the courage to use their *own* reason,' in Kant's words.

The recreation of strategy outlined in the pages that follow might thus best be described as 're-volitionary'. The primary 're-volitionary' aspect is a rethinking of the nature and 'position' of strategy, and two sub-fields seen as of utmost importance for strategy and management in the twenty-first century: managing change and business ethics. This 'rethink' can best be summarized graphically. The Modernist 'outside-in' view of Management, as the diagram below illustrates, is largely about bringing in a best practice strategy from above, then implementing change as a series of steps down through the company, and finally making sure that the organization's decisions and operations do not infringe general ethical boundaries.

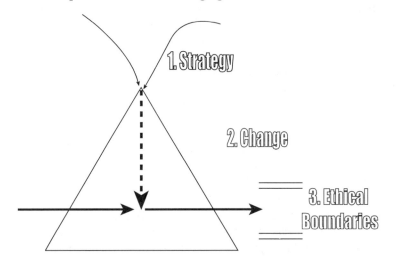

By contrast, *ReCreating Strategy* suggests an alternative way of thinking, where those within an organisation begin with:

- a focus on understanding their unique ethos; before
- using this to inspire strategic differentiation with regard to the direction/s that they believe they should take; and then
- feeding these developments back into how they should adjust, or change *and* remain the same, over time – 'surfing' the past rather than dismissing it in a way that builds upon their unique ethos. (See diagram below.)

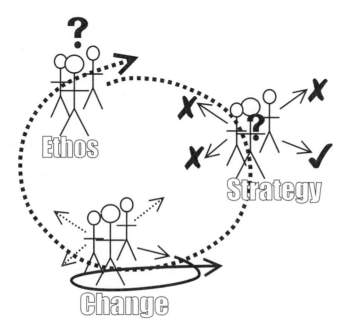

After deconstructing the Modernist triangular, hierarchical 'outside-in' approach to management and strategy, *ReCreating Strategy* now seeks to promote seeing things from the 'inside-out' in this way.

Part II's development of this alternative view is divided into three chapters. In Chapter 5, 'ReConceptualizing Business Ethics', business ethics is shown, on account of its Modern constitution, to draw only on one aspect of ethics – the general code of behaviour outlining duties to stakeholders. The purpose of such codes is to ensure alignment within current norms. They are, therefore, concerned with *commonality*. Hence business ethics is increasingly out of step with what it most seeks to influence – strategy – which, as we have begun to explore, must increasingly be about developing *difference*. By rethinking the history of business ethics so as to incorporate Premodern notions of *ethos* that focus on knowing and accentuating one's differences within a community, an alternative, more rounded and potentially more effective, approach is developed.

By reconceiving corporate strategy as originating where the word was developed (Ancient Greece), rather than where it is often assumed to have been born (twentieth century America), the idea that strategy must represent one specific action is challenged in Chapter 6, 'ReConceiving Strategy'. The Greek's saw strategy as the fruitful combination of design and opportunism. It happened in many forms in all areas of organization and was consequently reflective of life in general. Thus, they would have had difficulty fathoming the largely fruitless debate that gripped the strategy literature over the past decade as to whether strategy is *either* planning, from the top of the triangle down, *or* emergence, from the bottom of the triangle up. *ReConceiving Strategy* uses the Ancient Greeks' approach to argue against choosing between different views of strategy. It recognizes that strategy relates to organizations, an aspect of life that all humans have experience of and to which all our traditions can be related. Hence, any framework that allows us to make divisions and generalizations toward discussing choices and decisions, be it Maslow's Hierarchy, Michael Porter's models, Chinese theology or the principles of weaving, may be usefully applied to mapping strategic differentiation and direction. However, we should be wary of using any such frameworks in a rigid, universal or representatively static manner. Given the developments described above it may be more fruitful if individuals exercise their own volition to oscillate between or mix and match frameworks like these and adapt them to their circumstances in order to articulate their own differences, rather than religiously apply them as a global blueprint. To 'shake hands' with them in ways that spark off creative solutions, or to use 'the "energy" of these frameworks and shape them in new and unexpected ways' for their own purposes (see p. 8 and p. 64).

Chapter 7, 'ReGenerating Change', questions conventional change management models and finds a remarkable similarity between them. It argues that this is largely due to change management research being a largely incremental Modernist affair, with later theories seeking to add complexity to, rather than fundamentally rethink, the 'past masters'. It then investigates a Premodern change process (from tyranny to democracy in Athens in 508 BC) to see if it might add to our understanding of change. By juxtaposing Modern change theories against the Premodern Athenian case, it questions largely undebated assumptions about change. This leads to a vision of time not as a straight line but as a spiral, with past, present and future intermingled. Hence change is an un-closed loop, not a linear, step-by-step, process, and there can be no successful change without constancy. Both insights indicate that the bringing of local traditions and differences from the past into the future is a crucial aspect in any organizational transformation: a recognition that brings change back around into, and draws further inspiration from, ethos.

Part II concludes by investigating how organizations may be drawn other than in terms of generic boxes-and-lines triangles in a way that enables a corporation's ethos, strategy and development through time to be depicted in an individualized and non-static manner. And this loops us all the way back around to *ReCreating Strategy's* very first Case Boxes from Chapter 1.

5 ReConceptualizing Business Ethics

By the end of this chapter you should:

1 Be able to distinguish between different approaches to ethics.
2 Understand how business ethics had conventionally drawn only from general 'written code' based approaches.
3 Recognize the limitations associated with this emphasis on general codes and values given Postmodern environments.
4 Be capable of making recommendations as to how an organization may use other approaches, in addition to code-based approaches, in order to develop an individualized sense of ethos.

The proposition 'Alternative A is good' may be translated into two propositions, one of them ethical, the other factual: 'Alternative A will lead to maximum profit.' 'To maximize profit is good.' The first of these two sentences has no ethical content, and is a sentence of the practical science of business. The second sentence is an ethical imperative, and has no place in any science.

Herbert Simon

Things have changed since Simon declared ethics to be no part of any science and since Peter Drucker and economist Milton Friedman's similar assessments that business ethics was no part of management, or a 'non-subject'. As mangers have come to wield more power in society, the claim that 'ethics is other people's concern, we just do the managing,' has ceased to wash. In addition, the 'freeing up' of access to global information networks, for which Lyotard's *Postmodern Condition* held out hope (see Chapter 2), has enabled an increasingly cynical public to find out more about what companies are doing in various locations and effectively network themselves against companies' actions if they see fit. Management has had to respond, and this response has seen the rise of business ethics. This last decade in particular has witnessed an increasing awareness in the importance of 'doing business ethically'. It is a sign of the times that companies such as Shell and British Petroleum now sponsor reports entitled 'Profits and Principles – Does there have to be a Choice?', reports which conclude that 'Tomorrow's successful company can no longer afford to be a *faceless* institution that does nothing more than sell the right product at the right price.' However, because of its Modernist historical conception of itself and because ethical approaches are generally sold by external consultancies, business ethics has come to emphasize general objective 'goods' and common codes or values, things that can be similarly applied to many organizations at once. Management has taken the application of 'ethics', 'philosophy' and 'values' to be about organizations developing the same externally imposed ideal or average identity, about imposing the *same face* on all.

Such an approach might work well in a world converging on one clearly defined universal set of values and if organizations were all the same, if they had the same bureaucratic structures perhaps and the same aims. But, paradoxically, the forces for globalization that are leading to an heightened awareness of business ethics are also driving a juxtaposition of local traditions that is leading some influential ethical theorists to question the belief in universal 'goods'. Hence, management's approach to ethics seems lacking in a world where people are increasingly aware that to not acknowledge that different local traditions can sponsor different beliefs as to what is good is both short-sighted and imperialistic, and where the cost advantages of applying universal business processes are not the only motivator for customers. The main reason why many commentators now confess that the codes of conduct and well-meaning missions that spring from business ethics have little impact on the formation of strategy, other than in a restrictive sense, and why most involved with strategy still fail to see business ethics as a particularly informative construct, is no longer that they believe that ethics has no place in business. It is rather that in a time where people are recognizing that 'best practice' copying cannot be applied to strategic thinking, business ethics is focussed upon how organizations should act 'in accordance' with predetermined boundaries, or be the same.

A good illustration of how ethics or values have entered into management in a limited and not strategically useful way concerns a recent evaluation of a financial services organization. This organization had, like many of their competitors, employed consultants to help them construct 'corporate values'. Seven were agreed upon:

- creativity
- integrity
- respect
- commitment
- professionalism
- teamwork
- humour.

However, reviewing the value statements of their competitors demonstrated that all these, apart from humour, were common across the lot. As the general manager exclaimed upon our presentation of this: 'If everybody is doing this then these are just hygiene factors. We need some added-value values.' A related example of the limitations of a Modernist, outside-in, approach to developing ethical values is outlined in Case Box 5.1.

Case Box 5.1　How External Consultants can Diminish an Organization's Ethos

The New Zealand Police have a reputation as being one of the least corrupt law-enforcement bodies in the world. Up until the early 1990s, this simple ethos or mission statement guided them:

> To work with the community to maintain the peace.

However, as was often the way with public service organizations in the 1990s, the NZ Police were increasingly encouraged to utilize external consultants in order to help them move closer toward 'best practice' and be seen to be more 'accountable'. One of the first services that such consultants generally offered was the creation of a new mission statement. Hence, after much development work, 1992 saw the launch of NZ Police's new mission statement:

> To contribute to the provision of a safe and secure environment
> where people may go about their lawful business unhindered
> and which is conducive to the enhancement of the quality
> of life and economic performance.

Curiously, while the later statement is five times longer it says no more of substance than the first (indeed, by making no mention of how, or by what strategy, its stated aims should be achieved – contrast 'To work with the community ...' with 'To contribute ...' – it says less). Subsequently, the second statement is far less memorable and more confusing in terms of how it might be operationalized.

1　What would have lead the consultants involved to come up with the 1992 statement?
2　Why might the 1992 statement mean less than the one it replaced?

Thus, there appears a discrepancy between current views of business ethics and the Postmodern environments that value individuality in which organizations must now act. In response, this chapter attempts to broaden our understanding of business ethics by incorporating a Premodern outlook. A vision where ethics was closer to what we now might call character or individual *ethos* than objective values and universal goods. It is an approach that business ethics has largely written out of its constitution.

1 The Modern conception of business ethics

With a broad enough perspective one may discern two basic approaches to ethics: codes of behaviour, and forms of subjectification.

- *Codes of behaviour* refer to general rules of conduct that exist above or *outside* of particular actors. These may be used to prove actions right or wrong and thus provide the means to channel individual behaviour in a common, normal or ideal direction.
- *Forms of subjectification* refer to individuals constituting or rejuvenating themselves as subjects of moral conduct from the *inside-out*, through the development of relationships for self-examination according to self-delineated rather than externally imposed criteria.

A similar distinction is often drawn between *deontic and aretaic* ethics:

- A deontic approach, from the Ancient Greek *deos* meaning 'duty' and 'fear', views ethical questions with appeal to some *external code of rights and responsibilities* toward others.
- An aretaic approach, from the Greek *arete* meaning virtues or personal excellence, is about working on an individual's particular character, purpose in life or *telos*.

Most ethical systems in most societies incorporate elements of both of these modes. But business ethics has focussed almost entirely on the *general deontic code*.

Business ethics' singularly Modern view

Chapter 4's discussion of culture illustrated how management has assumed that ethical behaviour is something that can generally be defined and measured, with both of the questionnaire based general 'culture grids' highlighted here including 'ethics' (or 'moral integrity') as one of their objectively measurable elements. One only need examine business ethics' mainstream literature to further observe this particular way of seeing. For example, *Blackwell's Encyclopedic Dictionary of Business Ethics* summarizes ethics in terms of the *deontic* and *aretaic* branches described above and notes that the *deontic* strands harbor business ethics' 'most popular and highly developed approaches', while its entry on a virtue approach explains that:

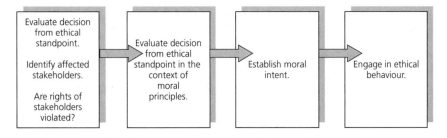

Figure 5.1 A leading textbook's model of ethical decision making

Source: Charles W.L. Hill and Gareth R. Jones, *Strategic Management: An Integrated Approach, fourth edition*

> It is not clear … that any kind of business could fit the virtue model. [It] distinguishes between the internal and external good of practices. The virtues help us to achieve the internal good of a practice (e.g., effective teaching in academia); external goods such as wealth inhibit the development of those virtues. Business necessarily involves a focus on the external good of wealth, and so precludes the virtues.

Consequently, *Blackwell's* explains that what managers need from business ethics is 'an orderly way to think through the moral implications of a policy decision – a perspective and a language for appraising the alternatives available from an ethical [that is, a *deontic*-objective] point of view.' A top-selling strategy compendium similarly informs us that business ethics is about 'the codes of behaviour over and above everyday behaviour that professional and business people agree among themselves constitute the proper way to deal with the general public and each other.' A leading strategy text explains what business ethics should subsequently do in the 'model of ethical decision making' reproduced in Figure 5.1.

In management and strategy an ethical standpoint consequently means taking an objective ethical position, identifying how action may impinge upon 'stakeholders', evaluating stakeholder rights relative to general or external moral principles, and then using the outcomes of this analysis to provide restrictive boundaries. Business ethics is thus devoted to codifying general principles, about the study and development of collective charters that provide rules enforceable by objective bodies for individual people, organizations, industries and professions to act in accordance with. On this view, ethics is nothing to do with *arete* or subjectification. Indeed, we are told by leading texts that individuals cannot 'create their own morality'; that 'the managers role if it were derived from ethical theory would focus on society and other individuals rather than on self-interest.' Why this particular constitution should be the case may be better understood by considering the history that business ethics acknowledges. *Blackwell's* tells us that while the field is 'at least as old as commerce itself, in the modern period [and it is from here that their discussion begins] we can date it from the industrial revolution.' Given this point of origin, it may be no surprise that the establishment of business ethics 'piggybacks' upon the particularly Modernist views of this period.

As Chapter 2 outlined, the seventeenth and eighteenth centuries represent Modernism's first flowering. Thinkers here sought to move beyond reliance on tradition and custom and the acceptance of individual difference with regard to the constitution and purpose of all things, including humans. Newton's method was increasingly applied to the 'human race' so as to abstract the general characteristics of the 'species' and difficult to measure particularities were put to one side or seen as 'secondary'. These general characteristics were then used to establish universal 'tables' comprising categories and measures that could be used as universal backdrops against which particular cases could be assessed. Rather than constellations of unique relationships within particular communities, people became discrete objects *subject to general laws and norms*. Medical science developed general norm tables by averaging the data gathered in Modern bureaucratic hospitals and clinics, institutions that in turn administered life on the basis of the norms thus defined. Psychiatry and 'psychology' did the same by studying cases and gathering statistics in asylums run according to bureau-cratic principles, while 'criminology' drew from centrally organized penal systems. Indeed, the belief that society as a whole could be seen in this way (with bureaucracy as *the* form of organizing and where an individual's behaviour could be detached from his circumstances and traditions and iso-lated as a 'case' to be judged against general laws, where the common ideals and procedures for operations in society could be specified in advance), sup-ported the belief in a science of ethics that worked toward the provision of general norms of moral action. Consequently, in the period that business ethics takes to be its origin, the word 'moral' only pertains to what is *univer-sally* good or *generally* right, and ethics is correspondingly defined as the science of 'how we ought to live', with an emphasis on the general 'we'.

Modernist developments also added further to the advance of codes of conduct. Given Modernity's dismissal of the influence of 'surface' traditions and the belief in liberty and equality, general codes of behaviour became a necessary social component. Without recourse to the guidance of tradition, belief in some overriding restrictions or rules of practice, rules not thought subjective or infringing upon 'basic human rights or norms', became neces-sary. Hence, in addition to general laws of normality, *common codes* of prac-tice outlining patient's or criminals rights, doctor's responsibilities and so forth, became increasingly commonplace.

By the nineteenth century the development of common norms and common codes led thinkers like Sidgwick to declare that a new 'ethical science' was arising from the application of 'the same disinterested curio-sity to which we chiefly owe the great discoveries of physics.' Indeed, Modernism appeared, by this time, to have gone a long way toward fill-ing the gap left by the dismissal of traditional beliefs. The eighteenth and nineteenth centuries' ethical doctrines matched developments in other sciences in rejecting the Aristotelian view of people as having a specific *telos* comprising their many individual roles that implied case-specific ways of acting toward particular ends. At the same time, the Modern bureaucratic/triangular way of seeing, with general norms below and detached objective observation points above particular instances, encouraged seeing ethics as the perfection of general codes as opposed to the development of a particular arete toward a specific *telos*. Moreover, the Modern perspective, mixed with the egalitarian and self-sacrificing Christian vision of the period, saw Modernity dismiss an *aretaic ethic* as 'selfish'. In fact, an *aretaic* approach came to be regarded as not really ethics at all. It was, subsequently, forgotten.

With ethics separated out from an individual's particular being, the idea of ethical codes, missions or values as things that could be objectively measured, generalized, abstracted and transferred to others from the outside-in, best-practice style, became possible, then prevalent, and eventually the only way of thinking an organization's ethics.

2   The historical limits of business ethics

When ethics emerged as something that management should be concerned with (according to *Blackwell's* 'with Baumhart's revealing 1961 study,' the first to show 'that ethical issues and problems were important because they were found in every industry, in most companies, and on all levels of the managerial pyramid'), it reflected the heritage described above. Its influences are limited to the Modernist top-down triangular perspective and the subsequent quest for general codes outlining common norms. *Arete* is not part of its consciousness. After business ethics arose as 'a field in its own right' in the 1960s, it looked back to the halcyon days of the eighteenth and nineteenth centuries for an origin. Correspondingly, its development mirrors the fate of ethics in general since this period (see Chapter 2) and business ethics subsequently mirrors its limitations with regard to having practical effect. This chapter explores three such limitations:

1   Business ethics' attempts to outline essential goods and to satisfy all people led to approaches that were *difficult to apply to a company's particular direction*.
2   It also led to approaches that were *so bland as to be next to meaningless*.
3   Then, in an attempt to take a firmer stance, business ethics reverted back to the economic logic of efficiency that *added nothing more to the economic models* that companies were already using.

It then outlines an alternative way of thinking about an organization's ethics.

Limited application

Stakeholder theory, which is claimed to be based on utilitarian principles and maximizing the happiness of all concerned, is currently business ethics' most highly developed approach with respect to actively influencing an organization's decisions. Stakeholder theory advocates writing down an organization's duties to those potentially effected by its future development. Its limitations may be explored with reference to the most widely regarded mission statement outlining a corporation's duties with regard to stakeholders: Johnson & Johnson's *Credo*. The *Credo* is indeed something that J&J see as a very important guide to their decision making. Its prominence has contributed greatly to J&J's deserved reputation as one of the world's most ethical companies.

At the end of 1982, J&J fell victim to industrial terrorists who claimed to have injected cyanide into an unspecified number of Tylenol capsules. Seven people in the Chicago area died. A leading strategy textbook outlines what happened next:

> J&J immediately withdrew all Tylenol capsules from the US market, at an estimated cost to the company of $100 million. At the same time the company embarked on a comprehensive communication effort targeted at the pharmaceutical and medical communities. By such means, J&J successfully presented itself to the public as a company that was willing to do what was *right*, regardless of the cost. As a consequence, the Tylenol crisis enhanced rather that diminished J&J's image. Indeed, because of its actions, the company was able to regain its status as a market leader within months.

The *Credo* (shown below), it was argued, had shown J&J the way. However, in February 1986 another person died in New York after taking a tainted Tylenol capsule and many commentators revisited the case. In 1983, shortly after the first crisis, J&J had developed 'caplets', smooth-coated capsule shaped tablets that could not be penetrated with a foreign substance. Some now argued that if J&J's first responsibility really was to 'doctors, nurses, patients and mothers and fathers' (see the first line of the Credo), then the capsules should have been replaced with caplets. James Burke, then chairman of J&J countered that if 'we get out of the capsule business, others will get into it' and that to do so would be, in any case, a 'victory for terrorism'. Others were more cynical, pointing to J&J's huge investments in capsule-making facilities, a survey that 59 per cent of capsule users would not be willing to switch to caplets, and projections that such a move would result in $150 million pre-tax charge against first-quarter earnings and cost the company between 60 and 80 cents a share. These things, they argued, made doing 'what was right' seem like the wrong thing to do. It was claimed that, in reality, J&J's 'final responsibility' to 'stockholders' (first line of the final paragraph) had triumphed over their 'first'.

OUR CREDO

We believe our first responsibility is to the doctors, nurses and patients, to mothers and
fathers and all others who use our products and services.
In meeting their needs everything we do must be of high quality.
We must constantly strive to reduce our costs in order to maintain reasonable prices.
Customers' orders must be serviced promptly and accurately.
Our suppliers and distributors must have an opportunity
to make a fair profit.

We are responsible to our employees, the men
and women who work with us throughout the world.
Everyone must be considered as an individual.
We must respect their dignity and recognize their merit.
They must have a sense of security in their jobs.
Compensation must be fair and adequate and
working conditions clean, orderly and safe.
We must be mindful of ways to help our employees fulfill
their family responsibilities.

Employees must feel free to make suggestions and complaints.
There must be equal opportunity for employment, development
and advancement for those qualified.
We must provide competent management, and their actions
Must be just and ethical.

We are responsible to the communities in which we live and work
and to the world community as well.
We must be good citizens – support good works and charities
and bear our fair share of taxes.
We must encourage civic improvements and better health and education.
We must maintain in good order
the property we are privileged to use,
protecting the environment and natural resources.

Our final responsibility is to our stockholders.
Business must make a sound profit.
We must experiment with new ideas.
Research must be carried on, innovative programs, developed
and mistakes paid for.
New equipment must be purchased, new facilities provided
and new products launched.
Reserves must be created to provide for adverse times.
When we operate according to these principles,
the stockholders should realize a fair return.

Johnson & Johnson
This credo has been reproduced courtesy of Johnson & Johnson

But is it really a drug company's role to act as 'big brother'? Surely all J&J
could do was offer people advice and alternatives, then it was up to the individual? If J&J had done all that these critics seem to have expected it would

soon be bankrupted, which would compromise all of its other stakeholder responsibilities. The FDA (Federal Drug Authority) concluded that it should not direct or pressure J&J into such an action, and that the decision was 'a matter of J&J's own business judgement.' In any event, it is hard to see how the *Credo*, on its own, could provide J&J with the 'right' judgement as to what the company ought to do.

In addition to recognizing such limitations with stakeholder approaches, companies are also increasingly concerned about what statements like 'we are responsible to our employees' in their codes can be taken to mean. As organizations increasingly act across national boundaries, notions of 'responsibility' are problematized. Does this mean that companies are 'responsible' to employees in all the countries in which they operate in the same ways? Should these employees' healthcare benefits, insurance and even salaries be the same? These increasingly asked questions, in combination with increasingly bold lawyers and litigious interest groups, are now making companies balk before committing their duties to paper.

The above examples do not suggest that J&J is an unethical company (their commitment to their credo has been exemplary). Rather, they illustrate the limitations of any general *deontic* ethical code. The proliferation of information technology, mobile populations, multi-national corporations and so on, has brought about an environment where different cultures and traditions wash across one another, resulting in the disintegration of the set homogeneous socio-cultural canvas and the objective viewpoint with which such codes work best. The increasing acceptance of diverging interests and the recognition that measuring and comparing 'stakeholder utility' is impossible, make balancing stakeholder benefits an unworkable and ultimately frustrating objective.

Limited meaning

From a Modernist perspective there seem two responses possible upon recognizing the limitations described above: either make codes more detailed, so as to represent every eventuality; or boil things down to essentials, so that they do not specify particular responsibilities that could be criticized or prosecuted. The first response has resulted in some mission statements so convoluted that they could not possibly be remembered or applied. And still they fall short of anticipating every eventuality in a complex world. The second response has been more commonplace. However, the drive to create shorter, more abstract but still all-encompassing mission statements and corporate values, tied up as it has been with most companies using the same set of consultant advisors and the effects of internal group-think, has made 'mission' the past decade's most popular target for corporate satirists. Most prominent is Scott Adams, creator of the Dilbert cartoon strip. Adam's combination of biting wit and keen knowledge of corporate foibles make his commentaries strike a chord with most managers. About mission statements he writes:

If your employees are producing low-quality products that no sane person would buy, you can often fix that problem by holding meetings to discuss your Mission Statement. A Mission Statement is defined as 'a long awkward statement that demonstrates management's inability to think clearly.' All good companies have one . . . such as this: 'We will produce the highest quality products, using empowered team dynamics in a new Total Quality paradigm until we become the industry leader.'

Other Dilbert examples of inanely meaningless, but plausible given the conditions described above, missions include: 'We enhance stockholder value through strategic business initiatives by empowered employees working in new team paradigms.' As with most of Adams' humour, it is funny because it is scarily close to the truth. (Indeed, Adams has posed as a management consultant and impressed management boards with mission statements like 'to scout profitable growth opportunities in relationships, both internallly and externally, in emerging, mission inclusive markets, and explore new paradigms and then filter, communicate and evangelize the findings').

Case Box 5.1, at the outset of this chapter (p. 183), provided one example of an organization attempting to import a general, abstract statement that meets external criteria while not disenfranchising anyone or anything which ends up 'fudging' and saying less, but there are many others that could be pointed to. The root of most of the problems experienced by one company that we worked with recently could be traced to its mission statement:

> To satisfy the needs of our customers, shareholders and employees with *exceptional business efficiency* and *superior service*.

It a turned out that this statement confused most employees (let alone customers) as they sought to make real decisions because it did not acknowledge its internal paradox. For example, customer service and repair teams claimed that it gave them unexplained mixed messages. If they were called out to a repair job at 5 p.m., should they respond and bill the overtime to the company (= superior service) or leave the job until the next morning (= greater efficiency)?

In a similar vein, other commentators have criticized mission statements like these for setting vacuity and indecisiveness in stone. One recent newspaper article in the *Guardian* bemoaned missions such as a gas company's 'Piping gas for you'; a university's 'Setting new challenges, creating new opportunities'; and a government department's 'Investing as people' as pointless on grounds of the 'inversion test'. If you invert sentences such as these you get a ridiculous statement for the organization (that is, 'Not setting new challenges …'), indicating that a company has not really made a substantive decision regarding its character.

Not unlike the criticisms levelled at Modern art as it disappeared toward essential nothingness (see Chapter 2, p. 57), the codes, values and mission statements promoted by a business ethics influenced by Modernism are now criticized for attempting to satisfy all without offending any. Criticized for being so devoid of meaning for the particular organizations they seek to serve that they are little use as positive guides to action. Subsequently, many researchers and practitioners now see these kinds of mission and stakeholder ethics as 'wishy-washy,' 'blandening,' 'empirically problematic' or worse 'fundamentally misguided and incapable of providing better governance.'

Limited development

Also paralleling the history of Modern ethics, business ethics' search for a universal overriding good that appears more tangible, justifiable and practically applicable in response to the problems described above has seen it fall back upon the economic logic that many thought it might overcome. In an attempt to provide more concrete or less 'wishy-washy' guidelines for business ethics, the language of economics is blended with utilitarianism. 'Moral common sense is [at the end of the day] disciplined by a single dominant objective: maximizing net expectable utility,' explains the *Blackwell Encyclopedia*, and this generally 'manifests itself as a commitment to the social value of market forces.'

Primeaux and Stieber's recent output in business ethics's leading journals is exemplary in this regard. They advocate identifying the 'principles of business itself' as firm foundations upon which 'the ethics of business should be drawn.' These principles turn out to be 'defined in terms of neo-classical economics' because 'the firm's ethics should be economically determined.' Unsurprisingly, the principles or foundations of business ethics turn out to be 'economic efficiency,' 'profit maximization' and 'opportunity cost.' Consequently, to find a 'common ethical language,' Primeaux and Stieber argue that we must understand profit 'as a means of representing human achievement and social good' and define the 'inherent ethical absolutes of business in terms of economic efficiency.' Thus, we may situate 'ethical decision making for business within opportunity-cost decision making,' and 'reserve judgment, in the final analysis, to the market.' Or, in other words, 'accept profit maximization and the efficiencies of profit maximization as the primary standard of judgment.'

Business ethics' interpretation of history frames it as the provision of general codes to be applied from above and spoken in the Modern terms of the general 'utility of all concerned.' In the final analysis, because agreement as to what this tangibly might mean, and how it might then have practical effect, has proved elusive, the 'general good' arrived at amounts to 'efficiency'. Hence, it is easy to see why strategists should now find business ethics, thus conceived, to not be a particularly useful concept. It is a logic, based on the micro-economic theory of the firm and offering only common assumptions about the way that capitalist economies work, that provides no guidance for differentiated or 'value-added' decision making, a 'hygiene factor'. It brings us, back to where this chapter began, the idea that ethics only makes sense to business if it is subsumed into economics. That, as Mathur and Kenyon's recently published *Creating Value: Shaping Tomorrow's Business* claims, 'financial performance must be the ultimate yardstick of business' and that 'business merely has an ethically neutral, financial reason for existing.'

Companies are people too?

No wonder, given the limitations described above, that the manager described on p. 183 should feel disappointed after having gone though a 'value development' exercise with expensive consultants only to find that his organization needs some 'added-value values' to *really* guide its strategy. Recognizing the limitations of a solely *deontic* code-based approach is one reason why people have begun to wonder whether the *aretaic* channel might be worth re-connecting with to provide such guidance. Another reason is that there is growing evidence to suggest that people do not conceive of companies as lists of objective stakeholder responsibilities, mission statements or lists of values. Rather, it appears that they tend to make sense of them as if they were like other *people*. Hence, while they are increasingly concerned with a corporation's efforts to be ethical in a *deontic* sense, people are at once happy to accept that different companies will, and in fact should, have a 'face' that is unique. They do not expect a corporation, any more than an individual, to be able to be all things to all people, and do not seem to trust them when they attempt to be.

For example, market research carried out into terrestrial television channels in the UK has revealed that people attributed particular characters and, correspondingly, different standards to each channel (see Case Box 5.2). Perhaps this highlights a Postmodern paradox: that in a poly-dimensional world it is better to have a particularly clear sense of one's different 'personality' so that customers can make well-informed choices as to who they want to connect or relate to, rather than attempting to represent or capture all things or try dutifully to be all things to all people?

Perhaps this is why Jaguar never really suffered the problems that other cars did as Modernist essentializing practices led to their designs looking increasingly bland and 'samey' (see Case Box 2.1 on p. 75). The aim of their 'focus groups' was not to determine the average of what a cross-section of people all thought was 'good' (or at least 'not bad'), but to ensure that at least 90 per cent of such a group could *identify* a new prototype, without badging, as *a Jaguar* – as a continuation of the particular Jaguar 'personality'. Whether the car appealed to the majority of the people that made up the focus group was not so important.

By the same token, when British Airways unveiled its new 'global identity' in June 1997 the multi-ethnic liveries that were daubed on tail fins and promotional materials over the traditional Union Jacks were meant to consolidate BA's sense of itself as 'the world's favourite airline' in the new 'global village'. It seemed to make good sense. But by the year 2000 the fins were being repainted in red, white and blue and ads were featuring odes to 'Britishness'. Apparently, it was not the protests from within the UK (from Margaret Thatcher down) that hurt BA as much as the protests from groups of Asian customers. They felt that the Union Jack had personified a *particular* type of service that they wished to associate with and that BA's inconsistency was messing with this. Seemingly learning from this failed attempt to be all things to all people, Lufthansa was recently reported to be putting pressure on British Midland (in which it had a 20 per cent stake) not to drop the word 'British' from its name as it sought to expand its presence in the marketplace. Lufthansa's management believed that the British association connected the company to a *unique and particular **ethos***.

Case Box 5.2   Channel 5

Channel 5, Britain's newest terrestrial (non-cable) television channel, has a problem. It, unlike its competitors, does not have a personality. Consequently, viewers do not know what to expect from it and, subsequently, seem less likely to 'tune in' or build a relationship with it.

British researchers have recently demonstrated that viewers tend to have clear images in their minds about the personalities of the television channels they watch. BBC1 was seen as staid and 'establishment', but reliable – 'the Queen Victoria of channels'. BBC2 was seen as an 'enthusiastic educator – something between an old professor and a trendy teacher, with a touch of social worker keen to save the world.' ITV was seen as jolly, lively and 'more normal', but also a bit 'dodgy', with something of a 'used-car business' about it. Channel 4 was identified as a 'Richard Branson' – entrepreneurial, dashing and risk-taking, often pushing the boat out a bit too far, but then this suited its character.

The researchers also found that people do not apply the same ethical standards to each channel. For example, it appeared that one reason for making a customer complaint was if a programme delivered something *at odds* with the customer's anticipations of the channel's personality, thereby causing dissonance that led to the relationship between viewer and channel to be questioned. A racy programme shown on Channel 4 would receive less complaints than the same programme shown on BBC1 – partly because of the profile of the people tuning in to each (those watching Channel 4 were likely people who had already decided that their ethos was okay with them), but also due to 'viewer expectations'. Using the same logic, when Channel 4 recently took over the rights to show cricket matches from the BBC, it knew that it would have to show them in a more dynamic, less traditional way – otherwise viewers would wonder 'what on earth is happening to Channel 4?' The message seems to be that customers tolerate difference more than inconsistency.

Channel 5's problem is that their programming seems particularly inconsistent: an unruly mix of half-baked game shows, 'soft-porn' and 1960s wildlife programmes. It is hard to see any positive pattern to it and thus it is hard for any significant segment of the population to 'connect' with. This is partly due to circumstances beyond its control. It is young and it could be said that it is still finding its way – no infant arrives with a personality completely intact). Plus, just after a highly successful launch where the Spice Girls were used as the channel's spokespeople (indicating a bright, optimistic, youthful image), the 5 Spices became 4, and those 4 seemed to go their own separate ways, making it difficult for Channel 5 to build upon the initial success of the launch.

However, confusion still seemed to rein regarding what 5's character should be 18 months after the 'personality research' described above came out. Channel 5 executives recently announced that the channel was going to reposition itself dramatically – moving away from its salacious programming to become a 'family broadcaster emphasizing popular entertainment.' However, this did seem to have been compromised somewhat when one Channel 5 senior executive was reported to be demanding that his channel be allowed to show more explicit sex.

Channel 5 is not the only channel that is working on its personality. ITV has recently launched separate cable-only channels, with related but slightly different personalities, that will allow it to show a more diverse range of programming without compromising its 'flagship' identity, and the BBC is reportedly not entirely happy about the staid Queen Victoria image. The BBC's public service remit is to 'serve all people', and, in response to what its own research defines as an increasingly fragmented and multicultural market, different delivery methods and more consumer choice, it is currently asking itself how, BBC1 in particular, should change its 'personality' to better match the new environment.

1   Is Channel 5 doing the right thing in its attempts to 'rebrand' itself?
2   If you were advising the BBC, what would you suggest they do about BBC1's person-ality? Should they get rid of the 'Queen Vic' identity in order to move with the times?
3   What can we learn about organizations and strategy making from this research into the way that people relate to television channels?

Sources: This case draws on 'Who's Your Favourite Television Channel', *The Times*; '"Channel Filth" Plays the Family Card', *Guardian;* 'Channel 5 Boss Demands Explicit Sex on Television', *Independent*

---

3   *Ethos*: the aretaic alternative

Ethic. A. adj. (now usually ETHICAL.) 1. relating to morals (i.e., 1. Concerned with the distinction between good and bad or right or wrong, 2. Adhering to conventionally adhered to stan-dards of conduct). 2. Treating of moral questions and of ethics as a science. B. sb. 1.a. The science of morals. b. A scheme of moral science. 2. The department of study concerned with the principles of human duty.
Ethos. character, a person's nature or disposition 1. The char-acteristic spirit, prevalent tone of sentiment of a people or community; the 'genius' (i.e., distinctive spirit) of an institution or system.

The Comprehensive Oxford English Dictionary

Ethics and ethos have come to have very different meanings, despite having a common root in the Greek ἦθος. As we saw with a number of words in

Part I, Modernism's quest for greater representative accuracy combined with a desire to identify universal norms has seen the meaning of ethics become what previous sections have demonstrated to be the basis of our limited understanding of what business ethics is. While the recent emphasis on business ethics in corporations has been useful and helpful for many, the limitations associated with the *deontic* code-based approach that it promotes and the recognition that people seem to connect to organizations as if they were particular people is now encouraging some to look to *aretaic* alternatives. Alternatives that are about developing upon a *characteristic spirit* or *distinctive 'genius'* rather than conforming to the same standards and common duties.

The development of these alternatives to business ethics draw from the rethinking of ethics in general that has taken place over the past few decades, where Modernity's emphasis on foundational rule-based codes has been increasingly questioned. Prominent among the questioners is Michel Foucault. Foucault questioned the 'search for a form of morality acceptable to everybody, in the sense that everybody should submit to it.' He found that with the Postmodern idea that an *essential* human 'self' may not be a natural given, the view of morality as obedience to a code of rules was now declining. Foucault believed that we must take advantage of this breech by establishing an alternative approach to ethics, one where we 'give style to our characters by surveying all the strengths and weaknesses of our particular nature and fitting this into an artistic plan.' However, Foucault found that such an approach had been lost in our times. He consequently decided to seek such an alternative by looking prior to Modernity's dismissal of *arete* and forms of subjectification. He found himself drawn to the Ancient Greeks – particularly the ethics of Aristotle.

'Good,' Aristotle stated, could not be 'a common characteristic responding to one Idea,' as life contained too many different 'categories'. Subsequently, Aristotle sought to reaffirm the more common Greek understanding of ethics that Plato (with his view that 'goodness' could be a single form) had attempted to overcome. During the early phases of Modernity, Aristotle's thinking was targeted as symbolic of all that was wrong with the Premodern thinking. Moderns, firm in their newfound belief that the goal of science and philosophy was the discovery of *general* truths and *universal* propositions, were far more inspired by Plato's arguments for ideal forms that could be abstracted in order to direct general progress. Thus, 'Aristotelianism', the dominant mode of thought in the West until the seventeenth century, was dumped, and the Greek's approach to ethics, tarred with the Aristotelian brush, was thus forgotten. That it consequently remains largely untouched by Modern thought made Foucault think that it might be capable of stretching our thinking today. Perhaps the Greek's alternative thinking can also be revisited in order to provide an alternative theoretical basis with which to reconceptualize business ethics?

Aristotle began with the notion that the end of any action was *eudaimonia*, which translates as 'happiness', but in a quite particular sense. *Eudaimonia* is not 'pleasure' as Emotivists might see it, for it cannot be short-lived. And the happiness that Aristotle expected the virtuous actor to pursue was not, as the Utilitarians would have it, the whole world's 'general happiness'. It was rather the *individual* happiness of a particular actor. The *eudaimon* is thus the person who fulfils himself by achieving his 'heart's desire', and he who does so is, according to Aristotle, 'virtuous'. However, because Aristotle recognized that there are many ways people could fulfill themselves and thus many different ways they could pursue *eudaimonia*, to act in accordance with virtue depended on one's particular character or combination of characteristics. 'Virtue,' he therefore claimed, 'is a purposive disposition *relative to the individual.*'

Aristotle's *Ethics*, as we have seen in Chapter 2, consequently involved three elements:

- the unreflective individual;
- the individual as they could be if they fulfilled their particular character and purpose in life (*telos*); and
- the moral bearing that would allow one to 'fare well' toward this aim.

Ethics here, therefore, hinges upon knowing one's *telos*, an awareness that could only come from self-reflective contemplation or 'subjectification' – making oneself a subject of personal inquiry and reviewing what one knows about oneself and the traditions to which one relates. If one knows oneself, he is aware of what his particular character and subsequently his *telos* is, and 'is' can therefore indicate 'ought' with regard to what one must do to act ethically. Knowing one's *telos* would also enable one to know the difference between one's current abilities and what one could be, so that one could begin to contemplate the 'bearing' that could help them 'carry' themselves to their *telos*.

This individualized approach to ethics, combined with the fact that ethics was, for the Greeks, a practical subject, meant that general behavioural codes could not be appealed to. Because practice is contingent on the particularities of the situation faced, ethics could not be treated with the same clarity as mathematics or chemistry. However, in keeping with ancient notions of education (see Chapter 2), an individual's moral tutelage could be further furnished by stories, left to posterity, of virtuous people making particular decisions. However, these could not be imitated as 'best practice', they could only inspire one toward self-reflection and developing a sense of one's own virtuosity. Moral tutelage came from connecting these examples to one's own experiences and traditions and learning not by imitation but by comparison with one's own particular strengths and inspirations. Hence, ethical precepts or principles could only be related to specific situations by means of the sort of perception born of a *'prudence'* gained from a reflective understanding of one's *telos* and a familiarity with analogous situations.

'Prudence' required one to develop a teleological understanding by which one could keep 'faring well' on one's 'life journey'. This wayfaring, claimed Aristotle, could be informed by the 'Doctrine of the Mean'. This suggested that each individual virtuous act exists between two vices (for example', between a 'rash' and a 'cowardly' action exists a courageous one; or between 'bankruptcy' and 'self-serving' exists what company X must do to be ethical). However, this 'doctrine' could not provide general prescriptions either. Virtuosity was not about adhering to a universal behavioral mid-way point, but acting in accordance with one's particular disposition and abilities or one's own individual 'midway point'. The contemplative, virtuous person would know his character and his own particular limits when faced with a situation. He would also know which 'side of vice' he would more likely veer toward (was he more 'coward' or 'hothead') so that he could guard against this.

Consequently, we can say that Helmsperson X will be prudent, therefore virtuous, therefore morally correct, if upon confronting a particular helming situation he can:

1 know his purpose or *telos* as a helmsperson;
2 connect to the traditions and stories of what good helming might suggest in such a circumstance;
3 know what the two vices (for example, too ponderous or too rash) either side of a good action might be;
4 know how his disposition might lead him to one or other of these courses of ruin; and
5 know how his *particular* skill-set within this ought subsequently be put to good use.

This means that Helmsperson X might act in ways that are different than those chosen by Helmsperson Y or Z if they were faced with the same circumstances. Just as the characters of television channels described in Case Box 5.2 added to the community of television, all three added to the helming community. Because people would be aware of the different *ethos* of each, and the subsequent strengths and weakness of each, informed choices could be made as to which might best be chosen for particular purposes.

Knowing one's *telos* would enable one to know where best to direct their energies *and* the price one must pay for this direction, because connecting to a specific *telos* means making choices (the great blues trumpeter, for example, will find that this ability will often distract him from attending to life's other pleasures or even other styles of trumpet). Consequently, the virtuous person, according to Aristotle, had an *eudaimonia* that was subject to imperfection. That is to say, one could not be master of all trades or generally good. Aristotle illustrated this by noting that everybody knows that 'Those who have a great many friends and greet everybody familiarly are felt to be friends of nobody.' Aristotle claimed that if one's network (of interests or friends) became too large then they would veer into the vice of obsequiousness. Here they would be faced with the joy of one friend or interest or 'stakeholder' conflicting with the sorrow of another, thus being unable to be a virtuous actor. The difficulty that the Greeks would have with the application of stakeholder theory is readily apparent.

The claim, quite logical from a Modern (or Judeo-Christian) perspective, that this approach to ethics is purely self-serving and anarchic may be countered by noting that *ethos*, with a subtle difference of intonation, also meant 'custom'. *Ethos* may be egotistical, but for the Greek's ego was wrapped up in building with manners and traditional links with one's past and one's communities. An individual character always implied a particular series of relationships – with friends, family, workmates and the community at large – and the traditions embodied in these. Instead of Modernity's scientific approach which separated out the individual as a discrete object subject to essential general principles, people here were conceived as dynamic constellations that could be worked upon. The Ancients took for granted a view of the self not as something pre-given to keep pure and unsullied (as in the Christian conception of soul or a Modern material object), but as constituted by one's particular developing community of relationships and the subsequent 'crafting' of these (hence Foucault's analogy of the 'artistic plan'). Consequently, *eudaimonia* could not come from self-aggrandizement. It required securing the recognition of the communities within which one acted. Thus, the ultimate consideration for the prudent individual, having reflected on his character, is how his differences could *complement* those of his peers (for example, how Helmsperson X's differences complemented Helmsperson Y's).

Knowing one's strengths and limits, the virtuous person would seek to be recognized as different from others and at once be 'completely integrated', 'on good terms with himself' or 'self-loving' and thus consistent in his character. This would enable him or her to win the recognition and trust of others within the wider community. Consequently, for the Greeks, virtuosity was characterized by an effort to give one's own life a unique story in which one could recognize oneself, be recognized by others and in which 'posterity could find an example'. But this example could never be *the* generic 'best practice' example.

A Postmodern return to an Aristotelian *ethos*

The influence of this thinking on the likes of Heidegger, Nietzsche and Foucault is clear. Heidegger's half existentialist idea of 'throwness' – that we have choices but at the same time these choices are limited by our being cast in particular directions by our past individual connections and traditions – is a notion that we will explore in greater detail in Chapter 7. Nietzsche, whose belief that universal codes could only ever be artificial and limit constructions was discussed in Chapter 2, also believed that the Greek attitude toward a personal ethics offered interesting ways of thinking beyond Modernism. Inspired by the Presocratic philosopher Diogenes, Nietzsche liked to remark that rather than general codes, 'what is truly irrefutable', in any philosophy, is what is 'personal' and that 'image of any individual could be conveyed with *three anecdotes*,' more than with any number of general principles.

Following Nietzsche, Foucault argued that 'arts of existence' had been lost as Christianity and then Humanism's focus on commonality downplayed individual difference. Here a self-ethics could only be equated with self-absorption, self-centeredness and irrationality. Thus, the pre-Christian Greek idea of the relation with oneself and the nurturing or crafting of this relationship also particularly inspired him. In contrast to an approach to ethics that provoked the self to define itself in terms of a system of rules posited as universal, this was an attitude that enjoined a commitment to the elaboration of an 'oeuvre [or body of work] that carries certain aesthetic values and meets certain stylistic criteria.' A process of shaping and developing the self according to personal standards in relation to particular communities.

Not seeing a dichotomy between being self-focussed and community-minded, the ethics that Foucault subsequently promoted (which he termed 'self-aesthetics') did not see the individual as separate from social relations. Foucault noted that 'the pleasures of the other' must be seen *in conjunction* with the pursuit of a self-aesthetics, concluding that self-aesthetic practices are not something that the individual invents by himself, but patterns that an individual finds in his culture that he must work with. For Foucault as for the Greeks, ethics or *ethos* is thus about 'deportment', about finding a way of 'carrying oneself' in a community in a manner that is distinctive enough to enable others to recognize you as a member of the community *and* think you exemplary in your difference; about leaving an impression so as to stand out *and* complimenting a community so as to be remembered favorably.

Moral philosopher Alasdair MacIntyre gives good reasons why Foucault and other's recovery of *ethos* may be pertinent now. He argues that those who sought to apply the Modern methods to morality created an unresolvable tension. In a humanistic manner typical of the times, they believed that everyone had the same potentiality, disconnecting the way an individual 'is' from implying how they 'ought' to act. Thus, they took the first and the last elements of Aristotle's ethical scheme: the untutored individual and the moral precepts that allow him to pass from this to something better, but wished to remain silent about the second, silent about *telos* or particular ends. Hence Moderns required a general, secular end that appeared neutral and disinterested and, as we have seen, this turned out to be 'efficiency'.

Consequently, MacIntyre claims that we now possess only a simulacrum of morality. We continue to talk and act as though we have recourse to frameworks for thinking about and resolving moral issues but, in reality, moral debates can find no terminus. Moral questions thus end up going unresolved or being answered in terms of an impersonal economic efficiency. MacIntyre asserts that as we recognize that removing particular traditions and individual ends from morality results only in anarchic individualism hemmed by homogenizing and 'blandening general codes' that defer substantial debates, we must return to an Aristotelian ethics. 'Blandening general codes' seems to be where the emphasis on ethics and values in management and strategy has thus far led us. Perhaps such a return to an Aristotelian ethics or *ethos* might also provide a means of offering organizations something that they can use positively, rather than restrictively, to inform them as to *particular* strategic directions?

Ethos driven strategy

Twofold arguments concerning the good and bad are put forward by those who philosophize. Some say that good is one thing and bad another, but others say they are the same, and that a thing might be good for some persons but bad for others, or at one time good and another time bad for the same person. I myself side with those who hold the later opinion.

The *Dissoi Logoi*, author unknown, Fifth century BC

How might the idea of recovering an *aretaic* approach to ethics and the analogy that an organization is like an individual character, distinctive spirit or particular genius, positively influence an organization's development?

At the outset it would encourage organizations to base action not on ethical questions like 'what is expected of us?', 'how can we conform?' and 'how do we act in accordance?', but instead to focus them upon questions such as:

- 'Who are we?'
- 'If our organization was a person, who or what would it be like?'
- 'How and why is this different from the 'personality' of our competitors?'
- When faced with particular circumstances, 'How must we act in order to be true to or consistent with our character, personality or "distinctive spirit"?'

Ethos-driven strategy would consequently begin with a desire for those within an organization to know 'itself', develop its own 'artistic plan', 'oeuvre' or 'style'. Actions would be scrutinized less from the perspective of how they directly effect external stakeholders and more on the degree to which they flow from and reinforce an internal character. Hence, organizations would not seek to please everyone. For example, customers' would not always be right (some customers' particular wants cannot be met while staying true to Company X's virtues and so should be referred on to others within the community, like Company Y or Z, whose character is more in tune with such demands). An *aretaic* approach would, in this way, encourage organizations to develop and promote 'their legitimate strangeness' (to appropriate René Char, Foucault's favourite poet).

How could an organization's 'legitimate strangeness', character or *ethos* be further developed? The following paragraphs explore two ways. The first, which picks up on this chapter's earlier mentioned example of the financial services company that decided it needed 'added-value values' (which we shall call *Virtue Finance* for the purposes of this discussion), comes by way of Diogenes, Nietzsche and Aristotle. The second draws upon Deleuze's summary of Foucault's attempt's to 'think differently' about ethics.

Returning to *Virtue Finance*, which found that almost all of its 'values' were shared by its competitors (that is, they were 'hygiene factors'), how might one begin to develop its differentiated *ethos* (or 'added-value values')? Nietzsche and Diogenes' notion a character being able to be captured in 'three anecdotes' is one way. Exploring its one somewhat unique corporate value, 'humour', and probing what *Virtue Finance* people actually took that to mean beyond the abstract adjective, teased out stories like this:

> There is a particular broker who is a 'Spurs [Tottenham Hotspurs Football Club] supporter who always calls us as opposed to our bigger rivals, even though he's advised otherwise, because he enjoys the mid-week banter with the people here who support other London teams. The banter usually takes longer than the business!

This may not seem much. However, it indicates several differentiating virtues. For example, virtue finance is about:

- developing personal relationships with its buyers and suppliers;
- keeping staff for lengthy periods so it can develop these relationships;
- not being large and gray and all business;
- knowing how not being the biggest is a weakness, but it's smallness can be made a virtue or a strength if they work at it, and so on.

Thus, a suitable way to begin to reflect on and understand an organization's *ethos* would be through highlighting a few such anecdotes towards developing a profile or 'oeuvre' (a 'body of work') rather than a restrictive code. Such exemplars may be sought in reflection upon the organization's:

- traditions and history;
- stories of how employees have done, or do, things;
- key defining crises faced in the past and how it responded to these;
- ability to do things in the present as a result of this past;
- historical relations with others and how these shape its make-up;
- view of what it expects of itself; and
- image is perceived in contrast to others.

Such an oeuvre is likely, due to the personal idiosyncrasy of its elements, to be more memorable and more difficult for competitors to replicate than a code or list of principles.

Applying Aristotle's doctrine of the mean can further develop an organization's *ethos*. If anecdotes, like the one from *Virtue Finance* above, characterize virtues, what actions either side of them indicate vices?

On the one side, the abovementioned broker could call virtue finance and be met with a *surly matter-of-factness*. The effect of this action would be more damaging to X's standing than the same action would be to another company's (for example, a bigger, cost-focussed organization) because coming from X such behaviour is unexpected and confusingly inconsistent.

On the other side, if X's small talk became *too familiar* it could seem unprofessional.

This *familiarity* is likely the 'side of vice' that X's disposition is more likely to veer toward. Thus, it needs its people to be particularly on guard against it.

The profile that emerges from such a process would work strategically as does a novelist's sketch of a character. This usually incorporates a profile of a character, his or her purpose and key historical relationships with others, in order to enable an author to begin with an idea of the range of reactions a character ought to have to situations that emerge as the narrative unfolds. Hence virtue finance knows, for example, that its *ethos* ought to promote a strategy that:

- involves the brokers with whom it has close relationships with in some capacity in evaluating its future development; and
- is wary when considering growth opportunities and efficiency measures (such as timing telephone calls) if they impinge on its virtues (for example, the personal touch; long-standing relationships).

And *Virtue Finance* knows, in this manner, how its particular character should be maintained and developed as it has some idea of what type of character it is and can easily imagine how this type of *ethos* would develop over time.

This ethos-driven approach might be given more structure through the application of Deleuze's summary of Foucault's investigations into thinking ethics differently. Deleuze saw Foucault's work in terms of four 'folds of subjectification'. These folds distinguish an individual and are shaped differently by each subject, be it a society, field of knowledge, organization or person. But in each case it takes four folds to constitute a distinctive ethical whole.

1   The first fold concerns the *material part of the being* around which everything else folds. At a personal level, the Greeks saw this as the body and its pleasures, the *aphrodisia*. For Christians it was the flesh and its desires

and was treated very differently. An organization might question itself here along the lines of:

- What is the core business or resource/s around which everything hinges?
- How are these to be spent and restrained?
- What needs to be done to ensure that they are sustained and replenished?

2 Next is the fold of *power relations or the rules that one follows* as it is always according to particular rules that one monitors one's material being. Thus, it makes a difference whether one chooses to evaluate oneself in terms of natural, divine, scientifically rational or aesthetic values, for example. Here an organization may ask:

- What 'rules of living' are we bound by?
- What codes do we look up to and wish to evaluate ourselves against?
- What rules are applied for making decisions about our direction?

That codes are incorporated here indicates that an *ethos*-driven approach to strategy would not seek to dismiss general codes, credos or principles – its aim is rather to add to the ethical 'folds' that may be related to and to encourage seeing codes, in themselves, as not the be all and end all (see Case Box 5.4 at the end of this chapter, on p. 211).

3 The third fold is that of *knowledge*. How does an individual seek to know their self? For the Greeks this was primarily through contemplation about one's self and one's relations with friends, gods and traditions; for Christians it is more dependent upon one's relationship with God; for Modernists the truth of human workings will be revealed by science. Of this fold, an organization may ask:

- What relationships are particularly important to us in defining our self? (Again, this will require making choices and seeing certain relationships are more important, or bigger, than others – in the same way that the Premodern map in Chapter 2 showed the church and the homes as larger than they materially might be [see p. 34])
- Whose reactions allow us to see our self reflected?
- What research allows us to know ourselves and how we are seen by others?

4 The final fold is the *line of the outside*. This constitutes an 'interiority of expectation' in which the individual recognizes him or herself as different from others. For the Greeks, the aim here was to define a unique but complimentary and thus aesthetically pleasing life story. Organizations may correspondingly ask of themselves:

- What particular things do we (and don't we) do?
- How will this difference in the way that we carry ourselves enable us to be recognized?

- What do we see as our *telos* or particular *raison d'être*? How do we want to be remembered?
- What is this organization's style and how is that different from others?

This leads us back to, and should replenish thinking about, the first fold or the material core of the organization (see the digram below).

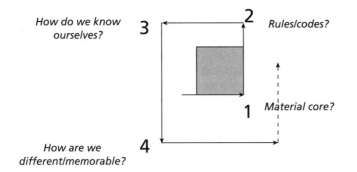

Underlying all of this is the simple idea that organizations are like characters, like particular people. When we as individuals relate to others we capture all this complexity easily. We understand that our friends have a particular ethos that indicates all sorts of things about them, but it may not be the same as our own. Because we know this, we have an idea of how they might act in particular situations. They do not always refer to codes of conduct, but we still consider them ethical, in their own way. If we wanted to describe them to another in anything more than a superficial sense, we would likely characterize them by relaying a few anecdotes. Organizations are like people too.

Mission revisited

This ethos-based way of looking also encourages us to revisit 'mission', a concept that was largely thrown out with the bathwater on account of examples of it becoming subject to the sort of satire described earlier and management's desire to quickly move on to 'the next big thing'. Mission statements were rightly derided as they were increasingly doled out by external consultants and academics rather than developed from within, and subsequently became increasingly bland, 'samey' and timid.

Our word 'mission' is a derivative of the Indo-European *(s)meit*, meaning to throw or send. One of the first senses of *meit* appears to have been to throw dung at a wall to dry for fuel, hence the word 'smite' from the meaning 'spot on the wall, where the dung strikes'. Stemming from this is the Latin *mittere* or *missus*, meaning to let go, to cause to go, to send, throw or

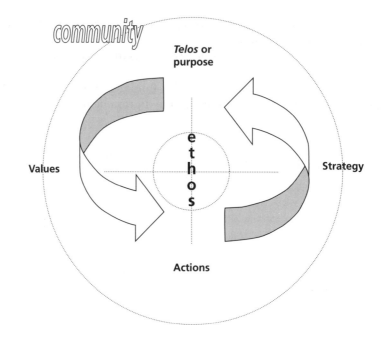

Figure 5.2 The circle of corporate ethos

Source: After A. Campbell, D. Young and M. Devine's Ashridge Mission Model in A. Campbell, D. Young and M. Devine, *A Sense of Mission*

cast. Hence the emergence of *mission* (the task on which one is sent or feels compelled to act out) and related words such as *missile* (a weapon thrown forward), *dismiss* (a sending away), *demise* (death, a sending away), *emit* (send forth), *permit* (send through) and *premise* (a foundation or proposition sent forth). Extrapolating this into an organizational context, one can see mission as the particular intent, spirit or 'genius' that constitutes an organization's trajectory that casts and carries it into the future in a particular direction toward its particular goals and targets. This is, of course, quite close to the concept of *ethos* being developed here. Perhaps the best framework for thinking about an organization's mission is that developed in the early 1990s at the Ashridge Management Centre in the UK. The Ashridge model outlines four elements that, if they reinforce one another to the point where the whole is greater than the sum of the parts, create a 'sense of mission' far more helpful than any grand mission statement. The organization whose '*behaviour standards*' match its '*purpose*' and whose particular '*values*' reinforce its '*strategy*' is generating this sense of mission whether it writes anything down or not.

We may return to it to inspire a further means for conceptualizing an alternative, ethos-based approach to an organization's ethics and, subsequently, their strategy. Here we may say that a strong ethos emerges if an organization's '*telos*' is reinforced by particular '*values*', which inspire particular 'actions' by employees which then both drive and reflect the organization's 'strategy' for working towards its *telos* (see Figure 5.2).

We can use this diagram to reflect on the success of the NZ Police's traditional *ethos*: 'To work with the community to maintain the peace' (see Case Box 5.1 on p. 183). These words reflect the *telos* of the force, convey a particular set of values, and a sense of how staff should act toward achieving a particular strategy. In a quick sentence it reflects the mission of the people who have served the force, conveying a particular *strategy*, a particular *purpose*, a particular set of *values*, and a sense of how staff *behave*. Over time these things have reinforced one another and gathered strength and meaning so that the 'mass' of mission or *ethos* that they embody is far more than the combined weight of the individual words mentioned above. And this ethos has been able to be replenished even as the community around them has developed. (*The Economist's* 'To take part in a severe contests between intelligence, which presses forward, and an unworthy, timid ignorance obstructing our progress,' which has served it since 1873, or the *Independent's* 'Great minds don't think alike,' are other good examples). You may further examine how the four elements can create a virtuous circle and generate a sense of *ethos* or, if they are out of alignment, create a virtuous circle and subsequent downward spiral, by working through Case Box 5.3 below.

Case Box 5.3 M&S – recreating a virtuous circle

Until the early 1990s, UK-based retailer Marks and Spencer (M&S) thrived with a purpose or telos that they articulated as:

To continually raise the standards of the working man and woman.

On the clothing side of their business they achieved this by following a *strategy* of working closely with local, mostly British, suppliers and developing long-standing relationships with them. These relationships enabled them to provide quality fashions that were by no means avant-garde but had a certain functionality and 'weight' that became a style in itself. This reinforced a set of *values* that one might, for want of better words, call a 'solid, dependable, decent Britishness' and complementary *actions* from staff who were experienced, knowledgeable, discrete and courteous. This fed back into the *strategy* of selling through high street stores that, while by no means the swankiest of salons, had a particular up-market department store gravity to them. Whether you liked M&S or not, you could not deny that they had an *ethos* and many people sought to associate with them, if not for all of their needs then at least for some.

However, the environment around M&S changed. New competitors entered the market place, either seeking to sell at a lower price through reducing costs by sourcing from outside of Europe, or moving into the high-end or the fashion market through leading-edge design, or by selling more units by mail or over the Internet. In the meantime, M&S had become sluggish and complacent about its traditional relationships. For example, they did not seem to work as closely with their suppliers on fabric or product development, and it was hard to see how 'raising the standards of working people' was served by *strategies* like their refusing to accept payment by credit card at a time when most people who worked used one.

As things deteriorated new executives were brought in. The easiest *strategy* for them to focus on was cost reduction. The easiest way to do this was to start sourcing from cheaper suppliers overseas. When traditional suppliers that lost business as a result protested, M&S blamed them for not having kept up with fashion. Those traditional M&S suppliers who remained were understandably nervous. The product quality in M&S stores diminished, and they were not particularaly 'fashionable' because M&S had lost the knack of working with suppliers to ensure this. And, in any case, new relationships like this took time to gel. This strategy also took M&S into realms where they could be accused of dealing with unscrupulous companies. M&S claimed to be unaware of their new supplier's links and past dealings. In any event, M&S still could not compete on cost because the fixed costs associated with their traditional stores and staff was always going to be higher than their new competitors. The 'British decency' *values* were compromised, staff morale was effected and how staff should *act* became less clear. Profits continued to decline. Younger executives and external consultants blamed the problem on M&S appealing to an older constituency (despite the fact that this was the fastest growing segment of the economy, in both number and spending power). The company would have to appeal to younger people as older people, they claimed, would die (which was true, although most of them not for another 40-odd years).

But younger people did not buy the fact that M&S could be a new character overnight, others did not see them as an authentic high fashion provider, and older customer segments felt disenfranchised. Profits continued to fall. In reaction, more costs were cut, HR spending was reduced, and more foreign suppliers incorporated. All of which further comprised the traditional values and *actions* of M&S employees. The *telos* of continually raising the standards of working people now seemed a long way off.

At the beginning of the twenty-first century, with new M&S initiatives being reported in the media every other day (from in-store cappuccino bars, to exclusive designer ranges, to an emphasis on fuller figures, to more exotic lingerie, to more sourcing of supply outside of Europe, to scrapping the traditional carrier bag), most would agree that M&S is very unsure of its *ethos* within the retailing community. Most would be hard pressed to say what M&S stands for (although the food side of the company, which could still be associated with the 'continually raising the standards of the working man and woman' *telos*, appears to have achieved this quite well). By not maintaining, working upon and developing key relationships while being true to their core ethos, a once virtuous circle has, over time, turned vicious for M&S.

1   Use the 'circle of corporate ethos' framework to depict the rise and fall of M&S.
2   If you were advising M&S in the year 2000, what would you suggest they should do to reinvigorate their once strong corporate ethos?

The limits of *ethos*: 'authenticity'

'Authenticity' can be taken two ways. Firstly, philosophers like Heidegger claim that to simply absorb the ways and traditions handed down by our friends, family and culture is to be inauthentic. To be 'authentic' means critically questioning how things like this influence your character and then, to some extent at least, consciously shaping your own identity in the light of this self-reflection. Taken this way, it might appear that the frameworks that may be used to develop a more individualized or *ethos*-driven approach to ethics, developed in the paragraphs above, would give corporations' license to do as they feel *and* then claim to be both ethical and authentic. However, while it is important for organizations to consciously reflect on their ethos if they are to be authentic, a second sense of the word 'authentic' and an increasingly networked society guards against organizations simply picking this or that *ethos* 'off the shelf'.

To be 'authentic' also means that your identity must be based on something genuine. It cannot therefore be invented out of thin air. It must be based on some characteristic. Indeed, in the words of David Lewis and Darren Bridger's recently published *The Soul of the New Consumer*, while it clearly helps in this day and age if a company's identity is connected with something creative and original, these creative or original aspects must connect to genuine aspects of the past, a particular:

- time, and/or
- place, and/or
- event or series of events,

in order for that identity to be 'authentic' and that company to be considered *credible*.

As Aristotle insisted, the virtuous person must reflect some consistency of action over time if they are to be trusted. Thus, a company can reflect on the past and change but it cannot completely betray its history or traits any more than a friend can convince you that he is a new person because he is wearing a new outfit. For example, although a group of managers from a large British-based multinational bank decided that their company's ethos was like 'James Bond' (see Case Box 6.3 on p. 257 in the next chapter), it was recognized, on reflection, that building a strategy on this character would not work: 'Bankers as Bonds? Our customers would not buy it.' And while British Petroleum may have had good internal reasons for changing its identity to 'Beyond Petroleum' in 2000, the move was criticized in newspaper editorials from London to New Zealand as inauthentic 'beyond belief' given that less than 1% of BP's revenues came from renewable sources of energy. Those editorials claimed that BP actually stood 'unmatched in the annals of British business for its contribution to keeping industry supplied with the energy it needs'. BP should be proud of this background and build upon it, they argued. It should 'proclaim itself for what it is, instead of masquerading, quite absurdly, as some kind of rival to Greenpeace.' These arguments seemed to strike a chord, and it was not long before BP was downplaying the change.

Thus, organizations cannot choose an *ethos* willy-nilly. Hewlett-Packard's emphasizing the notion of their being different because they are, at core, like inventors in tin sheds (See Case Box 6.3 on p. 281), washes because this rings true with their history, as does Jaguar's emphasizing how they have always being about 'little bits of history repeating'. Even new organizations have to work with and build upon the character or traits of those who have formed it if they are to be 'authentic' in this second sense.

Moreover, companies have to operate within communities. So, while a company, like a character, cannot be all things to all people, it must be something to enough people. It must have some network of others that choose to relate to it. No character can afford to be disenfranchised. To connect this point to the first, Warwick Business School often shows a video to their course participants called *Roger & Me*. It is about filmmaker Michael Moore's attempts to get the then CEO of General Motors, Roger Smith, to visit the city of Flint, Michigan, the birthplace of GM, to see for himself the disintegration of the social fabric of the town since GM closed down their factories there. Often such films are shown in relation to case studies illustrating how other companies have been good and highlight how GM's decision was evil. However, most who watch the film say they would not necessarily change the decision to relocate to climes where production costs were lower. The thing that galls, and which subsequently caused GM the most damage when the film came out, was that GM appeared to be unwilling to confront the issue. They appeared unwilling to be up-front and straight about the choices they were making, and seemed to believe that the community that was once important to them was now nothing to do with them. Conditions may have meant that they had to change their relationship with Flint, but they should not have washed their hands of the implications of their decision.

Thus, from an *ethos*-driven perspective, a company like Bodyshop ought to honour its hometown and keep its interests there because it is upon such values that the company *is* explicitly founded and profits from. To not do so would be inconsistent. But the same need not apply to a company like GM that competes on different bases. However, companies like GM, as with all companies from this alternative ethical perspective, must be forthright about their differences and the choices that they have made. Then individuals have the free access to the information they need in order to choose whether they wish to connect to them or another organization given their particular needs.

It is interesting to note that recent cases indicate that developments in information technology may be enabling a more *aretaic* approach now by exercising an influence similar to that of the public communities in which Aristotle thought. Influenced by a greater transparency promoted by 'community discussions' on the Internet, many companies are currently 'recrafting' their characters. Nike (see Case 4 on p. 308 in Part III) and McDonald's are prominent examples of organizations who have had to re-evaluate and re-shape their virtues in light of these developments while recognizing that they cannot completely change their strategic direction or satisfy all stakeholders at once.

4 Business ethics reconceptualized

Traditionally approaches to business ethics have often alienated many organizations by assuming that there is a general sense of 'angelic good' that must be aimed for. While this may be possible for trendy niche-players, it means that for others ethics becomes 'something for other people', or something to be paid not much more than lip service. While all organizations must operate within communities and thus respond to certain standards of acceptability if they are not to be ostracized, just because an organization seeks to focus on lowering costs or serving an older demographic does not mean that it cannot think ethically or have values. A more *aretaic* or *ethos-driven* approach may enable many companies to more substantively think about and debate their ethical standpoints and bring ethics on to the agenda in places where it has not previously been.

This does not mean that we should overthrow conventional approaches to business ethics (see Case Box 5.4). Rather, in a Postmodern way, a more Premodern *aretaic* appreciation should be *added* to the Modern focus on *deontic* codes in order to give people within organizations more to think on, bounce around and create with. But we should recognize that in environments not dominated by bureaucratic commonality, where people have less faith in general goods, or products and services that please all people (or plans that authentically satisfy all stakeholders), environments where organizations cannot be 'best friends with everybody', the concept of *ethos* may proactively inform a company's direction in ways that business ethics thus far has not.

In reconceptualizing this alternative approach to ethics we must be wary of slipping back into the same Modern traps. Because organizations are 'thrown' by the wash of the past into the future in unique and historically influenced directions, every one has a unique history and, subsequently, a *unique ethos* to be built upon. Thus we must beware of seeking to transplant 'best practice' *ethos* from one organization to another and using external consultants considered expert because of their detached objectivity and having performed similar tasks across a large number of organizations. Academics and consultants should no longer advise what an *ethos* should be. If *ethos* is about exploring what comes from the 'inside-out' rather than what might be imposed from the 'outside-in', then the onus for developing *ethos* must fall back on to people within particular organizations. They are the people who embody that company's way of proceeding and best know the company's idiosyncrasies or 'genius'.

By encouraging organizations themselves to develop the differences that make individual personalities and organizations endearing, the Premodern concept of *ethos* may fruitfully connect the realms of ethics and strategy. Such a move is explored in Case Box 5.5 and developed in more detail in the following chapter, 'ReConceiving Strategy'.

Case Box 5.4   Discussions Toward a Code

In March 2001, a spokesperson for the campaign for an oath to set global ethical standards for scientists announced that they were 'dropping the future pursuit of it.' It wasn't so much a lack of interest or failing to see it as an important issue that had stalled it, as the inability for the many bodies concerned to agree the wording of a common code. However, as one executive director of a leading scientific research society said: 'I'm sceptical about the practicality of an oath that can be widely applied, but the spirit of the discussions that led toward the oath may be more important than the oath itself.'

1   Why might discussions toward an ethical code be more important than actually determining that code?

Source: This case draws on 'Science Body Snubs "Impractical" Ethics Oath', *The Times Higher Education Supplement*

Case Box 5.5   From Jack Dee to 2-D

In the early 1990s Jerry Goldberg, brand manager at Scottish Courage Breweries, oversaw the appointment of an up-and-coming deadpan comedian Jack Dee as the spokesperson for John Smith's Bitter. 'When John Webster at DDB (the advertising agency responsible for the campaign) suggested Dee we weren't worried about whether he'd be big,' reflected Goldberg. 'The fact was that his personality suited the brand's "no-nonsense" positioning.' Five years on, the Jack Dee campaign, with 50 awards to its name, was widely regarded as having helped propel John Smith's from number 16 to number 4 in the UK beer market, toppling Tetley's from its market-leader perch in the 'Bitter' segment for the first time. In December 1995, John Smith's sales were almost two percentage points behind Tetley's. Three years later, they were 4.5 per cent ahead.

In 1998 Scottish Courage decided to replace Jack Dee as the personification of John Smith's.

The Jack Dee campaign had re-energized a beer with a long, solid history; a beer that had personified the honest, straight up, 'no-frills just good taste' ethos of a bitter first brewed in Tadcaster, Yorkshire 240 years ago. Now a new creative team from the agency GGT came up with 'no-nonsense man', a cardboard cut-out synthesis of the essential 'average bloke' pictured, in various guises, with a pint of John Smith's.

Jerry Goldberg's successor as brand manager explained that the new 'no nonsense man' campaign would take 'the 'no-nonsense' proposition one step further – our new frontman is the ultimate no-nonsense celebrity.' Scottish Courage's marketing manager claimed that 'No-nonsense man aims to show the beer's down-to-earth positioning in an involving way. It conveys all the product-values. It has the potential to become a cult star.'

Even though Jack Dee was by no means everybody's' favourite comedian, the momentum generated by the Jack Dee image had helped put John Smith's in a position where it looked well placed to leapfrog Guinness as the UK's third top-selling beer (after Carlsberg and Fosters). However, after the launch a survey by *Campaign* magazine showed that 67 per cent of people thought the 'no-nonsense man' image was less effective than Jack Dee. A year on and the general consensus among industry and media commentators was that 'no-nonsense man' lacked the impact of the previous campaign and that, despite Scottish Courage not giving up on him, he was 'not catching on'. No-nonsense man had not become a 'cult star'. John Smith's had not overtaken Guinness.

By 1999 Goldberg had moved on to become brands director for lagers at Scottish Courage and was overseeing another highly successful campaign – Fosters' 'He who thinks Australian, drinks Australian.' Jack Dee hosted the British Advertising and Design Awards that year. One magazine's review of the night describes how 'the audience loved it when he riffed about "the days when John Smith advertising used to win awards" and baited "Anyone here from GGT?" with a "You haven't won anything".' Whether he was genuinely bitter or just being funny was hard to tell. But then it always is with Jack Dee.

1   What did Jack Dee provide for John Smith's that the average or ideal cardboard 'no-nonsense man' cannot (comparing the no-nonsense man concept with Figure 2.11 [see p. 52] might provide some food for thought)?
2   As the case mentions, Jack Dee was never the most popular of comedians. Would a more generally appealing comedian have been even better for John Smith's?
3   How could the Jack Dee *ethos* help Scottish Courage at once revive and change John Smith's brand and corporate values *and* help focus a strategy for John Smith's?
4   Does the 'He who thinks Australian ...' ethos 'work'? If so, why?

Sources: The case contains elements from 'Lager Than Life', *Marketing*; 'John Smith's in £10m Sales Push', *Marketing*; 'Media Case Study: John Smith's', *Marketing*; 'Cardboard Cut-out with Cult Status', the *Scotsman*; 'Live Update', *Campaign*; 'Design and Advertising Brave an Uneasy Alliance, *Campaign*.

6 ReConceiving Strategy

By the end of this chapter you should:

1 See how conventional theories of strategic management have built upon, and been limited by, Modernist assumptions.
2 Have a working knowledge of some of the classic frameworks for thinking strategy.
3 Understand that a Postmodern approach to strategy would not dismiss these generic frameworks, but rather connect and criss-cross them with particular networks.
4 Be able to use these and frameworks drawn from other sources, in combination with the ideas with regard to *ethos* covered in the previous chapter, to develop particular organizational strategies.

The intellectual can no longer play the role of the advisor. The project, tactics, and goals to be adopted are a matter for those who do the fighting. What the intellectual can do is provide the instruments of analysis.

Michel Foucault

Radical art never creates anything new: it simply shifts the emphasis.

Michael Craig-Martin

A young lieutenant of a small Hungarian detachment in the Alps sent a reconnaissance unit to spend a night in the icy wilderness as part of their survival training. It began to snow immediately, and unexpectedly continued to snow for two days. The unit did not return. The lieutenant feared that he had dispatched his own people to death. However, on the third day the unit came back. Where had they been? How had they made their way? 'Yes', they told the lieutenant, 'We considered ourselves lost and waited for the end'. Given the nature of the exercise, they did not have any maps, compasses or other equipment with which to ascertain their position or a probable route out. 'We spent the best part of a day arguing over which way to go. But then one of us found an old tattered map in a seldom-used pocket. That calmed us down. The map did not seem to quite fit the terrain but eventually we discovered our bearings. We followed the map down the mountain and after a few wrong turns eventually found our way'. The relieved lieutenant asked if he could see this life-saving map. 'This isn't a map of the Alps!' he exclaimed. 'It's a map of the Pyrenees!'

Of all the stories I have told to MBA and Executive courses this, borrowed from a chapter by Karl Weick, is far and away the most popular and most remembered. The notion that the value of a map, just like the value of a strategic framework, comes not so much from its ability to objectively represent the essence of things, but from its 'social' ability to *focus minds and help people toward a particular course* clearly strikes a chord.

If an organization's strategy can best be described as its movement in space and time, or its 'course' – where it goes and where it does not go – strategic frameworks, ideas and theories should be to an organization what the map was to the Hungarian soldiers. Once one has an idea of their *ethos* or purpose, such maps help people *think* and *talk strategically* by offering them a language by which complex options can be simply understood and communicated or *mapped*. It enables a group to focus in order to learn more about themselves and what they want to achieve and locate themselves in relation to their environment. At the same time these maps can help people *act strategically*, getting the group beyond indecision so that they can begin the process of doing their own *mapping* and taking a course, giving people the confidence to act and a knowledge of what behaviors or skills must be put in place in order to make that action effective.

In other words, strategic frameworks or maps help people to do their own mapping, thereby kick-starting an oscillating thinking–acting process which instills a momentum that brings other choices and possibilities to the fore. It may not get people down the mountain in a straight line, but it gets things moving, and when things move other opportunities come into view that inspire further action. In short, the interaction between the general map and the mapping of a particular course helps *orient* and *animate*, and no course is likely to be effectively taken without a measure of each of these things.

Indeed, one useful way of ascertaining whether or not an organization has a 'good strategy' (beyond the obvious *post-hoc* financial measures) is to ask whether it is oriented *and* animated. Some companies are all *animation* without really knowing who they are, where they are in relation to others, and what they are really trying to achieve. Sometimes they get lucky. Mostly they don't. Some organizations are all *orientation*, spending forever questioning and plotting and positioning themselves in the market, developing elaborate mission statements and systems models that represent every conceivable variable. By the time they feel ready to act the world has moved on. Orientation without animation can drain the animating life-blood out of a company. The key seems to be appreciating these two spirits in tandem, as illustrated below.

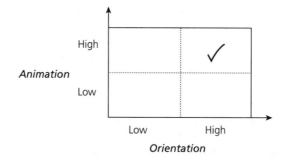

If *ethos* can help one orient or 'know' oneself and indicate which courses of action might be possible and appropriate given one's 'throwness', strategy maps or frameworks can help communicate this orientation and build it into animation.

   Despite the chord that the Alps story, and the subsequent motto that strategy is about orientation *and* animation, strikes with managers, writing on strategy almost disappeared up an alley of its own making in the 1990s as academics lost sight of how the maps or analytical instruments they made helped people strategize. 'Turf wars' were fought over which school of thought or set of models most accurately represented the way in which strategy really happened or set of criteria by which strategic decisions should be made. Some said strategy was instigated at the top of the organizational triangle and required logical forethought and rationally *designed* plans that positioned or oriented the company. Others argued that strategy might be formalized by those at the top, but in reality this was where the 'rubber met the sky' – strategy actually happened at the 'base' of the company. Here salespeople met customers, research scientists met test tubes, and people were animated. Good ideas developed on the ground would then *emerge* into policy from the 'bottom-up', as shown here:

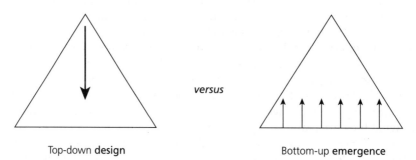

Top-down **design**   Bottom-up **emergence**

Some claimed industrial economics as the discipline to which we must look for foundations. Others countered that psychology, history and political science were far more useful means of grasping the strategy nettle. By 1997, the disagreements had become so fractious that eminent professors wrote despairing editorials claiming that:

Something is amiss, either the practitioners cannot keep up with theorists frequent changes of mind or the theorists still cannot decipher the practice. Were the many decades of vigorous development wasted? Does anybody at least *know* what strategy is?

If we could not answer this without contradiction then how could we begin to develop strategy as a serious science?

How people use maps in their everyday lives may provide the insight necessary to get beyond this ultimately fruitless line of questioning. Let's say you have arranged to meet a friend at a small pub in the country. It is about a three-hour drive from the city where you live. How many maps would you use to get there? Probably many:

- a motorway map to plan the direction of the route, key interchanges, how long it should take you and so on before you set out;
- a street map of your city to determine the best exit and how you might get there;
- a map indicating the location of service stations if you found you needed to stop for gas or other supplies;
- a more detailed road map would be useful if you encountered roadworks on the motorway and wanted to find a quicker alternative route;
- a map drawn on the back of an envelope by your friend the last time you met, indicating the key turns and landmarks as you leave the motorway exit and approach the pub (a map not unlike those Premodern vistas with their oversized churches and symbolic images – see Figure 2.5 on p. 34) would come in handy; and
- the map in your head of the personality of the friend who drew the envelope map would help you understand what he was trying to express in his drawings.

In addition you will consult road signs along the way and your onboard navigational system if you have one. If you have passengers you will likely debate some options with them in terms of the maps and signs and their histories of similar journeys.

The point is that for even a simple journey no one map exists over and above all the others that captures all the information and knowledge (attempting to create one would likely result in an unholy mess), and no one map can be objectively defined as the best. You get where you are going by combining a knowledge of your particular purpose or *telos* with a number of different maps and perspectives: maps compiled by a number of different people from different disciplinary lenses that provide differing images. What helps you in mapping and taking a course is a montage of fragments from these images networked together in your mind for the purposes of that particular journey. In the perilous situation that the Hungarian army platoon found themselves, one map that people had faith in, no matter how dubious, was better than none. In the more everyday example described above many maps are better than one.

Given this, this chapter suggests that it is not important to ascertain 'what strategy is' without logical contradiction; or whether strategy is top-down planning *or* bottom-up emergence; or which framework is the best or cutting edge. It is more useful to see what we can understand about our particular organizations by looking at how strategy might develop through *each* of these lenses. This chapter argues that it is also limiting to think organizations *just* through the Modernist triangle, a traditional notion that the 'top-down' versus 'bottom-up' debate seems to reinforce and an assumption that has pervaded Modern strategic thinking, as we shall explore further on in this chapter. It is not helpful to argue whether economics *or* psychology *or* ethics provides the correct background, we need to understand strategy and make strategic choices (that is like arguing that an Atlas is better than a London Tube map). It is more useful to ask how the various frameworks each provides may help individuals understand themselves or configure particular strategic courses. It is not useful to argue, for example, as many are currently, that Michael Porter's conventional strategy frameworks are too simplistic to be of any use in today's real world. This misses the point that the strength of a simple, not overly detailed map (the back of the envelope, the Tube map), is its simplicity not its accuracy.

Perhaps a more radical approach to strategy would be not to seek the revolutionary overthrow of the old views in favour of a 'new model army', but to see if the traditional energy of the 'old' approaches can be appreciated, though in different ways – using the value of their language but shifting the emphasis? But before we do this we have a little history to think differently.

1 Modern strategy: the triangle and the objective grid

Strategy, as we tend to understand it today, is clearly fashioned upon the Modern 'geometry' described in Chapter 2. Alfred Chandler, the father of management history, is widely regarded as having developed strategy's foundational definition in 1962: 'The determination of the basic long-term goals and objectives of an enterprise.' This definition, premised upon the scalar hierarchy and division of labour diagram reproduced in Chapter 3 (p. 83), made strategy something determined by those at the top and passed down the structure. Other works considered 'foundational' include Drucker's 1959 *Long-Range Planning*, Kenneth Andrews' 1971 *Concept of Corporate Strategy* and, in particular, Igor Ansoff's 1965 *Corporate Strategy*. Ansoff is listed as primary among those that 'applied the concept of strategy to management' and is subsequently regarded, even by those who oppose his ideas, as defining the 'basic concepts' or 'premises' of strategy. If F.W. Taylor is the first man of management, Ansoff is the first man of corporate strategy.

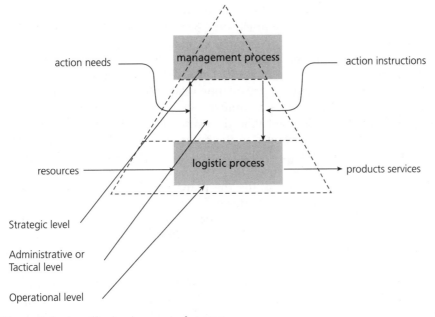

Figure 6.1 Ansoff's development of strategy

Source: H.I. Ansoff, *Business Strategy*, levels superimposed

Strategy as the apex over the input→process→output mechanism

Ansoff began his work by identifying a problematic gap between reality and theory. The increasing complexity of business environments in the 1950s and 1960s, compounded by increasingly predominant multi-business firms (in keeping with the evolution described by Chandler), had, Ansoff argued, created a desire for foresightful ways of positioning companies in order to exploit environmental change. However, the current theory set included only a business policy approach that assumed a company could stipulate what it would do on any occasion (that is that assumed simple, predictable environments) and the prevailing microeconomic theory of the firm. This theory saw organizations in terms of a model now very familiar to readers of this book: a simple function turning resources or inputs into outputs through a production function. This model assumed that managers just manipulated the factors under their control to maximize efficiency – a model that provided for no differentiation between different firms' positioning. Ansoff subsequently defined strategy as 'a rule for making decisions pertaining to a firm's match to its environment' and set out, in his words, to 'enrich the theoretical conception of the firm'.

Simply speaking, this 'enrichment' involved Ansoff adding a layer called 'management process' on top of the microeconomic 'resources→

logistic processes→outputs' model, and then outlining three distinctive action or decision areas: administrative or tactical, operational and strategic (see Figure 6.1). *Administrative* action related to establishing the central stem of management and logistic processes. *Operational* action related to the maximization of operational efficiency within the process parameters set by the administration. *Strategic* action related to establishing the organization's relationship to the environment: it is, therefore, carried out by the 'men at the top' – those best placed to gain an objective or 'global' view, forecast and represent changes in the environment and rationally control corporate development accordingly. Strategy imposes operating requirements. The administrative structure provides the climate for meeting these. The operational level then fulfils the plans provided from above. What is now called the 'classical' or 'design' school of strategy thus perceives strategy as separate from, overseeing and proceeding organizational action in a linear-hierarchical manner. It is about developing the most accurate objective grid or map of the environment possible and then orienting the company.

While Ansoff acknowledged that a theory that was useful for analysing real world behavior would 'have to integrate and interrelate the three major decision areas' (operational, tactical and strategic), he stressed that 'to reduce the theory-building task to manageable proportions' we must begin by 'study[ing] each class of decisions separately'. In order to master the complex whole of the firm's 'problem', Ansoff, in a Modernist fashion, had broken it down into constituent parts. His 'separations' inspired a Cartesian language that spoke of the *strategic mind* as above and separate from *operational matter*.

The influence of Ansoff's separations can be seen in textbooks that now speak of a hierarchy of strategy from corporate to business to functional levels, of a hierarchy of control from strategic to tactical to operational levels, and of the importance of recognizing the difference between strategy and tactics. Ansoff's stated aim to: 'synthesize and unify into an overall analytic solving the total strategic problem of the firm [the] partial analytical insights into strategic business problems'; had resulted in the formalization of the triangular hierarchy over the mechanistic input-output equation and all that that assumed about management. Thus, strategy is defined in teaching texts as the:

> ... planning, directing, organizing and controlling of a company's strategy related decisions and actions.

Or, in other words, the achievement of management's universal principles but at a higher level and for the longer-term, so as to coordinate a Modern organization's divisions. Ansoff accordingly pays tribute to 'pioneers like Taylor, Mayo, and Fayol beg[inning] to apply science to management', given that it was their models that he was building upon. However, as Ansoff goes on to say, because they focussed upon operational productivity 'historical progress in management had been from the "inside out"'. His enrichment, concerned as it was with overseeing the positioning of the firm in relation to the global environment, would focus strategy on the 'external' and look top-down from the outside-in.

However, despite Ansoff's separation of strategic management as above and beyond the input→process→output system of operations and his claim that a satisfactory theory of the whole firm would 'have to integrate and interrelate the three major decision categories', after breaking the firm down, Ansoff's modeling ultimately rested upon the pioneering language of efficiency that was seen to underpin operations. Ansoff explained that while firms had 'traditionally and historically' been regarded as solely economically motivated toward the purpose of increasing 'return on investment', and toward this 'end' had 'developed a measurement of efficiency – profit – common and unique to [them]', this had recently been the subject of much debate. However, having identified that the object at the operating level of a firm is always 'to maximize the efficiency of the firm's resource conversion process', when finalizing his model of the firm he concluded that seeing as:

> ... there is no general agreement on a proper philosophical basis for business objectives ... our framework for formulating objectives was made adaptable to a variety of different management attitudes, *so long as the underlying concept of the firm is that of an efficiency-seeking organization which meets the objectives through the mechanism of making and selling goods and/or services.*

Ansoff and Chandler's triangular-hierarchical image of strategy built upon the input→process→output logic of efficiency and the central administrative stem, thus replicating the form that came out of 1959's foundational reports into business schools that were being implemented as they wrote (see Chapter 3). These reports concluded that in order to counter the disparate 'organic' growth of programmes with differing contributing 'specialisms', it had to be realized that 'economics has traditionally provided the only theoretical framework for the study of business.' Economics thus became the central stem according to which other business courses would be related. Having outlined the central gaze and then using this as a basis to determine a properly ordered range of contributing subjects, the studies advocated the standardization of the curricula's super-level or 'sharp end'. They recommended the development of 'capstone courses' that would allow students to 'pull together what they have learned in the separate business fields.' These tips of the educational triangle would become courses in the field that Chandler and Ansoff were marking out: corporate strategy. As Andrews noted in 1969: 'The establishment of Business Schools provided the basis for the education of strategic managers and the divisionalized structure of organizations [that is Chandler's form characterized by the division of labour, scalar hierarchy and coordination] provided the form for them to work within'.

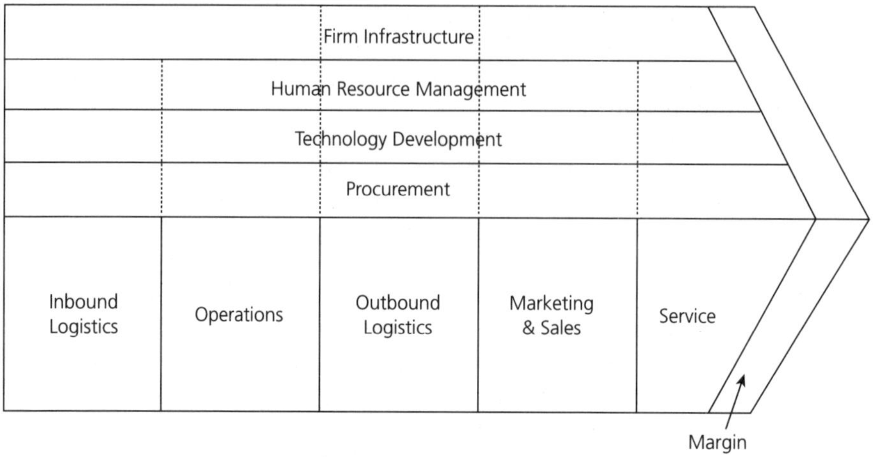

Firm Infrastructure				
Human Resource Management				
Technology Development				
Procurement				
Inbound Logistics	Operations	Outbound Logistics	Marketing & Sales	Service

Margin

Figure 6.2 Porter's 'Generic Value Chain'
Source: Michael E. Porter, *Competitive Advantage: Creating and Sustaining Superior Performance*

The grids beneath the triangle's apex

If Ansoff and Chandler consolidated the view of an organization as a triangle and positioned the strategist at the top of it looking down, it is Michael Porter (who we encountered at the outset of this book) who more than anyone else who provides the general grids upon which strategists can position their companies from on high. Porter, whose PhD is in industrial economics, has a great ability in distilling large amounts of detail into easy-to-follow frameworks that seem to make sense. He also has the happy knack of issuing a new one every five or so years. We briefly examine three of these here: the 'Value Chain', the 'Five Forces of Industry' and the 'Generic Strategy Matrix'. (NB: as with the previous chapter's ethos frameworks, this logic being outlined here seems to stick better when you draw it yourself – particularly if you apply them to arenas that you are familiar with).

The value chain

Porter's 'value chain' (Figure 6.2) clearly shows Porter's debt to what he considers the essence or 'heart' of strategy. Its geometry and categorization of space is Ansoff's 'classical' view (compare Figure 6.1 on p. 219). Its linear chain of process functions with 'tactical' and 'strategic' aspects layered on top provides an ordered framework with which to consider how the various processes within the firm are adding value to the outputted product or

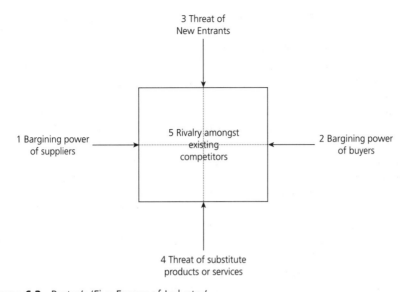

Figure 6.3 Porter's 'Five Forces of Industry'

Source: Michael E. Porter, *Competitive Strategy: Techniques for Analyzing Industries and Competitors*

service. If, upon analysis via this tool, certain things are found not to be adding value above what they cost to perform, they should be 'addressed' or eliminated. This will result in *greater margins* (the gap between the cost of producing something and what you can sell it for).

The five-forces of industry

The line of the value chain extends both ways to become the horizontal line of Porter's Five Forces of Industry (Figure 6.3). This framework enables a focus upon the aspects that will determine that industry's average margins. On either end of the individual firm's value chain is the *first* and *second* force: the *bargaining power of suppliers*, which, if high, can increase the cost of inputs thereby reducing margins; and the *bargaining power of buyers* (which could be individual consumers, retail outlets or added-value manufacturers depending on the commodity in question). If the bargaining power of buyers is high, average selling prices, and hence margins, decline.

The *third* force is the *threat of new entrants*. If entrepreneurs and senior managers in other industries observe high margins being achieved in an industry, they are likely to bring their expertise and other resources into that arena. Unless, that is, the cost of overcoming the 'barriers to entry' (for example, the initial investment required, the specialist knowledge needed to be developed) are perceived to outweigh the benefits to be gained.

The *fourth* force is the *threat of substitute products or services*, things that buyers might use instead if the industry's prices are perceived to be too high, and the 'switching costs' (for example, inconvenience of purchase and use, breaking of existing contracts) are low enough. For example, the more expensive or difficult air travel becomes, the more likely it is that people will consider trains where possible.

Finally, the laws of supply and demand indicate that the more competitors there are in an industry, the lower the average margins. Subsequently, the *fifth* and final force is the *rivalry among existing competitors*.

Obviously, Porter argues, companies and other investors want to put their money into industries where the margins are high, and the Five Forces is a useful framework for analysing relative margins and how these might change over time. For example, 15 years ago the pharmaceutical industry experienced very high margins. There were a relatively small number of *competitors*, all of whom were well established and reaping the rewards of being a long way up the 'experience curve'. Hence, rivalry was largely 'gentlemanly' and the market divided in such a way that all the main companies profited. Competitive positioning and existing relationships with customers and suppliers were well staked out. The set up costs for a new player would be high and returns would also be a long time in coming, given the lead-time necessary to develop and test new drugs and the importance of a 'solid' reputation. Because of this, the barriers to entry were high and, subsequently, the *threat of new entrants* low. The *bargaining power of suppliers* was low, given that the basic ingredients for most drugs was cheap, plentiful and produced in 'developing countries' in need of foreign currency. Because governments and insurance companies had become complacent about costs and un-well individuals had little choice but to take what registered medical practitioners prescribed, the *bargaining power of buyers* was low. And, relatedly, there was little *threat of substitutes*.

However, things have changed. Increased awareness about alternative and complimentary medicines has increased their social legitimacy and increased the *threat of substitutes*. *Buyer power* is also up, with governments in particular getting more savvy about how they fund healthcare and paying particular attention to using generic or unbranded drugs where possible to reduce costs. Supermarket chains, previously just buyers, are seeking 'backward integration' into the industry in order to bring their own-brand alternatives to market. Individual consumers have more choice and perceive the switching costs away from the established brands as less risky. In light of the above, government agencies like the FDA are revisiting patent law restrictions and required testing periods, further reducing the barriers to entry. The *threat of new entrants* is therefore on the up and with it further *buyer power*. An increased awareness of the conditions in the developing countries in which the basic elements of drugs are produced is forcing the pharmaceutical companies to take more care in the dealings with *suppliers*. And, in response to the resulting declining margins, *competitive rivalry* has become more fierce, with mergers and takeovers more prevalent as firms within the industry seek to rationalize and cut costs by increasing economies of scale and other companies seek to move into new segments to increase their overall unit sales.

The generic strategy matrix

Having looked inside the firm with the value chain and at the forces acting on the industry within which firms compete with the Five Forces, Porter's Generic Strategy Matrix, or GSM, focuses on how firms position themselves in relation to their competitors in an industry. In effect, it looks further into the fifth-force window of competitive rivalry. At the core of the GSM is the concept of 'competitive advantage', the idea that all companies must do something that their competitors do not, or even better cannot (when 'do not' becomes 'cannot' one can talk of the firm having a '*sustainable* competitive advantage'). In typically stark fashion, Porter's GSM offers an organization two choices: either focus on doing what you do at a cost that is less than your competitors, or make sure that you add value in a unique way by investing in technology, design, tailor-making or branding, thereby differentiating your product from the standard. This will cost more, thus meaning that you will have to set your price higher than your competitors, thus meaning that you may not sell so much. But because some will be willing to pay a lot more for what you do, your margins and profits will still be healthy. Porter creates a two-by-two matrix out of these cost and differentiation columns by crossing competitive advantage with 'competitive scope'. Here the choice is broad or narrow (Porter is suitably vague about what this means exactly; it could mean the number of different products produced, the number of distribution channels used, or the number of markets sold in). Narrow versus broad is also seen as an either/or choice. The worst strategic sin, according to Porter, is to be 'stuck in the middle', to not be willing or able or aware enough to position oneself in one or other box. Failing to do this will result in a company falling between stools and becoming a master of nothing. Hence, a simple two-by-two grid emerges comprising the four generic strategies that a company can rationally choose between (see Figure 6.4).

One may simply illustrate the grid by examining the car industry. In the *broad cost* segment are big, long established players like Ford, General Motors and Volkswagen. They have big ranges, huge distribution networks and sell all over the globe. Their costs are cut through the advantages of their economies of scale, and large sales mean small margins can equate to huge profits. More *differentiated* companies who also sell a *broad* range through a wide distribution network include Volvo, Audi and Saab. Those focused on *cost* but with smaller volumes and *narrower* targets include Seat, Skoda, Hyundai and Daewoo. Those focussed on *differentiation* but with more *exclusive* targets include Jaguar, Rolls Royce, Ferrari and Aston Martin. In the last two decades, the Japanese manufacturer Toyota has profited from moving from cost focus into broad cost, while German manufacturers like BMW and Mercedes have moved up into the differentiation as opposed to the

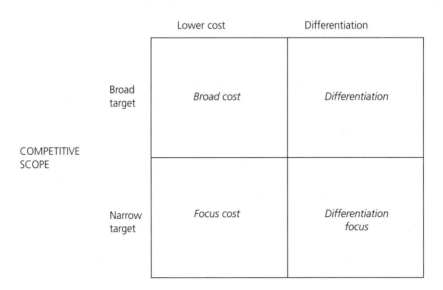

Figure 6.4 Porter's 'Generic Strategy Matrix'
Source: Michael E. Porter, *Competitive Strategy: Techniques for Analyzing Industries and Competitors*

differentiation focus segment. Honda seems to defy Porter's logic by being somewhere in the middle, suggesting that they need to choose a strategic position fast. Applying the GSM can enable strategists to see where their company is in relation to the competition, rationally decide where it is best for them to be and then develop a plan or design of how to get there.

Does strategy come from the top of the triangle down or from the bottom up?

The 'basis' of strategy was consequently defined by its not being administration or tactics or operations or processes. This, combined with the view of strategy as about 'thinking' and operations as about 'doing', combined with a view of organizations as hierarchies where the further up one is the more thinking and less doing one does, meant that strategy was seen as the preserve of senior managers at the top ('those at the bottom lack the ability to detach themselves from the minutia of everyday tasks' – see Case Box 3.2 on p. 129) and a detached, objective and logical process. The view is that strategy means executives, crucially staying above the action, carrying out a rational plotting and planning process whereby grids like Porter's are used to orient the company. This orientation then leads to the provision of explicit plans for operational action. This conception enabled the Modernist need to determine things positively, without logical contradiction, to be satisfied. From the 1960s to the 1980s, strategy was unquestioningly defined as a firm's *explicit long-term designs or plans*. However, in the late 1980s and 1990s a number of academics attempted to surpass or overthrow the conventional view, either by trumping it with more detailed models that more accurately represented the complexity that became apparent when one studied the 'real world', or by dismissing the whole 'design school' perspective and the heritage on which it was based.

Not being satisfied with the simplicity of models like Porter's, some constructed more complicated contraptions (there are many examples, but that shown in Figure 6.5 serves as an illustration). Unfortunately, the more complex things became, the more difficult the models were to apply, particularly in environments perceived to be 'fast moving', and such modelling quickly became the stuff of satire (see Figure 6.6).

A more revolutionary approach was to completely overturn the idea of strategy as a top-down map-drawing, rational positioning and planning affair. Writers like Hamel and Prahalad began to wonder whether strategy was actually more about an 'unwritten pattern of behavior' or 'intent'. Indeed, in our new fast-paced world they argued that there was no time to carry out a formal planning process. Others chimed in that perhaps the classical design school 'got the notion of strategy all wrong, "the wrong way around".' Strategy, claimed Richard Pascale, actually happens from the 'bottom-up'. Consequently, a revolutionary Gary Hamel concluded that 'the essential problem in organizations today is a failure to distinguish *planning* from real *strategizing*', suggesting that what is required 'is not a little tweak to the traditional planning process but a new philosophical foundation'. We must 'cast off industrial conventions,' and overcome the old 'reductionist, elitist and easy, positioning' approach to strategy. Along these lines, Ralph Stacey begins his *Dynamic Strategy for the 1990s* by criticizing the traditional view of strategy and the frameworks developed by the likes of Porter, explaining that he:

> ... uncompromisingly rejects the conventional strategic management framework, with its trite future-mission statements and flimsy strategic plans, as unrealistic, impractical and essentially static. I ... propose more appropriate ways. The real cutting edge of strategic management lies in handling the unknowable, and the cast of mind generated by the conventional approach is a positive hindrance to such an endeavour ... in the dynamic business world of the 1990s it is totally inappropriate.

Dynamic Strategy's back cover consequently boasts of 'rendering traditional long-term planning, the grand design, redundant.'

This revolutionary perspective is usually traced back to the ideas of Henry Mintzberg and the so called 'emergence school' of strategy. In the early 1970s, Mintzberg's research found that real managers were far less rational and foresightful than the management literature supposed. In the

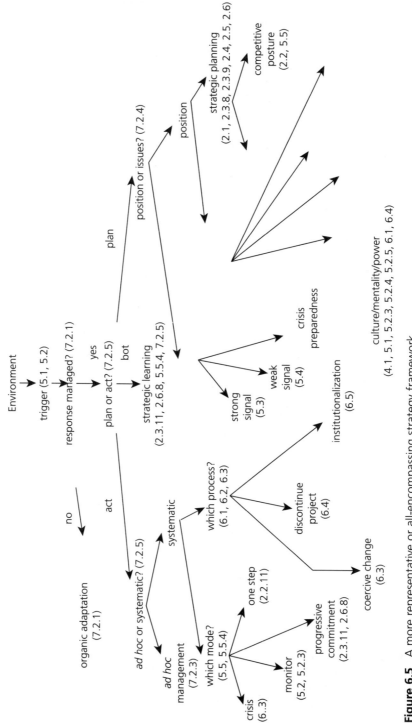

Figure 6.5   A more representative or all-encompassing strategy framework

Source: 'Tree of strategic management' from H.I. Ansoff, *Implanting Strategic Management*

Figure 6.6 The dangers of increasingly representative detail

Source: 'Dilbert' cartoon

early 1980s, as we have seen (Chapter 4), he developed an 'organic' view of organizations, developing something a bit 'cuddlier' than the standard mechanistic 'boxes and lines' hierarchy (Figure 4.3, p. 145). Mintzberg's next initiative, issuing a challenge to the 'classical' view of strategy, shows the influence of these two earlier projects. He now argued that Ansoff and others' view was dependent on the fallacy that 'thinking' and 'doing' are separate. Managers were not rational, logical, 'clean sheet' forecasters – their courses were influenced by politics and historical or cultural patterns of behavior over time. Thus, Mintzberg found that the interaction crucial to strategy does not happen between top executives and the environment, it occurs where employees at the operational base of the organization interact with one another and react to or anticipate customer needs and wants or spot gaps and opportunities. Over time, the animation that goes on here creates patterns of behavior that filter up the apex to be formalized in plans, but the real 'strategizing' does not come from the top.

To illustrate this idea, Mintzberg liked to relate stories such as how 3M's strategy was influenced more by one scientist playing around with adhesives and papers and coming up with Post-It notes rather than by its formal plans. And how Honda's research extrapolations of the US market led it to leave behind the little bikes it sold in Japan and develop big 'American style' bikes for their entry into this new market. Honda's big bikes flopped and the company was about to pull out of the US. But then people who had never thought about riding a motorcycle before started asking where they could get one of the little 50cc bikes that Honda's employees were riding around US cities to make deliveries. After this news filtered up the company, Honda decided to enter the market with its small bikes. The rest, as they say, is history.

Hence, Mintzberg argued that the notion that 'strategy making could be reduced to a series of steps proved to be *reductio ad absurdum*.' In addition, he claimed that environmental turbulence and decision-making complexity is such that forecasting the future environment, in order to set plans to determine positioning for the future, is impossible. In any case, Mintzberg argued that truly creative strategies are the result of the opportunistic synthesis of different ideas and aspects rather than detached analytical thinking within a set of constructs. Thus, real strategy stems from a direct knowledge of local contexts and there can be no 'formal techniques' for strategy.

Mintzberg's early attempts to conceptualize an alternative view to Ansoff's incorporated planning argued that strategy happens as a potter crafts a pot – with an initial plan of action, but also reacting to the particular nature of the clay and what takes form during the process to arrive at something quite different from what was originally pictured. He called for an 'opening up of the definition of strategy' to include patterns, perspectives and ploys, *in addition* to planning and positioning. However, things became increasingly polarized in the first half of the 1990s. In so doing, they reflected two of Modernism's key tenets: objective representationalism (that the purpose of knowledge is to represent, without logical contradiction, the 'ways things really are' or the linear, functional causes of actions) and the notion of organization as a triangle.

The 'What is strategy?!' crisis

Opposing schools of thought are problematic for any field seeking to develop as a Modern science (see Chapter 2). Hence, the more people dwelt upon the fact that there were alternative and seemingly opposite and contradictory definitions of, and causal links in, strategy, the more there appeared to be much at stake. One way around this problem was to ascertain an 'evolutionary chain' that demonstrated how various schools had built on one another toward an understanding that is moving ever closer to representing the truth. A good early example of strategic management seeking to make sense of its development in this manner is Ellen Earle Chaffe's *Academy of Management Review* paper 'Three Models of Strategy'. Here the unscientific existence of different schools is seen as being due to the 'evolution of the strategy construct proceeding sequentially through [a] hierarchy, beginning at [the] machine level'. 'During the past 20 years', Chaffe explains, 'the strategy literature has greatly evolved. Today, in fact, it has almost arrived at the point at which it is capable of reflecting the actual level of complexity at which organizations operate.' On this logic, the 'Emergence' paradigm would come to be categorized as cutting edge: a superior, more representative, view of how strategy really is. This seems to have sorted out the 'more than one school' problem. However, the ensuing sense of superiority also seemed to fire up the emergence side.

Hence, the 'fighting talk' of Stacey and Hamel mentioned earlier, and Mintzberg's own later conclusions, that 'strategic planning' 'has never been strategy making' and that 'the term "strategic planning" has proved itself to be an oxymoron.' Indeed, Mintzberg's best-selling book, *The Rise and Fall of Strategic Planning*, begins with 'This history book of sorts ... traces the story of [strategic planning] from its origins around 1965 through its rise to prominence and its subsequent fall.' Mintzberg and other emergence theorists subsequently came to argue less for 'opening up' the definition of strategy to incorporate views beyond planning. Rather they began to claim that the view of strategy as planning was downright wrong: that top-down planning was actually *the opposite* of real strategy.

As things became more polarized they also became more personal. Those who had invested their reputations in an approach that was now being flippantly dismissed as 'old hat' fought back. In a series of papers, Ansoff criticized Mintzberg's use of single case studies like 3M and Honda, claiming that they made it 'difficult for Henry to claim universal validity for his emerging strategy model.' Mintzberg's descriptions of the environment as an unpredictable force were met with Ansoff's claim that his:

> ... cryptic statements beg all kinds of questions: whose environment is being discussed; what kind of influence does the force exert on organizations; under what circumstances is it exhorted; what impact does it have on strategic behavior, etc.

Moreover, Ansoff compared Mintzberg's notion that planners cannot manage complexity to 'a child's perception of the adult world.' For a descriptive statement to be valid, Ansoff remarked, 'it must be an accurate observation of reality,' and the design school's views held up because his observations showed that 'modern versions of planning are alive and well' and that 'the levels of success in organizations which are aligned with the environment were substantially higher than in organizations that were out of alignment'. In an increasingly heated exchange Mintzberg gave as good as he got.

Mintzberg was backed up by those emergence writers already mentioned, while Porter, still the number one heavyweight in the division, sided with Ansoff, arguing for a 'reconnection' with 'the classics'. The 'new [emergence] dogma' has, according to Porter, short-sightedly rejected positioning – 'once the heart of strategy'. This has led to a number of problems, the root of which is 'the failure to distinguish between operational effectiveness and strategy' and a subsequent lack of focus on real strategy, due to the mistaken belief that strategy happens 'further down' organizations. 'Operational effectiveness,' writes Porter (Ansoff termed it 'operational efficiency'), relates to 'practices that allow a company to better utilize its inputs,' and this should be taken as a given from a strategic point of view.

By the late 1990s, the debate between emergence and design was being described as 'tectonic' and spoken of as a 'crisis', indicating how fractious, and seemingly fundamental, it had become. However, amidst the shifting plates there did seem to be at least two related aspects that were not contested:

- As we have seen, the polarization of the debate, and using language like 'top down versus bottom up' to describe it, reinforced the view of organizations as triangles.
- All the protagonists have a shared vision of history.

The paragraphs below explore the second similarity in more detail.

Mintzberg's ideas were made 'reactionary', and consequently a mirror image of his top-down opponents, once he identified Ansoff as where corporate strategy began and what he was opposing. As we have seen, even those who criticized the design perspective accepted the idea that Ansoff and Chandler conceptualized *the basis* of strategy. In keeping, when all camps looked before the 1960s they saw the same conventional historical backdrop. Ansoff, explaining that the concept of strategy is 'relatively new', continues that:

> Its historical origin lies in the military art, where it is a broad, rather vaguely defined 'grand' concept ... Strategy is [here] contrasted to *tactics*, which is a specific scheme for employment of allocated resources.

Perhaps it is not surprising, then, that Stacey is dismissive of strategy's ancient military associations as he sees them as promoting a simple top-down design approach analogous, in his words, to a 'general who deploys his forces tactically within a grand war strategy.' In his first major article that criticized the conventional hegemony, Mintzberg similarly bemoaned strategy's Greek military origins for encouraging the view of strategy as an exercise in detachment and rational planning. Those few textbooks that engage with history reinforce the view. 1999's *Strategy and the Business Landscape* by Pankaj Ghemawat, for example, begins its 'Origins of Strategy' chapter with:

> 'Strategy' is a term that can be traced back to the ancient Greeks, who used it to mean a chief magistrate or military commander-in-chief. Over the next two millennia, *refinements* of the concept of strategy continued to focus on military interpretations. Carl von Clausewitz's attempted synthesis in the first half of the nineteenth century is a particularly notable example: He wrote that whereas 'tactics [involve] the use of armed forces in the engagement, strategy [is] the use of engagements for the object of the war.'

However, there is a resonance here with earlier sections of this book that might make us a little suspicious of this outlook. First, this vision of strategy's history is very much like that undermined here in Chapter 3. It is, once again, the Modern idea that we have only been clever or disciplined enough to understand management or strategy properly in Modernity, but, if we do look further back we can see more simplistic (rather than different) notions of this which we must refine and surpass. The key discoveries or advancements are those that reinforce the assumptions that we have made common practice (for example, 'tactics is not strategy'). Was strategy really never thought differently?

Second, that the answer to this should be 'not really' is made even more suspect by this chapter's earlier discussion on how people relate to the different perspectives provided by different maps or frameworks in 'everyday life'. Here, the idea that design and emergence would be seen as an either/ or, or the idea that one would need to be seen as an advance on the other, would appear strange. This realization also questions the notion that there must only be *one* true perspective of strategy that most objectively represents the way things really are.

2   An alternative origin for strategy

Having our suspicions aroused in this way, we might wonder whether there is not a way of rethinking the conventional origins that appear to reinforce these dubious distinctions, a manner that might enable us to get beyond the either/or's of design versus emergence. A history that might lead us to think strategy differently?

Reconceiving the history of strategy

'Strategy' is, in actual fact, one of the few words whose origin we can trace almost to the exact year. It derives from the Athenian position of *strategos*, a title coined in conjunction with the reforms of Kleisthenes of 508/507 BC. After the break up of the Peisistratid tyranny, Kleisthenes was given the job of developing an administrative structure that would help usher in a new form of limited democracy. His major reform was the institution of ten new tribal divisions as military and political sub-units of Athens. However, in an attempt to dissipate traditional regional rivalries, each of the new units cut across the 'space' of traditional regional boundaries to incorporate particular villages from all parts of the district. This created a matrix structure with each 'slice' designed to be the district of Athens in microcosm (these arrangements are discussed in greater detail in Chapter 7). Kleisthenes decreed that each of the ten new tribes would be commanded by an elected *strategos* – a title developed by compounding *stratos*, an army 'spreading out' over the ground (in this way *stratos* is allied to *stratum*) and *agein*, 'to lead'. The ten incumbent *strategoi* formed a council that made policy recommendations to the general assembly in Athens and commanded the armed forces.

The restructure paralleled increasing military complexity, which was also leading to a 'spreading out' of activities. Warfare had developed to a point where sides relied less upon ritualized head-to-head infantry confrontations and increasingly upon a network of many different types of units fighting on several different fronts, depending on particular circumstances. The proliferation of naval forces, mercenaries and political alliances at this time further multiplied the variables that commanders had to connect if they were to be successful.

Hence, the organizational form shaping the conception of strategy incorporated hierarchical elements, as it was primarily associated with leadership, but it was at once different from the Modern triangular view. Strategy *was* about detached top-down forethought, planning and positioning in advance of corporate action. However, as the frontlines were believed to be good places from which to read the mood of events, to implement, adapt and change plans as events unfolded, *strategoi* were at once expected to be at, or connected to, the local nodes or fronts where action took place. Militarily, strategists were expected to be present in the thick of battle at least some of the time, and politically their skill lay in cutting across traditional spatial boundaries and being at or relating to different locations. Subsequently, strategy *also* emerged at the 'front'. Further, given that this organizational form operated on many different fronts at once, depending on particular circumstances, strategy, and particularly military strategy, had to 'spread out' according to the form that the organization took at a particular point in time.

This amorphous, fluid and multi-faceted view of the organizational form indicates that a number of aspects would be of strategic importance:

1 Given that the *strategos* could not physically be in all places at all times, some sense of *ethos* was required to ensure that they would be there 'in spirit'.

2 Those at the 'operational' level needed to be prepared to step forward in this spirit and seize strategic opportunities. Something that the Athenian

training system and organizational structure, which was arranged into modular units representing the whole in microcosm, encouraged.

3 Able deputies, or what we might call middle managers, were key to the development of strategy, in making decisions as to which opportunities to pursue and which to pull back from, and ensuring that the various parts of the whole were kept in contact.

Strategy, for the Ancient Greeks, consequently occurred at all levels and parts of what we would see as the organizational hierarchy, as a blend of what we call strategy, tactics and operations. However, it is perhaps more correct to say that they likely operated with a visibility more like a Premodern microcosm-web or a Postmodern rhizome spreading along particular strata than a Modern triangle. Given this conception, the Greeks would have had trouble comprehending the Modern wars between the top-down design and bottom-up emergence schools of thought.

Correspondingly, the ability of a *strategos* lay in appreciating paradoxes. In the ability to meld past, present and future in creating an *ethos*; in the ability to oscillate between detached simplistic plans and practical expedients and opportunities on particular fronts; and in being a part of an organization able to go in any direction as opportunities emerged. On the view inspired by this alternative origin, strategy *is* about planning, forecasting and positioning (such aspects are helpful to provide impetus, coherence and understanding). But it is *also* about breaking plans, opportunism, emergence, patterns, ploys and expediency, which are helpful given that there is always some *chaos*, some void in understanding, that makes the future impossible to forecast.

Indeed, it is this *chaos*, this lack of predictability about what might be 'unconcealed' in the course of events, that enables those with impetus to change tack, subject themselves to different elements and provokes innovative approaches. Strategic ability came from an awareness that human travels are shaped both by the order of things, the actions that one's traditions and experiences inspire from within, an ability to shuttle from ordered detachment to chaotic reality, and from traditional frame to frame as need be in one's particular strategy making process. Not surprisingly, given this way of seeing (clearly based on an appreciation of *metos*, Chapter 2 [see p. 29]), the metaphor used to describe a skillful strategist was a *kubernetes*, the helmsperson on the fighting ships that surfed inshore currents. This view encouraged seeing strategy as about working to incorporate corporate direction while working with prevailing patterns and conditions, not about starting with a 'clean sheet'.

Hence, the Ancient's definitions of strategy and strategists were suitably 'ample', and to a Modern way of thinking often implausible. Aineias' *How to Survive Under Siege* saw strategy broadly as about exploring how 'human ability and other resources might deployed to best advantage'. This was expanded on in Frontinus' *Strategems* which defined strategy as 'everything achieved … be it characterized by foresight, advantage, enterprise, or resolution.'

The best known description of what it took to be a strategist comes from Xenophon. The strategist, he argued:

> ... must be ingenious, energetic, careful, full of stamina and presence of mind, loving and tough, straightforward and crafty, alert and deceptive, ready to gamble everything and wishing to have everything, generous and greedy, trusting and suspicious.

The Ancients' approach to educating *strategoi* followed this type of 'over-determined' or 'ill-defined' thinking. They recognized that there was no transferable universally prescriptive and logically consistent approach that could be developed to represent reality (cf. Alexander's statement to Aristotle on how he could never say what he would certainly do in a particular situation until that situation arrived; and Themistocles' greatness being said to be due to his ability to 'do precisely the right thing at precisely the right moment' rather than any particular technique). Consequently, the Greeks favoured story-telling as a means of 'refreshing the vision' and firing each strategists unique telos without 'forming his character by mere imitation' as expressed by Plutarch (see p. 24 in Chapter 2). Many of the most refreshing stories concerned Pericles (see Case Box 6.1).

Case Box 6.1   An Alternative 'First Strategist'

Historians thought Pericles a great strategist for being methodical in his *'making plans and then going forward'* and being unimpressed by placing faith in fortune, luck and 'reckless impulses'; *and* for his *recognizing the disadvantages of following plans* and subsequent unpredictability. He argued that competition created some crucial situations that must be exploited with boldness rather than planning, coining the phrase 'opportunity waits for no man'. His preparedness to disregard plans as much as make them appears to have been based on a number of assumptions. On the one hand, goals made in advance of events could never be realized exactly, and that 'there is often', as Thucydides pointed out, 'no more logic in the course of events than there is in the plans of men.' On the other hand, adherence to plans made prior to action could stifle the potential gains provided by the sort of opportunistic creativity that can only occur as events, problems and contingencies unfold. (Hence, as Thucydides notes, 'To face calamity with a mind as unclouded [by preconceptions] as may be, and quickly to react against it – that, in a city and in an individual, is real strength.')

Pericles himself attributed his strategic success to his ability 'to see what must be done and be able to explain it in such a way that people could understand what this meant for them.' Indeed, ancient historians claim that the most striking proof of Pericles' greatness lay in his ability to persuade the sovereign Athenian citizenry to adopt courses that on first glance seem so hard to grasp. (Or reducing complex and dynamic circumstances into 'trite future-mission statements' and 'flimsy strategic plans', to use Stacey's words [p. 227]). However, in so doing, Pericles was a master at doing something very subtle: connecting an organization's past, present and future, intertwining this with people's own beliefs, and indicating what these connections meant in terms of the course that should be taken. Plutarch writes of Pericles as like a great *kubernetes*, working with 'people's hopes and fears as if they were rudders'.

Pericles' skill in this respect is most obviously manifest in his 'Funeral Oration' issued around 430 BC during the first year of the second Peloponnesian War. The Funeral Oration was an annual event whereby a leading citizen would be chosen to speak in honour of those Athenian's who had died at war. This had not been a good year for Athens. Many had died and there was great uncertainty as to whether, or in what manner, Athens should continue the War.

The traditional format of the Oration was to first praise the actions of mythological and past military ancestors, second to praise the acts of the warriors of the generation previous to the one present, and third to praise for the actions of those who had fallen in the previous year. This then provided the context for exhorting those present to a particular strategic course. However, while Pericles acknowledged such a pattern, and even followed its outline, he also boldly departed from it by subordinating these themes to a sketch developed by picking out what he saw as the key elements of the *ethos* of Athens. Why?

Firstly, Pericles claimed that outlining the distinctive spirit for which the fallen had given their lives would be a greater testament and embodiment of their actions. Secondly, he argued that past deeds were often portrayed in too rosy a fashion, and that 'praise spoken of others' was only advantageous 'up to the point where each believes himself capable of *doing* the things he hears of.' Pericles was primarily interested in the past that was useful for 'offering encouragement' for the present.

Beyond his introductions, his very first words on the Athenian organization were: 'We do not seek to copy others.' This becomes the Oration's base note, with the remainder laced with continued references to how Athens is 'different', 'unique', 'the opposite of most', 'an example to others rather than imitators'.

Pericles first picks out Athens' particular form of democracy. While others see it as a motley aggregate of different systems ('a supermarket of constitutions' in Plato's words), Pericles claims it is a paradoxical but judicious mix of equality and individual merit. He then builds on the theme of paradoxical characteristics to develop his picture of Athens:

'Athenians appreciate diversity and tolerates many ways of life while all obey laws both written and unwritten.'
'Athens boasts more local traditional ceremonies and rituals than others while being the most global of cities where products of all nations may be enjoyed.'
'Athens combines a concern for self and for state.'
'Athenians establish memorials to both their successes and their failures.'
'Athens is both relaxed and prepared.'
'Athenians are wise and thoughtful, but they are not soft: "We combine boldness with reasoning about the business we are to take in hand, whereas for other people it is ignorance that produces courage and reasoning produces hesitation."'

These paradoxical differences and strengths enable each Athenian to 'profit from the greatest variety in life and the maximum of graceful adaptability.'

'Such is our city', Pericles concludes.

'I have spoken at length about it to give a firm basis of proof to my praise of the men who have gone before', but also, Pericles goes on, 'to instruct you that the contest is not on the same terms for us and for those who do not similarly enjoy these advantages'. In other words, 'your ethos is different, therefore your strategy must be conceived on different terms from that of others'.

Thus: 'You must not consider the advantages of this *ethos* not simply as a theoretical matter ... In your actions you must every day fix your eyes on the strength of our city; you must become lovers of it. When it appears great to you, you must realize that men have made it great, by daring, by recognizing what was needed.'

'The men who fought and died', he explains, did so 'nobly judging that it would be wrong to be deprived of [this *ethos*]; and it is right that every single one of those who are left should be willing to struggle for it.'

'These men met their fate in a manner worthy of our city. The rest must judge it right to adopt an equally daring attitude.' By following in their spirit you grant them 'the most distinguished of tombs – not the one in which bodies lie but rather the one in which their glory remains recorded for ever on every occasion for word or deed ... their lives in every man's heart an unwritten memorial, of their purpose rather than their accomplishments.'

In this light, Pericles explains, your 'glory is great', and your strategy clear, 'if you do not fail to live up to your own nature.'

1   Why do you think the Greeks considered Pericles to be a great strategist?
2   How might strategy or management now be thought differently if we saw Pericles rather than Ansoff or Taylor as a key point of origin?

Sources: This case draws on 'The Life of Pericles' from Plutarch's *Parallel Lives*, Herodotus' *The Histories,* and Thucydides' *The Peloponnesian War* (many translations of each are available)

From their foundation myths to their belief in a myriad of personable gods and goddesses the Greeks assumed the unresolvable tension between and mutuality of *chaos* and *cosmos*. The coming together of these two spheres made life what it was. In keeping, it seems that strategy, for the Greeks, arose in the coming together of design and emergence in the same way that *metos* required working with both *cosmos* and *chaos*. The Greeks did not see wisdom as being able to represent the way the world really was, but as the ability to recognize the world of 'being', of forms, laws or *maps*; and the world of 'becoming', of the multiple, the unstable and the unlimited – the world of *mapping*.

Strategy, like *metos*, existed in neither of these domains. It was characterized by an ability to oscillate between the two, to be 'polyvalent' and sufficiently wily and supple to bend one's course of action, to be able to pick out a number of different elements, frameworks or perspectives with which to inspire actions toward particular purposes. It is for this reason that Odysseus was given the epithet 'resourceful' and described at the outset of the Odyssey as 'expert in all ways of contending' (or 'genius versatile' as an earlier translation puts it). His greatness lay in the ability to connect to the right interpretation or experiences, lived or heard, so as to arrive at the best course for him given the way the situation was unfolding.

How strategy's conventional history saw the past through the eyes of the present

Strategy, according to the alternative history outlined above, is originally and fundamentally about the interplay of design and emergence in the same way that *metos* required working with and shuttling between *cosmos* and *chaos*, plan and circumstance, map and mapping. Planning or design provided necessary preliminary orientation and impetus, but once underway the art of strategy lay in 'working with the flow' as unforeseen opportunities rendered plans less than optimal in order to build a momentum and keep things animated. This alternative history presents a very different conception of strategy's foundations from the conventional view. So, how did Stacey, Mintzberg, Ansoff and others come to see the views of the Greeks as just a simple or 'less educated' version of the top-down design view? Simply by seeing history in terms of their present.

When *strategoi* emerged into English in the fifteenth century as *strategem*, it still meant either any 'operation or act of generalship' or any act in 'devising expedients, artifice or cunning' in keeping with its alternative origins described above. By the middle of the seventeenth century, Boyle still noted that 'stratagems are as Lawful as Expedient.' However, as the word *strategy* arose in English in the middle of the nineteenth century, the *Oxford English Dictionary* makes it clear that it emerged as 'distinguished from tactics, which is the art of handling forces in battle or in the immediate presence of the enemy', or a formal military plan. As the shift took place, there was some ambiguity of meaning. For example, in the first half of the nineteenth century, James claimed that 'strategy, something done out of the sight of the enemy, *differs materially* from *tactic*; the later belonging to the mechanical movement of bodies, set in motion by the former', while MacDougall wrote of '*every point* on the theatre of war being a strategical point.' However, by the end of that century, what strategy is becomes positively established as *only* the thinking and planning that goes on 'before hostile armies or fleets are brought into *contact* (a word which perhaps better than any other indicates the dividing line between tactics and strategy).' By 1901, Hornung found it remarkable that 'Raffles was both strategian and tactician, [because] we all now know the difference between the two.'

Consequently, we may relate the changes in the meaning of strategy over the past three centuries to two specific historical developments:

- Modernity's particular separation of mind and body, thinking and doing – a separation that valued the lack of contact, or objectivity, over connecting to things, that became commonplace in the West as the words linking back to *strategos* shifted emphasis.
- Technological developments and the increasing size of military organizations. Here, weapons and information technology had increasingly enabled commanders to see the advantages of removing themselves from the operations of war outweighing those of being at the frontline, enabling *thinking* and *planning* to be increasingly removed from *doing* or *action*. This, combined with the increasing size of armies, promoted hierarchical, bureaucratic military organizations requiring mechanistic universal rules and procedures, to ensure control and coordination.

As labour was specialized and divided in this manner, strategy became a top management task associated with planning in advance of action, differentiated from the tactics, and operations conceived as taking place further down the hierarchy, toward the frontline.

Hence, the etymological development of the conventional Modern meaning of strategy relies upon the emergence of Modernism's particular triangular-hierarchical way of viewing. The Greek's lack of this made them see strategy differently. But for writers like Mintzberg and Ansoff, looking at the world with words shaped by this Modern gaze, it is difficult to recognize the Ancient's different approaches to strategy unless they can be made to fit a stream of development that flows directly into present conventions. (This is partly why Sun Tzu, who *did* distinguish between strategy and tactics, is seen as a key historical figure far more than the Greeks mentioned here).

Mintzberg, Ansoff and others view of the history of strategy is a backward vision that promotes seeing present conventions as fundamental. Consequently, their Modern interpretations of Premodern approaches to strategy represent another example of unwittingly limiting the field by seeing the past through the eyes of the present. But what if we combined the Ancient's view of strategy with the Modern in a Postmodern manner? Might we then reconceive strategy? The next section explores another way of looking at strategy – a way that gets beyond the recent academic debates – combining both:

- Premodern notions of the subjective networked web and the interaction between design and emergence, *and*
- Modern grids born of the over-and-above design approach.

The former enables us to incorporate the developmental *animation* that is often lost sight of by the design approach. The latter enables us to utilize useful maps and grids thereby aiding *orientation*, a factor lost sight of by many of the theorists who sought to overthrow the top-down view and its 'flimsy models.'

3   Modern grids + Premodern webs: A Postmodern approach to strategy

I am a great lover of these processes of division and generalization; they help me to speak and think.

Plato

If the Alps story is the anecdote most remembered by my strategy students, the strategy model that most say they retain and apply is this simple expression:

$$\text{Cost} + \text{Margin} = \text{Selling Price} \quad (\text{or } C + M = SP)$$
$$\text{Margin} \times \text{Units} = \text{Profit} \quad (\text{or } M \times U = \Pi).$$

The beauty of these two equations is that any strategy for any for-profit company may be analysed (and indeed should be justifiable) in these terms. A viable strategy must, over time, enable margins and profit to improve via:

* reducing costs; and/or
* increasing selling price; and/or
* increasing units sold.

There are infinite routes to this, but if a strategic course cannot be justified in these terms it is hard to see why a company would follow it. People like the model because it is easy to remember, and it enables them to quickly assess proposals and ask pertinent questions.

In general terms we can see the value of this simple model by using it quickly to break down how companies have, in the past, tended to seek to achieve a competitive advantage in terms of things that are easy to measure (handy if you are 'accountable' and are subject to 'performance appraisal').

* The first, and most easily measured route, is *cost reduction* through increasing efficiency.
* The second has been investing in new technology in order to increase *selling price*.
* The third most common route has been to increase *unit sales* through aggressive marketing.

However, as with the problems described with regard to best practice copying in the introduction to Part II of this book, as these three routes have become increasingly easy and quick to copy or 'reverse engineer' they have become hygiene factors (that is, not routes to sustainable competitive advantage). Consequently, we are witnessing an interest now in less tangible but more difficult to copy means of increasing selling price or unit sales through things such as an idiosyncratic *ethos* or history (see Chapter 5).

In particular terms, the value of the model can be seen as it is blackboarded up in front of a group of executives. They hear little of what is said for the next five minutes as they input and analyse their own concerns in terms of its logic.

One gets a quite different reaction when one puts up a slide of a more complex and likely more representative model, such as the one shown in Figure 6.5 on p. 228 – usually a mixture of eyestrain, perplexity and disengagement, as people sit back and wait to have its technology inputted into them. The detail incorporated into representations like this generally prevents people from being able to see, or feed in, their own particular situations and subjective interpretations. Getting too caught up in developing all encompassing world-views hinders, in other words, the mapping process (that is, things become all orientation and no animation).

Perhaps this highlights another Postmodern irony. In a complex world where more individualized approaches are required, simpler frameworks are more useful than more complicated ones. The more complex or 'representative' a model is, the more it bounds rationality, closes off debate, alienates people and prevents them incorporating their own ideas or networks of relationships. The more basic maps, on the other hand, require interpretation, connection and 'play' to bring them to life, thus encouraging people to get involved in them and subsequently take ownership of them. In fact, while *maps* must be perceived as having some sympathetic connection with the situation faced (it is not that 'anything goes' – the Hungarian soldiers would not have been aided by a tin of beans or an album cover), their lack of 'accuracy' inspires a greater compulsion to take ownership by using these maps as a starting point and then doing one's own *mapping*.

A good illustration, and perhaps the most famous 'Postmodern map', is Harry Beck's 'London Underground' (see Figure 6.7). Here geographic representation is eschewed for 'short hand'. It may not be rational in an objective sense, but Beck's map makes no claim to represent things the way they really are. But it is memorable and open to individual customization (as Beck said, it 'must be thought of as a living and changing thing, with schematic "manipulation" and spare part osteopathy going on all the time'). Anyone who has lived in or visited London will make their own lives understood as they network themselves in relation to particular parts of it. It is not reality (look above it for that), but its symbols have become a shared language and people interact with it to schematize their lives in ways that are useful to them in plotting their particular course. The Postmodern city may be, in Harvey's words, a 'labyrinth, honeycombed with such diverse networks of social interaction oriented to such diverse goals that the encyclopaedia becomes a maniacal scrapbook filled with colourful entries', but we still use schema to make sense of and communicate our individuality in labyrinthine times.

This may lead us to question those strategy academics that dismissed outright conventional strategy frameworks as 'presumptuous' and 'always too simple to capture the complexity and irrationality of life.' This attitude is not particularly useful for people who want to pursue individual courses. It is hard to engage in mapping particular courses if you do not allow any maps (indeed, Columbus may not have found a passage to India, but he would not have left home if he tore up the charts he had at his disposal, no matter how imperfect they were). In such circumstances things become all animation and no orientation, encouraging the frantic grabbing at buzzwords to no lasting effect. Hence, this attitude can only result in a debilitating schism between strategy academics and strategy practitioners. But this schism may be overcome if we take a Postmodern view and cease to see the discovery of representative-prescriptive models of strategy and management as our aim.

In Plato's later works (lesser known because they were not regarded as so significant in Modernity), we sense a questioning of his earlier universal idealism, perhaps influenced by his pupil Aristotle. In Plato's *Phaedrus* Socrates says:

> I am a great lover of these processes of division and generalization; they help me to speak and think.

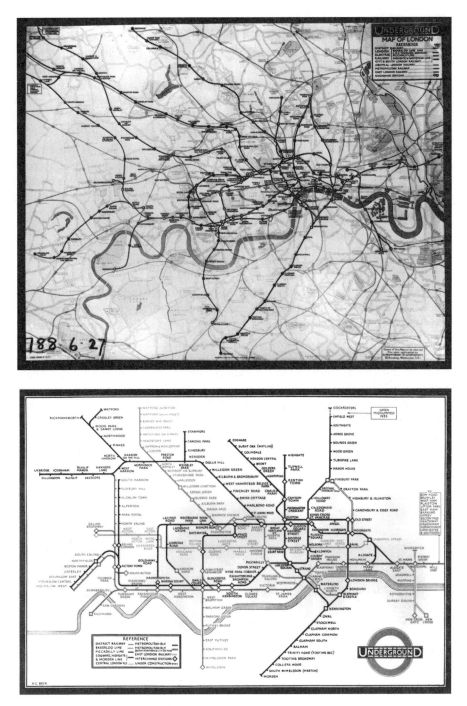

Figure 6.7   Mr Beck's Underground map (bottom) and the more geographically representative map that it replaced (top)
Source: The London Transport Museum

There could perhaps be no better motto for using strategy frameworks in a Postmodern manner. To paraphrase Foucault, it may no longer be appropriate for academics and consultants to play the role of the advisor, the project and goals to be adopted being a matter for those who 'do the fighting.' However, what they can do is provide useful 'divisions and generalizations' that help people 'speak and think' their own strategies. And this is what Porter's models and others like them (see the Bibliographical Notes, pp. 340–4) offer us. It would be a pointless shame to toss them out, given that they do provide people with useful languages (or 'trees in their heads' to borrow from Deleuze and Guatarri). What might be more radical would be to shift their emphases a little, so as to use them in a more knowing, playful and individualized manner, while questioning and rethinking their linearity and either/or distinctions.

Rethinking Modernist assumptions and grids

While we might wonder at Porter's ruling Japanese approaches to strategy out of court (Chapter 1), one consistent thread through all of his work is the idea that strategy is about choosing an identity or 'position', to use his terminology, that is different from your competitors. This is all in keeping with the ideas expressed in Chapter 5 here with regard to *ethos*. However, as Chapter 2 argued, conventional Modern notions of identity are now being rethought. The Postmodern recognition of the 'rhizomatic and relational character of life' and the subsequent 'breaking down of conventional categories' has particularly led to a questioning and rethinking of:

- the idea of a 'unitary stand-alone self';
- 'the linearity of things';
- 'being all things to all people'; and
- making 'either/or distinctions.'

We can combine this questioning with Porter's conventional language to rethink the shape of strategy. Again, mapping these things with a pencil and paper helps things 'stick'.

For example, the shape of the value chain is problematized as companies realize that they do not need to keep all parts of the chain 'in-house' and linear. Rather than attempt to do or be 'all things', they can just focus on one or two core aspects and outsource the rest to other identities who can focus on these things better and with whom they can link. Perhaps, given the advance of information technology, this web can spread simultaneously across national or continental boundaries. Given this, it makes less sense to talk about the linear value chains (see p. 222) of unified stand-alone companies and more to talk of 'value networks' or 'constellations' (contrast the diagram below with Figure 2.4 on p. 22). While this form may still draw from Porter's language, it is more like a Premodern web than a Modern line. And what was key then is key now: knowing your particular strengths within a community and developing and maintaining relationships with other members through placing yourself in their shoes – an understanding that enabled one to be separate from another contributor while 'participating in their being' or working with them.

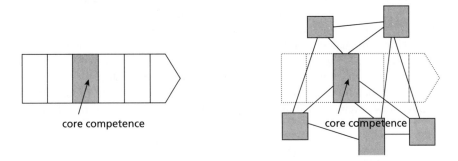

core competence

This focus on networking has seen the rise of 'strategic alliances' – the idea that paradoxically companies should both compete and collaborate. In the airline industry, for example, while company's 'value chains' are increasingly webs, as provisions such as catering, cleaning, marketing and fuel are contracted out, another web of connections or alliances (for example, OneWorld; Star Alliance) runs between companies (see the diagram below, based on Figure 6.4 on p. 226). These amount to an aggressive form of defense, as they protect against the *threat of new entrants* (to use the language of the Five Forces [Figure 6.3 on p. 223]) as it is hard to set up a new company that can instantly develop these relationships. These relationships also question Strategy's conventional either/or choices. Alliances help to reduce costs by enabling buying in bulk, thereby reducing *supplier power*. At the same time they hook customers into relationships with frequent flyer programmes that increase the perceived switching costs of moving to a company outside of the alliance thus reducing *buyer power*. This enables the selling price to edge up. Indeed, companies who are part of a prestige alliance reduce their costs *and* give themselves a differentiated advantage.

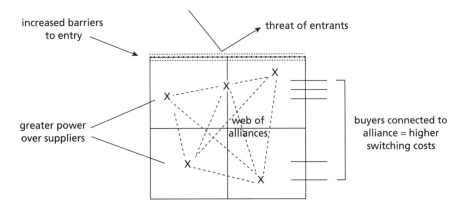

Other conventional either/or distinctions may also be questioned. The combination of globalization and localization is encouraging firms to look at ways they can cut across conventional categories. Hence, through alliance partners an airline can focus on its local difference and responsiveness within a narrower scope while being networked to a broad global market through an alliance.

Other companies are looking at ways of networking local differences in countries that we might associate with lower cost and cities that we might associate with focus-differentiated design to achieve low cost-focus *and* differentiation *and* high unit sales, thereby dominating the broad-cost segment. (For better and for worse – see the Nike case on p. 308 in Part III). Some companies are looking to develop more individualized relationships with customers, something that can be much better understood if one replaces the one big 'five forces' arrow to buyer power with lots of different little arrows as in the diagram below.

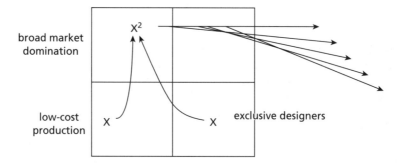

Indeed, the breakdown of these either/ors, discrete stand-alone entities, and linear chains of production, suggests that it might be better to use frameworks like Porter's to talk about how particular firms are seeking to 'glocalize' by employing 'lo-glo' strategies, rather than to ask whether a company is going global *or* not. Instead of thinking of companies deciding to become more centralized or more decentralized, perhaps it is more useful to examine how they achieve 'centralized-decentralization.' Rather than struggling when doing a SWOT analysis (strategy's most basic framework where one notes down a company's Strengths, Weaknesses, Opportunities and Threats), to figure out whether a particular characteristic (for example, 'being relatively small') is a strength or a weakness, one can recognize it as both. Seeing as no one company can be all things to all people, and there is no generic strategic best practice, it is a matter of seeing this smallness as related to a company's *ethos* and setting out to do things that bigger companies cannot do.

Case Box 6.2   Deconstructing and reconfiguring the value chain

Levi-Strauss is a great brand and it makes great jeans. But then so do a lot of other companies nowadays. In order to continue to be at the forefront of casual-wear and related products, Levi's are re-thinking how they add value. Using the traditional linear input-process-output view of adding value, clothes' manufacturers take inputs like fabrics and fixtures, use the company's information systems and knowledge to subject these inputs to value-adding processes (such as design and assembly), and then distribute outputs to customers who pay for the finished product and then go on their way. Levi's have attempted to deconstruct these assumptions and look at ways in which they can *involve* their customers in the value-adding process so that they become part of the 'Levi's community'.

Flagship stores, such as those in San Francisco and London, now contain a 'Levi's customization area'. Here customers can photograph themselves and input these images into computer terminals that allow them to see what various outfits from the Levi's range would look like on them. Then they can become part of the value-adding design team by testing out how customized alterations (different cuts, or washes, or buttons, or pockets, or rips, or stitching, or patches and so on) would look on them. Finished designs can then be taken to an in-house construction team that works with the customer to develop what is wanted. Information on individual customers can be kept for return visits and aggregated to provide insights into popular trends.

Moreover, the London store has been refurbished into a combined store and club/arts venue. It incorporates a 'chill-out' area, Internet stations, plasma screens, ISDN links, a suspended two-tier DJ booth designed by DJ Paul Oakenfold, and a record outlet called Vinyl Addiction. It can be transformed into a 500 capacity venue with facilities to host club nights, live music, fashion shows, film screenings, comedy nights and exhibitions.

1   How would you draw the Levi's 'value adding' system described in the case above?
2   What advantages might Levi's gain by re-conceiving the conventional value chain?

We can explore these Postmodern shifts of emphasis in more detail by returning to the car industry. Case Box 2.2 (p. 75) indicated the way in which Postmodernism may mean the co-habitation of globalization and localization. In the car industry, for example, it would be foolish to suggest that a continued globalization or homogenization is not happening. VW's development of the 'new' Beetle has been enabled by a global chassis that is the same for a Seat or a Golf, and Ford's quirky Ka is just a Fiesta with curves. Hence, best practice and standardization will play a continuing role in cutting the costs of production. However, something else is happening too. Globalization is, paradoxically, enabling smaller 'local' marques to survive or even thrive.

Networks created via alliances and 'soft mergers' now characterize the car industry. Some of these webs appear to work particularly well. One such concern is the Ford Group's incorporation of Jaguar. After initially attempting to impose 'The Ford Way' upon Jaguar (according to Jaguar people at least), Ford management took a step back. They recognized that they benefited from being associated with a Jaguar that maintains its own identity within the focussed differentiation segment and now leave it to do its own thing to a large extent. Thus it does not undermine the distinctive *differentiated* Jaguar style, but helps out wherever possible, particularly on *cost reduction*. This 'soft merger' relationship is similar to that with Volvo. Ford seeks to increase its average selling prices through association with Volvo's differentiated competitive advantage (safety technology) while using its operational expertise and global muscle to reduce Volvo costs.

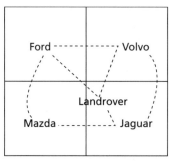

Thus, one can understand the Ford Group's strategy by superimposing their particular web of relationships over Porter's general grid (see Figure 6.4 on p. 226), as shown in the diagram above. It is no longer a question of global *or* local, or either/or choices between cost and differentiation, but a question of thinking in terms of individual webs and knowing how the different identities that make up your web can best interact with one another.

Other companies and groups in the automobile industry may also be quickly and simply analysed in this manner. VW works well by networking identities (Skoda and Seat, VW, Audi, Bentley) in all four segments of the GSM, although they may have difficulties reconciling the relationship between Skoda and Seat and VW and Audi marques if their identities come to be perceived by the buying public as too similar. Chrysler and Daimler have sought to become a broader global player by sharing their own particular geographic foci and expertise. BMW succeeded in enabling Rover to produce the 75, a car competitive with its own marques in the broad-differentiated segment. But making Rover marques into BMWs could only cannibalize sales and create internal tensions. By contrast, one of the things that British Airways has done well in recent times is re-focusing its identity from 'stuck in the middle' to the broad-differentiated end of the market by spawning a low-cost airline called 'Go' to compete against new entrants in the cost-focus end (see diagrams below).

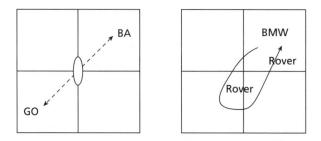

In sum, while Porter's notion that companies must be clear in understanding their positioning still rings true, his frameworks' emphases on either/or choices and singular bodies and linearities may require questioning and rethinking. The key thing when using and adapting such frameworks is that organizations 'know themselves', that they know how and why they are different and then seek to develop or make the most of this. For example, while Honda may indeed be 'stuck in the middle' and subsequently damned by Porter's generic logic, so long as Honda is clear why its *ethos* leads it to be oriented there and how it can be animated to accentuate and profit from the difference of 'being in the middle'. Frameworks like the ones described above and in Case Box 6.3 can help rather than hinder this orienting/ animating process – if they are mixed, matched and developed in an individualized-descriptive rather than a generic-prescriptive manner.

As Case Box 6.3 indicates, complexity may be better addressed on a case-by-case basis, bolting on the bits of framework that suit rather than seeking to apply one complex model that fits all, or polarizing the debate and/or using nothing. For example, managers as they become more resourceful and connect to more frameworks and languages can create montages that help them understand particular situations. By, for example, bolting a PEST analysis (like SWOT, but focussed on listing Political, Economic, Social and Technological forces and scenarios that may impact on an industry) onto the Five Forces to facilitate a fuller discussion on the factors influencing their industry, or by combining, and Porter's Diamond of National Competitive-advantage [the Five Forces] to discuss a local industry's competitive advantage in a global marketplace (see the Bibliographical Notes for more information on these frameworks).

One may even connect to 'retro models' to analyse and see the dangers of unquestioningly taking fragmenting value-webs (see p. 245) as a general best practice. For decades the Boston Consulting Group (or BCG) matrix has helped organization's think about how, given that there is usually a 'life-cycle' associated with a product or service, they need a portfolio of things at different growth stages:

1 New products, or *question marks*, that may exhibit low market share and market growth but could be the next big thing.
2 *Stars*, that may have low market share but fast market growth and the potential for high market share if the growth continues.
3 *Cash cows*, who have the large market share but for whom the growth has waned.
4 *Dogs*, those products that have crossed over into declining market share.

One of the most common problems we are now seeing with taking the web and hub approach as a 'be all and end all' is companies who cut themselves back to focussing just on their cash cows, believing this to be the same as their *ethos*.

An airline, for example, may cut costs by joining an alliance and focussing mainly on its Asian segments while its 'partners' take care of the rest, but it also becomes a very small company with limited opportunities for growing new stars. This makes it a static concern that could fade away if others can nibble at the limited things that the company now does. A spectacles manufacturer may decide that what it does best, or its 'cash cow', is making basic lenses, import in other components, and close down its research and development arm. This cuts costs, obviously. However, it may only be a matter of time before that company's suppliers seek to forward integrate into making lenses themselves and decide that it is unwise to supply their competitors. Or a matter of time before another company with an R&D facility patents a new approach that changes the market, turning cash cows into dogs. Organizations must retain the ability to develop or rejuvenate their *ethos*, otherwise short-term cost-cutting can mean long-term failure.

Case Box 6.3   Porter's Power

Power, a pub/restaurant group, has grown fast through successful acquisitions. It now owns many big name brands, including 'Mr Beef', 'M.J.'s and 'Pizza Court.' To aid the company's coordination as it grows, managers need to think through how these various 'characters' relate to one another. The diagram and dialogue below came about as the result of encouraging a group of these managers to use Porter's frameworks to express their own ideas about where the company was going, with a particular emphasis on Mr Beef.

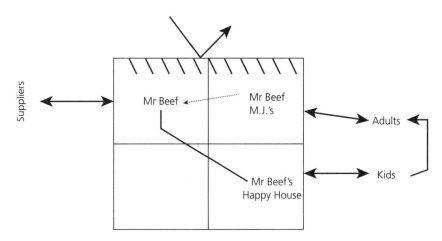

Manager 1: 'Basically, I saw Mr Beef as being a family pub/restaurant, but a bit better than the competition – differentiated. However, over time this has been kind of forgotten. It's been easier to focus on cost reduction and it's drifted back into the broad-cost segment. The interesting development is Happy House [*Happy House is a children's restaurant/playground that had been established within a number of Mr Beef pubs*]. These have proved really popular and are differentiated and focussed on kids, obviously. So, what do we do? Perhaps we need to revamp Mr Beef and move it into the differentiated end again?'

Manager 2: 'Maybe, but there it's almost directly competing against M.J.'s

Manager 1: 'And surely Mr Beef is such a big chain now that we should be in the broad-cost segment? If you add in that part of Porter's Five Forces of Industry, that's where we can really exercise power over suppliers by using our size as a buying strength.'

Manager 2: 'But what about the disparity between Mr Beef and Happy House? If we continue with your bringing in the Five Forces and look at the other side of things, buyer power, we all know that for family pub/restaurants it's kids who often make the buying decision. We can't afford to damage that link by letting Happy House slide the way of Mr Beef.'

Manager 3: 'Sure, but if we realize the difference and the relationship between the two, then surely we can benefit at both ends of the value chain; a strong link into key suppliers and a key hook into a special type of buyers.'

Manager 4: 'Yeah, in a way, if we could do this, and get the best of both sides, then this could be a source of competitive advantage hard to replicate. It would create a real barrier to new entrants up at the top of the box there.'

1   How did using basic strategy frameworks aid these managers?
2   While the above discussion may not represent a *pure* application of the logic of Porter's frameworks, how have these managers benefited by using and 'customizing' them?

The identities of this organization and its business units have been disguised.

Webs and networks as frameworks

Given what has already been said in this chapter about not seeing strategy as just an either/or choice between top-down planning and emergence, frameworks that enable us to analyse how strategy can be enabled or thwarted by networks at 'the bottom' would also be useful. The only problem being that bottom-up emergence theorists have generally been more interested in dismissing existing frameworks than creating alternatives. The result has been a number of 'happy' cases like 3M and Honda Motorcycles, mentioned above. These are worth adding to our 'map kits' as they highlight the importance of being open to ideas coming from all over a company and following up on the opportunities that subsequently emerge. However, there is more that we could connect to from this perspective if we look a little deeper.

The most thoughtful attempt to provide something tangible that can be used to think about strategy in terms of emergent networks is the 'resource-based view' (RBV) of the firm. Throughout the 1990s, this approach, popularized through a series of papers by Jay Barney, has gathered momentum within strategic management circles. The RBV argues that each organization is made up of a unique constellation of:

- *physical resources* like land, offices and machinery;
- *financial resources* like access to capital;
- *human resources* like experience and expertise; and
- *organizational resources* like reputation, culture and traditional relationships.

The best way to record these resources and relations is not to list them, as is often the way when company's seek to record their competencies, but in a systems diagram (see below) showing how the various resources connect to, build upon and reinforce one another.

The conventional list of competencies, represented below, is static. It does not illustrate how, for example, this particular company's reputation is what it is because of its employees, production facilities, links with suppliers and so on. The list seems to imply that if a competitor were to assemble the six parts on this list they would match this company. The RBV web of relationships and the tacit knowledge embedded within them is a tangible illustration of how the whole will always be greater than the sum of the parts, and how these relationships cannot be engineered – they have to grow organically. Because a system of relationships is organic, it is reflective of a particular geographical location, a particular history, particular and emergent relations between employees within the firm, and then between them and suppliers and customers and so forth. Therefore each organization's RBV web will be unique. This is important to recognize, because in an age where firms have become very good at copying what they can through best practice benchmarking and reverse engineering, historically determined interrelationships and the knowledge embodied in them, are difficult to quickly replicate. For this reason it may be claimed that tacit 'knowledge webs' will, along with other difficult to copy aspects like ethos, become increasingly valuable sources of an organization's competitive advantage.

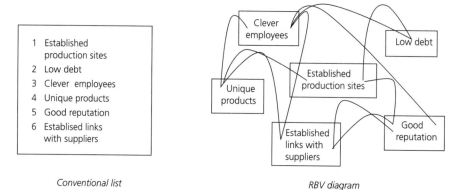

1 Established
    production sites
2 Low debt
3 Clever employees
4 Unique products
5 Good reputation
6 Establised links
    with suppliers

Conventional list   *RBV diagram*

Looking further there are many other fruitful approaches that we might borrow from philosophy, history and psychology to analyse how strategy can be shaped, for better or for worse, by emergent webs. Foucault's notion that networks can cut across traditional spatial boundaries in order to facilitate or repress the flow of knowledge and new ideas and actions, is one way of examining how strategy practices are shaped in ways that may not be planned from the top down (see Case Box 6.4). The 'further reading' list for this chapter recommends others.

Case Box 6.4   Networks Shape Strategy

When Heinz Fischer arrived as head of human resources at Deutsche Bank he found that women accounted for fewer than one in six at the managerial level despite making up half the bank's workforce. Experience had shown him that companies that pursue diversity enjoy better performance, largely because their strategies subsequently reflect a cross-section of society rather than just one particular category. So, Fischer invited 30 women employees to a workshop to discuss the obstacles they faced. The most critical barrier the women identified was the lack of informal networks of the type used by men, such as the golf course or the drink after work.

While the 'emergence school' has shown us the importance of looking at strategy as influenced by those further down an organization, it often presents an overly rosy view of the effects of 'bottom up' influence and does not provide many tools for analysing how this happens. Particularly good examples of such processes can be seen in many of the 'fly on the wall' documentaries about organizations that have become popular in recent times. These provide palpable 'real life' examples of how particular networks of relationships can 'skew' the implementation of top-down strategies. And how these same networks selectively filter information about emergent ideas so as to influence the decisions made further up. Often these networks draw further strength from connections with people beyond the company walls. One way of analysing this behavior is to 'diagram' the key interactions. (Indeed, a San Francisco-based design company called Future Farmers now provides a website *http://theyrule.orgo.org/* which maps the relationships between key players in US corporations).

This is not a new idea. William Foote Whyte's groundbreaking ethnographic study *Street Corner Society* built diagrams mapping the interactions between individuals to understand relationships between group structure and individual performance. Whyte found that the influential people were those with the most key 'connections'. Michel Foucault also challenged preconceptions about power by arguing that power does not exist in 'bodies of authority' (for example, the government, the police, the media, the education system) but in the relationships (tangible or otherwise) between these bodies. Hence, protesting through directly confronting such bodies may cause the network (consciously or subconsciously) to manufacture opinion against the protest and make traditional bonds stronger (a simplistic example of direct student action against university councils in response to increased fees is provided in the diagram below).

The best form of resistance, therefore, is to organize alternative networks of like-minded individuals who can help the cause behind the scenes. Many disenfranchised groups, particularly within the US, have now taken up Foucault's thinking.

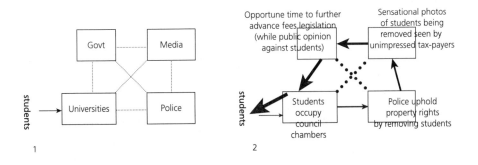

The same logic can be applied to understand particular organizations. Pilar Conde, a managing director at JP Morgan, says that people often misunderstand 'networking': 'They ask "Why do I need a network to be successful? If I do my job well my manager will recognize me." But everyone in a position of power has used a network.' Furthermore, we have found that after practicing on a 'documentary' case, diagramming relationships in their own organizations is a powerful way for managers to begin to understand how their company's strategy is actually realized, and how and why certain individuals may, or may not, be influencing things.

The problem described in the first part of this Case Box may be understood in the theoretical terms described above. Women, or any under-represented group, find it difficult to influence agendas as they emerge from the bottom, or steer strategies as they are handed down from the top, because they lack the 'common interest' networks drawn upon by others in corporations to 'grease the wheels'. Directly confronting these networks would likely create counter-productive 'underground' forms of resistance. The best solution is to form alternative networks.

In response to the problems outlined by Heinz Fischer above, Deutsche Bank encouraged the establishment of a 'women's network' within the company. This network then decided to extend its web beyond the organization. The Bank's female executives organized and hosted the first *Women in European Business Conference* in Frankfurt in March 2000. Around 400 delegates were anticipated. More than 1000 women attended.

1   Are you part of a network, at work or in any other sphere of life? How would you diagram it? How does this network facilitate and inhibit the development of new ideas, ways of behaving or strategies?
2   Have 'outsiders' ever threatened that network? How did the network respond?
3   How would you make your network more effective?

Source: This case draws on 'Women's Sociable Route to Success', *Financial Times*

---

4   Strategy reconceived

Our strategy was to accept the physical power of Banksides' mountain-like brick building and even to enhance it, rather than trying to break or diminish it. This is a kind of Aikido strategy: you use your opponent's energy for your own purposes. Instead of fighting it, you take the energy and shape it in a new and unexpected way.

Herzog & de Meuron Architects

A recent paper in the *Academy of Management Review* by David Knights described Porter's GSM as a classic example of the 'myth of progress that underlies the demand for stable and positive management knowledge.' Knights claimed that despite the fact that Porter's model is too simple to reflect reality for managers, they continue to cling to it. Furthermore, he argued that Porter's condemnation of those who fail to choose between cost and differentiation and stay 'stuck in the middle', and the fact that Porter's representation has become the reality for managers detracts from giving attention to 'subjectivity' by 'disciplining modern management regimes into emulating it.' This may well be so, but if managers think of the GSM as not representative of reality, and use such models subjectively, with input or modification to develop individualized insights, frameworks like Porter's provide great frames upon which ideas can be expressed and used as a starting point for debate as to a company's course. In Wittgenstein and Heidegger's words (p. 57) they offer a shared language that provides the *'necessary appearance of foundation'* – exceedingly useful if one wants to make and communicate ideas about taking a particular direction.

Indeed, one of the main reasons that frameworks like these continue to be popular is that their simplicity enables people to interpret them subjectively, weave their own language into them and express them in ways that the people they work with can quickly relate to. Moreover, their simplicity enables people to customize them or nomadically combine them into their own particular 'hot rod'.

While it is correct to say that conventional strategy frameworks are 'trite' and 'flimsy' and that strategy is much more than this, the call to make them 'redundant' may be a case of throwing out the baby with the bath water. While things are more complex than a two-by-two matrix, particular strategies spring from the oscillation and interaction between 'local' individuals and purposes and 'global' frameworks. As with the Hungarian army example (p. 214), these maps do not need to represent the world all in one. They animate and orient, provide a shared language, and act as sounding boards and points of convergence. So long as they are recognized as such there is no need for belittling them – strategic thinking is richer for them.

Hopefully, after years of debating which map or perspective or recipe best represents what strategy really is, we might now see the value in having many images at our disposal. One is more likely to reach a particular destination by oscillating between an underground map and a London A-Z *in combination* with a map drawn by a friend on the back of an envelope *in combination* with asking a few people for advice along the way. These, *in combination* with other environmental signs seen on your travels, will provide a basis for constructive debate with those travelling with you and, subsequently, a further platform for developing impetus.

Most of the maps that strategic management has conventionally drawn upon have been based on the fields of economics, psychology and statistics, as indeed are most of those described in this chapter. However, as the first part of this book demonstrated, this is more due to particular historical contingencies than fundamental necessities. If, for example, General Lee's plan (see Chapter 3, p. 129) had come to fruition we may have been just as likely to use frameworks drawn from biography, linguistics and geometry. Recognizing this should encourage us to begin to incorporate frameworks from other fields that we may be familiar with *in combination* with those already widely used, so long as they can help us articulate and bounce back and forward potential courses of action and choices.

While there are many 'processes of division and generalization' that can help, none of these maps should prescribe what you must do. Each individual must bring his or her particular purpose and understanding into the mix in order to analyse his or her situations – which brings us back to *ethos*.

Nigella Lawson provides a useful parallel in bemoaning the 'tyranny of the recipe' in her recently published *How to Eat*. Having a number of good recipes is a starting point, she explains, but a good chef must be more than this – he or she must have their 'own individual sense of what food is about.' Too often in the past managers have fallen under the spell of the tyranny of this year's recipe for corporate success, just seeking to replicate it before realizing that everybody is doing the same inferior copy of the original. A recipe can inspire added value, but only if it is infused with a different approach or *ethos* and given a new twist. Thus, it is important to focus on one's individual ethos before and during the preparation and 'cooking' process.

Raban's *Soft City* (see p. 62) provides another good analogy in describing the Postmodern relationship between the individual and their 'topography':

> For better or for worse the city invites you to remake it, to consolidate it into a shape you can live in. Decide who you are, and the city will again assume a fixed form around you. Decide what it is, and your own identity will be revealed.

There could be no better expression of the worth of exploring many different strategic frameworks on equal terms, to see how they may be useful to connect to in order to help you individually understand your organization's identity. The onus is, first and foremost, on individual organizations and their employees to *know who they are*. Know this and you can use many different frameworks to good purpose (they fulfill functions related to the second and third 'folds' of subjectification [p. 204]). Do that and you will develop a further understanding of your own *ethos* and that of other companies and be able to use more frameworks to greater effect. And on it goes, with the strategist becoming ever more insightful and resourceful. In this way a symbiotic relationship between *ethos* and strategy frameworks or 'recipes' can emerge (see Case Box 6.4).

Plutarch contended that we should read the ideas and models of others, not in order to copy them but as a means of refreshing our own vision and animating our own unique style. Similarly, we may see strategy as arising from the oscillation between an *ethos*, the maps or models of others, our own best-laid plans, and the unfolding chaotic realities in which we must act toward particular purposes. *ReCreating Strategy's* deconstruction and rethinking leads us to reconceive strategy as the oscillation that orients and animates us toward our purpose or *telos*.

In any event, Postmodern paradoxes and the realization that organizations must increasingly accentuate their differences as their similarities become hygiene factors means that it may no longer be useful for 'gurus' – be they consultants, academics or chefs – to prescribe the content and purposes of an organization's strategies. That is a matter for those who determine particular goals in specific contexts, those who 'do the fighting' – you. Outsiders looking down on local practices have driven strategy for long enough. It is time for the strategic identity of corporations to arise from the 'inside-out.' Hopefully the maps and models described here will help you refresh, orient and animate your own strategic vision.

Case Box 6.5   Ethos + Strategy

After working through the Channel 5 case (Case Box 5.2, p. 194) as a preparatory exercise, a group of middle managers from a bank, based in the UK but increasingly, through mergers and acquisitions, present in other countries, settled down to discuss the ethos of their corporation and its current strategy. They began to think of the corporation in terms of its personality.

This was not an easy exercise for them, indicating that the corporation's personality or *ethos* was not particularly clear. One thing they were clear of, though, was that one of their leading competitors had recently got it all wrong. Barclays Bank had just launched a media campaign extolling the virtues of their 'bigness'. Celebrities like Anthony Hopkins and Robbie Coltrane told the camera that 'people want things "big" – and they want a big bank.' According to the research done by these managers, people may have wanted some of the benefits that a big bank offered, but they also liked the idea of dealing with a bank that 'felt' small, who valued particular personal relationships.

Eventually, they came up with three possible personality types: James Bond, the current CEO of the Bank and Michael Palin. After some discussion, Palin was thought best. The idea of Bond appealed to many, particularly the male members of the team. However, it was quickly decided that while his British, suave demeanor and his unruffled 'shaken not stirred' character could fit nicely, his risk-taking and attitude to women (an interesting character to have a 'fling' with, but not a very safe long-term bet) probably did not fit the image the Bank wanted to present. Many thought that having a well-liked CEO step forward and lead the company from the front, in the spirit of Victor Kiam or Richard Branson, would have been particularly powerful. However, others countered that his personality could be problematic given that it was not well-known to those out-side the company and that the 'heart' would be pulled out of the corporation when he, inevitably, left. So in the end it was Palin – the ex-Monty Python turned world-travelling documentary maker – who won out. He was British, but had made a second career of combining this very British nature with embracing foreign cultures and appearing com-pletely sympathetic to their differences. His TV shows were the epitome of the 'when in Rome' ethos. He was also, said one manager 'a nerd, but with a broad good nature and a sense of humour underneath it – unlike James Bond you can associate this with a Bank.'

While they could not have avoided thinking of strategy while thinking of characters, the managers then turned to focussing specifically on how the articulation of this per-sonality or ethos could help them articulate their strategy. They began with the staples: Porter's Generic Strategy Matrix and Porter's Five Forces.

They placed Palin firmly in the middle of the competitive advantage distinction between costs and differentiation. 'It's a very Palin like position', said one manager. 'He just understands different perspectives.' They also felt that his wide-ranging appeal ('you can watch his show with the kids and even teenagers kind of like him because of the Monty Python connection') put him firmly at the broad end of the broad/narrow scope distinction.

'I guess this fits with our strategy,' another manager continued. 'Like all banks we're increasingly having to cut processing costs. Globalization is increasingly giving up oppor-tunities to do that. At the moment we're switching a lot of our data processing and clearing stuff to India and places like that.'

Another interjected: 'But we maybe have to be careful about this, what with concerns with business ethics and so on.'

'Sure, sure, we can't abuse different people – maybe the Palin image can help us formulate our approach to that. But we have to cut costs to compete. But at the same time one of the strongest things our market research is telling us is that most of our customers like having a branch. They like the idea of a branch manager or someone they can talk to in a branch about them. So, one of the ways that we are going to try and differentiate ourselves increasingly is by having a strong local branch presence while others are closing theirs down. So I guess what I'm saying is that we have to look both ways – toward new suppliers for cost saving and to existing and new customers to differentiate, even though keeping the branches open and staffed costs us a lot.'

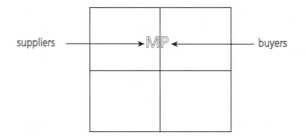

There was general agreement about this logic and the figure presented above (based on Figure 6.4, p. 226) was developed. Another manager expanded on it: 'And we do, through our traditional presence in the High Street, have a broad appeal – in fact, we have to cover a lot of fixed costs so we really have to be broad to shift the 'units' needed to perform.'

Moving on to expansion issues, the Bank had recently announced two new initiatives: an Internet banking option and a tailored investment-banking arm. These two companies had been launched under different names, to avoid diminishing the brand image of the parent. However, all the managers present believed that it was important to realize how the various parts of the expanding company fitted together so that the most could be made of the synergies and cost reductions available to the group.

It was suggested that the Internet banking operation enabled the company to put forward a low-cost bundle of products and services to a particular market, while the personalized investment banking advice offered by the other arm sat in the differentiated and more exclusive segment. 'Together', said one manager, 'perhaps they could be seen as "the Palin children" – the same sort of values having been bred into them but they are more dynamic, more focussed on what they want to do and a little bit less risk averse' (as the figure below seeks to represent).

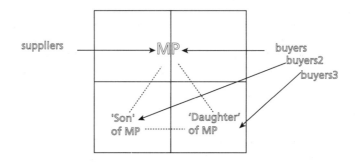

Nobody present knew whether Mr Palin would have been receptive to an approach with a proposal that could have led to these ideas being used in the public arena. Neither did anyone know whether Mr Palin had any children. But perhaps neither of these things mattered, for the time being at least. A group of managers had a clearer idea of what their organization was and what it was not and could, from there, begin to think about how they would move into the future.

1 Why shouldn't the bank have gone with the CEO or Bond? Surely these 'characters' would have been more personal or more exciting?
2 How are ethos and strategy related?
3 Outline the ethos of your company or an organization that you are familiar with. How should it be driving that company's strategy?

The identity of this organization has been disguised.

---

7 ReGenerating Change

Change

By the end of this chapter you should:

1 See how recent models for thinking organization change have developed incrementally upon one another, and be able to link the assumptions that underlie this development to a Modernist approach.
2 Recognize, through reading the Premodern change story, that change could be thought otherwise.
3 See how managing *change* may benefit from seeing past, present and future as interwoven and 'surfing' key traditions so as to ensure *constancy*.
4 Be able to individually draw organizations in ways other than through triangles and bureaucratic organizational charts, so as to enable the communication of a particular *ethos*, strategy and path of change over time.

---

1 Modern change: generic linear models

In 1985 an Academy of Management symposium on managing change concluded that:

> (1) organizational change and redirection, the process of making and keeping organizations competitive in changing environments, is an important topic; (2) many executives were wrestling with just these issues, and had some interesting insights to share; and, most importantly, (3) an examination of what these executives and their organizations were doing would probably reveal that, in fact, many of the things being tried were consistent with research and theory in organizational behavior.

That this call was well received is indicated by the fact that the inaugural issue of *The Academy of Management Executive*, launched with the express purpose of better linking the research of academics and the practice of managers, took five papers from the symposium and published them as its first special forum. The signs were readily apparent that what would emerge from this 'new' emphasis on managing change would indeed be 'consistent with existing theory in organizational behaviour'. For example,

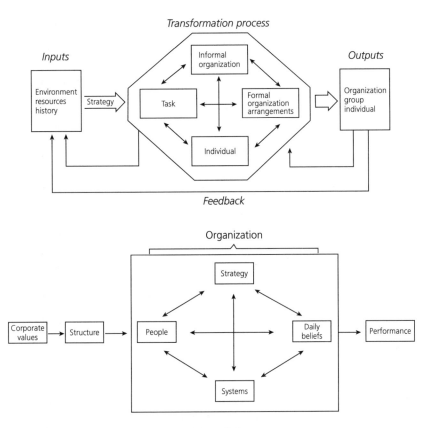

Figure 7.1 Input→Process→Output vision of change

Sources: Top, D. Nadler and M. Tushman, 'A Model for Diagnosing Organizational Behavior', *Organizational Dynamics*; Bottom, R. Beck, 'Bank of America Change Agenda', *The Academy of Management Executive*

the only diagram in the five papers (The Bank of America model, Figure 7.1, bottom) looks uncannily like the input→process→output models described in earlier chapters of this book (compare it with Figure 4.1 on p. 138 and the diagrams on pages 86 and 47) and is the image of one published by Nadler and Tushman in 1980 (Figure 7.1, top).

Much the same models of change

Since this symposium, a dramatic expansion in the number of attempts to develop theoretical frameworks for guiding change, based upon the examination of practice and experience, has occurred. However, despite an expansion in numerical output, a review reveals a certain 'sameness' among the

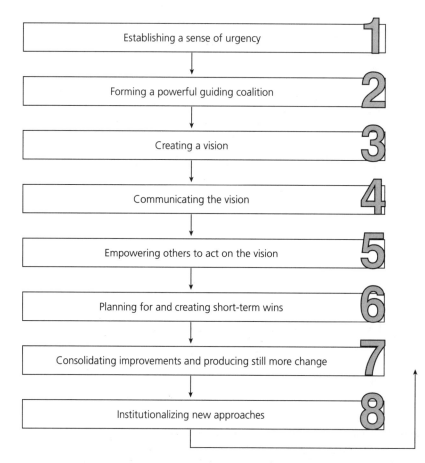

Figure 7.2 Kotter's change management framework
Source: J.P. Kotter, 'Why Transformation Efforts Fail', *Harvard Business Review*

many authors who have applied themselves to this issue. This can be seen by the way that John Kotter's framework of eight steps, recently published in the *Harvard Business Review*, replicates almost all that has been said in applied management fora on this subject. 'Over the past decade,' Kotter claimed, 'I have watched over 100 companies try to remake themselves.' Kotter concluded that 'the most general lesson to be learned' from his observations of the 'more successful cases', was that 'the change process goes through a series of phases [or] steps.' These steps are shown in Figure 7.2.

Other commentators may have outlined their ideas in other ways, but they are easily assimilated into Kotter's steps. Identifying a compelling need for change or creating *a sense of urgency* is seen as crucial by Beer, Johansson et al., Tichy, Nadler and Tushman, Stace and Dunphy and a book published by consultants PriceWaterhouse Coopers titled *Better Change: Best Practices for Transforming your Organization.* (See the Bibliographical Notes at the end of the book for full details of these and the other publications mentioned in this chapter). All of these sources and others, like Beck, Chen and Larkin and Larkin, emphasize the need to develop, effectively *communicate* and *empower others* to work toward a *vision* of a future organizational state. We are reminded of the particular importance of being aware of the politics at work in an organization, gaining commitment and *forming a guiding coalition* by PriceWaterhouse, Johansson, Tichy and Sherman, and Nadler and Tushman, while *emphasising short-term wins* and *consolidating improvements*, integrating and *institutionalizing* new approaches and forming a *platform for further change* are highlighted by re-engineering exponents and most of the above.

While almost all of the authorities mentioned above are American, Kotter's eight steps seemed to also ring true with the best of European theory. The 'model' that emerges from Pettigrew and Whipp's *Managing Change for Competitive Success*, published four years before Kotter's article, seems very similar to Kotter's 'eight steps'. In a study of competitive change in a number of UK industries, Pettigrew and Whipp identified 'nine similarities':

1 Building a receptive context for change, legitimization.
2 Creating a capacity for change.
3 Constructing the content and direction of change.
4 Operationalizing the change agenda.
5 Creating a critical mass for change within senior management.
6 Communicating need for change and detailed requirements.
7 Achieving and reinforcing success.
8 Balancing the need for continuity and change.
9 Sustaining coherence.

Of these nine steps the only thing that the American works seem to not incorporate is the notion of 'balancing continuity and change', and even Pettigrew and Whipp describe this as a 'secondary mechanism' as opposed to a 'primary feature'.

A very Modern homogeneity

There are perhaps two main reasons for the homogeneity of change management theories in the 1980s and 1990s and both can be related to Management's Modernist heritage. The first relates to the way in which *theory and practice have been linked*, or the way that empirical research tends to be informed by the models one already has in one's head. The second is the *common point of origin* that all of these theories, often unwittingly, share.

First, their continued sameness since the Academy sought to 'learn more from practice' is likely due to the fact that practitioners, looking for ways to categorize what they have done, have often done so in collaboration with academics and external consultants. For example, the commonality between

Nadler and Tushman's 1980 model (Figure 7.1, top) and that developed by Bank of America managers a couple of years later (Figure 7.1, bottom) is likely due to the external consultants that the Bank's vice president credits in his *The Academy of Management Executive* paper for 'having helped bring the model to fruition,' being very familiar with the Nadler and Tushman approach.

Second, when in 1985 The Academy of Management symposium called for theoretical frameworks for guiding the management of change based upon the examination of practice and experience, the view of the authors of these frameworks were already influenced by earlier research and theory in organizational behavior. While Smither's scholarly review found that the subject of managing change is 'relatively new [and] lacking a long history of theory and research,' it does stretch back further than 1985. It began, according to management texts that go a little deeper, with 'eminent social psychologist Kurt Lewin.' In the early 1950s, Lewin discovered what textbooks to this day call the 'three basic steps that summarize what's involved in the process of changing people and organizations.' These steps – 'unfreezing→moving→refreezing' – were reconfirmed by authorities such as Ed Schein in the 1960s. Figure 7.3 shows how others, all the way to Kotter, would subsequently follow Lewin's lead.

In the mid-1970s, Tushman, looking back on the history of his sub-discipline noted that 'though published more that 15 years ago, *The Dynamics of Planned Change* by Lippit, Watson and Westley, continues to be the foundation of much that is current in organizational change literature' and that this work was 'based on the Lewinian tradition.' Indeed, Lippit et al.'s model seems an obvious extension of Lewin's, with two more 'mezzanine' steps simply being inserted into Lewin's original three. In the 1960s and 1970s a number of authors developed Lippit et al.'s model to create a seven-step process called 'the planned change model'. Blake and Mouton's influential studies of the mid-1960's also resulted in a change management prescription of 'six phases' similar to what went before it. Placing these alongside the 1990s approaches of Kotter, Tichy and Devanna demonstrates how Lewin's 'original' view has been carried forward, albeit with added increments that make the later theories seem 'new and improved'.

Given the context of its development, this homogeneity with regard to managing change is underpinned by a number of related Modernist preconceptions:

1 Change is a general, linear input→process→output process (see Figures 7.1 and 7.3).
2 Change comes from the top or outside-in and then works its way down (see Figure 7.2). In Kotter's words, top people must first provide a vision or, as the Bank of America's VP noted, 'strategic changes must start at the top of the organization with the CEO and his or her management team.'

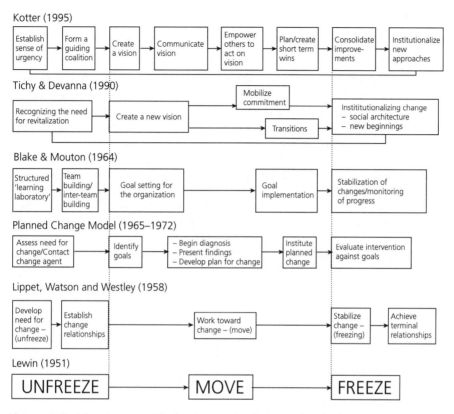

Figure 7.3 The incremental development of conventional change management frameworks since 1950

3 The logic of Modern science encourages the distilling of the essence of 'hundreds of cases', rather than looking at the individuality of one. For example, Greiner's 1972 classic *Evolution and Revolution as Organizations Grow* begins by claiming that research into change had been too 'heavily empirical without attempting more generalized statements about the overall process of development' (although he does cite Chandler's *Strategy and Structure* as the 'notable exception').

4 Related Cartesian assumptions lead us to break down the complexity of change into its 'component parts' which can then be ordered into a series of steps. Greiner, for example, tells us that 'organizations move through five distinguishable phases of development.'

5 Further, these steps can be developed into general theories that have predictive power and thus can be applied prescriptively. In order to 'arm' managers, Greiner goes on to provide 'a prescription for appropriate management action in each of the five phases.' While some

mainstream change models do move beyond a singular prescription, these models still tend to classify organizations into a limited number of categories and then offer prescriptions for how to manage organizations in each.

6 Connected to these predispositions is the Modern idea that time and history move in a linear and step-by-step manner, with the new being separate from the past and, because knowledge is cumulative, distinctly better or 'more advanced' (that is past→present→future). Subsequently, Lewin's three steps mirror Hegel's thesis→antithesis→synthesis dialectic. On this view, organizational change, and thus frameworks for managing organizational change, should be linear and processional. While a number of the models described above add a feedback loop at the end of their strings, one only needs to read a few MBA projects that apply such models to see how this format still encourages a Cartesian, straight line, step-by-step, approach to managing change.

7 In keeping, past beliefs and traditions are not what managing change is about. Hence management experts tend to focus on changing tangible, material things in the present for the future. These 'things' are often arranged into four categories: 'organizational structure', 'tasks', 'technology' and 'people'. While the 'people' category seems to offer scope for exploring beyond the material present, generally what has concerned experts under this heading are still empirical 'tangibles': decision-making approaches, interpersonal and inter-group relations and re-education.

8 Finally, in true Modernist fashion, change and constancy are seen as either/or choices. Because the theorists and institutions described above tell us that organizational change is imperative, constancy is seen as secondary, at best.

Of course, none of this is to say that that the models that have come from looking with these Modern predispositions should be dismissed. They can all be used as processes of division and generalization in order to speak and think, in the same way as the 'energy' or language of classical strategy frameworks can be utilized and modified in individual settings. However, given that we can now see them as somewhat 'samey' and hence limited, perhaps we should seek additional frameworks that may inspire us to think about managing change differently?

While Nadler and Tushman remind us that the meeting of academic minds and practical experience sought by The Academy in 1985 spawned 'more successful examples of planned organizational change than ever before', Kotter explains that the fact that many organizations still do not do change as well as they could is likely because 'we have relatively little experience in renewing organizations'. These comments exhibit further Modern assumptions that limit our ability to see different ways of managing change: the assumptions that knowledge and development is cumulative, and that people have only been seriously concerned with organizational change in recent times. Certainly the level of specialized academic energy focused on developing theories to account for and prescribe best ways of managing organizational change over the past two decades is unprecedented. But does this mean that people did not think about and enact change prior to the Modern formularization of generic models? More to the point, in enacting change Premoderns likely thought change differently, given that the language of the Modern approaches described above did not influence them. If we wish to challenge our common conventions, perhaps we should suspend our assumption that the past has been surpassed and should therefore not be dwelt upon?

In this spirit, this chapter returns to the alternative origins of strategy outlined in Chapter 6 to investigate a 2500-year-old example of managing change: Kleisthenes' transformation of Ancient Athens toward democracy. We shall see that it exhibits all of the 'critical success factors' outlined in the Modernist frameworks above, but this finding offers little scope for insight and development in itself (apart from the fact that it may induce a little humility). More interesting is the way this Premodern example differs from, and hence challenges and adds to, what is present in our current models.

Kleisthenes' reforms provided the basis upon which classical Athens developed into a society possessing an innovative culture that could boast of being unique among its competitors, and members who were intra- and entre-preneurial, creative, multi-skilled and self-reliant. These qualities are still sought by organizations. However, the difference between organizations that exist within a sociopolitical organization and sociopolitical organizations themselves, and significant cultural differences between Ancient Athens and other societies, warn against direct application from ancient to modern contexts. Hence, what emerges here is not a new prescriptive general theory nor a one-best way, but a juxtaposition of two traditions – Modern theories and Premodern practice – in order to enable you to oscillate between them and inspire you to think differently.

2   A case of Premodern change: toward *demokratia*

The district of Athens incorporated large coastal tracts, arable plains, olive-growing lowlands and mountainous highlands. It was ruled by nine *archons* appointed from the ranks of the aristocracy and a council comprising those citizens who had been *archons*. Mirroring its geographical diversity the district traditionally split into four geographically distinct tribes, divisions that promoted an environment where factionalism and infighting was prevalent. In response to growing social unrest along these 'party' lines, Solon, a leading *archon*, was appointed in 594 BC to re-draft the Athenian constitution.

Solon sought, in his words, the ideal of *eunomia* ('Good Order') to 'put an end to works of faction' via the provision of a set of new laws and more equality before the law or, in his own words, 'the establishment of just boundaries between individuals, so that conflicts should not occur ... laws alike for base and noble, fitting straight judgement to each.' Solon saw himself as a 'marker' or 'boundary stone', protecting all with the 'strong shield' of his laws. However, despite his best intentions, internal friction and confusion concerning the constitution of Athens continued to develop. Unfortunately, three factions re-emerged: the parties of the Shore, the Plain and the Highlands, each joined by territorial allegiances and differing economic interests. Various attempts to establish a tyranny grew out of these factions. All were thwarted until 561 BC, when Peisistratos, leader of the Highland party, seized power. These were not unsuccessful times for Athens initially, but after Peisistratos' death in 527, the citizenry became increasingly disaffected with his sons' reigns.

The Spartans, always keen to destabilize their Athenian rivals, helped overthrow the tyranny in 511 BC. After this, a struggle for power began between Isagoras and Kleisthenes, whose family had opposed the Peisistratids and had subsequently been in exile for most of their reign. Isagoras at first held the upper hand, and with the support of one of the two Spartan kings, expelled Kleisthenes and his supporters from the city. Isagoras then sought to dissolve the ruling council of *archons* and make himself and 300 of his friends masters of the city. However, upon hearing this, citizens gathered *en masse* to besiege Isagoras' party in the Acropolis and Isagoras surrendered. Kleisthenes was then recalled, in Aristotle's words, as the people's 'leader and champion'. Kleisthenes' management of the transition from the state described above is divided here into three parts:

- vision for the *future*;
- reorganization of the sociopolitical structure of Athens in the *present*: and
- the development of Athenian myth from the *past*.

However, as we shall see, Kleisthenes did not treat these elements as isolated steps. Rather he interwove them.

Vision: the *future* in the present

The prescriptions offered by Modern theorists enable us to note that the background leading to Kleisthenes' elevation got him off to a good start. He came in with a mandate for change, a sense of urgency in the air and a groundswell of support that would have helped in developing a powerful coalition. How he managed to garner the support of the people in the first place, however, is an interesting question. While his family's traditional opposition to the tyrants would have helped, he must have offered more to continue to endear him to others in these turbulent times. To have been regarded as having *metos* enough to lead, Kleisthenes must have had some ideas regarding how best to steer Athens into a difficult future (that is, a plan) and a target towards which this plan was set (that is, a vision) that inspired his supporters and focused their energies.

Research suggests that Kleisthenes' offered the people his vision of *demokratia*. The word came from the combination of two: *demos* (people) and *kratos* (power). In effect, it meant a broadening of the political franchise, increasing the powers of the citizen *assembly* in relation to the council of *archons* and making it easier for people to become citizens. However, given the propensity for competition and conflict to manifest themselves as factionalism within the Athenian system, the development of a unified populace would have been a necessary precondition to the development of a workable democratic system. Kleisthenes' vision must, therefore, have been something very near *'demokratia* through unity'. In contrast to Solon, whose laws sought to contain the negative aspects of the existing system, Kleisthenes offered a vision of a different system – but one that reconnected fragments of Athens' past.

While *demokratia* was a relatively new word, the behaviour and values that it embodied dovetailed well with existing and emergent Athenian values. If *demokratia* was to work, it required a reciprocal relationship between state and individual. The citizens of Athens would be expected to maintain and protect their city, to become more involved in the affairs of state in return for freedom and protection from the corporate body. Relationships between fellow citizens, due to the Athenian's traditional belief system, were already thought to be based on reciprocal connection, as were those between humans and gods (see Chapter 2, p. 21). A similar understanding between citizen and state would not have been incongruous and would have fostered the further development of a reciprocal sense between citizen and corporation. At the same time, pressure to participate was also induced by the Athenians' way of life being a public affair. Fellow citizens already judged citizens' political performances informally, on a day-to-day basis, and it was difficult to hide disinterest, mistakes or carelessness in such a society.

Kleisthenes' vision also sat well with developing military methods that promoted unity and reciprocal sacrifice of the individual citizen towards the good of the whole corporate body, and the rise of the whole leading to the betterment of the lot of the citizen. *Hoplites* had, by this period, become the regular Athenian fighting force. The *hoplite* phalanx would fight in close formation in rows, one behind the other, with each having a heavy bronze shield for defence. When the phalanx took form, a wall of shields would be presented to the opposition, one man's shield protecting part of himself and his neighbour. Long spears would then be thrust towards the advancing enemy. Each phalanx moved like a ferocious tortoise with spikes, encountering great difficulties when trying to reverse. When in proper formation it was extremely effective, but when ranks were broken individuals were easily picked off, and as Tyrtaios wrote 'when one flinches, the courage of all is perished'. In contrast to earlier 'heroic' warfare, each *hoplite* relied on every other for his security. By the turn of the fifth century BC, stories of these military methods were embedding into myth and history.

Kleisthenes' vision benefited from appearing both *unique* in its time (enabling Athenians to differentiate themselves from other organizations) and *resonant* with Athenian traditions. Traditions that the pursuit of this vision, in turn, developed.

Structures: forms in the *present*

As the organization's vision for the future changed, its form in the present required 'rewiring'. It was important that present structures were developed so as to consolidate and institutionalize the types of behaviour required throughout the re-orienting organization, and enable 'short term wins' toward its vision. The Athenian system's traditional propensity for factionalism or infighting was clearly contrary to 'demokratia through unity'. Consequently, Kleisthenes' structural strategy reflected a need to unify previously disparate factions while discouraging the emergence of new ones. It sought the difficult objective of ensuring some form of corporate continuity in turbulent times while developing new structures that emphasized and enabled the behaviour required if *demokratia* was to succeed.

According to Herodotus, the most memorable feature of Kleisthenes' structural reforms was the creation of ten new tribes that cut across traditional geographic categories. All of Athens' existent *demes* (local wards) were separated into three distinct geographical groups or *trittys:* coast, city and interior. These were then divided into 10 parts. Kleisthenes established new tribes by an amalgamation of one of the 10 coastal groups of *demes*, one of the 10 city groups and one of the 10 interior groups. Being based on existing local communities, the *demes* naturally varied in population. However, they were blended in a manner that gave each tribe an equivalent number of citizens, while at the same time fulfilling what Aristotle described as the requirement of 'mixing up the people so that more men should have a share in the running of the state.' The best way of expressing the organization that Kleisthenes sought is diagrammatically (see Figure 7.4).

The new tribes fulfilled both military and political functions. Each had their own assembly, which met regularly in the civic centre, and each furnished the Athenian army with a regiment. These shared tasks enabled the tribes to cohere and the nature of *hoplite* warfare described earlier (each tribe became a military unit and *demes* would fight as *hoplite* phalanx within this structure) promoted the rapid development of a positive *esprit de corps*. The short-term gains that came from a wider franchise feeling themselves more deeply involved in the running of the organization were added to when the Athenians repelled a larger invading Persian force at the battle of Marathon in 490 BC. This victory gave the Athenians enough confidence to enact for the first time another of Kleisthenes' new policies – *ostracism*. This was designed to guard against the re-emergence of tyranny by giving Athenians the

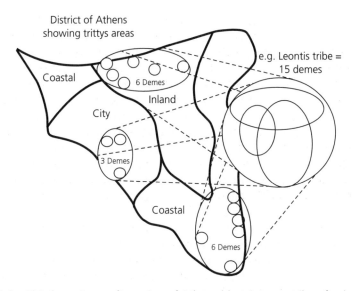

Figure 7.4   Kleisthenes' reconfiguration of Athens (showing one tribe often)

Source: S. Cummings and J. Brocklesby, 'Toward Demokratia: Myth and the Management of Change in Ancient Athens', *Journal of Organizational Change Management*

opportunity to vote out of the city, for a period of 10 years, any resident that had become too powerful.

The 10 tribal councils came together as the city council. This body acted as a steering committee, setting the agenda for the sovereign body of state in the new system, the citizen *assembly* in which all citizens could take part. Each tribal council would take its turn as the presiding administrators of the state for one tenth of the year. This board administered the running of, and implemented the decisions made by, the assembly and resided at the council chambers in the city. While these rotational boards took care of administrative functions, the key speakers in the assembly were generally the 10 *strategoi* (see Chapter 6, p. 233).

Kleisthenes' innovations weaved traditional geographic divisions with the new tribal project teams who came together for specific functions. The Athenian reformer sought benefits similar to those that are sought today via a matrix structure: enhanced coordination, better communication and improved motivation and commitment to the corporation as well as to one's own immediate task, precisely the actions that would be required of the new system if *demokratia* through unity was to be achieved.

Beyond the overall structure of the Athenian organization, Kleisthenes implemented other changes. Within each *deme* sat a number of *oikoi*, extended family communities, and *phratries*, exclusive religious kinship groups based on descent. The *oikoi* and *phratries* had traditionally been more influential than the local *demes*, and many *oikoi* had formed strong relationships (effectively 'old-boy' networks) with others of similar status. Such ties were also manifest within and between *phratries*. Those alliances that were traditionally powerful controlled significant political influence. Before Kleisthenes' reforms, one had to be admitted to a *phratry* to be a citizen, and to achieve this required satisfying the *phratry*'s controlling families that one's genealogy was common to theirs. Through his 'people-mixing' matrix structure, combined with increasing the sociopolitical significance of the *demes* and broadening the franchise, Kleisthenes' structural reforms sought to make the redevelopment of power centred on traditionally privileged *oikoi* and *phratries* difficult. He did not directly confront or oppose their existence, but provided new networks around them.

Kleisthenes passed the *phratries*' control over the right to citizenship to local *demes* who were given the responsibility for registering those who met citizenship requirements, regardless of genealogy. In addition, citizens were required to use their *deme* name as part of their own (for example, 'Krateas of Melite'), socially reinforcing the *demes*' significance. This, combined with the mixing of people into the new tribes, led to a popular saying about Athens at this time that highlighted its uniqueness compared to other states: 'Don't judge a man by traditional tribes.'

Further significance was granted to the *demes* through Kleisthenes' decision that it should be they that elected those from their ranks who would sit on their tribe's ruling council. Each *deme* was allocated a number of places that its citizens would fill on this council depending upon the *deme*'s population. Every year *demes* elected a set of citizens deemed suitable for the role and presented this list to their tribe. Each *demes*' allocation would then be drawn by lot from this set – a blend of human determination and fate left to the gods. No one name appears on council representative lists more than twice, indicating (given population figures) that some form of job rotation, whereby all citizens were at some point expected to fulfil this role, was in effect.

In order to achieve positions of higher influence in the organization, one no longer needed to belong to a *phratry*. Prominence in local *deme* politics, structured along similar lines to those of the tribes and the corporation as a whole, became increasingly important. Consequently, a citizen with corporate aspirations had to undergo a basic political and administrative apprenticeship in his *deme*. This structure, in conjunction with the military organization that it coupled, enabled values that could be related to the vision to surface and solidify at the 'frontline', rather than just be espoused from above.

Kleisthenes' method was one of working with what already existed and not forcibly terminating the old bodies while creating the new. While working the local *demes* into the new organization's design provided initial logistical difficulties, it created an excellent basis from which Kleisthenes was able to build the new structural form from 'bottom up' as well as 'top down'.

This ensured local continuity. On the other hand, he did not oppose the continuation of the traditional tribes, the aristocratic council of *archons*, or the *phratries*. They were left to decay organically as their influence waned.

Myth: the *past* in the present

While Kleisthenes' vision and structural policies exhibited wisdom similar to that espoused by conventional management models, his use of 'myth' to integrate these developments does not. One clear reason why myth is not at the forefront of conventional thinking as it contemplates organizational change is the modern association of myth with fictional, unsubstantiated falsehoods. This, however, is a very Modern slant on the word.

The etymology of myth again traces changes in Western beliefs. For the Ancient Greeks, *mythos*, at its most basic level, meant 'word', but it could be used in many different variations: rhetoric; conversation; a thing said, fact, or matter; a threat, command or mission; something thought, an unspoken word or purpose; a saying, proverb or rumour; a tale, story or narrative; or a professed work of fiction. That it could refer to both what we might call tangible and non-tangible things, the present and the imagined, indicates the extent to which the Greeks 'felt' the presence and influence of both the seen and unseen (or heard and unheard). Thus the Greeks created the word *panic* (after Pan) because they felt the presence of a real invisible being who swayed the emotions of flocks and herds and thus named what they were conscious of. Clearly *mythos* was seen as crucial in the shaping of being in the Premodern mind, but the word has since become a more abstract expression.

The Romans, as was their habit, did away with much of this ambiguity. Their '*mythus*' mostly referred to fable. (But one secondary meaning is of myth as analogous to *plasmata*: the 'former', 'moulder' or 'shaper' – linking to our modern phrase 'life-blood'; it was noted, for example, that myth was the '*plasmata* of history'). While the fifteenth, sixteenth and seventeenth centuries see myth being used to mean 'measure' or 'to show', these meanings have fallen away. Since the mid-nineteenth century, myth has meant either 'a purely fictitious narrative usually involving supernatural persons, actions or events, and embodying some popular idea concerning natural or historical phenomena', 'an untrue or popular tale – a rumour' or 'a fictitious or imaginary person or object'. It seems that while the Greeks' broader meaning of the word was, at least in part, shaped by their feeling the presence of invisible beings who swayed the emotions, by the nineteenth century, Modernist sensibilities had deemed such aspects to be other and lesser than objective provable structures and facts. What could not be seen, positively identified and proven to be materially true must be falsehood. For the Athenians, myth was an accepted part of everyday life, a means of conveying values, meanings and beliefs in the present towards the future. They had a very real 'presence'.

Greek myths were intimately bound up with the ways of the gods and goddesses. Most prevalent were the 12 Olympians, but they co-existed with a myriad of lesser deities, regional gods and goddesses and semi-historical figures. As we have seen (in Chapter 2), each deity had their own spheres of interest and people would connect to a god, or gods, depending upon who was seen as presiding over that area of concern to which their current situation related. Kleisthenes sought to identify and promote aspects that reiterated the merits of his vision of the future and helped consolidate and institutionalize his structural developments in the present from within Athens' existing system of myths.

It was traditional for a Greek corporation's identity to be personified by a mythic figurehead. In keeping, Kleisthenes sought to promote 'heroes' for each of Athens' new tribes. Tradition has it that in order to imbue the new tribes' heroes with religious credence, the priestess at the oracle of Delphi was provided with a list of 100 heroes from which the oracle was to select the religiously sanctioned 10. However, the characteristics of the 10 fitted too neatly with Kleisthenes' vision and structural policies for us to believe that their selection was by chance. Indeed, recent research has argued that Kleisthenes attempted to influence the priestesses' selection from behind the scenes, in all likelihood submitting his own top-ten list of preferred heroes.

Unlike the four original tribes' heroes (the four sons of Ion), the new Delphi-approved heroes were all Athenians except for Aias who was added because he had been a neighbour and ally (indicating a key relationship to be nutured). They comprised four kings, one son of a king and a sixth whose role in myth looked like a king's. Centralizing elements were clearly stressed, but the new figureheads did not represent passive central authority. Each was connected with previous unifications of Athens.

The one notable absence on the list of heroes was Theseus, the Athenian tradition's primary unifier. While it was clearly Kleisthenes' objective to promote unity, Theseus' presence at the head of one tribe would have overshadowed the other representatives, thus hindering the development of a sense of tribal equality. In any event, Kleisthenes required Theseus elsewhere in his schema, as we shall see. He did, however, ensure that the spirit of Theseus was present within the new family of tribal heroes. Both his son Akamas and father Aigeus were in the ten.

The new tribes were named after their heroes and each hero became a tribal role model and symbol to be linked with. A 'shrine' to each hero acted as a centre for the tribe, with documents placed there for public viewing, and the 10 heroes were represented in art and came to be used in political rhetoric. In a speech following a major battle, Demosthenes, for example, praised the dead in general, before turning to each tribe and tracing a connection between the courage and patriotism of the fallen and some element of their hero's story.

The worship of Kleisthenes' heroes can be associated with recognized public festivals already in existence before 508 BC, their connections to the tribes being additions – elements added to old observances rather than substitutions. As symbols at the head of each tribe, they added another dimension to Athenian mythology, without undermining the activities of established deities. For instance, the four old tribes' hero myths continued to function, but in contrast to the Kleisthenic heroes those of the old tribes seem to have been not particularly 'personable' and they became increasingly obscure.

Kleisthenes' policies with regard to the local community aspect of the organization reflect similar tolerance. While the *phratry* 'brotherhoods' operated in ways contrary to Kleisthenes' vision, they where not quashed. Neither were the religious practices of the *phratries*. Nor did the promotion of the new tribal myths require the *demes* to alter their religious practices. Each locale had its own important cults but Kleisthenes did not seek to tamper with these to make them more consistent with his objectives. *Deme* practice in the districts did not need impinge on that of the new tribes and vice versa. It was when the *deme* member came to town for tribal congregations or joined with citizens from other parts for the performance of civic or military duties that he became aware of the importance of the tribal division. Here a global sense of 'tribalness' would be engendered, but at no stage did one need lose the sense of belonging to a local *deme*.

Theseus, as we have seen, was the primary unifier in the Athenian tapestry, and it was for the corporation as a whole that Kleisthenes developed his myth. It is likely that Kleisthenes felt that if Athens were to be great, it would have to develop for itself a proud mythological past that it lacked in comparison to other Greek states (note *The Illiad's* lack of Athenian heroes). The exploits of Theseus were obviously suited to playing a part in this development and the similarities between the Kleisthenic reforms and the exploits of the heroic creator of Athens were too good to miss. As Plutarch's biography of Theseus tells it, he too had:

> … conceived a wonderful and far-reaching plan, which was nothing less than to concentrate the inhabitants of the district of Athens into a capital. In this way he transformed them into one people belonging to one city, whereas until then they had lived in widely scattered communities, so that it was difficult to bring them together for the common interest, and indeed at times they even fought one another.

The most popular hero in Athens at the time of the Kleisthenic transition was Herakles. The contrast between Herakles and Theseus is an interesting one. The huge Herakles, generally depicted holding a rudely-wrought club, achieved tasks through physical toil and smashing those who got in his way. Unlike Herakles, Theseus was an indigenous Athenian hero who achieved his objectives more through guile and strategic alliances than 'smash and grab'. It is plain to see why Kleisthenes would have preferred Theseus as a corporate symbol and he invested heavily in promoting Theseus' deeds in civic buildings and monuments. Given that producers of the 'lesser' arts and crafts like pottery took their lead from these larger forms, Theseus soon usurped Herakles' primacy as the hero with the highest profile.

Kleisthenes' management of myth reflected a desire to work with rather than against 'the grain'. Heroes and myths were not simply added or removed. Rather, elements were picked out and enhanced. Instead of seeking to overthrow or ignore tradition, Kleisthenes' initiatives worked with it. The reformer's new structure sought to address present and possible future factions in Athens, promoting the behaviour necessary if his vision was to be realized. The Athenian mythic past was managed in such a way as to reinforce these aims and integrate structures in the present with a vision of the future. Gradually, the new structural and mythological associations and symbols, stressing *'demokratia* through unity', became more widely regarded than the old. It was not so much that particular elements had their DNA genetically modified (just as with *ethos* – see Chapter 5 – one could not 'engineer' or 'manufacture' an Athenian identity), as particular elements were pruned, fertilized and propped up to make them grow faster than others.

3   A Premodern approach

When a man weaves the laws of the land, and the justice of the gods that bind his oaths together, he and his city rise high.

Sophocles

Athens' actions following 508 BC are described by historians as 'dazzling in their self-confidence and heady with success' and the decades that followed witnessed the Athenian confederation of alliances (which Herodotus described as successfully incorporating many cultural 'divergences' and 'varieties of speech') become the most powerful in the Mediterranean. These achievements were in no small part due to the management of the transition into *demokratia*. While the similarities between Kleisthenes' approach and the models outlined at the head of this chapter are many and will have been noted, four interconnected threads to Kleisthenes' programme, that do not figure in the conventional management literature, are presented below.

i   A vision that brings the past into the present toward a future

Kleisthenes' success seems in no small part due to his harnessing of existing, but perhaps under-appreciated, traditions and values and his articulation of a positive vision of a better system that at once projected these traditions into a future. Solon, by contrast, offered to make the current system less bad by appealing to the grand notion of 'good order'. Solon's method for achieving this, the construction of objective boundaries, reflected a rational approach to the problem of politics where the gods and the unseen did not play a significant part in affairs, where Man completely determined his own destiny. The idea that 'a mere mortal could override the gods – the great unwritten, unshakeable traditions,' to borrow from Sophocles' *Antigone*, placed Solon's reforms directly against public currents. Also, the notion that just boundaries and marker stones between individuals would see conflicts avoided was perhaps too idealistic in not seeing competition and *chaos* (an influence even on the gods and goddesses, the greatest Athenian role models) as an inherent feature in the system, to be worked with rather than marginalized. Solon's ideal of 'good order' lacked congruence with existing norms – Kleisthenes' vision, albeit less 'noble', did not.

ii Seeing future, present and past as interwoven

Kleisthenes seems to have assumed that an organization in transition must be treated as a complex system, and that a vision is far more likely to be achieved if it is interrelated with congruent structural and mythological elements. Hence, each of the three elements of the Kleisthenic programme described here – structures in the *present*, vision for the *future*, and mythology from the *past* – was connected with, and thus exhibited resonance and congruence with, the other two. The formal structures under which the organization was to operate and the mythological beliefs that bound those structures together and gave them life at once encouraged and reinforced one another. At the same time, they promoted the values that were necessary for the achievement of the vision. The matrix organization structure encouraged 'cross-department' communication that enhanced tolerance that encouraged unity. This, in turn, encouraged further participation in the new tribes and councils leading to *demokratia* and enhanced worship of the tribal heroes. This reinforced unity, and so on. Kleisthenes' processes set Athens on a virtuous spiral.

This notion of interweaving future, past and present often gets lost in Modern change management analyses. This may be attributable to the linearity of Modern models. Hence, many current-day organizations do not achieve Kleisthenes' level of congruence with regard to change, and suffer as a result. For example, it is no good changing everything to employ a vision along the lines of 'increased accountability and efficiency' and implement 'matrix structures'. Despite the fact that both have been fashionable in recent times, one undermines the other (matrix structures by nature require more time of organizational members). This forces members to make their own choices of which 'master' they will serve and which they will compromise, thereby undermining one (or both) and likely bringing about a vicious spiral of decline (see Case Box 4.3 on p. 162).

iii Integrating material and mythic dimensions
(or change as 'surfing' the past)

In Nietzsche's words, 'without myth every culture loses the healthy natural power of its creativity: only a horizon defined by the myths completes and unifies a whole cultural movement.' From this perspective, an appreciation of an organization's myth systems would seem a crucial aspect of change management. However, such an appreciation is largely overlooked in the mainstream literature on organizational change. Perhaps this is not surprising. Modernity's adherence to scientific-positivistic knowledge proclaiming reality to be expressed in distinct physical entities has likely dulled our appreciation of the importance of mythology over the past 300 years. This adherence finds myth a difficult 'object' to deal with and subsequently sees myth classified as 'secondary', at best.

Kleisthenes' structural reforms created a matrix of new and extant groups, some large, some small, some compatible and some mutually exclusive. However, these groups were carefully integrated with a mythological system. Mythology was an acknowledged part of everyday life for the Athenians. While Modernity has sought to separate myth from history, and differentiate science from myth, myth is still very much a part of our lives. Then, as now, it helps to form our values, beliefs, horizons and the way we view the world. Kleisthenes worked with the Athenian corporation's mythic history as a means of infusing pride in the organization's past and providing for its future. However, less tangible aspects like mythology may not come so easily to corporate actors imbued with Modern paradigms. Hence, we observe many managers today being either too aggressive in managing such aspects, seeking to impose a transplanted 'best practice' type 'mythology' from the top down; or being too passive, avoiding these aspects in favour of issues of structure or technology which are more easily grasped. In light of this, the homage paid by Kleisthenes to myth in his programme for change, his active-passive approach of not forcefully quashing the old system but actively developing positive aspects from within, provides unusual food for thought.

Perhaps the best analogy to express this Premodern approach is to 'update' the Ancient Greeks' favourite metaphor for describing an effective strategos: the *kubernetes*, the helmsperson on ships used for inshore fighting who, while he may use his skill to work with the current, will not succeed by working against it. The approach taken by Kleisthenes, and which may inspire us, seems akin to 'surfing'.

It goes without saying that no surfer can make waves; he or she must work with what the gods give them. But a competitive surfer's skill is related to their ability to pick out from all the waves occurring in the environment at that time, the ones that suit their objectives and particular style, and then riding or promoting them for all they are worth. In organizations, too, it is a matter of identifying and connecting to those historical currents that one wants to repeat and build upon toward the future.

iv Change requires continuity

In *The Physics* Aristotle develops the idea that 'there must always be something that underlies, out of which things come to be', examining how we are only able to recognize something as having changed if something about it or what it does has remained the same. On this view, the presence of traditions enables a connection between past, present and future so that we may at once recognize an 'object', an individual or an organization, as being 'the same being' and as 'a being that has changed'. In keeping, all three Kleisthenic dimensions described above are embedded in the paradoxical notion that managing change requires providing continuity. In managing change today many overlook this, approaching the process as a matter of replacing old with new, always asking 'How will we change?' but seldom asking 'How will we stay the same?' The most obvious recent manifestation of this view in management theory is seen in the 'discontinuous thinking', 'start with a clean sheet of paper', 'obliterate and start over', and 'wipe the slate clean' rhetoric of business process re-engineering.

Perhaps managing change is not so simple. Organizations have histories and traditions, and it is difficult to make people forget them. Given this realization, it may be more fruitful to attempt to work with rather than against the past. Many 'old' aspects of changing organizations are often not inconsistent with the achievement of 'new' ideals. Yet in Modernist mindsets, with a binary either/or set up where old = negative; new = positive, the 'old' is often dismissed as a whole, to detrimental and unnecessary effect (see Case Box 7.1 on p. 281). Such a scenario was avoided in Kleisthenes' Athens. The positive aspects of the existing structures and systems were identified and promoted: enlisted to help propel the organization into Kleisthenes' vision.

This brings us back to the philosophy of Heidegger and his idea that we are 'thrown' by the past into the world, unfolding into the future in unique and historical determined directions. It is this historically directed unfolding that gives every culture, and every individual, a unique point of view. This recognition should lead us to be cautious of seeking to transplant approaches from one organization to another, and it encourages people engaged in transformations to really connect themselves to the unique traditions of the organization they are seeking to redirect.

All of this may seem to indicate that organizations are prisoners of their pasts. However, in a way, Heidegger's view may enable those who seek change greater freedom. Recognizing that it is throwness, rather than any foundational basis, that directs our actions, enables questions to be asked about often-unquestioned assumptions. We are encouraged to question the way in which historical events have shaped, bent, thrown or 'ricocheted' supposedly fundamental modes of operating. This does not, however, mean that we are 'absurdly free' and that 'anything goes'. Our tradition-directed unfolding makes certain decisions and paths for the future unlikely or impossible, and thus likely to be ultimately frustrated. However, we can achieve some sense of liberation in recognizing why this is so, and we can in this way broaden our horizons and re-orient things to an extent: 'even if only within the limitations of [one's] throwness,' to use Heidegger's phrasing. Or, by sticking something of a rudder into the current rather than 'thrashing about' or being thwarted by the flow and unaware of why this is so, to use the language of the *kubernetes*. Indeed, this seems very much in keeping with the surfing metaphor mentioned above.

Combining the elements described here, we can say that if an organization is to continue it must keep something of its 'self' as it becomes different.
Kleisthenes was careful to identify, and then worked hard to ride, those
waves within Athenian myth and traditional sociopolitical past that reinforced the value of his vision. This knowledge was then used to integrate
and develop structural changes in the present towards the vision. All the
components of the change process were developed to reciprocally reiterate
one another, 'pinballing' the organization closer to Kleisthenes' view of its
destiny as time unfolded. It appears to have worked like a 'catch-stitch',
whereby the needle always takes the thread back before moving forward. A
maneuver, which while it takes more time, effort and resources, will hold
and move with the fabric more than a quick, linear straight stitch.

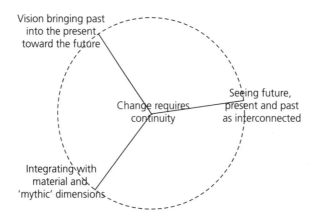

As depicted in the diagram above, change here is seen as revolutionary
in the Premodern sense – with things coming around while at once becoming different. Unlike a solely Modernist perspective, where the aim seems to
be the provision of a generic objective backdrop of steps to be followed
based upon a 'collation of best practices from several organizations' that any
organization can 'measure itself' against, the 'Kleisthenic' approach makes
an emphasis upon knowing and developing a particular local organization
according to its own terms a necessity. Which brings our discussion on
regenerating management back to where it began – with the notion of working from the individual *ethos* of the organization out.

We can also loop this back around into our discussion on strategy to see
how this Premodern thinking may again be pertinent in Postmodern times.
If we take our basic strategy equations from Chapter 6 (p. 240):

$$C + M = SP$$
$$M \times U = \Pi$$

We can say that the three main routes followed by organizations toward increasing margins in the past few decades have been:

- Increased efficiency + Outsourcing + Increased accountability = **Cost** reduction.
- Increased technology + Positioning = **Selling price** increase.
- Increased marketing + Increased production = **Unit** sales increase.

All of these routes are increasingly achieved within changing organizations through the use of external consultants employing 'best practice' from the outside-in, and hence, because of the circumstances already described in this book, are increasingly replicated and common. Because most organizations have subsequently followed these routes they are increasingly hygiene factors. In response, *ReCreating Strategy* has outlined two other routes to competitive advantage that are difficult to replicate:

- developing a particular authentic character, identity or ethos (Chapter 5); or
- focusing on embedded networks of knowledge relationships (Chapter 6, p. 251).

Both of these aspects come from or rely upon *the past*. Hence, in a world where these aspects are increasingly imperative, managers of change must be maintainers and developers of myths, stories and traditional relationships. A bit like Kleisthenes.

Case Box 7.1   Four Weddings and a ...?

1   In May 1998 at the end of another disappointing English football season, Liverpool FC took what seemed to be a fairly insignificant step. In a small article in *The Times*, Nick Szczepanik reported it thus: 'Manchester United recently claimed to have moved football shirt design forward with their new zip-front shirt design, but Liverpool have moved in the opposite direction with a distinctly traditional look to their new home shirt, launched today. The design, more or less identical to that of the Bill Shankley era [Liverpool's "golden age" of the 1960s] is bound to evoke memories of Ron Yeats, Ian St John and John Toshack [famous past players].' Indeed, while Manchester United has been far and away the best team in the UK over the past decade, Liverpool is perhaps the one English team that could boast a past more glorious than United's. At the turn of the millennium, *The Times*' ranking of all English Football League clubs, based on their performance since the League's inception in 1872, showed Manchester closing in fast from second place but Liverpool still as number one. Szczepanik, however, seemed somewhat skeptical of the shirt change: 'One unfortunate side-effect could be that the underachievement of the present squad may be thrown into even sharper relief by the similarity of their new kit to that worn by multi medal winners of the past.'

However, with the benefit of hindsight, one might see this change of kit as symbolic of a more substantial rejuvenation at Liverpool. Shortly afterwards, Gérard Houllier, a Frenchman who spent a good part of his youth in Liverpool studying for his Masters and teaching in Liverpool schools, was given sole charge of the team. After 18 months at the helm, Liverpool's aim of consistently finishing in the top three of England's Premier League ('a financial necessity', explains Liverpool director Noel White) appears a realistic one for the first time in a long time. Both die-hard fans and shareholders alike seem united behind Houllier, quite an achievement given the general sense of suspicion regarding a 'foreigner' being appointed, and the 'divisive' and 'unprofessional' influences that were at work in the clubhouse when he took over.

On reflection, most commentators see the secret of Houllier's success as his 'going back to old values to heal new divisions', 'blending foreign and local talent', or his ability 'to thread foreign players' technique with the ebullience of the emerging players from Liverpool's youth academy.' Many feared that Houllier's appointment would see the club's 'grass-roots' undermined as the side followed the approach of other English clubs under foreign leadership with more emphasis on signing overseas talent and less on 'growing their own' (London's Chelsea, for example, now often play without any Englishmen in their team). However, Houllier is clear that 'our best signing is probably our youth academy. It represents an investment of £12 m. [But] the tradition of players going through the youth development system has got to be kept.' Liverpool's traditional strength of investing in home-grown youth means that while clubs like Arsenal and Chelsea bypass English youth to buy wholesale from abroad, they fielded seven players from the local region in the 1999/2000 season. While Liverpool must buy in certain players to remain competitive on a global scale with the Manchester's, Real Madrid's and Juventus's, Houllier believes that the investment in the Academy is a crucial element in maintaining continuity with the past.

And now the team is playing with almost the same passion, perseverance and commitment that Houllier claims to have 'loved' when he first watched Liverpool from the Anfield terraces in 1969. 'What we have is embryonic,' says Houllier. 'The team is starting to have some personality … and we're leaving the century in a good way.'

2   Hewlett-Packard was founded by Bill Hewlett and Dave Packard in a garage in a small mid-Western town in the US at the height of the 1930s'depression. Along with IBM, it grew to become the most successful computer company in the world, and all the while the company's existing employees and its new recruits were inspired by the circulation of what where called 'Bill and Dave stories'. However, in the 1980s and 1990s the company fell upon relatively hard times and appeared to be losing its focus in a market where differentiation was becoming increasingly important. On 15 November 1999, under the leadership of new CEO Carly Fiorina, HP announced a new global campaign. 'We must reinvent ourselves,' claimed Fiorina. At the heart of this reinvention was a theme of 'going back to the garage'. Advertisements featured a small wooden garage at twilight with a light burning inside, over the top of which were printed messages such as: 'The original company of inventors started here. It is returning here. The original start-up will act like one again.'

3   In an article in the *New Republic* at the beginning of 2000, Joseph Stiglitz, former chief economist with the World Bank, offered a stinging critique of his former organization and the IMF (International Monetary Fund), 'fixer' of the economies of poor countries. Wrote Stiglitz: 'Critics accuse the institution of taking a cookie-cutter approach to economics and they are right. When the IMF decides to assist a country, it dispatches a mission of economists. These economists frequently lack extensive experience in a country; they are more likely to have first-hand knowledge of five-star hotels than of the villages that dot its countryside. They work hard, poring over numbers deep into the night. But their task is impossible. In a period of days, or at most weeks, they are charged with developing a programme sensitive to the needs of the country. Needless

to say, a little number crunching rarely provides adequate insights into the development strategy of an entire nation.' Given their limitations, Stiglitz claims that country teams have been known to 'compose draft reports before visiting. I heard stories of team members copying large parts of the text for one country's report and transferred them wholesale into another. They might have got away with it, except the "search and replace" function on the word processor didn't work properly, leaving the original country's name in a few places.'

The views of Tony Dolan, principal of Baraka Agricultural College, appear to support Stiglitz's. 'The models used by the IMF and World Bank,' he explains, 'tend to judge development in terms of industrialization. So, if countries like ours want funding, they have to show how it will be channelled into big industrial projects.' Not only are such projects potentially damaging to the sensitive ecosystems within the countries that the IMF seeks to help, Tony explains that they are often simply not feasible in countries where the infrastructure – electricity, clean water, roads – is not yet able to support existing needs. At present, for example, the College has to make preparations for at least three lengthy power cuts a week.

Baraka College was founded in 1974 and is managed by a group of Franciscan Brothers. Its ends are more or less the same as the IMF: 'To respond to the needs and aspirations of the poor.' However, their stated philosophy indicates very different means: 'Baraka promotes sustainable agriculture and rural development through education, training and extension programmes that focus on recognizing the environment, natural and human resources as the foundation of economic and social activity. In the current demographic, economic, environmental and social realities of East Africa, the most appropriate response is that of *sustainable agriculture and rural development*.'

From humble beginnings, Baraka now attracts students from all over East Africa. It seeks to train these students to get more out of their land, and enable them to spread this knowledge when they return to their homes. In contrast to some of the grander IMF sponsored projects, Baraka's latest initiative is the promotion of and training in beekeeping. This is an activity that is easily set up, does not take away resources from soil crops (indeed, the bees' activity improves yields of traditional crops such as coffee, bananas and sunflowers) and provides small farmers with invaluable extra income. In a land where subsistence farming is still very much the 'way of life' and the dominant mode of production, the College believes that this sort of ground-up development is far more practical and beneficial to local people at this point in time than an industrialization imposed from on-high.

4   At the beginning of the year 2000, Robin Cook, the British foreign secretary, approved a new campaign to 'rebrand' Britain. Twelve new posters were designed to replace decorations in British Embassies and Councils that had not been updated since the 1960s. While calculated to show that traditional images of Morris dancers and crooked teeth, flatulent Beefeaters and glossy Kodachromes of castles have been eclipsed, the posters sought to illustrate a sense of continuity with the past. Each is split down the middle, connecting 'Old England' with 'New Britain'. A frock by Sir Hardy Amies, the Queen's most respected couturier, is cut in half and joined at the hip with the right half of an outfit by John Galliano, the flamboyant Englishman who designs for Christian Dior. Julie Christie, the face of the 'swinging sixties,' fades into Kate Winslet. Sir Geoff Hurst, in his 1966 England kit, kicks at a ball that is melded with the one being chased by England's most recent international football sensation, Michael Owen. The late Benny Hill is paired with Mr Bean, and a horse painted by George Stubbs in the eighteenth century is 'cross-bred' with Damien Hirst's infamous 1990s 'pickled sheep'. Embassy staff and the general public

have welcomed the campaign, as has Mark Leonard who writes on national identity for the independent 'think-tank' *Demos*. 'It is a good use of money,' says Leonard. 'We could do with some of these posters at British airports and the Eurostar [train] terminal, too, just to remind us as well as visitors what Britain is about.'

? A former state-owned enterprise in New Zealand had just been privatized and bought by a US corporation. The new controllers brought about many changes. They needed to if the organization was to be successful in its new guise. Most managers were gung-ho about the structural changes that had been put in place and felt that the culture of the organization would not take long to catch up. 'From a structure point of view there's very little left to do,' claimed one senior manager. A senior director claimed that 'We have a people and a "mind set" problem. We were 25 000, we are now 15 000. Of those 15 000, 13 500 worked for the old organization. We don't have a structure problem.'

However, things did not come around as quickly as they had hoped. 'From a culture point of view,' said the first manager quoted above, 'there's quite a lot [of problems] because the people who are still here from the old organization are not in tune with the new direction and the values that the new management has put in place. Their's is a culture that does not work in a trading organization, sorry, full stop, end, not any of it. It has to be completely new.'

A year later, many believed that upon reflection many of the teething problems that the organization had in the first two years after the change were caused by the original assumption that 'everything must go' – that the old culture held nothing within it of use to the service organization of the future. Staff expressed their frustration and disappointment at the way things had developed by faxing cartoons to one another like those pictured below (Spot the Dog, an agreeable little terrier who would go anywhere and do anything to help people out, was the company's 'spokesperson').

The head of corporate strategy, a veteran with the company and one of the many we interviewed, summed up the feelings of many looking back with the benefit of hindsight at the change process:

> The old organization had a very strong ethic, a strong sense of 'family'. There was a strong sense of public responsibility and I think many who stayed in the organization over a long period of time stayed because of these values and a sense of service ... I think at the moment the family sense is shattered or strained. I think the sense of service, the spirit of service is not there because too many issues are being reduced to issues of profitability, accountability and 'incentivization', and this emphasis is devaluing those things.

1   What could this last Company have learnt from the previous four examples? Did the sense of family and public responsibility really have to be marginalized – or could a private sector service organization have been built upon this ethos?
2   What would you seek to surf if you were 'rebranding' Britain? What about another region, country or company that you are familiar with?
3   What similarities might you draw between the behaviour of the IMF and those consultants brought in to 'fix' the NHS described in Chapter 4 (Case Box 4.4, p. 171)?
4   Draw an alternative model of change management to those depicted in Figures 7.1, 7.2 and 7.3.

Sources: This case draws on reporting from 'Jersey Beat', *The Times*; 'Liverpool Show Way Forward', *The Times*; 'Best League Table in the World … Ever!', *The Times*; 'Managing to Put the Side Back into Mersey', *Irish Sunday Tribune*; 'IMF in Need of New Faith', *Guardian*; 'Eco Soundings', *Guardian*; 'Bill and Dave Show', *Human Resources*; 'Cook Sells Britain's New Look Abroad', *The Times*. With special thanks to Tony Dolan and all the staff and students at Baraka College

4   ReGenerating change: strategy from the inside-out

One of the main problems caused by our seeing organizations in terms of triangular-hierarchical charts (as illustrated right back at the outset of this book in Case Box 1.2 on p. 13), is the way it seems to influence our notions of change. Seeing all organizations in terms of the same hierarchical triangle has meant that recent big notions of change have been understood in these same generic terms. Thus 'organizational development', up until the 1990s, generally meant either 'adding more layers' or creating more subsidiary triangles, as illustrated below.

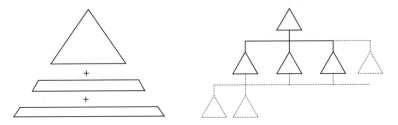

Then a 'revolution' occurred in the 1990s. This sort of accretion depicted above was associated with inefficient waste by BPR and 'rightsizing' (which generally means downsizing). The suggested remedy was 'delayering' or 'flattening the triangle' (effectively the same thing) or, in BPR's terms, removing the 'middle management' layer (see below).

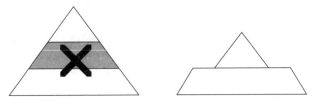

It is true that it was difficult to measure what middle managers materially did. Lower-level employees were seen to contribute because they interacted with the outside world and produced outputs, and you couldn't sack too many senior executives (could you?). However, many firms who had been BPRed soon found that they had lost something (even if they may not have been able to measure what it was exactly). If strategy happens top-down *and* bottom-up (rather than either/or – see Chapter 6), then good middle managers are imperative, a crucial lynchpin. They pick out and sponsor those opportunistic initiatives taken on 'the ground' that can be connected to the organization's ethos and strategic trajectory (if it is all bottom-up emergence then it is all 'animation' and no 'orientation'). And they make sure that 'pie in the sky' plans turn into actions or get knocked back 'upstairs' if they cannot be implemented (if it is all top-down planning then it is just all orientation). Organizations, it turns out, need good middle managers oscillating between 'top' and 'bottom' concerns more than ever. And so, after adding a whole load into organizations in the 1970s and 1980s and throwing a whole load out in the 1990s, back they now come (although they are now given less tainted titles like 'corporate knowledge officer', 'chief quality manager' or 'information manager').

But there are other ways of thinking. There is a way of reconfiguring change that does not gravitate toward the pendulum of simply either taking layers out or putting them back in that springs from such generic views. Warwick University runs a post-experience MA in Creative and Media Studies which seeks, among other things, to enable people from creative enterprises to interact with management and business interests in more fruitful ways. One of the biggest problems that programme director Chris Bilton has identified in this regard is that at a time when it is increasingly imperative that creative arts organizations have a dialogue with business concerns, most people from creative backgrounds believe that management has nothing to do with them. It is, they assume, all about economics, efficiency and hierarchy, and they are all about being creative (or what they see as the opposite of these 'management things'). This leads to another unhelpful either/or, or a 'double miss'. At a time when companies want to be more creative, very creative people do not feel they connect to them (so companies are left to 'hire in' unbounded creativity exercises like juggling and sand-castle building, things that do very little to substantially change mind sets 'on the job'). At a time when people in creative industries need to engage with business they are not engaging, which leaves people from professional management backgrounds to run things, often to the long-term detriment of creative organizations' capacity to create.

One of the things that we have been doing at Warwick over the past few years to rectify this 'miss' is to run a session for the MA students to 'deconstruct' the premises about management that they have bought into. To argue that management, organization and strategy can be about more than efficiency and triangles, we ask each student to draw freehand a 'picture' or map of their organization as they understand it – not in what they understand to be managerial terms. The results are not unlike the depiction of Kleisthenes' organization in Figure 7.4, particular scribblings

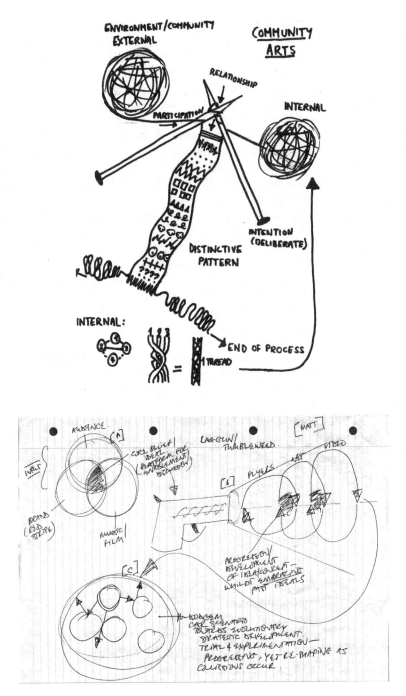

Figure 7.5 An organization as knitting (top) and an organization as tumbleweed/dodgems/raygun (bottom)

that reflect local understandings and unique 'geographies' in order to express particular ends. People draw their organizations as knitting needles, dodgems and rayguns, undersea worlds and train sets (see Figure 7.5). This provides a map or picture, like that used by the Hungarian detatchment in the Alps, which can be put before a group to explain how they see their organization's particular orientation. These pictures or maps can then inspire *mapping* in particular ways. What often happens during these presentations is that other members of the group upon seeing a particular image can say, for example, that 'it's all very well running a gallery like this train on that set of tracks, but, given the type of gallery you're describing, we need some people looking at developing some new tracks here and here for the future.' Or 'sure but we've got to be careful that we don't end up pulling too many carriages and slowing the whole thing down.' Or 'if that ray gun is to be effective then it has to shoot an increasingly wider beam, but not too wide.' These contributors can also draw what they mean on to the 'map', oscillating between one another's views, gradually forcing one another to greater levels of articulation. Before they realize it, these people are connecting into management and strategy issues, but in an individualized, interactive, and hence more creative and meaningful way. These individual pictures at once orient and animate change and communicate a specific ethos in ways that a generic triangle or organization chart can never do. We now use examples like these to inspire MBAs and executives to draw their organizations creatively and individualistically.

One of the main advantages of drawing organizations in this manner, as the pictures and Case Box 7. 2 illustrate, is that what gets drawn is easier to relate to an organization's *ethos*, far more relateable to a particular *strategic* trajectory, and far more able to 'develop' in order to understand and communicate consistency and *change* in a particular organization and what it is trying to surf.

Thus, these individual organizational 'scribblings' bring together the three interwoven spiral of elements that have made up *ReCreating Strategy*:

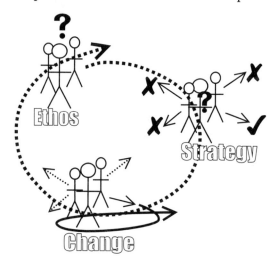

ReGenerating Change, ReConceiving Strategy and ReConceptualizing Ethics (see the figure above). And also, because they are internally or self-generated and hand drawn (it is interesting to see what gets lost when people attempt to replicate their map in a drawing package so they can incorporate it in their Powerpoint presentations), they only cost a little time.

Case Box 7.2   Folkdevils United

With four years' experience as a 'coolhunter' (young people picked out by companies to tell them what will be cool next year), Matt Hardisty was looking for a new challenge, one that would allow him to explore his interest in the creativity beginning to be show-cased over the Internet. He took a year out to do the MA in Creative and Media Enterprises at Warwick (he's responsible for the bottom picture in Figure 7.5), during which time folkdevil.com was born. Matt was awarded a distinction for his Masters and while continuing to guide 'folkdevil's' organic growth has joined Naked Communications as a Strategist. Quick to spot Naked and 'folkdevil's' rapid development, *Campaign* magazine listed Matt as one of its 'faces to watch' in 2001. Matt explains the symbiotic relationship between the styles of thinking that Naked and 'folkdevil' promotes:

> Configuring yourself to sell things used to be about defining a demographic or target segment developing something that provided the general function that that group wanted-then using economies of scale to reduce costs and then pushing the product on to them through one or two static channels. But Britain's cities have actually been awash with a new mode of marketing for quite some time. The division between the traditional creative disci-plines of music, clothing and art are dissolving for branded 'association'. Age is no longer con-sidered to be such a big measure, as the word 'youth' becomes blurred as we progress to targeting by 'lifestyle'. Brands have become 'cultures', creating immersive environments through which consumers can experience a brand's values. There has been an explosion in new, innovative types of channels. And this diminishing of traditional boundaries has led to a new creative fusion. Beyond bland 'sponsorship' and 'promotional activities', new processes of 'promotional symbiosis' have evolved whereby particular relationships are developed by net-working together a blend of micro and macro channels in order to convey a particular set of values or 'mythology' about a brand. An example of this new phenomenon can be seen in the fashion brand, skim.com. The label's clothing features a unique e-mail address on each garment, facilitating passers-by to contact the wearer in an attempt to traverse the on- and the off-line realms, and this helps build a particular sense of what 'skim' is about.

'It's all about how hard you push the boundaries,' Matt explains. 'And what we try and do at Naked is to help our clients think of themselves as not contained within tra-ditional boundaries or channels. We network a web of channels into a dynamic family that helps develop a complex relationship with customers to convey a sense of some-thing truly different in order to capture people's attention.' Matt draws the following figures to convey the concept.

One of Matt's latest projects for Naked involved connecting Reebok, local radio stations, skateboarding and BMX communities, various DJs, and people who wanted to have a laugh playing football, for 'The Sofa Games'. Inspired by Reebok's recent ads fea-turing under-active people being eaten by sofas, this involved temporarily transforming an urban area of Dublin into a playground featuring old sofas as goals for 5-a-side football and 'urban furniture' for skateboarders and BMX-ers, surrounded by 'chill-out'

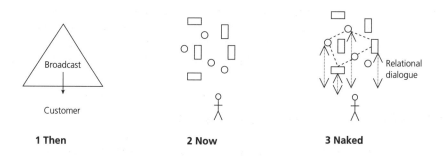

1 Then   **2 Now**   **3 Naked**

lounges serving drinks and food, all 'cushioned by an Irish backdrop of progressive nu-skool beats'.

This way of 'connecting' and building links or a 'relational dialogue' is very similar to that which inspires Matt's work with *folkdevil*. Here, partners are helped to think of their organizations differently: not as isolated fragments or separated stand-alone monoliths, but independent local units that are at the same time interconnected across traditional boundaries with other like-minded customers and organizations (Matt claims that the distinction between 'customer' and 'company' and 'competitor' is becoming increasingly irrelevant as things fragment):

> The Internet is enabling a new entrepreneurial spirit to emerge. No longer marginalized to the classifieds, fly-posting or word-of-mouth communication, new, local start-ups can now focus on particular niche characteristics and personal identities and then extend beyond their immediate geography and embrace a 'global' audience. But for all the cries of an emerging egalitarian environment (coupled with IBM's visions of 'Mom and Pop' stores selling olive oil from remote parts of Italy to 'cash rich, time poor' consumers in urban areas) the reality is that while these 'Folkdevils' [Matt's word for these new little 'glocal' players] are good at producing innovative content, they are bad at consolidating this into a viable ongoing organization. These independent enterprises behave like a quasi-cottage industry – 'folksy', which is good, but also introverted and detached. A cross-cutting collaborative network promoting independent talent is needed. To allow 'folkdevils' to progress beyond 'contacts' and facilitate business on a global basis, a new empathetic resource is needed to enable their dreams to become a reality – a 'virtual cultural intermediary' – to compensate for the increasing fragmentation in the workplace, and a means through which productive exchange can take place. That's where folkdevil.com comes in.

One way that folkdevil.com 'comes in' is through an individualized mapping technique. Matt explains this while free-handing a configuration of identities that he has been working on recently (see diagram on p. 291).

> Here you've got a radio station, a ticket seller, a record label, an info-Website and a couple of clothing labels – they share what we call the same 'tribal frequency', so they benefit by linking their marketing spends and subsequently developing a collective brand equity. But they all stay independent, which is what they're into it for. Collectively they hook into other Internet sites and channels that help convey their 'tribal freq', while these sites and channels also gain by association while staying independent and creative. Drawing things in this way helps them see how they can change with the new environment, keeping what they like about their histories – their independence and creativity – and growing for the future.

The recently launched 'Reading Room Media Network' provides an example of the independent/co-joined model that Matt and 'folkdevil' help develop. The Reading Room

Media Network's collection of organic sites showcase independent British talent, from record labels to filmmakers, while also providing credible content for the astute cultural consumer. Not only do the sites provide independent lifestyle brands (with little budget) with the ability to reach larger audiences, but allows a marketer wishing to target a 'fibre optic' audience the chance to communicate in a credible fashion across a previously illusive network of channels.

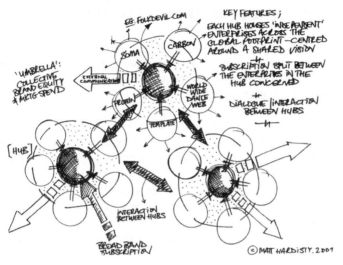

Matt believes that these united folkdevils are breathing a breath of fresh air into business: 'They are stamping out the earlier apathy of Generation X and the British condition of it being a crime to take anything too seriously.' Moreover, more traditional businesses must similarly rethink the way they perceive themselves as being configured. 'There is now a real need for many organizations to fragment and focus on particular vibes while sharing information and ideas about their often-common customers, and begin to collaborate and co-evolve in order to exploit the new opportunities presented by the multimedia economy,' says Matt. 'With central "sites" holding independent people together as a fluid entity,' he explains, 'the idea is that enterprises within the ecosystem can benefit from shared traffic across different ecosystems in a globally networked environment. So that they can grow without becoming the sort of monolithic corporations that by their nature dull the things that the people who started these enterprises are passionate about: creativity and independence.'

1   Can what Naked and 'folkdevil' do be captured with hierarchical triangles and straight lines?
2   What does the individualized mapping approach allow folkdevil to do for its partners?
3   What 'folkdevil' are doing is all very well for so called 'youth projects', but in what ways might what is going on here also be relevant for bigger more established companies?

This case was written in January 2001 and updated in February 2002. With special thanks to Matt Hardisty and the good people at Naked. Further resources on this emerging phenomenon can be found at www.folkdevil.com, with additional examples of community-sustained 'independence' available at the San Francisco based sites www.skinny.com and www.betalounge.com, and the Toronto based www.2Kool4Radio.com. If it's still up, The Sofa Games can been seen at www.sofagames.ie. Comments may be directed to matt@nakedcomms.com.

Epilogue: management and strategy, deconstructed, regenerated, recreated

In concluding *ReCreating Strategy* it must be acknowledged that in the years since the project that became this book was begun, strides toward more diverse and individualized approaches to strategy have been made. Some of the most visible examples include:

- A *McKinsey Quarterly* article published in 2000 entitled 'Best practice does not equal best strategy', and an increasing focus on companies developing their own *'next practice'* rather than copying yesterday's 'best practice'.
- A *California Management Review* forum discussing the state of strategy which concluded that both the emergence and design schools were right and, subsequently, that the most important strategic capability is 'agility', the ability to move from and to plan faster than one's competition, an idea not dissimilar to an oscillating *metos*.
- Bartlett and Ghoshal's *The Individualized Corporation*.
- Henry Mintzberg's *Strategy Safari* outlines many different strategy schools and similarly concludes that no one is better than the others and consequently welcomes the ensuing 'eclecticism'. (Although it has to be said his survey is constrained by only acknowledging schools that have established themselves in the past 40 years and relate to what Mintzberg describes as the 'strategy tree', with its branches 'the basic disciplines – economics, sociology, anthropology, political science, biology').
- Mintzberg's recent *Harvard Business Review* article 'Organigraphs: Drawing how Companies Really Work' offers a similar, but more structured, approach to redrawing organizations in an individualized manner to that described here.
- Floyd and Wooldridge's *Building Strategy from the Middle* is a further provocative attempt to reconceive strategy as occurring at all levels of the organization.
- Elsewhere, the big management consultancies, either under pressure from regulators or responding to what they now recognize as their weakness with regard to their bureaucracies and 'cookie-cutter' or 'one-best way' attitude, are currently seeking to reconfigure themselves and incorporate more difference within their networks.

ReCreating Strategy, by deconstructing the view that management must universally be about efficiency, mechanistic function, triangles, outside-in objectivity, science and economics, and showing how things could be otherwise, has attempted to add to this groundswell. But continuing to build this alternative swell into waves that more managers can pick out and surf requires that this book's limits be acknowledged. Because of the particular background of the author, *ReCreating Strategy* has leant heavily upon traditions such as those of the Greeks and the Maori and the ideas of the likes of Foucault and Feyerabend. There is far more that can be added in from your own particular backgrounds in this spirit in order to add to the Postmodern 'ocean of mutually incompatible alternatives' that creativity theorists like Koestler and Feyerabend called for. The more that goes in, the bigger the waves and the more there is to bounce off or oscillate between. This does mean that we toss out conventional approaches – management and strategy will still be about increasing efficiency, about doing more with less, about learning from consultants – but there is no reason why it cannot also be about doing less with more, or even stretching to find ways of doing something different that you and your colleagues believe in.

Part III of *ReCreating Strategy* provides a number of cases with which to hone your surfing skill. But first, a friend from your childhood needs your help (well, he might be a friend if you grew up watching a lot of British television). Before it was just a bunch of concepts that were being limited by management's association with Modernism. Now Postman Pat is under threat. *ReCreating Strategy* just got personal.

Case Box 7.3   Ethos + Strategy + Change: No Future for Postman Pat?

In December of the year 2000, the British Post Office announced that its corporate figurehead Postman Pat, an animated character whose television show has been entertaining children in Britain and other parts of the world almost since children's television began, would be dropped from its promotional and charity work. (If you are not familiar with Postman Pat, you may want to check him out at www.postmanpat.co.uk). Among other measures, Post Office employees will no longer be encouraged to visit local schools, fêtes and children's wards dressed as Pat. Instead their volunteer work will be directed toward a new campaign to encourage literacy. In the Post Office's defence a press officer said that it was nothing personal: 'We're not anti-Pat. We're just reassessing our priorities.'

These are certainly challenging times for the Post Office. Courier companies, many of them well-known global corporations, are eroding market share in what once was largely a monopoly for them. Society's values are also changing. However, David Thomas of the *Independent* has put up a spirited defense for the long-serving Greendale-based postie:

> I realise of course that, judged by the ruthless, market-driven standards universally prevalent today, Pat is a hopeless case. From the moment when, just as the day is dawning, he climbs into his bright red van, his life is a catalogue of professional misconduct. The Post Office was quick to confirm that his habit of letting Jess, his black-and-white cat, ride in the front of his van was a blatant contravention of health and safety procedures.
>
> Similarly, the incidents [from his television and book adventures] that repeatedly cause post to be lost, misdirected or damaged (one thinks, for example, of the occasion when Pat entrusts

the school mail to young Bill Thompson, who promptly drops it in a puddle) would be matters requiring disciplinary action. 'This is a very serious matter for a postman,' said my source.

But his most persistent failing is his seemingly incurable habit of allowing his close relationships with local folk to distract him from the swift delivery of the mail. 'We do like a postman to be community minded,' I was told by the Post Office spokesperson, 'but he's there first and foremost to do his job.'

This is something that Pat would do well to remember. No one could deny his fundamental enthusiasm. He's determined to do his deliveries, come wind, rain or snow. He has been known to use methods as various as inline skates, sledge and motorised super-speed scooter to help him on his rounds. But there's no escaping the degree to which other matters are liable to intrude.

In *Postman Pat's Washing Day*, for example, he begins his rounds with the observation that Granny Dryden has neglected to hang out her washing despite the sunny, breezy weather. He stops to discuss the matter with the rheumatically-afflicted pensioner, who reveals that her washing-machine has broken. Taking her dirty togs, Pat promises to deliver them to Mrs Pottage. He then drives to see Dorothy Thompson, with whom he has tea and a slice of cake, before discussing laundry issues with the Rev. Timms, Ted Glen, Miss Hubbard and George Lancaster ...

On the following morning, Pat delivers Granny Dryden's laundry to Mrs Pottage and stops for yet another cup of tea, only for his uniform jacket and hat to be thrown into the washing-machine along with the old biddy's unmentionables. This is by no means the only occasion on which Pat causes damage to his uniform (one remembers, with a shudder, the white paint he left all over his trousers on the occasion of Granny Dryden's redecoration), despite being contractually responsible for its upkeep. But the fact that Pat has to complete his round in a tweed jacket and deerstalker hat belonging to Mr Pottage is far less significant, in the great scheme of things, than the blatant time-wasting that has gone on beforehand.

Here is a man with no concept whatever of productivity or time-and-motion. And he is not alone. Consider Ted Glen, the local handyman. Pat visits him during his search for Katy Pottage's lost doll. Ted has agreed to mend toys, television sets, cookers, cake-stands, bikes, roller-skates, farm machines and house machines, 'more than you could count'. Yet he has no idea when he will fulfil these contractual obligations. Even when he does, his service is abysmal. Among his goods is a watch of Miss Hubbard's, of which he remarks, 'She brought it to be fettled, last Christmas.'

The service economy has made little headway on Greendale. But is the region's apparent refusal to move with the times really so counter-productive? Here we have a rural community that can sustain both a sub-post office (run by Pat's superior, Mrs Goggins) and Sam Waldron's mobile store. At a time when households are shrinking and the increasing autonomy of individuals as social and economic units is producing side effects of isolation and alienation, Greendale folk evince a strong sense of community.

When Granny Dryden's ceiling needs painting, Miss Hubbard provides dust sheets, Dorothy Thompson donates spare time while both Pat and Ted Glen volunteer their time to do the job for free – a task rewarded by cake and tea ...

This is a world which has no need for social workers, a world that looks after its own. When Ted Glen's design for Pat's scooter causes chaos, people do not sue or seek compensation. Instead they take the matter to PC Selby. He, in turn, talks to Mrs Goggins. She has a quiet word to Pat, who abandons his machine without complaint, secure in the knowledge that Dr Gilbertson is having words with his superiors in Pencaster to ensure that they get him a proper trolley for his parcels.

People feel better living in a world like that, and there are clear economic benefits. The Government spends £120 bn on social security, much of which could be saved if people were empowered to take local voluntary community action ...

Pat and Ted's working methods are less wasteful than they may appear to corporate accountants, who seem incapable of seeing the financial wood for the budgetary trees. In a country plagued by the longest working hours in Europe, staff everywhere find themselves burdened with ever greater responsibilities, while being offered diminishing professional security. No wonder that more than two-thirds of TUC safety representatives identify stress as the greatest health and safety concern in the workplace.

Stress is now the single biggest cause of absenteeism, and costs corporate Britain anything between £9 bn and £19 bn per annum in compensation payments, quite apart from the mammoth cost of lost days of work. The Government spends about £8 bn in incapacity benefits every year, quite apart from the drain on NHS resources.

If more of us were more like Pat – or if we were allowed to be – the social *and* economic benefits would be enormous.

1   The Post Office have decided to rethink their decision with regard to their continued association with Pat. They have asked you to formulate a case for keeping him. Can you develop an approach that enables the Post Office to change without dumping Pat? An approach that indicates a particular strategy that builds on the sort of ethos that Pat symbolizes while enabling it to move into the future?

Source: David Thomas's words are extracted from 'Why Pat Must be Saved for the Nation', an article first published in the *Independent*

PART III

CASES AND FURTHER SOURCE MATERIAL

Cases

Case 1   Interbrew and Huyghe of Belgium – A Tale of Two Breweries

The theme from *Hawaii-Five-O* plays on the radio as Wim Vannimmen, a young accountant, tours us around Browerij Huyghe. We step over discarded kegs, past machines that are 'currently under repair' and old bottles on the wall representing the fifty-plus varieties that are produced in the plant. As we go, Wim turns machines off and on to demonstrate their workings and jokes with various work mates in Flemish. Given the laid back way things work here, the frantic music in the background seems more that a little incongruous.

Two decades ago the Huyghe brewery was in trouble. It traces its antecedents in Melle near Ghent in Belgium to 1654, but the brewery as it is now was founded by Leon Huyghe, a brewery worker married to a brewer's daughter, in 1906. The brewery grew steadily by producing Pils and basic 'table beers'. By the 1960s it was supplying its own chain of 300 pubs in addition to filling several big government contracts, most notably to provide beer for hospital restaurants and railway workers. However, things went against Huyghe in the 1970s and 1980s. There had been as many breweries as there were villages in Belgium, but consolidation now meant that Huyghe did not have the relative economies of scale necessary to compete on cost in the Pils and table beer segments. Consolidation also turned 300 outlets from a relatively big concern into a minor one. Advances in distribution networks made competition less regionalized and subsequently fiercer. Government organizations like hospitals and railways began to question whether supplying their workers with beer, the traditional Belgian drink, was necessarily a good thing. 'This brewery would not be here now,' confessed Wim as we pushed past the boxes of yet to be sorted out memorabilia in the new brewery museum to get to the bar, 'if it wasn't for one thing: try this.' 'This' was *Delirium Tremens*.

According to Alain De Laet, whose father married into the Huyghe family, the creation of *Delirium Tremens* was 'coincidental'. De Laet, now manager of the brewery, explains how in 1988 a distributor asked for a strong blond beer for the Italian market. Brew engineer Patrick De Wael made a first experimental batch on 26 December 1988. 'It was dead on target,' claims De Laet. 'The process hasn't been changed a bit ever since.'

The distinctive features of *Delerium's* packaging also emerged serendipitously. The light-grey speckled bottle was the remnant of a failed campaign. Painted by a German company and three times more expensive than normal bottles (far too pricey to fill with Pils or table beer where the margins are much lower), these had been intended for a 'grand cru' for a German customer. After this deal fell through, they had sat in storage and were due to be destroyed – until a bottle was needed for the trial batches of *Delirium*. For some reason, the heavy beer (9 per cent alcohol) and the light bottle seemed to go together.

Another part of the eclectic but distinctive packaging mix is the label with its brightly coloured elephants, monsters and birds. The formulation of this is the subject of folklore that, like all good corporate stories, has varying versions. As Wim has it, De Wael, excited by his creation, immediately brought it to a small meeting of Huyghe staff and family members. After tasting it and agreeing it was good they sat down to drink more. 'After four bottles,' Wim explains, 'one of the group said, "If I drink much more of this I'll start to see pink elephants". After seven, eight, nine, somebody said "If I drink any more of this I'll be seeing monsters". After eleven, you know that movie by Alfred Hitchcock,' Wim says, pointing to the row of birds along the top of the label. 'Somebody said they'd start to see those birds from the movie.'

Jean De Laet, Alain's father, who was running things at the time, remembers it slightly differently. 'Initially, the label showed a skull, to clarify the link with the disease' (*Delirium Tremens* is an acute disorder following withdrawal from alcoholic intoxication – because seizures can last up to six days and involve terrifying hallucinations and violent tremors it can be fatal). 'But a student working with us once drew the now well-known pink elephant, and bingo!'

The name *Delirium Tremens* (born when an inspector from the Excise Office tasted the new beer and said 'If I drink too much of this, I'll get a delirium') is unlikely to have been approved by a multinational corporation, but despite the problems it has caused it works for Huyghe. 'In Britain, for example, some individual protested the name,' explains Wim. 'So, we dropped the '*Tremens*'. Apparently '*Delirium*' by itself doesn't have the same meanings. They also made us change the colour of the elephant from pink. We made it red. I don't know why red is better than pink, but it's not a problem – whatever they want, we just change things around so that they're ok. In Canada we have to have special labels with all kinds of warnings. In the US we were afraid of the reaction so it was called '*Mateen*' [after a famous Flemish-American brewer]. Initially, we also had problems from the Republican Party [whose corporate logo is an elephant]. But we sorted all that out and it's *Delirium Tremens* there now too, with the elephant. It's funny but it's no problem. The most important thing is that people really remember the beer.'

In a market where there are hundreds of alternatives this is crucial (over 1500 different internationally available beers are rated on the Beer Lover's Association website www.whoop.com/Ratings.htm, reflecting an increasingly global and diverse marketplace). 'What's in the bottle is important only after you buy the beer for the first time. If a beer stands out you might try it. If you like it then you'll buy it again, but you have to have bought it in the first place.' Wim expands on this, only half-seriously, by comparing beer with people. 'Naked, we are all more or less the same,' he says pointing to a row of beer bottles without labeling. 'But with clothes on – wow, some people really stand out.' He holds a bottle of 'fully clad' *Delirium* in front of the bunch.

According to Johan Peters, marketing director at Interbrew, Belgium's largest brewing group, the specialty beer market is all about 'discovery'. 'People like to feel that they've found something new – and if that discovery is associated with tradition then that's even better.' Huyghe is fortunate here in two respects. Distributors in its main export markets are generally surprised by the fact that *Delirium* is such a recent invention – the unusual bottle and art deco/art nouveau styling of the elephant (which matches the architecture of the brewery) seems to link it to another time. Secondly, *Delirium* has been 'discovered' by some very influential people. In 1997, beer guru Stuart Kallen surprised aficionados by declaring *Delirium Tremens* the world's best beer, despite the fact that it would make his life more difficult – 'If I simply mentioned a beer everyone had heard of, without the name of a drinker's disease, I would get more peace,' he wrote. In 1998 it won at the World Beer Championships. It is still one of only 12 beers rated a perfect 10 on *whoop.com's* list (9 of the 12 are Belgian). Subsequently, sales are booming. About two-thirds of the Huyghe's output is now *Delirium*. The vast majority of this is sold outside of Belgium where it attracts a premium price.

Wim is upbeat about the future. 'I don't know much about brewing, but I like beer and I really like working here.' When it is pointed out that the prospects for smaller breweries are seen by many commentators to be bleak (their cost structure makes it impossible to compete against the bigger players and most small Belgian breweries with strong brands are being bought up by big companies like Interbrew), he is philosophical. 'Interbrew aren't stupid,' says Wim. 'When they buy companies they do so because they are good breweries and they keep good breweries going. But in any case, this is a family company, they [the family] want to retain control. It means the difference between really being a part of things or just being an 'owner'. And we have certain advantages the way things are. What we can do is when a buyer comes to us from Guadeloupe or New Zealand or wherever – we deal with over 45 countries – he comes and visits us and talks to *us*. It's a nice trip for him. Then if he only has a small shop we can make up a mixed pallet, half a crate of this and that, whatever he wants. So, he walks away with a ready-made shop of specialty beers.' ('We have a target of two new beers every year,' says Wim, with an enthusiasm for product proliferation that few accountants would share.) 'Interbrew can't do that. Hopefully, if that goes well he'll come back to us for another pallet and maybe one from another local brewery and we'll grow bigger together.'

Developing the point, Wim explains that 'We can even tailor-make a beer to suit a client's needs.' A claim proved by a quick look around the warehouse piled high with surplus labels for different niche-fillers like the sweetly named *I Love You* beer made for a German distributor. In keeping, Alain De Laet describes Huyghe's philosophy as 'meeting the demand of the customer as good as possible, and as it were, providing "made to measure". Important customers asking us for a new beer must be able to get it. We are open to all possibilities.'

In response to just such a request from American distributors obviously aware of the demand that *Delirium's* success has created, Huyghe have recently launched what Wim describes as *Delirium Tremen's* 'dark sister' – *Delirium Nocturnum*. A traditionally-brewed dark beer with a sweeter aftertaste that also utilizes the pink elephant/grey bottle packaging. It is also proving to be a big seller. However, Wim is puzzled by the suggestion that this is a brand that could run and run, the idea that a whole *Delirium* family could be built. 'First,' he explains, 'traditionally there are really only two types of specialty beer: Trippel [the blonde *Tremens* style] and Dark. You can't just make up new traditions. Second, *Delirium* is successful because it is different, because it stands out. You don't want to damage that. A new line would have to be labelled differently, without elephants – maybe with a gorilla or something ...'

Interbrew's new plant next to its global headquarters in Leuven, a student town on the other side of Brussels from Ghent, is altogether different. After watching a video outlining the rich history of beer in the region, the tour guide (a professional tour guide) appears a little guilty. 'One of the questions we get asked most frequently,' she explains, 'is where are all the people. The truth is that there are very few people here, apart from the computer operators in the control room.' This operation, all polished steel vats and piping, is state of the art. The factory, only a few years old, produces around 10 million units of *Stella Artois*, Interbrew's flagship brand, each day. Across the road, the old plant is now producing smaller runs of specialist brands, like the famous abbey beer *Leffe*, which are now an integral part of the Interbrew 'family'. Both operations benefit from being able to avail of an alternative to Europe's increasingly overburdened roads – the original 'beer canal', channeled 300 years ago by the Artois brewery's foresightful founding fathers.

Interbrew, recently formed through the merger of Belgium's two largest breweries – Artois in the northeast and Piedboeuf in the southwest – appears to benefit from the best of the old and the new at Leuven. They have recently grown very big and very global very fast. Since 1992 Interbrew have made 24 acquisitions in 14 countries. However, it is also a family business, still privately owned by people steeped in brewing tradition. Up until a few years ago one of the senior family members and largest shareholders worked the night shift in one of the plants. He had to be told that his multi-million dollar status meant he did not need to work in the factory any more.

According to CEO Hugo Powell, Interbrew's seemingly paradoxical aim is to become 'the world's local brewer. Our global approach is based on strong regional platforms and supported by our great ability to adapt to local markets and cultures.' Ludo Degelin, director of operations and manager of international technical support explains the approach in greater detail. He begins by reviewing some of the approaches favoured by Interbrew's competitors. Anheuser-Busch (AB), the world's largest brewing group, tends to buy up local production facilities (important given the high distribution costs associated with beer) that can then be converted and standardised to produce their global brand – *Budweiser*. 'It's a good strategy that has worked well for them, but it works because they started from such a large base and they have a huge global brand. We start from a different position and in any case I don't think their approach suits us,' Ludo explains. Guinness attempts to match local tastes (and take advantage of different licensing laws) by varying their recipe. Hence, the Belgian Guinness is stronger than in Britain where the excise regime is a lot stiffer, and the African brew is both stronger and sweeter than the Irish. A lot of mileage can be got out of one brand in this way. However, Ludo believes this strategy is becoming problematic as drinkers increasingly move across national boundaries and are confused by the variation in what they assume to be the same product.

Interbrew, by contrast, looks to acquire breweries with brands that have a strong local identity and are market leaders. Unlike AB they look to *develop* these brands. 'It is difficult to recreate the emotional attachment that local people already have for these beers,' claims Johan Robbrecht, who works with Ludo on aspects of packaging development, 'they are deeply rooted in the community, linked to particular sports and so on.' However, Interbrew does change some things. In Ludo's words, while they do not alter the taste of a local brew too radically, they do seek to 'clean up the production, using our technical experience and expertise, and then effectively re-launch it. Once this is done we offer the local management the opportunity to brew *Stella*, which we are building as our global flagship brand. However, [unlike *Guinness*] they must be able to produce it using the Belgian recipe so that it tastes as close as possible to the *Stella* brewed in Leuven.' And, importantly, Ludo adds, 'it must come into the local market at a premium price.'

Stella's premium status in Europe came almost by accident, thanks to what Ludo and others acknowledge was 'great work' by Artois' UK partners. As lager became popular in the important UK market around 20 years ago, brewers there looked to the Continent for licenses to brew strong European brands in the UK. Carlsberg and Heineken allowed their partners to change the recipes according to UK tastes and licensing laws, meaning flatter brews with lower alcohol levels. Whitbread, with whom Artois joined forces, did not go down this route.

Adapting a recipe to British tastes seemed sensible at the time (it certainly saved money by bringing it under the 5 per cent level – a marker in the UK excise system). However, as British drinkers have become more 'educated' this 'adaptation' strategy has proved problematic, with Heineken and Carlsberg's premium image being compromised. In response, they have launched new 'export' brands alongside their British variants, a move that Ludo believes can only further confuse the public as to their beer's 'identity'. In contrast, Whitbread's approach to brewing *Stella* 'Belgian style', combined with effective marketing, has seen it become the number one premium lager in the UK.

Over time, Interbrew aims to operate high-volume local brands that generally tap into that area's traditional masculine sporting culture in tandem with *Stella* as the premium more refined brand 'over and above these', to use Ludo's words. In this way, Ludo believes that Interbrew avoids pitfalls such as those encountered by Heineken as they attempted to penetrate Eastern Europe. In one country in particular, the approach was to discontinue local brands and replace their production with Heineken. This caused local resentment with Heineken seen as a foreign intruder even though local people produced it. Then, because of Heineken's global branding, it had to be sold at a price that very few drinkers in the East could afford (any lower would diminish the value of the product in neighboring countries). Ludo sees the way that Heineken now follows the same approach to international development as Interbrew as a vindication of Interbrew's strategy. However, he stresses that tolerance for local difference must have its limits. Just adding more and more brands to the portfolio creates logistical and organizational problems, and the cost savings that can be made by discontinuing brands that are not performing must be realized in a company of Interbrew's size. Plus, it has to be admitted that some of the local brews are not, in Ludo's diplomatic words, 'as good as they could be'. Indeed, corporate marketing director Johan Peeters points out that there are some global constants in beer. 'For example, if a beer is colder people will drink more of it; physiologically this is true, this is why Guinness are brewing colder now. And all people appreciate a beer that is more consistent and technically better brewed.' However, Ludo and Johan agree that beer is also connected to human emotions and traditions. So, if you are going to change production approaches, recipes or temperatures, it must be done gradually. That local people do not like to see their traditional tastes trashed appears to be another 'global constant'.

The advantages of associating with tradition in brewing are not just to do with personality and emotion. One of Interbrew's biggest success stories of recent times has been the white beer *Hoegaarden*. Interbrew purchased the small brewery that made the beer and then set about using it's international distribution network and marketing expertise to push this old beer into the consciousness of new consumers. Other brewers, in particular Heineken and Guinness, quickly copied *Hoegaarden*. According to Peeters, some of Guinness' difficulties with their *Breo* white beer stem from the fact that unlike Interbrew and Heineken, who linked into established white beer making expertise (and past mistakes), Guinness attempted to develop *Breo* themselves. Given that beer, and white beer in particular, is a 'live' product, thousands of batches are necessary to discover a beer's temperament and iron out inconsistencies. Hence, a tried and tested brew is an extremely valuable starting point.

While Interbrew's 'glocal' strategy is proving extremely successful, it has also created new conundrums for its managers. Most obviously the fast growth combined with the desire to develop rather than discontinue local brands means that the cost-cutting rationalization and restructuring generally associated with big conglomerates is difficult to achieve. However, Interbrew believe that the benefits of their approach outweigh the costs associated with their not taking a globalization strategy *à la* AB.

Less predictable, but just as palpable, are the ways in which local developments can increasingly present global difficulties. The recent merger of Artois and Piedboeuf brought together *Stella* and *Jupiler*, Belgium's two most popular lagers. Thirty years ago *Stella* was the clear local market leader with *Jupiler* a poor second, but the past decade has seen the situation reversed. *Jupiler* now commands around 40 per cent of the local Pils/lager market, with *Stella* at between 10 and 15. However, *Stella*, particularly given its established success in the UK market, is clearly the stronger global brand and has been developed accordingly (*Jupiler* is not marketed in any significant quantities overseas). One could argue that to continue with *Stella* in a Belgian market where it can only make significant headway at the expense of another Interbrew brand makes little sense. Indeed, it seems contrary to Interbrew's global strategy of only backing market leaders in local markets.

Globalization presents opportunities as well as problems, though. Stefan Descheemaeker, vice president responsible for mergers and acquisitions, believes that with the way things are going the notion that the global headquarters could be in London or Frankfurt rather than in Leuven is one that has to be considered (due to the pace of growth Interbrew's offices now spread across a number of sites in Leuven and a purpose-built corporate HQ outside of Leuven has been mooted). Again though, the economics of such decisions, as Stefan and others in Interbrew realise, are not clear-cut. There are certain advantages that come from the association with Belgium, and with the brewing history of Leuven. Ludo Degelin, for example, is clear in his view that Interbrew's continued global success is linked to the continued health of Belgium's local 'beer-café culture' and that the company's essence must continue to be strongly linked with the region.

Despite the challenges associated with their rapid internationalization, Interbrew has little option but to grow quickly given the nature of developments in the brewing industry. Analysts predict that five or six players will dominate the world market by 2005 (Interbrew are currently about the sixth largest). Stefan Descheemaeker explains the situation with a simple diagram, with 'profitability' on the vertical axis and 'size' on the horizontal. Between the axes he draws a 'U' shape. 'In the future only the smallest micro-breweries and the largest groups will exist. You cannot survive in the middle.' This scenario seems to bear out Wim's optimism about Huyghe's future, but others paint a slightly different picture. Johan Peeters suggests that the micro-breweries with strong local brands will still be visible, but only as shells: 'Museum's for tourists who want to feel good, who want to believe in the emotions and traditions of beer.' The beer itself, he believes, can be brewed better and less expensively using the likes of Interbrew's size and technical know-how.

1 Draw a diagram that illustrates Huyghe's competencies or strengths. Outline why Huyghe's approach works in the light of recent Postmodern developments.
2 How should Huyghe build upon the success of *Delirium*?
3 Can an independent Huyghe survive?
4 Diagram and explain the reasons for Interbrew's success.
5 Should Interbrew maintain its HQ in Belgium? Give reasons for your answer.

6   Should *Stella* be phased out in Belgium? If it is to remain, how would you seek to differentiate it from *Jupiler*?

This case was written in 2000 with the assistance of Johan Robbrecht and Kathleen Van den Berghe (both MBA graduates from Vlerick Business School in Ghent). Special thanks to the staff at Huyghe and Interbrew who gave so freely of their time and their opinions. The views expressed here by individual staff members should not be seen as necessarily indicative of corporate policies.

Case 2   Tayto Ireland and Walkers UK – Crisp Wars

Ireland's leading brand of crisps (or 'potato chips' as they are called in some countries), 'Tayto', has dominated the Irish savoury snack market for 40 years. Every week the Tayto Group produces and sells eight million packets of crisps and snacks in a country with a population of less than four million. This means that, on average, every Irish person consumes almost 100 packets a year.

However, Tayto's position is now under threat. British company Walkers, backed by the muscle of its parent company Frito Lay and Frito Lay's owner, the giant Pepsico corporation, launched the UK's most popular brand of crisps in the Republic of Ireland on 17 March 2000 (St Patrick's Day). According to Andrew Hartshorn, Walkers' brand manager for Ireland, Walkers intends to capture a 'substantial share of the [Irish] market quickly.' Indeed, Walkers appear to not only want to eat up market share, but to change the way Irish consumers see crisps. While Taytos generally come in dinky 25 gram bags and are replete with the skin shavings and blemishes of the potatoes they once were, Walkers is a crisp without blemish. They come with a minimal trace of vegetable oil in bigger servings with a modern foil bag decorated in the global Frito Lay format.

While Walkers is now backed by an American parent, Tayto has recently gone the other way, returning to Irish ownership after US firm TLC Beatrice sold it to the Irish drinks company Cantrell & Cochrane.

All of Ireland's crisps were imported from the UK until Mr Joe Murphy from Donabate, County Dublin founded the Tayto Company in 1954. Murphy, an enthusiastic crisp-eater, found the crisps available in his day to be bland and insipid (the only flavouring option available amounted to a little bag of salt contained in each packet for 'self-sprinkling'). He launched his crisp company on O'Rahilly Parade in Dublin with one van and eight employees, some of whom were to work for him for over 30 years.

Murphy's biggest claim to fame was his invention of cheese and onion flavoured crisps – a flavour perfected by one of those original eight, Seamus Burke, on what was effectively nothing more than a kitchen table. Cheese-and-onion is now the top selling flavour in Ireland and in the UK where Murphy's innovation was quickly copied.

Originally Tayto's were produced by hand using two sets of deep-fat fryers. But the company grew quickly, aided by the financial association with Beatrice who first acquired a stake in the company in 1965. Factories were built in Rathmines, Harold's Cross and Coolock, all in the Dublin area. Tayto now employs over 250 people and boasts a low staff turnover as testimony to the family atmosphere of the company.

Tayto's supply and distribution chains go deep into the Irish fabric. It only uses Irish potatoes grown under contract by farmers with whom Tayto have been associated for many years, and it has developed an intricate distribution network. Tayto's distributes its crisps through one of the largest direct van sales operations in the country, with 10 regional depots located through Ireland serviced by a roving fleet of 35 Tayto's vans. This provides a 99 per cent domestic distribution level – a quite remarkable feat given the still rural nature of large parts of Ireland.

To further consolidate these channels a central distribution centre was created in 1996 in Ballymount, Dublin. The centre is fully automated and contains 10 automated loading bays, with the capacity to hold in excess of 150 000 cartons of crisps. All types of outlets are serviced by this system: supermarket chains, pubs, newsagents, garage forecourts, off-licenses and independent owner-operator stores, and Tayto guarantees that each customer receives fresh product through weekly service calls.

The result: almost every shop in Ireland – from the biggest supermarket to the smallest independent corner grocer to the most remote petrol station – prominently displays Tayto crisps, a big factor in a market where it is estimated that approximately half of all sales are impulse purchases. Finding an Irish person, or anybody with a connection to Ireland, who is unaware of the brand is a difficult task. Indeed, the way in which some Irish speak of Tayto crisps seems to indicate a kind of spiritual attachment. In a recent survey of brands, Tayto was rated the third biggest Irish brand and first in the grocery sector.

While Tayto holds a domestic market position enjoyed by few indigenous consumer brands (in 1999, it held 60 per cent of Ireland's crisp market, and the second highest selling brand, 'King Crisps', is also owned by Tayto), it has no official export business in an increasingly global savoury snack market. However, there are what could be called 'independent initiatives' that bring Tayto crisps to the world. It is often claimed that there are more Irish living outside of Ireland than within, and packets of Tayto are regularly dispatched to Irish emigrants from friends and family at home. Martin McElroy, an Irishman now living in Philadelphia, has developed an agency that now orders over 100 000 bags of Tayto a week which he sells through local wholesalers: 'It's wonderful to see the reaction of all the Irish people here when they walk into a shop and there is a box of Tayto Cheese & Onion,' claims McElroy. 'But the Americans are really developing a taste for them too. In fact, I can see that Tayto will be regarded as the luxury import in the same way that many American products such as Nachos are regarded at home [Ireland].' The crisps are retailing for $1 a pack, twice what they sell for in Irish stores.

Walkers can also trace its history back 500 years. As a local pork butcher in Leicester in the English midlands, Walkers began producing crisps as a way of utilizing staff and facilities in its small factory while meat was heavily rationed after World War II. It began to expand into other British regions around 20 years ago. In recent years, with the backing of it's new parents and the help of a big marketing budget wisely spent, particularly on television advertisements featuring British soccer stars, it has become the UK's second most powerful grocery brand after Coca-Cola. Walkers now boasts annual sales of well over £300 million and 65 per cent share of the UK crisp sector.

Walkers/Frito-Lay/Pepsico are taking the Irish launch of its products very seriously. It has given away more than a million free packets of crisps and made an Irish variation on its theme of soccer-star television advertisements staring Roy Keane, an Irish midfielder who now plays for Manchester United and is one of the highest paid players in the English football league. Andrew Hartshorn explains that the huge marketing budget that Walkers is currently using to push its crisps in Ireland is a 'long term investment' – a strategy which is part of a bigger global picture. Success in Ireland, Europe's fastest growing economy and Walkers first overseas target, will help the company develop the knowledge, experience and confidence necessary to launch into other European countries.

Evidence from Northern Ireland does not bode well for Tayto. While the Tayto brand (owned by a different company in the North) is still widely regarded, Walkers replaced it as the best-selling crisp in just three years. However, there are many cultural and business factors that make the Republic a different market – not least of which is the clout of the myriad of smaller independent stores who still contribute a much higher percentage of sales than in Britain or the US and with whom Tayto's has long standing relationships. Tayto's managing director, Vincent O'Sullivan, subsequently believes that Tayto can compete against the might of the multinational threat: 'We're not going to give away market share to anyone,' insists O'Sullivan. 'What [Walkers] are going to find out is that it's a very competitive market with strong local brands.'

1   Can Tayto survive in the face of the threat from Walkers and the global brands like Pringles that are sure to follow?
2   Develop a strategy for Tayto built around what you believe to be the ethos of the company.

Sources: This case draws from www.taytocrisps and 'The Crisp Wars', *Cara Magazine*

Postscript: Joe 'Spud' Murphy died in November 2001. Many obituaries were published in the newspapers of Ireland and Britain expressing the individuality and kindness of the man and hailing him as the very acme of the Irish entrepreneurial spirit

Case 3   Ottakar's UK – Living With the Amazons

The most talked about new company at the end of the twentieth century is almost certainly Amazon.com. It is attributed with having changed the way that we think about shopping. Some say it has challenged traditional notions of economics and strategy. All of a sudden retailers can broaden their scope and increase sales quickly and dramatically without the traditional costs associated with employing a bigger sales force and setting up new branches, depots or dealerships. All sales can be processed at a central depot and mailed out from one huge warehouse, with the saving made from not having to maintain a chain of real-world stores passed on to happy customers. Amazon's ubiquitous website (www.amazon.com) and its clean, efficient 'white space' style is increasingly familiar to book-buyers, and increasingly copied by retailers moving into Internet sales. In order to overcome the one barrier that Amazon has to increasing international sales, the high cost of international postage and customs duties added to the selling price of their books making them less attractive to those overseas, it is now looking at setting up bases in other countries. Recently, Amazon has established an arm in the UK. The formula is the same (compare www.amazon.com with www.amazon.co.uk) but sales are processed and the books dispatched from a centre in the UK.

The big question now being asked in book retailing circles is 'How can any company compete with Amazon?' More generally, people are asking whether any form of traditional retailing can survive in the face of their market share being eroded by online providers unencumbered by traditional cost structures.

Ottakar's is a UK chain of bookshops that has built a reputation for strongly individual high street shops staffed by book enthusiasts. It is described by one recent newspaper report as 'rather traditional and vaguely quirky'. Ottakar's came into being in 1987, when its current managing director James Heneage saw an opportunity to establish a chain of bookshops offering high levels of service in English market towns – those places bigger than villages but smaller than cities. At the time the idea of a national chain of bookshops was relatively new. Waterstone's and Dillons were opening branches within Britain's major cities, but otherwise the competition consisted of regional chains, like WH Smith, and the independent booksellers that existed in every town.

Ottakar's started life as three branches in southern England. It acquired a small chain of west country shops in 1990 on the back of the success of the original three. In 1992 Heneage was able to point to enough evidence of a successful formula to persuade backers to refinance the company so as to enable a more rapid expansion. Over the next eight years Ottakar's grew to encompass 72 branches employing over 800 staff throughout the UK. In 1998 the company was successfully floated on the London Stock Exchange.

'The secret of great bookselling,' according to Heneage, 'lies in the recruitment of people who enjoy a passion for books and are able to articulate that passion to their customers.' Subsequently, he claims that 'we recruit on love and knowledge of books above all else.' And, contrary to a lot of recent management thinking advocating bringing in people who have been successful in one field to shake up an organization operating in another, Ottakar's have a policy of not recruiting from outside the book trade at the management level.

Heneage describes Ottakar's today as 'a paradox. On the one hand it is a national book chain striving to offer uniform excellence in range and service over 70 branches. On the other hand it is a collection of intensely individual bookshops, run with great autonomy by staff whose commitment to books is matched only by their commitment to provide a bookselling service tailor-made for the communities they serve.'

Ottakar's results through to the end of 1999 have been impressive, with sales of £13.2 m in 1996 with a before-tax profit of £0.7 m, increasing to sales of £57.3 m and a before-tax profit of £3.1 m. According to Heneage, this success 'has been founded on allowing … individuals [the] freedom to create very original and individual shops.' However, for Ottakar's, as for any book seller, the main threat looming on the horizon is the market share being gobbled up by Amazon. In response, Ottakar's has recently developed its own 'Net strategy'.

Jim McClellan, who writes on e-commerce for the *Guardian* newspaper, claims that the assumption in e-commerce 'seems to be that successful first movers have probably got things right so all competitors can do is copy their approach, perhaps tweaking it slightly.' He expands upon this view using the example of online book retailing: 'Amazon showed how to do it and all subsequent sites, from Net-only concerns like BOL and Alphabet Street to real-world chains like WH Smith and Waterstones, have imitated their basic model. So much for the Net as a hotbed of innovation and experiment.'

Lacking the size or market clout of the chains mentioned by McClellan and saddled with the fixed costs of real-world stores unlike the Net-only operators, Ottakar's has been forced to come up with something different. Heneage claims that Ottakar's Internet strategy is to 'faithfully reproduce local branch individualism and expertise.' As opposed to Amazon's clean lines and universal sites, Ottakar's has attempted to get every one of its branches to create its own Website, one that reflects their own characteristics and passions. 'Our shops are locally oriented,' explains Heneage, 'we want to portray that online.' When one logs on to www.ottakars.co.uk one is imme-diately taken to a page listing local sites divided by region, each of which can be 'walked into' at a click. Each site has its own low-tech 'homely homepage' look, with pictures of local staff, inside and outside views of the store, details of particular in-store events featured prominently, and maps of where the store is highlighting local traditions and landmarks drawn by the staff themselves (see below – others can be seen on the Ottakar's site).

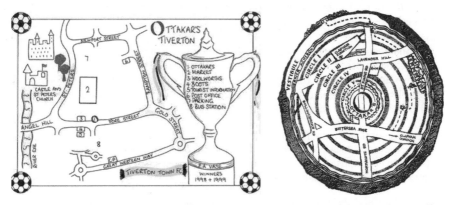

Heneage's hope is that these attempts to localise the website will bring Ottakar's staff in behind the initiative, and in this way their quirky passion will bring home to people the things lacking from Net-only bookstores. 'The main idea behind the site is to bring the enthusiasm and knowledge in our real-world shops on to the Net. Our staff knows a great deal about books. That's why people come back to us.'

Staff expertise is available through a number of features. 'Ask the Expert' enables people to post enquiries that can be answered by a local staff member or referred on by local staff to somebody else they know within the organisation who is better qualified to answer. People can read reviews of books recently read by staff at their local store and tap into a network of reviews posted by Ottakar's staff from around the country. Other innovations include a daily quiz (recently copied by Waterstones), a book gossip column and links to Ottakar's micro sites devoted to specific areas or genres like science fiction.

One aspect of Ottakar's new strategy that has proved surprisingly popular is the option for the customer to collect books purchased on their website from their nearest store. It seems that many prefer this more tactile approach to waiting for books to be posted, wondering when they are going to arrive, worrying that they will not be at home to receive delivery, and incurring the extra cost associated with mail delivery. Once these customers come in to collect their books they are likely to browse around and con-verse with Ottakar's staff. Unlike the Amazons of this world, whose approach is to cut out the middleman (that is, the bookstores) and pull customers away from the high street, Ottakar's is taking an opposite view. It sees the Internet as a way of enabling cus-tomers to develop a stronger relationship with local stores and, subsequently, pulling them in. One could counter that once customers get more comfortable about purchas-ing online they will care less and less about local identity and relationships and more and more about getting books as cheaply as possible. But at this point this seems to be a gamble that Ottakar's is prepared to take. While lower and lower prices on books seem to be the way that companies are seeking to build up traffic and sales through their sites,

Ottakar's says that it will only match the discounts offered on the lead titles and new books (prices that they will replicate in the real-world stores). They will not discount backlist titles in the way that Amazon and others do.

While the interest, customer reception (most surveyed really liked the different, local feel of the sites) and Net-sales achieved in the first few weeks after the launch were very encouraging, the first financial results following the initiative raised some eyebrows. Ottakar's saw turnover rise by 27 per cent but pre-tax profits tumble in the financial year 1999/2000. Subsequently, the yearly dividend to shareholders was reduced to 1.5 pence per share from 2.25 pence the previous year. Heneage blamed Internet set-up costs and Ottakar's store expansion programme, admitting that 'new store sales performance was disappointing.' However, he described the results as an 'aberration' and a 'savage hic-cup'. Shareholders, however, were understandably nervous.

Moreover, most website experts seemed unimpressed by www.ottakars.co.uk. An objective analysis carried out by James Wallis in *Doors* assessed the UK's nine major booksellers sites according to 'prices', 'service' and 'usability' and placed Amazon first and Ottakar's last. Of Ottakar's Wallis wrote:

> Ottakar's website is confusingly over-designed, which distracts you from what you are looking for, and it scores low for usability, even though the search and delivery options were good (including free shipping to your local branch of the chain). Prices were disappointing – all books are at the recommended price. Needs a thorough rethink.

1 Despite the early losses would you persevere with Ottakar's Net strategy?
2 Does a small traditional 'bricks and mortar' company like Ottakar's have any chance of succeeding, or will the might of global Net-based companies like Amazon eventually be too much for them to compete with?
3 Much of the advertising about the Internet claims that those organizations that do not embrace it will be no more in 10 years' time. Do you think this is true? Will e-commerce eventually make 's-commerce', or real-world shops, obsolete?
4 If Ottakar's 'homely' local strategy is a success, what could Amazon do to counter it?

Sources: this case draws from www.ottakars.co.uk; 'A New Chapter', *Guardian*; 'Expansion and the Net Take Toll of Ottakar's', *The Times*; 'Site Test', *Doors*. This case was written in 2000 and revised in 2001

Case 4   Nike – From Beaverton to the World

Nike was founded in 1964 when Phil Knight, a former collegiate track runner, put an MBA project he had done into practice with Bill Bowerman, his former coach at the University of Oregon. At a time when established companies like Puma and Adidas were manufacturing in high-wage economies, Knight's project had shown that decreasing transport costs would mean that higher margins could be gained by sourcing shoes from countries with low labour costs. Nike began by importing shoes from Japan. However, one morning Bowerman was standing in his kitchen and had an idea. He made an out-sole by pouring a rubber compound into a waffle iron. The waffle trainer was born and Nike became a design company rather than just an importer.

Knight and Bowerman's personalities provided other elements that paved the way for Nike's initial success: a love of athletics, an appreciation of the views of real athletes and a relentless appetite for competition. 'Every time I tour people around [the Nike 'campus'],' explains Geoff Hollister, who ran track with Knight at college and is one of Nike's longest serving employees, 'I show them a picture of Phil Knight running behind Jim Grelle.' It was Knight's customary position, Hollister continues, 'Grelle was a champion and Knight never caught him – but he never stopped pursuing.' Another Oregon athlete, Steve Prefontaine, a ferocious competitor and a notoriously rebellious individual, became the initial 'patriarch' of the Nike culture, always prodding his friend Knight to improve the quality and design of his shoes.

Initially, Nike outsourced all its production to plants in Japan. However, in the early 1970s, as costs there began to rise, production was switched to Taiwan and Korea. Due to the relative inexperience of shoe manufacture in these countries, Knight relocated some of the more complex tasks to Maine and New Hampshire. But in 1982, the same year that Maine passed a new industrial accident law entitling claimants to have their legal fees paid by their employers, this was moved back to Asia. Since this point only Nike's headquarters and design facilities have been located in the US (Nike's HQ, or 'campus' as it is called, has always been in Beaverton, Oregon). At the end of the twentieth century, Nike employed 13 000 people in US, while its 350 subcontractors employed nearly 500 000 in plants in China, Vietnam and Indonesia.

Nike's success can be best understood by examining the way in which Knight created a company where the corporate values, strategy and the actions of those who worked there all reinforced the original purpose 'to always strive for number one'.

Knight's passion for athletic excellence attracted employees with a similar outlook. Nike has subsequently attracted a weirdly diverse collection of young (the average employee age is 31) and confident individuals. According to Nelson Farris, another of Knight's former track teammates and a Nike employee for 25 years: 'We like employees who aren't afraid to tee it up.' The 'campus' culture is subsequently pervaded with an 'athletistocracy' that places athletic achievement above everything else. An article *in The Sunday Times* recently claimed that for this generation, the words 'I work for Nike', seem to have the same appeal as 'I work for NASA' did 30 years ago (in fact, Nike has many ex-NASA people on its staff and was the first to use the air-cushioning sole system developed by NASA engineers). 'If the automobile captured the popular imagination of the 1950s,' says Steven Langehough of the Cooper-Hewitt Design Museum, 'today the athletic shoe has become a more democratic symbol of identity and prestige in multi-cultural America.' Nike employees seem to have developed a particular pride that has come from being at the forefront of this revolution. Once part of 'the fraternity', they are famously devotional. Many have tattoos of Nike's trademark 'swoosh' on their bodies.

Nike's corporate values are powerfully expressed in their marketing. The swoosh speaks of a no-nonsense emphasis on speed and performance that now ranks alongside McDonald's Golden Arches, and Coca-Cola's red and white logo as being recognized by 97 per cent of Americans. In fact, Nike largely stopped using its name in advertisements in the 1990s because it became unnecessary in conveying what Nike stood for. The one tag line that Nike has consistently used in conjunction with the swoosh is the now ubiquitous 'Just do it'. This was born in 1988 when an advertising executive told Nike staff that: 'You Nike guys, you just do it.' It is the second most recognizable slogan in the US after the Marlboro Man.

These actions and values connected to a strategy consistent with Knight's original vision. Nike shoes sell for up to US $90 (well above the industry average), while Nike's contracted factories in under-developed countries pay as little as 20 cents an hour.

When the costs of production in a Nike base rise through a country becoming more developed, Nike simply switch to a cheaper alternative. Indeed, economists have coined the term 'the Nike indicator' to denote how far a country has to move up the development scale before Nike would depart. Thus, the cost of producing a Nike shoe is only around 4 per cent of the retail price. Nike then spends the difference on hiring the best designers and marketing experts in the US and on paying superstar athletes like Michael Jordan, Tiger Woods, Mike Tyson and Michael Johnson (not to mention dozens of other individuals and teams) to promote Nike products. In 1997, Nike spent two and a half times what its closest rival, Reebok, did on marketing its brands. The resulting marketing 'pull' means that despite high prices Nike also leads on units sold.

In the word of one commentator, the ethos generated within Nike enabled it to 'instill its products with a kind of holy superiority.' And this 'holiness' and the continued growth that ensued saw Nike go from strength to strength. Its share price rose 3686 per cent in the period from 1980 to 1997. Nike overtook Reebok to become market leader in sports shoes in 1988 and in the three years to 1996 more than doubled sales, moving from a 32 per cent share of the market in 1994 to 45 per cent in 1996. In the three years to 1997, the group tripled in size with worldwide sales up to $9 billion and profits to $800 million. Nike's latest growth initiative is a push into soccer, where, thanks to a huge marketing budget, it was beginning to make significant inroads by the time of the 1998 soccer World Cup in France. The Nike Globe that formed the focal point of Nike's promotions in Paris during the Cup symbolized Nike's view of itself as a global icon.

Since achieving number one status in sports footwear (where it now sells hundreds of different models), Nike has pursued an increasing number of new initiatives. In 1990, Knight claimed that the goal for the next decade was to be 'the market share leader and the most profitable brand in all 39 footwear, apparel and accessories lines in which we compete.' In 1992, he made it clear that he wanted Nike to be not just the world's best athletic shoemaker but 'the world's best sports and fitness company.' Indeed, Nike's vice president Mark Parker has recently claimed that the sports business 'is not just a better definition [than the shoe business] of what our epicenter is but what we are all about.'

In an interview in the *Harvard Business Review* in 1992, Knight described the transformation taking place in his company. 'For years we thought of ourselves as a production-oriented company, meaning we put all our emphasis on designing and manufacturing the product. But we understand now that the most important thing we do is market the product. We've come around to saying that Nike is a marketing-oriented company.' The new emphasis on marketing saw Nike seek to exploit and ram home the 'rebel' image, with 'Just do it' supported with slogans like 'You don't win second, you lose first'. It also saw Nike move into further pastures.

These included 'redefining retailing', with the launch of Nike Town stores (described as being 'more like theme parks that shops') and 'redefining and expanding the world of sports entertainment', with a joint venture with a Hollywood talent agency. The aim here was to package up events that Nike endorsers like Charles Barkley and Michael Jordan were involved in – such as exhibition matches and movies – into programming, sell time to associated sponsors and then peddle the package to media companies. Nike's director of advertising outlined the potential: 'Forget the business Nike's in at the moment. This is going to boom across the map, and massive amounts of money can be made.' Nike also sought to be more fashion conscious in its product design, a move that worked exceedingly well, according to fashion journalists. *Vogue* described Nike's new

Air Terra Humara as a shoe 'with the sort of nautilus-like shape of a camera's shutter; a shoe like the kind of long lever that clicks along the teeth on the gear of a clock; the hub of a very cool wheel ... the longitudinal slits sing of side-to-side stability.' Nike's vice president of corporate communications proclaimed that 'We see [these initiatives] as a natural progression. We are not a shoe company.' In 1996, Nike was increasingly slapping its swoosh on everything from sunglasses to footballs to batting gloves and hockey sticks. Phil Knight predicted that Nike would double its sales within the next five years. His stated objective for Nike in that year's annual report of was the ' "Swooshification" of the world'.

1998, however, would see a turn in Nike's fortunes. A turn that would lead the normally gung-ho Knight to admit to *Advertising Age* that: 'Everything we have tried over the past six months simply has not worked.' Profits fell 69 per cent at the end of 1997. Analysts predicted that Nike's share of the world athletic market would drop from 47 per cent in 1997 to 40 per cent. The share price, which stood at $72 at the beginning of 1994, hit $30 in August 1998. Standard & Poors subsequently downgraded its outlook on Nike from 'stable' to 'negative'. What happened? Two things, in a nutshell: the global community decided that it was not so keen on Nike's 'personality', and the fickle world of fashion appeared to turn its back on its products.

In September 1997, an organization made up of inner-city high school students and parents left their Nike shoes outside Nike Town New York in protest at Nike's underpaid foreign workers. As part of their ongoing appeal the students wrote 150 letters to Michael Jordan and Nike over a four-month period. They received one form letter in return. This event caught the public eye, adding weight to a media investigation that had begun to collate alleged abuses at Nike's foreign factories. The claims made included the use of children, sold to the factories by brokers, making footballs in Pakistan; daily wages in Indonesia that did not cover the cost of three simple meals; human rights abuses, including a group of women forced to run around a plant until 12 collapsed with heat exhaustion in Vietnam, and reports of workers being beaten with unfinished shoes in Korea; poor air quality caused by petroleum-based solvents leading to breathing problems, eye infections and hallucinations in some Asian factories; paying well under the minimum wage and the lack of sick pay and compensation even for industrial injuries in many countries. The anti-Nike fire was fueled by Internet sites like www.boycottnike.com and www.nike-sucks.com.

It transpired that Nike were doing little that was different from other sportswear manufacturers at this time. However, Medea Benjamin, director of *Global Watch*, admitted that Nike would continue to be targeted because it was 'the biggest and it sets the trends. I wish we had the resources to look at Reebok, Adidas and Converse, but we don't.' Indeed, it was not just that Nike was the biggest, it was also the loudest. As Thomas Bivins, Professor of Public Relations at the University of Oregon, argued: 'When a company goes out of its way to create an image, it is going to be a big target.'

Nike responded as if they were mounting a legal defence. They sought to distance themselves from the factories, denying that they were in any way responsible for what went on in them. They didn't directly pay anybody at the factories and didn't set the policy within the factories – it was none of their business. After this failed to wash, Nike's PR spokesperson declared that 'In a country where the population is increasing by 2.5 million a year, with 40 per cent unemployment, it is better to work in a shoe factory than not have a job.' Nike seemed to believe that the global community would be hushed if, firstly, it denied the problem; secondly, it was told that Nike did not own the factories – so it was nothing to do with them; and, finally, if what they did was no worse than what other operations near their production facilities did. But matters just got worse.

In January 1997, Andrew Young, former US ambassador to the UN, visited Nike plants in Vietnam, Indonesia and China and declared that they were 'as clean and modern' as any in the US. However, the big news story on Young's claims turned out to be the realization that he was paid by Nike for his visit and only had a few hours in each factory, during which time he was shepherded by Nike staff and only introduced to appropriately briefed members of staff. In the US, stories like these saw Nike-bashing become a spectator sport with Michael Moore, famous for *Roger & Me*, a film that had criticized the behaviour of General Motors, and cartoonist Garry Trudeau, lampooning the company. In Britain, the magazine *Big Issue* begged its readers to boycott Nike. One newspaper article drew links between Nike and Mike Tyson, declaring that 'Nike is one bad dude.' Even Nike's recent success in moving into soccer came to be tarred by the brush of their now dubious reputation. After Brazil's defeat by France in the 1998 World Cup Final, many came to believe that Nike had bullied Brazil's coach into playing Ronaldo (the superstar picked out by Nike as the global icon for their soccer range) even though he was obviously unfit.

In the fashion stakes, even Nike's own designers have admitted in interviews that 'we're just not cool any more.' Marketing guru Peter York claims that 'Nike [knows that they are] not what matters at the moment,' and that this recognition has lead to there being: 'an air of desperation about them now. They're doing too many special runs and limited editions, trying too hard to keep their cool. They've had brilliant brand marketing, but their brand stretches are unproven.'

Compounding these problems, Nike's failure to meet sales targets saw the value of stock in inventory rise by 50 per cent. Nike began to sell off stock in bulk, at a discount, creating a 'grey' market prayed upon by supermarket and discount store chains who began to sell cut-price Nike's under tag lines like 'Just do it for less'. In short, the brand was becoming too common to be cool, and Nike's image was becoming one of 'establishment' rather than 'rebel'.

While Nike is still a brand leader in training and athletic shoes, boasting a 33 per cent share of the world market and 40 per cent of the US market, its competitors are making up ground with the previously under-performing Adidas, and other small niche or 'lo-glo' competitors like Camper and the 'ecologically-sound' Ecco, making the biggest gains.

Adidas has recently settled on a strategy of reviving interest in the concepts of teamwork, fair-play and 'excellence without attitude'. Their new campaigns seek to subtly rebuke what is seen as Nike's personal glory ethic while celebrating skilled, smart play. One campaign featured Kobe Bryant (a basketballer who is to team play what Jordan is to individual performance) executing moves before unselfishly passing to a team mate to score. Other ads also mock Nike's 'winning is everything' ethos, with bylines like 'Take the bronze, take the silver, take the gold, take your own approach, take it very seriously, don't take it seriously at all, take what you want.' Adidas subsequently improved its European footwear sales by 42 per cent in 1997, and it is making significant inroads in the US. Its recent acquisition of the French ski manufacturer Salomon is now helping it exploit the trend for extreme sports-related wear.

The industry's number two, Reebok, is also trying to refocus after a period of decline. A decline that Reebok chairman Paul Fireman partly blames on their initial response to Nike's ascension in the 1990s. 'As Nike pulled away, competitors [like us] began to ape their look,' Fireman explains. When Nike began to suffer from a lack of what industry insiders call 'freshness', the likes of Reebok were caught out too. With hindsight, Fireman admits that: 'we were fools to follow'. Add to this the global 'shoe mountain' left by the glut of unsold product and Reebok and others now recognize that it has become very difficult to sell sportswear, especially at the high-yield end of the market. Reebok's response to Nike's more recent moves into marketing, fashion and entertainment is interesting in the light of this: 'More power to them,' argues Fireman. 'We're happy to see them trying to do so many things. It just means that they're losing focus and taking their eye off the ball.' As part of its refocus, Reebok has also stolen a march on Nike with its mission statement, now printed on its shoe boxes. It reads 'We will not be indifferent to the standards of our business partners around the world.'

Phil Knight originally refused to comment on the protests against his company, then denied all charges of slave labour, then labelled his accusers 'activists'. However, 1998 marked what the *Financial Times* called 'a stunning reversal'. Knight came out and personally responded to the criticisms. He explained that 'Basically, our culture, and our style, is to be a rebel, and we sort of enjoy doing that.' However, he conceded that 'Now that we've reached a certain size, there's a fine line between being a rebel and being a bully, and yeah, we have to walk that line.' Nike announced it would sever ties with three Indonesian contractors because of their 'unacceptable working conditions'. Knight announced that it would take students to its factories to demonstrate that they were not 'sweatshops'. It increased wages by up to 40 per cent for individuals in entry-level footwear manufacturing jobs in Indonesia and improved air quality by switching to water-based rather than petroleum-based adhesives. It also increased its minimum working age to 18. In May of 1998, Knight unveiled a plan to improve the conditions of 350 000 Nike workers in Asia. Moreover, it set up the website www.nikeworker.com where it invites people to log-on to gain information about Nike's production practices and 'other important human rights issues'. A measure of the success of these initiatives is that the third annual 'Protest Nike' day scheduled for the end of 1998 failed to draw any protesters. The Transnational Resource and Action Center, one of Nike's most vocal critics, also admitted that relations with Nike were much improved.

There was more to come, however. Later that year Knight explained that Nike would undergo a 'holistic reorganization' as it struggled with what it stood for. Nike spokespeople admitted that the company had made poor decisions in every area: design, marketing and sponsorship as well as offshore employment. Nelson Farris, a Nike employee for 25 years, admitted that 'I've been to Chinese-run factories and though we improved upon that, it obviously wasn't good enough. We got caught … None of us was smart enough to figure out the Asia thing, but we should have been looking at what we were doing wrong. Now we're looking at how we run our company. Are we making the right product? Is our service, our advertising, good enough? Are we good enough people?' The bad publicity had certainly had an impact on the mood of Nike's employees. Farris continued, 'When you pick up the newspaper and everyday you're being told how bad your company is, sure it's going to effect you. It has demoralized a lot of people. It's been very difficult to deal with that. We haven't been as on top of things as we'd perhaps have liked. We've got to learn to do business much better, we've got a lot to do internally. We've been far, far too arrogant, and we know it.' Tom Clarke, Nike's Chief Operating Officer, who confessed that 'We'd gotten stale on design,' was philosophical. 'You grow a lot and then you need a period when thing aren't booming to ask what works and what doesn't.' Suddenly the company whose strength of mission meant that it seldom stopped to question anything was pondering everything.

Nike has launched many new initiatives as a result of this pondering. It is developing 'sub-brands' as a means of spreading its expertise without damaging the core brand. Tiger Woods now has his own label, a swirling yin-yang logo reflecting both his club speed and his Buddist beliefs, and Michael Jordan has been given his own line, with a logo based on an amalgam of the Ferrari, Porsche and Mercedes badges – 'to give it some heritage' says Tinker Hatfield. Nike is also pinning a great deal of hope on a new high-tech line called Alpha, differentiated from other Nike products, and a 'great outdoors' range called ACG (All Condition Gear).

Despite initial teething problems, the move into soccer is being persevered with. 'The great thing about designing soccer-boots is that you don't have to try and figure out a fashion element,' says one designer who has been with Nike 19 years. 'You don't have to compromise like you do in basketball shoes say. When we design shoes for basketball, the company always looks at the fashion element first.'

In response to the threat from the low-cost chains selling Nike product, Nike themselves have opened a chain of outlet stores in the US that sells excess inventory at a discount.

Also, the company that had always relied solely on its *aretaic* approach to ethics – its 'personality' – issued a new *deontic* code of conduct which adds much more detail with regard to specifying what its duties are onto its previous statements of philosophy (see 'The Nike Philosophy' and the Nike 'Code of Conduct' below).

Finally, Nike is attempting to 'soften' its image. In 1998, 'Just do it' was watered down to 'I can' in the US. (Although there was some uncertainty as to what would happen to 'Just do it'; some Nike spokespeople claimed that it would not disappear, it would just be 'largely replaced', while others suggested that 'I can' would just *augment* 'Just do it'). 'At a time when cynicism in sports is at an all-time high, 'I can' is an effort to return to a focus on the positive,' said Bob Wood, Nike's marketing vice president. The *Financial Times* announced that with the 'unveiling of the new softer "I can" slogan to replace "Just do it", Nike may be about to take an evolutionary step.' However, some industry watchers were not so convinced, and many customers seemed confused.

Reebok and Adidas plan to match Nike on the technological front, but are changing the way they sell, parting company with many of their high-priced athletes. However, Nike's connection to the stars is one thing that has yet to be changed. The link seems an integral part of the company. Many of its offices are named after athletes (Knight's office is in the John McEnroe Building). The essence of Nike, according to Bill Sapporito, who has done extensive research into the company, is that it is 'built by pretty good athletes to serve great athletes, a place where work is play and play is damned serious.' But not everybody thinks that this sacred cow should be preserved. Mike Perry, director of the London arm of Nike's advertising agency, argues that Nike must 'get back to some core brand values. I think we've seen enough of this superstar stuff.'

1   Use frameworks from Chapters 5 and 6 to describe why Nike was so successful in the 1980s. Outline how things came apart in the late 1990s using the same templates. How has Nike's ethos or personality changed through the years?

2   Should Nike stick with the 'athletistocracy' and 'superstar stuff', or should it follow Adidas and Reebok's new emphasis on playing down individual greatness?

3   Will the new 'I can' slogan help Nike walk the fine line between being a rebel and being a bully and give the company the focus that it seems to have lost? Would you have supported the introduction of 'I can' in place of 'Just do it'? Would you have supported the idea of one running alongside or augmenting the other?

4   Which of Nike's other new (post-'97) initiatives would you have supported, which would you have disagreed with, and what else might you have suggested?

The Nike Philosophy (c. 1992)

NIKE Inc. was founded on a handshake.

Implicit in that act was the determination that we would build our business with all of our partners upon trust, teamwork, honesty and mutual respect. We expect all of our business partners to operate on the same principles.
At the core of the NIKE corporate ethic is the belief that we are a company comprised of many different kinds of people, appreciating individual diversity, and dedicated to equal opportunity for each individual.

NIKE designs, manufactures and markets sports and fitness products. At each step in that process, we are dedicated to minimizing our impact on the environment. We seek to implement to the maximum extent possible the three 'R's' of environmental action: reduce, reuse and recycle.

There Is No Finish Line.

The New Nike Code of Conduct (c. late 1990s)

NIKE Inc. was founded on a handshake. Implicit in that act was the determination that we would build our business with all of our partners on trust, teamwork, honesty and mutual respect.

We expect all of our business partners to operate on the same principles. At the core of the NIKE corporate ethic is the belief that we are a company comprised of many different kinds of people, appreciating individual diversity, and dedicated to equal opportunity for each individual. NIKE designs, manufactures and markets products for sports and fitness consumers. At every step in that process, we are driven to do not only what is required, but what is expected of a leader. We expect our business partners to do the same. Specifically, NIKE seeks partners that share our commitment to the promotion of best practices and continuous improvement in:

1. Occupational health and safety, compensation, hours of work and benefits.
2. Minimizing our impact on the environment.
3. Management practices that recognize the dignity of the individual, the rights of free association and collective bargaining, and the right to a workplace free of harassment, abuse or corporal punishment.
4. The principle that decisions on hiring, salary benefits, advancement, termination or retirement are based solely on the ability of an individual to do the job.

Wherever NIKE operates around the globe, we are guided by this Code of Conduct. We bind our business partners to these principles.

While these principles establish the spirit of our partnerships, we also bind these partners to specific standards of conduct. These are set forth below:

1. Forced Labor (Contractor) certifies that it does not use any forced labor – prison, indentured, bonded or otherwise.

2. Child Labor (Contractor) certifies it does not employ any person under the minimum age established by local law, or the age at which compulsory schooling has ended, whichever is greater, but in no case under the age of 14.

3. Compensation (Contractor) certifies that it pays at least the minimum total compensation required by local law, including all mandated wages, allowances and benefits.

Sources: this case draws on 'Critics Can't Stop Swatting the Swoosh', *Footwear News*; 'Is it Time to Jump on Nike?', *Fortune*; 'Nike's New Sneaker Challenge', *WWD*; 'Is Nike No Longer Cool?' *Financial Times*; 'I Will Just do it Better, Hope Nike', *Financial Times*; 'S&P Downgrades Nike', *WWD*; 'Can Nike get Unstuck', *Time*; R. Goldman and S. Papson, *Nike Culture*; 'Shoe Giants are Caught on the Hop', *European*; 'Down at Heel: can Nike Change Direction?', *The Sunday Times*; 'Nike to Sport a Smaller "Swoosh"', *Financial Times*; 'Nike's Plea: Judge us by our Actions', *Financial Times*; 'Nike Seeks a Footpath Back to Growth', *Financial Times*; 'Nike Takes the Pain in its Stride', *Financial Times*; 'Nike Agrees to Show Students its Factories', *Financial Times*; plus the websites mentioned in the text above. Special thanks to Kay Hammond (Warwick Business School MBA) for additional research

Case 5   **Natural History New Zealand**

'I hate management,' says Michael Stedman, managing director of Natural History New Zealand Ltd. (www.naturalhistory.co.nz). This is the first thing that Stedman says, after stepping out of his office to make coffee and asking if I take milk. 'We've just hired a "Human Resources" manager, whatever that means. I hate the idea of it, but I suppose we have to now.' The reason that he begrudgingly accepts such specialists is that his company has grown from 30 employees to 130 in the past two and a half years. It is now a major contributor to the economy and social fabric of one of the world's southernmost towns – Dunedin.

He goes on: 'I hate the way "management" separates people from other people, putting them up here [he picks out a space above his head with two hands], away from the people who are the reason the company exists [he makes a triangle shape with his hands and marks out the bottom of it]. We exist because we make f...ing good programmes – they make the programmes. Why do I have a car park outside the building when everyone else has to park in the public car park, why isn't that rotated or something?'

'Would you be more comfortable with a company shaped like this,' I offer, drawing a web shape on the back of my note pad – a mess of interconnected boxes spreading out like an octopus's arms.

'Sure. But the problem is that you draw something like that and everybody thinks the MD is there [he points to the box in the middle]. The way I like to think of it, my job is like being Susan Devoy's squash ball [with a pencil he draws a line that bounces from one box to the next]. I'm doing my job when I'm bouncing around the different parts of this company, connecting ideas and sparking things off.'

I suggest that squash (a sport not unlike Racketball where a small black ball is hit inside a rectangular court and in which good shots often involve the ball ricocheting off a number of walls) and Susan Devoy (a New Zealander and former world squash champion) may not be immediately recognizable to many readers, and offer pinball as an alternative. The last thing you want to happen in pinball is watch the ball slip meekly down the middle and out between those flapping arms. A high score is a result of the ball bouncing off the elements, doubling and redoubling the sum of the parts.

'Sure. I know I'm doing my job when I can walk down the corridor, in and out of offices stirring things up. When everybody here feels comfortable saying "Stedman you f...wit". But with a smile,' he grins.

Natural History New Zealand (NHNZ) has been around for 30 years, and Stedman has been with the company for 21 of those. There is only two reasons he can think of to justify his move into the arena he claims to hate: 'Because I didn't want to be told what to do by f...wits who didn't know what they were doing, and because I didn't want to see this place close.'

Closure was a distinct possibility just a few years ago. NHNZ was a department of Television New Zealand (TVNZ) and dying a slow death. It was making local programmes about local wildlife – which it had by this point filmed many times over – to a very small local audience (New Zealand's population is just over 3 million). When the previously state-owned TVNZ was privatized it began to focus more on cost cutting. NHNZ was an obvious target.

Three options presented themselves to TVNZ. First, they could inject a lot more money into NHNZ, enough to enable it to compete in an increasingly global marketplace. Second, they could close the place down. This, however, would have incurred a lot of bad publicity and cost around NZ $16 million in redundancy payments and breach of contract settlements. Third, they could sell. After much dithering, TVNZ put NHNZ up for sale. Much to their surprise they received 10 offers for NHNZ from all parts of the globe.

In a decision that Stedman attributes to some strange sense of antipodean loyalty, an Australian Company was TVNZ's preferred buyer. 'But it was a company that we could have bought. They were too small. They couldn't have given us anything that we couldn't already give ourselves.' Stedman told TVNZ executives that he would leave and take the rest of NHNZ's staff with him to set up their own company before he'd watch it be sold to the Australian buyer. TVNZ eventually relented and agreed to sell NHNZ to Stedman's preferred choice: Rupert Murdoch's Fox Corporation. The Australian company has since gone under. Stedman collects an article, recently published in a trade newspaper, from his desk. 'It says here that "The turning point in the company's demise was missing out on the highly desirable Natural History New Zealand". Now, I don't think for a minute that's why they really went down, but it's nice to know that's how we were perceived, and still are perceived.'

What can Fox do for NHNZ that the now defunct Aussie player could not? Stedman taps on a little red book on the coffee table in front of him. 'In this book is a global empire of distributors, partners and buyers – the Fox "empire". It means that the programmes that we make, which previously had a pretty limited audience, can now be channeled globally through this network. And people who wouldn't previously have thought of coming to us to commission or co-produce programmes now know about us. Because we're part of this book too.'

Was he not worried about NHNZ being subsumed into the Fox 'empire'? 'I'm not a nervous person,' Stedman explains, 'but I was pretty nervous when I went to New York to meet Rupert Murdoch, sitting there waiting for my allocated 10-minute slot. But when I went in he was just sitting on a stool in a corner of his office, eating a piece of fruit. An hour and a half later we were still talking. Not about business, but all sorts of other things – families, globalization, pollution. But the most important thing to me was that he had seen about six of our programmes, and he could remember them, and he liked them. We talked a lot about the programmes and why he thought it was important for Fox to move into the wildlife arena. He said, "We make programmes. You make great programmes. Just keep making great programmes and don't worry about profits. That will take care of itself – if we keep making good programmes".'

'The only thing I was really worried about then was the name. I worried that maybe we would have to become 'Fox Wildlife' or something. But when we met with the Fox people – and they came to us, in fact we've seen more Fox people in the last two years than we ever saw TVNZ people, they come here for weeks at a time, often with their families, and they really got into it, no suits and ties. They're really interested and inquisitive, and so we figured out pretty early on, "Hell, they're just like us". Anyway, they said "There are two things that are crucial to keep in your name: Natural History and New Zealand. You don't need Fox in there". They said, "You guys just keep doing what you do, if you need any help let us know, and we'll help connect that to our partners and our global sales and distribution networks".' This, in a nutshell, explains what Fox saw in NHNZ: *New Zealand* and *Natural History*.

'Being from New Zealand is our biggest asset,' Stedman explains. 'Whenever we entertain potential clients we really play this up – New Zealand wine, New Zealand food … the whole thing.' He reasons that people really like the association with New Zealand. It triggers positive associations for those who have had contact with New Zealand before, and a positive curiosity for those who have not.

NHNZ's corporate prospectus also highlights the importance of its 'Kiwi Heritage'. 'NHNZ is founded on a passion for telling the stories of New Zealand's unique animals,' it explains. Having been one of the first islands to have broken from the earth's primeval land mass, New Zealand's animals are certainly curious – a mix of prehistoric lizards and strange birds, many of whom have 'evolved' to the point of no longer being able to fly, on account of their not having to share the land with mammalian predators not born before New Zealand was set adrift. While not as vibrant or spectacular, in plumage or deed, as their better-known Australian and Asian cousins, they are just as idiosyncratic.

I relate Simon Schama's recent theories about how particular peoples are shaped by their geography, or the lay of the land that surrounds them, and suggest that a nation's character may also be shaped by its animals. Stedman doesn't buy it, but he likes Schama's notion of the link to the land. 'Yes, maybe this is why we get on so well with the Japanese – having grown up on a rugged isolated island pocketed with communities. They're always saying that we're like them, a bit quiet and introverted, relational, community oriented. They say we have very similar senses of humour.' Japan is NHNZ's fastest growing market. 'Australians on the other hand are much more extrovert, big and bold. It's a big wide-open land. I think this is why Murdoch gets a bum rap. He's no worse, probably a lot better, than other media moguls, but he's out there being up front and telling it straight. So others, particularly the British, label him a brash upstart Aussie … *ha ha ha*, the British hate him.'

However, in answering why the Kea, New Zealand's indigenous mountain parrot, has become NHNZ's corporate symbol and mascot, he does seems to indicate some connection between people and animals, albeit a more conscious or selective one than my earlier attempt at a theory. 'Hmm, it's been the Kea for a long time now, but we recently revisited it and decided that we were pretty happy with it. I mean, the obvious choice would have been a f…ing Kiwi, but who wants to be a fat, dozy, dull, nocturnal, flightless bird?' Examining the nature of the Kea makes it easy to see why NHNZ prefers this association. It is a bird of paradox: 'Hooligans, vandals and killers; but superb parents and resourceful providers,' says one source. 'Endearing and mischievous,' says another. The New Zealand Department of Conservation's website's entry on the Kea (www.doc.co.nz) runs as follows:

> *To survive in its harsh alpine environment Kea have become inquisitive and nomadic social birds – characteristics which help the Kea to utilize and find new food sources. It is thought to have developed its own special character during the last ice age by using its unusual powers of curiosity in its search for food. Their inquisitive nature often causes Kea to congregate around novel objects and their strong beaks have enormous manipulative power.*

One suspects that Stedman may also take a perverse pleasure in stories of Kea tormenting and often killing that other lumbering New Zealand stereotype – the sheep. 'You know, a Swiss scientist has determined that on its level of intelligence the Kea should be classified as a primate,' he says proudly.

However, Fox's interest in NHNZ stemmed not just from the New Zealand connection, but also from the fact that NHNZ had an established reputation for making what they describe as 'blue-chip natural history programmes'. It was this standing more than anything else that had made NHNZ 'highly desirable'. Their reputation stemmed from a number of factors, but particularly the quality of the scientific input into their programme making. NHNZ's Dunedin base clusters them next to a University (Otago) with a world-class reputation, particularly in zoology, biology and medicine. Dunedin is also New Zealand's most off-beat town and attracts people who seem unperturbed by elements that others would describe as 'harsh', including a good number of North Americans seeking an 'alternative lifestyle' (Otago University's advertising actually glories in the region's ruggedness). And it is the ideal 'jumping off' point to one of the world's most interesting, least understood and ruggedest wildlife arenas – Antarctica (NHNZ has made more films in Antarctica than any other production company). Dunedin is also home to a thriving computer graphics industry. These things, combined with a core of experienced staff used to working in tough conditions and with inadequate budgets (and, through their own curiosity in the film-making process, highly multi-skilled), made Natural History New Zealand an undervalued company with great growth potential in Fox's mind. The last thing Fox wanted to do was change a name that captured all that was good about the company.

The corporate ethos indicated above also feeds into NHNZ's growth strategy. Stedman sees his role as largely 'ambassadorial'. He and the sales team seek to connect what NZNH does with existing and potential clients and partners utilizing the global contacts that the Fox's little red book provides. It is all about relationships, Stedman says, and coming from where NZNH does, provides a point of differentiation here as well.

He struggles to put his finger on what it is exactly: 'New Zealanders seem to be unusually curious, and it's a genuine curiosity, but they seem to also be quite sensitive to cultural differences, so they don't push too hard. At the same time there's also an inquisitive naivete, but with brains.' (I mention a statistic that Air New Zealand use a lot in their marketing – that New Zealanders on average travel more miles in their lifetime than people from any other nation, 'Yes, that makes sense,' he says.) However, what he is trying to say becomes clearer as he relates one story from his past and two from NHNZ's present.

> One of my early coups came when I happened to be in LA. I went to a just-released movie called *Star Wars* and thought it was great. I was in my twenties working on a children's television programme for TVNZ and thought it would be great if we could do a feature on it, show a bit of footage, you know. So the next day I rang up the marketing manager of Twentieth Century Fox and we had a bit of a chat. I asked if he could let me have some stuff. He said 'Sure,' and asked where I was staying. The next morning, a huge package arrives, full of film,

posters, all sorts of paraphernalia. My US friends asked how I'd managed to pull it off, so I told them that I called the guy up and asked. They would never have thought of doing that. I was too stupid to know that I shouldn't. But the guy didn't seem to mind. New Zealanders often don't feel bound by the 'can'ts' and 'shouldn'ts' that you find in other places.

It's important to treat people how they like to be treated, but you have to make an effort to find out what this is. A few weeks ago I sent a fax to a Japanese manager and got nothing back. What do you do? Should I fax him again, should I phone him up directly? I mean, you don't want to be pushy. Anyway, I managed to get through to talk to his assistant and asked if I should send another fax. He said, 'Yes, keep sending faxes, he has a big pile of them on his desk, he likes getting them, sooner or later he'll come in and your fax will be on the top and he'll get back to you.' So I kept sending the faxes and he did, eventually, get back to me.

A lot of selling supposedly happens at these huge trade conventions. But after days of viewing and being sold to, a lot of people glaze over. You can sense this pretty quickly and if somebody's zombied there's not much point trying to sell to them. It's better to sit back and chat about something completely different: you can always send them an e-mail a couple of days later when they're more relaxed, away from the madness.

'Yes', Stedman says, returning to an earlier reference to close the circle, 'I think one of the reasons why Air New Zealand is such a good airline is that the staff seem very canny about what each customer wants – who wants to be left alone, who wants to chat, be flattered and asked questions and so on. They're open, they don't have preconceptions, but they very quickly seem to figure out what's going to go best. I'm not sure whether it's conscious, but it's good to watch.'

All of this seems to give NHNZ a real, albeit intangible, competitive advantage. Stedman relates what he believes to be perhaps the most satisfying thing he has ever been told by a client. 'A manager of a Japanese company said "You are the least arrogant company that we deal with." You've no idea how much that meant to us.' He contrasts the approach of some his competitors. The BBC? 'The BBC seems to still walk about with the remains of a colonial outlook; they think they're doing everybody a service by coming in to film other countries with the British approach. Plus they have a huge millstone around their neck – David Attenborough. I mean he's good, but it's hardly ground-breaking.' ('I'm more of a David Bellamy fan,' he adds, not surprisingly. 'I like his passion'.) The Americans? 'I was at a convention in Japan last week and this group of Americans decides to go out to dinner, on their own ... for pizza! I mean, how stupid is that.'

So far the marriage between NHNZ and Fox seems to be a happy and productive one. The exponential employment growth is one obvious sign, but there are others. The audience for NHNZ's programmes now spans 130 countries and is measured in millions rather than thousands, and, as it has spread its wings, it has picked up an increasing number of awards. Last year a series co-produced with Animal Planet, called *Twisted Tales* (which traces the strange relationships between particular animals and humans), won an Emmy for 'Outstanding Achievement in a Craft in News and Documentary Programming' for NHNZ writer-zoologists Ian McGee and Quinn Berentson. The next instalment of the series has been nominated again this year. Berentson claims that the series was 'quite easy to write because we both have twisted minds and we both think along the same lines.'

Programmes like *Twisted Tales* indicate a willingness to broaden NHNZ's scope beyond films of animals. This means moving, in Stedman's terms, into a number of 'natural extensions'. In the words of NHNZ's public relations and marketing people: 'We don't just work with wildlife. Our experience extends into genres such as adventure, travel and science, where we venture just as boldly to produce a variety of quality programming ... We now bring our traditional pioneering spirit to our work in every continent and throughout the world's oceans in pursuit of compelling, often unique stories.' Particularly high hopes are held for a new series entitled *Kill or Cure: The Bizarre and Curious History of Medicine*.

NHNZ has quickly become the world's second largest nature programming production company behind the BBC's Natural History Unit, something that Stedman is very proud of. 'The reaction from the BBC when they heard that we were 'going global' was interesting. First they were amused, then, when we didn't go under, they though 'hmm'. Then when we started stealing business off them they got annoyed. Now they hate us. We steal a lot of business from them.' Stedman is certain that NHNZ will overtake the BBC within the next couple of years.

The growth is enabling NHNZ to go further in doing something that Stedman has always thought important – reinvesting back into the local community. Beyond supporting the arts and scientific societies, NHNZ is always looking for ways to open up its facilities to budding local film-makers, graphic artists and musicians. Additionally, NHNZ, in collaboration with Otago University, has helped put together a new degree in communication and film production. Its not just 'corporate citizenship', which Stedman describes as 'bullshit, mostly', but, as he says, 'we depend on this community and we need people to keep coming through.'

However, NHNZ's recent success now presents new problems. Stedman is fairly clear as to what these problems are, if not what the solutions to them may be. The first two are likely obvious by now. The third is less so. First, there is the extent to which the company's personality is wound up with that of its MD. Stedman is patently aware that this is potentially not a good thing and 'is doing a lot to shore-up succession issues, because I'm not going to be around for ever.'

Second, Stedman knows that a lot of the positive energy within NHNZ has stemmed from the camaraderie felt by a core group who experienced the company nearly going under and from the feeling that comes from being the underdog in a global market made up of 'big fish'. In recognizing this he is also aware that this energy will be much more difficult to maintain as the company continues to grow and as the once little fish becomes the biggest.

Third, there is a phenomenon that Stedman has begun to sense in NHNZ that he claims to be particularly bothered by. 'Ironically, I seem to have created a company that is the opposite of the one that made me. When I started as a film editor I wanted to make whole films, not because of any particularly artistic vision, but just because I wanted to see how all the pieces fitted together. So, I stole some film stock from the storeroom, 'borrowed' a camera for the weekend, and got a mate in the developing room to develop it up for me (I think I paid him a crate of beer?). I wasn't supposed to do any of this, having been told not to touch or use any of the equipment beyond that needed to do my job. In fact, I came very close to being fired when I got caught late one night editing my film. Now, perhaps because of this, whenever somebody new starts here I tell them "Borrow whatever you like," "Use whatever you need," "Feel free to develop your own stuff." But it doesn't seem to be happening. It's not that they don't have their own ideas, but I think maybe they think, 'Ah well, I can always do it next week.' There's not the urgency and maybe that dulls the passion. Perhaps it's like unrequited love, Romeo and Juliet you know, if you're told you can't have something sometimes it makes you want it more, it stimulates you, makes the prize seem sweeter. I'm thinking maybe I should tell people "Don't you dare touch that f...ing camera".' One would have to check the nature books in more detail to find out if the Kea becomes less interested in making mischief, more dozy, dull and flightless, as his life is made easier and he is presented with all he needs.

On reflection, the essence of NHNZ's success is hard for Stedman to pin down: 'We make stories into programmes, programmes that when they leave the building everybody says "Yeah, that's what we do".' On the way out of his office, Stedman says 'Management, yeah, we have meetings where people say we need to go on management courses or bring in some consultants. Maybe we do.'

1 Diagram what you believe to be the elements of NHNZ's competitive advantage. How has the connection with Fox enhanced these things?
2 Industrial economists have begun to link socioeconomic factors within a country to the way in which local companies behave. Can even 'fuzzier' things such as relationships with the land and native animals be linked to the identity of companies from a particular region? If so, could the Kea identity be used as a basis for focusing NHNZ and determining the areas that it should expand into without dulling its competitive advantage?
3 If you were a new employee at NHNZ, how comfortable would you be with calling Stedman a 'f...wit'? What sort of things would have to happen to make you more comfortable doing this? What measures would you suggest to maintain the tight-knit identity and energy of NHNZ as it continues to grow?
4 Stedman's theory about staff motivation perhaps being linked to deprivation and telling people that they can't do things seems contrary to a view that has become unquestioned in management theory – that people need to be 'nurtured' and 'empowered' – but do you think there may be an element of truth do what he says? If there is some truth to it what does this say about universal theories of management?
5 Does NHNZ need to place more emphasis on sending staff on management courses and/or bringing in management consultants?

This case was written in July/August 2000. With special thanks to Michael Stedman, Andy Bean and the many others at *New Zealand Natural History* who generously gave their time and offered their opinions toward the preparation of the case.

Bibliographical Notes

Chapter 1: Deconstructing History, ReCreating Strategy

Throughout this book 'management', 'strategy' and 'organization' are often conflated. While this may annoy purists, it has been done in order to aid the flow of the text by not listing all three terms every time. In any event, that our view of one influences our view of the others is one of this book's main premises.

James Belich's analysis may be found in *The New Zealand Wars* (Penguin, Auckland, 1988). The Imperial quotations reproduced here (most of which are taken from mainstream histories from the 1920s and 1930s, a formative period in the history of New Zealand as an independent nation-state) are outlined and the background behind them well described by Belich. The popular contemporary high-school textbook referred to is Keith Sinclair's otherwise worthy *A History of New Zealand* (Penguin, Harmondsworth, 1980).

Michael Porter's critique of some of the emergent views of strategy that were becoming prevalent in the 1990s and his subsequent call for a reconnection with the heart of strategy can be found in 'What is Strategy?' (*Harvard Business Review*, November–December 1996). For a shorter synopsis with regard to Japanese companies being 'bad at strategy' see the interview with Porter entitled 'Debunking Japan's Model' in *The Wall Street Journal Europe* (January 15, 2001).

Michael Foucault's clearest 'statement of purpose' is issued in the introduction to *The Care of the Self: The History of Sexuality Vol. II* (Pantheon, New York, 1985). The introductory chapter gives a good outline of how he sees the elements of his earlier work adding up. Foucault's critiques of the constitution of psychology and psychoanalysis are published in *Madness and Civilization: A History of Madness in the Age of Reason* (Random House, New York, 1965); *The Birth of the Clinic* (Vintage, New York, 1975); and *Mental Illness and Psychology* (Vintage, New York, 1976). His thesis with regard to the notion that a subject and its objects can only emerge when particular cultural conditions encourage their constitution is outlined in *The Order of Things: An Archaeology of the Human Sciences* (Tavistock, London, 1970). *Discipline and Punish: The Birth of the Prison* (Allen Lane, London, 1977) describes Foucault's thinking with regard to the way in which a network of power sustains our beliefs, with particular regard to ideas of how miscreants should be punished for deviancy. The chapter entitled 'Method' in *The History of Sexuality: An Introduction* (Random House, New York, 1978) is a more focused discussion on Foucault's particular view of power and its function.

Gilles Deleuze's *Foucault* (University of Minnesota Press, Minneapolis, MA: 1988) is the best summary of Foucault's approach; *The Passion of Michel Foucault* by James Miller (HarperCollins, London, 1993), the most readable overview of Foucault's life and works. Frederich Nietzsche's contribution to Foucault's development is well treated here, but for more on Nietzsche's anti-positivist views one might consult his *The Genealogy of Morals* (Doubleday, New York, 1954), which argued that our understanding of what is 'Good' is a historical development rather than foundational.

Arthur Koestler's 'shaking' quotations are taken from the brilliant *The Act of Creation* (Hutchinson, London, 1976), probably still the best philosophical assessment of the act of creation available. Paul Feyerabend's *Against Method* (Verso, London, 1988) outlines a similar analysis spiced with Feyerabend's idiosyncratic and combative spirit.

The Captive State: The Corporate Takeover of Britain by George Monbiot (Macmillan, London, 2000) and *One Market Under God: Extreme Capitalism, Market Populism and the End of Economic Democracy* by Thomas Frank (Secker & Warburg, New York, 2001) provide a good overview of the increasing influence of business and management thinking in the Western world.

Good examples of the presentation of the Egyptians as seen through Modernist eyes in the history of management maybe be found in Daniel Wren's *The Evolution of Management Thought* (New York, Wiley, 1972 and 1994); or Stephen Robbins, best-selling textbook *Management* (Prentice-Hall, Englewood Cliffs, NJ, 1991).

For an overview of Christopher Alexander's architectural philosophy see Stephen Grabow's Christopher Alexander: *The Search for a New Paradigm in Architecture* (Oriel, Stocksfield, 1983). The excerpts that make up the table provided in Case Box 2.1 are taken from C.S George's *The History of Management Thought* (Prentice-Hall, Englewood Cliffs, NJ, 1968). J.D. Mooney's quotations in this box are from *Onward Industry: The Principles of Organization* (Harper & Row, New York, 1947).

Chapter 2: Premodernism, Modernism and Postmodernism

The focus is placed on the Ancient Greek's as representative of Premodernism firstly because it was their tradition that Modernism sought to transcend, and secondly because incorporating many Premodern styles of thought within 15 pages would be impossible. Indeed, even attempting to summarize the many nations and cultures that made up the Greek world in this space is difficult. Similar limitations should also be acknowledged with regard to the sections outlining Modernism and Postmodernism, which could be given 300 rather than 30 pages and still be criticized by some scholars.

The attempt to outline the Ancient Greek world-view must be prefaced with a number of provisos. That the Greeks were not one nation and that one of the points made in this chapter is that many schools co-existed within their 'thought-world' indicates that this chapter is a simplification and a synthesis. Further, in drawing upon material from Homeric, Archaic and Classical periods, it falls foul of scholars who insist upon contrasting the different cultures within this span of periods. If one wants to delve further into the complexities of this thought-world one might begin with J. Barnes' *Early Greek Philosophy* (Penguin, London, 1987) and *The Greeks and the Irrational* by E.R. Dodds (University of California Press, Berkeley, CA, 1951). The later is the first, and in many ways still the best, reassessment of the Greeks as more than just embryonic rationalists who laid the foundation stones for our Modernist ways. For more on how Premodern ways of seeing and knowing are different from Modern views see R.G. Collingwood's *The Idea of History* (Oxford University Press, London, 1960); M. Foucault's *The Order of Things: An Archaeology of the Human Science* (Tavistock, London, 1970); A. Gabbey's 'The Mechanical Philosophy and its Problems' in *Change and Progress in Modern Science*, (J.C. Pitt (ed.), Riedel, Dordrecht, 1985); and C. Taylor's 'Overcoming Epistemology' in *After Philosophy: End or Transformation?* (K. Baynes, J. Bohman and T. McCarthy (eds), MIT Press, Cambridge, MA, 1987).

A recent discussion of Pre-Socratic philosophy that takes the microcosm-macrocosm analogy very seriously is A. Capizzi's *The Cosmic Republic* (Kluwer, Amsterdam, 1990). J. Seznec's *The Survival of the Pagan Gods* (Princeton University Press, Princeton, NJ, 1953) reproduces a number of ancient microcosms in its plates. Frederich Nietzche's *The Birth of Tragedy* (various publishers) is a useful synopsis of the appreciation of Dionysian and Apollonian forces in the Ancient Greek world. Heidegger's essay on Greek notions of truth or *altheia* (reproduced in *Early Greek Thinking*, HarperCollins, New York, 1984) provides the basis for the analysis carried out of the concept in this chapter. D. Harvey's *The Condition of Postmodernity*

(Blackwell, Oxford, 1990) nicely describes the change of perspective from Premodern to Modern with particular reference to mapping, as does R. Helgerson's 'The land speaks: cartography, chorography, and subversion in Renaissance England' (*Representations*, 16: 51–85, 1986). *Metos* is well described by M. Detienne and J-P. Vernant's *Cunning Intelligence in Greek Culture and Society* (Harvester, Sussex, 1978).

Roy Strong's commentaries on Elizabethan portraiture (for example, *Gloriana: The Portraits of Queen Elizabeth the 1st,* Thames & Hudson, London, 1987) provide a good starting point for an understanding of the geometry of the Modern gaze. A.F. Chalmer's much read *What is this Thing Called Science?* (Open University Press, Mittou Keynes, 1999) 'drawing' of the scientific method, with mind over matter, clearly maps onto this. The cause of the Modern 'mind-shift' is put down to advances in scientific rigor and technology in most histories of science. However, A. Giddens' *The Consequences of Modernity* (Stanford University Press, Stanford, CA, 1990) gives a good account of the importance of the rise of Europe's nation states and organized capitalism and colonialism in shaping the Modernist way of seeing. S. Toulmin's *Cosmopolis: The Hidden Agenda of Modernity* (Free Press, New York, 1990) puts the case for the change toward privileging certain objective knowledge being related to a Europe fed up with divisiveness in the seventeenth century. R.S. Westfall's *The Construction of Modern Science* (Wiley, New York, 1971) and R. Dawkins' *The Blind Watchmaker* (Penguin, Harmondsworth, 1991) provide good accounts of the development of the Modern scientific method. *The Scientific Revolution in National Context*, edited by R. Porter and M. Teich (Cambridge University Press, Cambridge, 1992), builds upon these and describes the emergence of centralized knowledge institutions. The best concise combined academic review of all of these aspects is S. Shapin's *The Scientific Revolution* (University of Chicago Press, Chicago, 1996). *The Day the World Took Off: The Roots of the Industrial Revolution* (S. and D. Dugan, Macmillan, London, 2000) and the Channel 4 television series of the same name, provides a less academic but more compelling commentary. Immanuel Kant's *Critique of Pure Reason* (many translations are available) and other related essays outline where Modernism thought it was heading, in science and in ethics. A. MacIntyre's *After Virtue – A Study in Moral Theory* (Duckworth, London, 1981), describes the subsequent quest for a Modernist general code of ethics, the corresponding rise of bureaucratic rationality and performative efficiency as a general means and end, and the resulting conundrum that Modern ethics found itself in in the twentieth century. G. Vattimo's *The End of Modernity* (Polity, Cambridge, 1988) traces the decline of Modernism as the inevitable and dominant mode of thinking. A. Compagnon's succinct *The 5 Paradoxes of Modernity* (Columbia University Press, New York, 1994) does likewise, but with a particular focus on modern art and architecture's 'running out of steam'. The ideas presented in this chapter about the questioning of Modernism's averaging out of man's ideal characteristics (best illustrated by T. Levitt's

'The Globalization of Markets', *Harvard Business Review,* May/June 1983) may be connected to recent debates about how car air-bags may actually damage individuals who do not conform to the ergonomics and average body shapes upon which their design is based.

The best comprehensive survey of Postmodernism in all its forms is D. Harvey's *The Condition of Postmodernity* (details above). Important Postmodern documents include J-F. Lyotard's *The Postmodern Condition: A Report on Knowledge* and *The Differend* (Manchester University Press, Manchester, 1984 and 1991 respectively); G. Deleuze and F. Guattari's *Anti-Oedipus* (Viking, New York, 1977) and *Mille-Plateaux: Capitalism and Schizophrenia* (Athlone, London, 1988); and J. Derrida's *Margins of Philosophy* (Athlone, London, 1982). Umberto Eco's *Reflections on 'The Name of the Rose'* (Minerva, London, 1994) is a readable series of insights into the exhaustion of Modernism and the subsequent rise of the Postmodern view using the now famous novel as an exemplar. For something more focussed upon the impact of Postmodernism on management, B. Cova's 'The Postmodern Explained to Managers: Implications for Marketing' (*Business Horizons,* Nov./Dec. 1996) brings the issues down to earth in a simple, but not simplistic, manner. John Horgan's thesis regarding the diminishing returns to be had by continually applying the same scientific method is outlined in *The End of Science* (Little, Brown, New York, 1997). His idea may be linked to other critiques of the assumptions, unidimensionality and dominance of Modern science such as: F. Capra *The Web of Life: A New Synthesis of Mind and Matter* (HarperCollins, London, 1996); U. Maturana 'Science and daily life: the ontology of scientific explanations' (in *Selforganization: Portrait of a Scientific Revolution,* W. Krohn (Ed.), Kluwer, Dordrecht, 1990); P. Feyerabend *Farewell to Reason* (Verso, London, 1987); and T. Kuhn *The Structure of Scientific Revolutions* (University of Chicago Press, Chicago, 1962). The social theory that Lyotard takes aim against may be better understood by reading T. Parson's *The Structure of Social Action* (Free Press, Glencoe, IL, 1949). G. Burrell's 'recovery' of the concept of 'spiral time' can be found in 'Back to the future: time and organization' (in *Rethinking Organization – New Directions in Organization Theory and Analysis,* M. Reed and M. Hughes (eds), Sage, London, 1992).

Direct references not attributable to the above chapter lists are as follows. The Greek foundation myth is from R. Graves *The Greek Myths* (Cassell, London, 1981). Vasari's words are from his 16th century *The Lives of the Artists* (a number of translations are available). Foucault's quote at the beginning of 'The analogy of the microcosm' is from *The Order of Things* (details above), as are Crollius' words in the following section. The quotation from Demokritos, and those from the other Presocratic philosophers mentioned in this section, are from J. Barnes's *Early Greek Philosophy* (details above). Plutarch's analogy is from 'The life of Pericles' in *Parallel Lives* (many translations are available). The quotation that begins the 'Life as a circle' sub-section is from Aristotle's *Physics,* book IV. Umberto

Eco's comment on the Hermes myth is from *Interpretation and Overinterpretation* (Cambridge University Press, Cambridge, 1992). Montaigne's aphorisms can be found in *Michel de Montaigne: Four Essays* (Penguin, London, 1995).

A. Touraine's introduction to section 2 is from his 'Modernity and cultural specificities' (*International Social Sciences Journal*, 118: 443–57, 1988). Robert Boyle's beginning to the following sub-section is from his *Works* (book V – available in a number of forms). *The Making of the Modern World – Milestones of Science and Technology* is edited by N. Cossons and published by John Murray in association with the British Museum of Science (London, 1992). Kepler's words are from *Mysterium Cosmographicum* (a number of translations are available). Edgerton's *The Renaissance Re-discovery of Linear Perspective* is published by Basic Books (New York, 1976). Decartes' thesis is outlined in *On Method* (available in many forms). Nietzsche's 'we are at the top' exclamation is taken from *The Use and Abuse of History* (many translations available). Leibniz, Hobbes and Bacon's words are from Shapin's history (details above), and the related quotation from Lyotard is from *Political Writings* (University of Minnesota Press, Minneapolis MN, 1993). Hume's quotation is from his *Enquiry Concerning Human Understanding* (available in many forms). Turgot's *On Universal History* can be found in his collected *Oeuvres and Documents* (Felix Alcan, Paris, 1913). The inspiration for the triangular induction-deduction triangle diagram can be found in A.F. Chalmers' *What is this Thing Called Science?* (Open University Press, Buckingham, 1999). Hegel's ideas are outlined in A. White's *Absolute Knowledge: Hegel and the Problem of Metaphysics* (Ohio University Press, Ohio, 1983). John Murray of London first published Darwin's *Origin of Species* in 1859. Newton outlines his mission in *Opticks* (query 31 – available in a number of forms). Maclaurin's praise for Newton is from H.W. Spiegel's *The Growth of Economic Thought* (Prentice-Hall, Englewood Cliffs NJ, 1971). Sidgwick's words can be found in MacIntyre's *After Virtue* (details above). The quotations on modern architecture are from Compagnon's *5 Paradoxes of Modernity* (details above).

Lyotard's definition of 'postmodernism' is from *The Postmodern Condition* (details above). Parsons' beliefs are recorded in his *Essays in Sociological Theory, Pure and Applied* (Free Press, Glencoe IL, 1954). Baudelaire's words are laid out in Harvey's *The Condition of Postmodernity* (details above). Heidegger's 'necessary appearance' quotation is from *Introduction to Metaphysics* (a number of translations are available). The Geertz quotation that follows is from his *The Interpretation of Cultures* (Basic Books, New York, 1973). The 'bored architect' is from M. Filler's 'Building and nothingness' (*New York Review of Book*, June 12: 26–33, 1986). The words attributed to Wittgenstein and Heidegger in this sub-section are from *Philosophical Investigations* (Blackwell, Oxford, 1953) and *Being and Time* (Blackwell, Oxford, 1962) respectively. Deleuze and Guattari's two sub-section starting quotes are from *Milles Plateaux* (details above). Raban's *Soft City* is published by Hamilton (London, 1974). Foucault's 'discovering' quote is from *The Birth of the Clinic* (details above). Jencks' two quotations can be seen in 'Postmodern vs. late-modern' (in I. Hoesterev (Ed.): *Zeitgeist in Babel*, Indiana University Press, Indianapolis IA, 1991: 4–21). Schrodinger's 'argument' is from E. Schrodinger, *Physics and Nature* (Cambridge University Press, Cambridge, 1954). Kuhn's questioning of modern science is recorded in *The Structure of Scientific Revolutions* (University of Chicago Press, Chicago, 1962). 'What matters most is culture' is from Nietzsche's 'Twilight of the Idols' (*Germans* 4 – many translations are available). Levi Strauss' follow-on is from *Tristes Tropiques* (Plon, Paris, 1955). Lyotard's 'prudence' statement is form *The Differend* (details above). Levinas' view of the 'end of history' is described in J. Derrida's *Writing and Difference* (Routledge and Kegan Paul, London, 1978). Featherstone's paradoxical suggestion is from his *Consumer Culture and Postmodernity* (Beverly Hills, CA: Sage, 1991).

Chapter 3: Deconstructing Management's History

'The Conventional (but Fabricated) History of Management' is a summary-pastiche of the following management histories: J.D. Mooney's *Onward Industry: The Principles of Organization* (Harper & Row, New York, 1939 and 1947); L. Urwick's *Elements of Administration* (Pitman, London, 1947); L. Urwick and E. Brech's *The Making of Scientific Management – Volume I & II* (Pitman, London, 1953); R. Bendix's *Work and Authority in Industry* (Harper & Row, New York, 1956); J.G. March and H. Simon's *Organizations* (Wiley, New York, 1958); H.F. Merrill's *Classics in Management* (American Management Association, New York, 1960 and 1970); E. Dale's *The Great Organizers* (McGraw-Hill, New York, 1960); A.D. Chandler's *Strategy and Structure: Chapters in the History of the Industrial Enterprise* (MIT Press, Cambridge, MA, 1962); *The Visible Hand: The Managerial Revolution in American Business* and *Scale and Scope: The Dynamics of Industrial Capitalism* (Harvard University Press, Cambridge, MA, 1977 and 1990); B.M. Gross' *The Managing of Organizations: The Administrative Struggle* (Macmillan, New York, 1964); T. Caplow's *Principles of Organization* (Harcourt, Brace & World, New York, 1964); S. Pollard's *The Genesis of Modern Management* (Edward Arnold, London, 1965); E.F.L. Brech's *Organization – The Framework of Management* (Longman, London, 1965); H.R. Light's *The Nature of Management* (Pitman, London, 1966); C.S. George's *The History of Management Thought* (Prentice-Hall, Englewood Cliffs, NJ, 1968 and 1972): J. Child's *British Management Thought – A Critical Analysis* (Allen & Unwin, London, 1969); D.A. Wren's *The Evolution of Management Thought* (Wiley, New York, 1972 and 1994); H.R. Pollard's *Developments in Management Thought* (Heinemann, London, 1974); and W.J. Duncan's *Great Ideas in Management – Lessons from the Founders and Foundations of Managerial Practice* (Jossey-Bass, San Francisco, CA, 1990). Textbooks that provide histories of management are also incorporated (for example, S.P. Robbins' *Management and Organizational Behaviour – Concepts, Controversies and Applications* (Prentice-Hall, Englewood Cliffs, NJ, 1991 and 1996); S.P. Robbins and D. Mukerji's *Managing Organizations: New Challenges and Perspectives* (Prentice-Hall, Sydney, 1990); J. Greenberg and R.A. Baron's *Behavior in Organizations: Understanding and Managing the Human Side of Work* (Prentice-Hall, Englewood Cliffs, NJ, 1995); G. Dessler's *Organization Theory – Integrating Structure and Behavior* (Prentice-Hall, Englewood Cliffs, NJ, 1986); H. Koontz and C. O'Donnell's *Essentials of Management* (McGraw-Hill, New York, 1974); and H. Koontz's *Management* (McGraw-Hill, New York, 1980).

R.R. Locke's *The Collapse of the American Management Mystique* (Oxford University Press, Oxford, 1996), contains a nice critique of Chandler's perspective on management and history.

The Owen quotation is taken from R. Owen's *A New View of Society* (Woodstock, Oxford, 1813 and 1991). For a commentary on Barnard's 'Platonism' read T.C. Pauchant's review of 'Chester I Barnard and the Guardians of Management' (*Academy of Management Review*, 19: 823–9, 1994). T.K. McCraw's compilation of and commentary on Chandler's work is published as *The Essential Alfred Chandler, Essays Toward a History of Big Business* (Harvard Business School Press, Boston, 1988). On Williamson's views regarding the primacy of efficiency, read O.E. Williamson's 'Organization form, residual claimants and corporate control' (*Journal of Law and Economics*, 36: 351–66, 1983). Koontz's thesis about the problems with Management's lack on integration are developed in 'The management theory jungle' (*Journal of the Academy of Management*, 4: 174–88, 1961). The report on the ensuing conference is written up as H. Koontz *Toward a Unified Theory of Management* (McGraw-Hill, New York, 1964).

F.W. Taylor's *Principles of Scientific Management* was first published in 1911 (Harper, New York); it was reissued, as was Mooney's history (see above) in 1947 as *Scientific Management* by the same publisher to tap into the renewed demand for 'Management' after World War II. The Progressive era context of this work is well described by G.E. Mowry's *The Era of Theodore Roosevelt* (Harper & Row, New York, 1958); R. Hofstader's *The Progressive Movement, 1900–1915* (Prentice-Hall, Englewood Cliffs, NJ, 1963) and A.A. Ekirch's *Progressism in America* (Franklin Watts, New York, 1974). W. Lippmann's *Drift and Mastery* (Mitchell Kemerly, New York, 1914) indicates the scientific optimism of the period and S. Haber's *Efficiency and Uplift – Scientific Management in the Progressive Era* (University of Chicago Press, Chicago, 1964) is an excellent analysis of the rise of efficiency and scientific management in this period. G.H. Seldes' 'American efficiency in England' (*Bellman*, 22: 122–3, 1917) demonstrates the extent to which performative efficiency was still a foreign concept to most in other parts of the world in the early decades of the twentieth century. R. Kanigel's recently published *The One*

Best Way: F.W. Taylor and the Enigma of Efficiency (Penguin, Harmondsworth, 1997) provides a comprehensive and compelling overview of Taylor's life, work and times.

Stewart Clegg's work skillfully examines how Weber's thinking has been wrongly or one-sidedly appropriated by management (see S.R. Clegg's *Modern Organizations: Organization Studies in a Postmodern World*, Sage, London, 1990) and 'Postmodernism and postmodernity in organizational analysis' (*Journal of Organizational Change Management*, 5: 8–25, 1992).

The 'Barnard's Greek' Case Box refers to C.I. Barnard's *The Functions of the Executive* (Harvard University Press, Cambridge, MA, 1938 and 1968); H. Tredennick's *Aristotle's Metaphysics* (Harvard University Press, Cambridge, MA, 1936); and J.A. Smith and W.D. Ross's *The Works of Aristotle* (Clarendon, Oxford, 1908).

P.J. Powell and W.W. Dimaggio's *The New Institionalism in Organizational Analysis* (University of Chicago Press, Chicago, 1991) and J.W. Meyer's related analysis in 'The effects of education as an institution' (*American Journal of Sociology*, 88: 55–77, 1977) provides a method for analysing, and a commentary on, how educational institutes converge upon a standard form and the social effects of this, thereby fleshing out the somewhat cursory treatment of this with regard to American Business Schools in this chapter.

The two 'foundational reports' into the establishment of generic business schools are F.C. Pierson's *The Education of American Businessmen* (McGraw-Hill, New York) and R.A. Gordon and J. Howell's *Higher Education for Business* (Columbia University Press, New York), both 1959. The formation of the AMA is described, with first hand knowledge, by L.A. Appley's *Management at Mid-Century* (The American Management Association, New York, 1954). The research confirming the essential elements of Management is taken from J.F. Mee's *A History of Twentieth Century Management Thought* (University Microfilms, Ann Arbor, MA, 1963). The 'wider' alternative ABS curriculum referred to in this section is from D.L. Huff and J.W. McGuire's 'The interdisciplinary approach to the study of business' (*Washington Business Review*, June, 1960). The far narrower assessment from two years on is J.L. Meij's 'Management, a common province of different sciences' (*Management International*, 5, 210–234, 1962). Mosson's commentary comes from T. Mosson's *A Comparison of Management Education Systems* (Business Publications, London, 1965). However, perhaps the most comprehensive assessment of how the form and curriculum of the business school emerged is R.R. Locke's *Management and Education Since 1940: The Influence of America and Japan on West Germany, Great Britain, and France* (Cambridge University Press, Cambridge, 1989). B. Toohey's *Tumbling Dice* (Heinemann, Melbourne, 1994) is a surprisingly readable account of how modern economics came to be based upon the Modernist principles of physics. P. Mirowski's *More Heat than Light: Economics as Social Physics, Physics as Nature's Economics* (Cambridge University Press, Cambridge, 1989) is a more scholarly critique of this phenomenon. R. Dorfman, P.A. Samuelson and R.M. Solow's *Linear Programming and Economic Analysis* (McGraw-Hill, New York, 1958) investigates the coming together of economics and computer engineering in the middle of the twentieth century. The 1954 history referred to in 'The Formation of the Business School' is T.W. van Merte's *A History of the Graduate School of Business Columbia University* (Columbia University Press, New York).

The quotation at the head of 'The History of Management's Roots' is from R.L. Heilbroner and P. Streeten's *The Great Economists – Their Lives and Conceptions of the World* (Eyre, London, 1955). The 'longest serving' and still most widely read history of economics is E. Roll's *A History of Economic Thought* (Faber & Faber, London, 1992). The similarity of R. Lekachman's *A History of Economic Ideas* (Harper & Row, New York, 1964) shows how 'standard' the established history of economics has become. J.A. Shumpter's assessment of Aristotle is taken from his *History of Economic Analysis* (Allen & Unwin, London, 1954). For an alternative (that is non-Modernist reading of Aristotle's economics try S. Meikle's *Aristotle's Economic Thought* (Clarendon, Oxford, 1994). The standard perceptions of psychology and sociology's histories are from L.S. Hearnshaw's *The Shaping of Modern Psychology* (Routledge & Kegan Paul, London, 1987) and T. Bilton, K. Bonnett, P. Jones, K. Sheard, M. Stanworth, and A. Webster's *Introductory Sociology* (MacMillan, Basingstoke, 1987). M. Leontiades' *Mythmanagement – An Examination of Corporate Diversification as Fact and Theory* (Blackwell, Oxford, 1989) provides a nice critique of management's and management students' lack of any historical understanding.

K. Kipling and O. Bjarner's *The Americanization of European Business* (Routledge, London, 1998) offers a good range of perspectives on how European business has become more American in nature since World War II. On Urwick's view with regard to how management education should develop in the UK, see his *Education for Management* (Anglo-American Council on Productivity, London, 1951) and *Management Education in American Business* (American Management Association, New York, 1954). Other useful references that chart the emergence of British and other European business schools include T. Mosson's 'Introduction' to *Teaching the Process of Management: The Proceedings of an International Seminar* (Harrap, London, 1967); M. Wheatcroft's *The Revolution in British Management Education* (Pitman, London, 1970); R. Whitley, A. Thomas and J. Marceau *Masters of Business? Business Schools and Business Graduates in Britain and France* (Tavistock, London, 1981); and P.G. Forrester's *The British MBA* (Cranfield University Press, Cranfield, 1986).

Management Education and Development – Drift or Thrust into the 21st Century is written by L.W. Porter and L.E. McKibbon (McGraw-Hill, New York,

1988). R.R. Locke's lament about Europe's unquestioning adoption of the American business school is taken from 'Educational traditions and the development of business studies after 1945' (*Business History*, 30: 84–103, 1988). The other non-AASCB survey of business schools quoted at the end of 'The Lack of an Alternative Platform' is J.F. McKenna's 'Management education in the United States' (in W. Bryt's *Management Education: An International Survey*, Routledge, London, 1989).

'The lack of critique' contains elements of P. Drucker's *Management: Tasks, Responsibilities, Practices* (Butterworth-Heinemann, Oxford, 1991); D. Clutterbuck and S. Crainer's *Makers of Management* (Macmillan, London, 1990); P. Thompson and D. McHugh's *Work Organizations* (MacMillan, London, 1995); H. Braverman's *Labor and Monopoly Capital – The Degradation of Work in the Twentieth Century* (Monthly Review Press, New York, 1974); and a number of the teaching texts mentioned earlier. M.J. Piore and C.F. Sabel's critique of Chandlerian assumptions can be read in *The Second Industrial Divide: Possibilities for Prosperity* (Basic Books, New York, 1984). For a good example of how these views were dismissed by employing the very criteria that they sought to overcome, see K. Williams' 'The end of mass production?' (*Economy and Society*, 16: 405–439, 1987).

The critiques of the histories of economics and psychology described toward the end of this chapter are: S.T. Lowry's *The Archaeology of Economic Ideas* (Duke University Press, Durham, NC, 1987); R. Smith's 'Does the history of psychology have a subject?' (*History of the Human Sciences*, 1: 145–77, 1988); and G. Richards' *Putting Psychology into Perspective: An Introduction from a Critical Historical Perspective* (Routledge, London, 1996).

Direct references not attributable to the above chapter lists are as follows. Ansoff develops his vision of the shape of strategy in 'Toward a strategic theory of the firm' (in I. Ansoff (Ed.) *Business Strategy*, Penguin, Harmondsworth UK, 1969: 11–42). P. Selznick's methodological foundation is spelt out in 'Foundations of the theory of organization' (*American Sociological Review*, 13: 25–33, 1948). L. Gulick's view of the 'basic good' being efficiency is taken from B.M. Gross (details above). H. Fayol's writings may be found in *General and Industrial Management* (Pitman & Sons, London, 1916). Roosevelt's call for National Efficiency is taken from his 'New Nationalism' speech delivered in Osawatomie, Kansas, 31 August 1910. It is reproduced in Hofstadter's *The Progressive Movement* (details above). Pinchot's views are from Ekirch's *Progressivism in America* (details above). Emerson's '100% Efficiency' motto is taken from Haber's *Efficiency and Uplift* (details above). Parsons' version of Weber's 'Wirtschaft and Gesellschaft' is published as 'The theory of Social and Economic Organization' (Free Press, New York, 1947). The historian surprised by the empirical nature of economists in early business schools is T.W. van Metre, see *A History of the Graduate School of Business Columbia University* (Columbia University Press, New York,

1954). The quotation from Schmalenbach is taken from Locke's *Management and Higher Education* (details above). The history of Columbia University referred to is van Metre's (details above). The 'other commentators' mentioned directly after this can be found in B.M. Gross (details above). Touraine's assessment of sociology's founders is from *Modernity and Cultural specificities* (details above). The alternative non-AASCB study of business school's is J.F. McKenna's 'Management education in the United States' (in W. Bryt (Ed.) *Management Education: An International Survey*, Routledge, London, 1989: 18–54). Michael Hitt outlines his vision in 'Twenty-first-century organizations: Business firms, business schools, and the Academy' (*Academy of Management Review* 23: 218–24, 1997). The textbook quotation after Dessler's is from Greenberg and Baron's *Behavior in Organizations* (details above). Ironically, General Lee's alternative curriculum was noted in L.F. Urwick's *Management Education in American Business* (American Management Association, New York, 1954) which contains an appendix listing Washington and Lee University's record of the details. Michael Hammer's Business Process Reengineering quotes in case box 3.2 are taken from M. Hammer and J. Champy's *Reengineering the Corporation: A Manifesto for Business Revolution* (Nicholas Brealy, London, 1993).

Answers to Case Box 3.2: statements 2, 3, 6, 7 and 10 are from Taylor: statements 1, 4, 5, 8 and 9 are from Hammer.

Chapter 4: Management's Historical Limits

The quotation that begins this chapter is from W.P. Hetrick and H.R. Lozada's 'Postmodernity, organization and hyperchange' (*Journal of Organizational Change Management*, 5: 5–7, 1992). The section on management's Modern 'processing' of Postmodernism contains quotations from: P.O. Berg's 'Postmodern management? From facts to fiction in theory and practice' (*Scandinavian Journal of Management*, 5: 201–17, 1989); J. Hassard's 'Postmodern organizational analysis: Towards a conceptual framework' (*Journal of Management Studies*, 31: 303–24, 1994); A.F. Firat's 'Postmodernism and the marketing organization' (*Journal of Organizational Change Management*, 5: 80–85, 1992); P. Wendt's 'Comment – Economics as a postmodern discourse (in W.J. Samuels (ed.), *Economics as Discourse – An Analysis of the Language of Economics*, pp. 47–64, Kluwer, Norwell, MA, 1992); M. Featherstone's *Postmodernism* (Sage, London, 1988); R. Chia's 'From modern to postmodern organizational analysis' (*Organization Studies*, 16: 579–604, 1995); D. Boje and R. Dennehy's *Managing in the Post-Modern World* (Kendall Hunt, Iowa city, 1993); S.R. Clegg's 'Postmodern management?' (*Journal of Organizational Change Management*, 5: 31–49, 1992); R. Cooper and G. Burrell's 'Modernism, postmodernism and organizational analysis: An introduction" (*Organization Studies*, 9: 91–112, 1988); G. Burrell's 'The absent centre: The neglect of philosophy in Anglo-American management theory'

(*Human Systems Management*, 8: 307–12, 1989); C.J-N. Despres's 'Culture, surveys and other obfuscations' (*Journal of Strategic Change*, 4: 65–75, 1995); K. Gergen and T.J. Thatchenkery's 'Organization science as social construction: Postmodern potentials' (*Journal of Applied Behavioral Science*, 32: 356–77, 1996) and 'Developing dialogue for discerning differences' (*Journal of Applied Behavioral Science*, 32: 428–33). The paper that praises Victor Vroom's 'Unconscious postmodernism', P. Carter and N. Jackson's 'Modernism, postmodernism and motivation, or why expectancy theory failed to come up to expectation,' is reproduced in J. Hassard and M. Parker's *Postmodernism and Organizations* (Sage, London, 1993). A good view of how the pop-management literature saw Postmodernism as a 'new buzzword' is provided by V. Yarwood's 'Welcome to tomorrow: A guide to coping with chaos' (*Management Magazine*, June, 32–8, 1994). The decision that Postmodernism is, in actual fact, nothing new and hence to be dismissed is outlined in M. Parker 'Getting down from the fence: A reply to Haridimos Tsoukas' (*Organization Studies*, 13: 643–9, 1992). This note was a follow-up to 'Post-modern organizations or postmodern organization theory' (*Organization Studies*, 13: 1–17, 1992).

Much of this chapter is based on the changing nature of words and meanings through history. It is thus indebted to perhaps the most valuable resource work in the English language, *The Complete Oxford English Dictionary*, now available on-line (www.oed.com).

The section 'The Organization as a Mechanical Organism' is developed further in 'The Ghost in the Organism' by S. Cummings and T. Thanem (forthcoming in *Organization Studies* de Gruyter, Berlin). G. Morgan's *Images of Organization* (Sage, Newbury Park, CA., 1986) was republished in 1997 to widespread acclaim. All of the material from *Images* commented on in this chapter is reproduced in the 1997 edition. M.J. Hatch's textbook is titled *Organization Theory, Modern, Symbolic and Postmodern Perspectives* (Oxford University Press, Oxford, 1997). *The Science of Life* was compiled by H.G. Wells, J. Huxley and G.P. Wells (Cassell, London, 1931). Insights into Cannon and Henderson's thinking may be found in H.J. Henderson's *Pareto's General Sociology: A Physiologist's Interpretation* (Macmillan, Cambridge, Mass., 1935); and W.B. Cannon's *Bodily Changes in Pain, Hunger, Fear and Rage* (Arno, New York, 1932). B.S. Heyl's 'The History of the Pareto Circle' (*Journal of the History of the Behavioral Sciences*, 41: 316–34, 1968) provides a good overview of the workings of the circle. March and Simon's words are taken from J.G. March and H. Simon's *Organizations* (Wiley, New York, 1958) and H. Simon's, *Administrative Behaviour: A Study in Decision-Making Processes in Administrative Organization* (Macmillan, New York, 1957). The definitions of 'organization' are taken from O. Sheldon's *The Philosophy of Management* (Pitman, New York, 1924); E.H. Schein's *Organizational Psychology* (Prentice-Hall, Englewood Cliffs, NJ, 1965); S.P. Robbins' *Essentials of Organizational Behavior* (Prentice-Hall, Englewood

Cliffs, NJ, 1965); and S. Fineman and Y. Gabriel's 'Paradigms of organizations: An exploration in textbook rhetorics' (*Organization*, 1: 375–99, 1994). Mintzberg's 'organisms' are lauded by S.P. Robbins in *Organization Theory – Structure, Design, and Applications* (Prentice-Hall, Englewood Cliffs, NJ, 1990) and developed in H. Mintzberg's *Structure in Fives: Designing Effective Organizations* (Prentice-Hall, Englewood Cliffs, NJ, 1983). As we left the twentieth century, Ikujiro Nonaka's excellent works on the 'knowledge organization', employing an organic approach that appears to place learning above efficiency, did seem to offer hope that management was beginning to question these fundaments. However, even with Nonaka's work, the diagrammatic perspective is one that reduces and synthesizes organic behaviour into essential functions. 'SECI, *Ba* and leadership: A unified model of dynamic knowledge creation', illustrates Nonaka's diagrammatic synthe-ses of organic thought processes (I. Nonaka, R. Toyama and N. Konno, *Long Range Planning*, 33: 5–34, 2000).

The quotation at the head of 'The Object of Culture' section is from M. Casson's *The Economics of Business Culture* (Clarendon, Oxford, 1991). A.L. Wilkins and W.G. Ouchi's 'Efficient cultures: Exploring the relationship between culture and organizational performance' was published in *Administrative Science Quarterly* (28: 468–81, 1983). Those who warned against treating 'culture' as a discrete 'object' include A.M. Pettigrew ('On studying organizational cultures', *Administrative Science Quarterly*, 24: 570–80, 1979); T.E. Deal and A.A. Kennedy ('Culture: A new look through old lenses', *Journal of Applied Behavioral Science*, 19: 498–505, 1983); and T.J. Peters and R.H. Waterman (*In Search of Excellence*, Warners, New York, 1982). Edgar Schein's 'foundational' views on culture can be read in 'Coming to a new awareness of organizational culture' (*Sloan Management Review*, 25: 3–16, 1984); *Organizational Culture and Leadership* (Jossey-Bass, San Francisco, CA, 1985); 'Organizational culture' (*American Psychologist*, 45: 109–19, 1990); and 'Culture: the missing concept in organizational studies' (*Administrative Science Quarterly*, 41: 229–41, 1996). The two textbook ques-tionnaires referred to are from S. Robbins' *Organizational Behaviour – Concepts, Controversies and Applications* (Prentice-Hall, Englewood Cliffs, NJ, 1993) and J. Greenberg and R.A. Baron's *Behavior in Organizations: Understanding and Managing the Human Side of Work* (Prentice-Hall, Englewood Cliffs, NJ, 1995). The two 'more detailed approaches' are P. McDonald and J. Gandz's 'Getting value from shared values' (*Organizational Dynamics*, 21: 64–77, 1992) and R.H. Migloire and R.T. Martin's 'Use of a cor-porate culture index for strategic planning' (*Journal of Strategic Change*, 3: 95–105, 1994). R.R. Blake and J.S. Mouton's *How to Assess the Strengths and Weaknesses of a Business Enterprise* was first published in 1972 (Scientific Methods Inc., Austin, TE). G.S. Saffold's 'Culture traits, strength, and organizational performance: moving beyond "strong" culture' (*Academy of Management Review*, 13: 546–58, 1988) is a good overview of the 'strong culture hypothesis', while D. Meyerson and J. Martin's 'Cultural change: An integration of three different views' (*Journal of Management Studies*, 24: 623–47, 1987) looks at how culture has generally been seen by management as an 'integrating mechanism'. On the way in which Weber's view on the importance of culture have been overlooked by management, see S.R. Clegg's 'Postmodernism and postmodernity in organizational analysis' (*Journal of Organizational Change Management*, 5: 8–25, 1992).

The analysis of centralization versus decentralization using Derrida is developed in more detail in S. Cummings' 'Centralization and Decentralization: The Never-ending Story of Separation and Betrayal' (*Scandinavian Journal of Management*, 11: 103–117, 1995). The dialogue from Malcolm X is taken from *By Any Means Necessary: The Trials and Tribulations of the Making of Malcolm X* (S. Lee, Vintage, London, 1993).

'The External Expert Consultant and One-best Way Solutions' begins with ideas from A. MacIntyre's *After Virtue – A Study in Moral Theory* (Duckworth, London, 1981). On the rise of 'expert advisors' in Modernity see A. Giddens' *Modernity and Self-identity: Self and Society in the Late Modern Age* (Polity, Cambridge, 1991); M. Foucault's *The Birth of the Clinic* (Vintage, New York, 1975); and P. Feyerabend's *Farewell to Reason* (Verso, London, 1987). On the spread of outside consultants being 'bought in' from the outside, see D. Knights and G. Morgan's 'Strategic discourse and subjectivity: Towards a critical analysis of corporate strategy in organizations' (*Organization Studies*, 12: 251–73, 1991); J. Micklethwaite and A. Wooldridge's *The Witchdoctors: What the Management Gurus are Saying, Why it Matters, and How to Make Sense of it* (Heinemann, London, 1996); and G. Younge's 'Called to Account' (*Guardian*, 30 August 1999). Also well worth watching in this respect is the 1999 Channel 4 documentary series on the rise of management consultants entitled *Masters of the Universe. What is Enlightenment?* by Immanuel Kant, is available in *On History* (Bobbs-Merrill, New York, 1963).

Direct references not attributable to the above chapter lists are as follows. The lengthy 'impoverished state of affairs' quotation is taken from R. Chia (details above). The bracketed 'recent new management directions' are from 'Hard-nosed executives are turning to the world of creative talent in a pragmatic attempt to improve efficiency' (*The Guardian*, 30 September 2000), and 'Timely return of the people's business guru' (*The Times*, 14 September 2000).

Maslow's ideas can be found in 'A theory of human motivation' (*Psychological Review*, 50: 370–396), although it was the interpretations of others that led to the triangular view taking hold. *The Oxford Dictionary of the Business World* is published by Oxford University Press (Oxford, 1993). Elton Mayo's classic work is *The Human Problems of an Industrial Civilization* (Macmillan, New York, 1933). Munsterberg' *Psychology of Industrial Efficiency* was published by Houghton Mifflin (Boston MA, 1918). *The International Encyclopedia of Business and Management* is edited by M. Warner (Routledge, London, 1997). *The Science of Life* is by H.G. Wells, J. Huxley and G.P. Wells (Cassell, London, 1931).

The long quotation that begins the 'Building on the Modern mechanical organism' sub-section is from Arthur Koestler's *Ghost in the Machine* (Hutchinson, London, 1967). The 'leading undergraduate text' is J. Greenberg and R.A. Baron's *Behavior in organizations* (details above). Pascale and Athos and Peters and Austin's descriptions of cultural dimensions as 'techniques' are from R.T. Pascale and A.G. Athos *The Art of Japanese Management* (Simon & Schuster, New York, 1981), and T.J. Peters and N. Austin *A Passion for Excellence* (Random House, New York, 1985). Hofstede's ideas, referred to in Case Box 4.2, can be found in his *Culture and Organizations: Software of the Mind* (McGraw-Hill, New York, 1991).

The quote from Colin Carnall, which begins 'Centralization or Decentralization', is from his *Managing Change in Organizations* (Prentice Hall, London, 1990). The 'gushing' quotation from the UK 'excellence' study is from W. Goldsmith and D. Clutterbuck's *The Winning Streak Workout Book* (Weidenfeld and Nicholson, London, 1985). The quotes that follows it from the New Zealand 'excellence' study are taken from K. Inkson and B. Henshall's *Theory K – The Key to Excellence in NZ Management* (Bateman, Auckland, 1986). J. Naisbett's ideas are found in his *Megatrends* (Warner, New York, 1982). P. Drucker's contribution is from *The Concept of the Corporation* (Mentor, New York, 1964); and the text-book excerpt that follows this is from *Understanding Organizational Behaviour* by R.E. Callahan, C.P. Fleenor and H.R. Knudson (Merrill, Colombus OH, 1986).

Reporting on the anger towards the PETA poster and praise for Jesus as a management consultant can be found in 'Catholics half vegetarian Jesus poster campaign' (*Times*, 21 October 1999) and 'Disciples don suits for Christian poster campaign' (*Independent*, 16 September 1999). Shapiro and Kellaway's words are taken from the *Master's of the Universe* video (details above). Drucker's views on the central importance of management in a free civilized society may be seen in his introduction to *The Practice of Management* (Butterworth Heinemann, Oxford, 1989).

Part II: ReCreating Strategy

Warren Buffet's quotation and the ensuing German Telecoms example is taken from 'Best practice does not equal best strategy' by P.M. Nattermann (*McKinsey Quarterly*, Vol. 2, 2000).

Chapter 5: ReConceptualizing Business Ethics

The report 'Profits and Principles – Does There Have to be a Choice?' from which the quotation in the first paragraph in this chapter is taken, was published by Royal Dutch Shell in 1997.

A more academic critique of the limits of business ethics is provided in S. Cummings' 'The resurfacing of self-aesthetics as an alternative to business ethics' (in *The Aesthetic Organization*, S. Linstead and H. Hopfl (eds); Sage, Newbury Park, CA, pp. 212–27, 2000). B. Kjønstad and H. Willmott's 'Business ethics: Restrictive or empowering?' (*Journal of Business Ethics*, 14: 445–64, 1995) is another good critique of how business ethics are used only to provide general boundaries rather than something that might be developed individually. G. Starling's 'Business ethics and Nietzsche' (*Business Horizons*, May/June, 2–12, 1997) provides another, very entertaining, alternative perspective to business ethics.

The Blackwell Encyclopedic Dictionary of Business Ethics is edited by P.H. Werhane and R.E. Freeman (Blackwell, Cambridge, MA, 1997). Other good examples of how business ethics tend to be conceived of only from a *deontic* or external perspective can be found in T. Donaldson's *Corporations and Morality* (Prentice-Hall, Englewood Cliffs, NJ, 1982); T.L. Beauchamp and N.E. Bowie's *Ethical Theory and Business* (Prentice-Hall, Englewood Cliffs, NJ, 1993); and The Economist's *Pocket Strategy* (Penguin, Harmondsworth, UK, 1994). P. Primeaux and J. Stieber have published a wealth of material on how economic efficiency provides the measures of business ethics, including *Profit Maximization: The Ethical Mandate of Business* (Austin & Winfield, San Francisco, CA, 1995) and 'Managing business ethics and opportunity costs' (*Journal of Business Ethics*, 16: 835–42, 1997).

E. Steinberg's 'The defects of stakeholder theory' (*Corporate Governance Quarterly Research and Theory Papers*, 5(1), Oxford: Blackwell, 1997) is a good overview of views against adopting stakeholder-based approaches given their limitations. The debates raised here are developed further in the 1999 edition of *The Academy of Management Review* (Vol. 24, no. 2). Scott Adam's views on mission statements are taken from *The Dilbert Principle* (Boxtree Press, London, 1997).

Foucault's interest in ethics is described in M. Gardiner's 'Foucault, ethics and dialogue' (*History of the Human Sciences*, 9: 27–46, 1996). Aristotle's *Ethics*, often published as *The Nichomachean Ethics*, is available in a number of formats, including *Aristotle: Ethics* (Penguin Classics, Harmondsworth, 1976). J. Urmson's *Aristotle's Ethics* (Blackwell, Oxford, 1988) is a good academic summary of some of Aristotle's key themes and differences relative to Modern thinking. The connection between the thoughts of Foucault, Aristotle, Nietzsche and Diogenes is covered in J. Miller's *The Passion of Michel Foucault* (Simon & Shuster, New York, 1993). Gilles Deleuze's understanding of Foucault's work in terms of the four folds of subjectivity is developed in *Foucault* (University of Minnesota Press, Minneapolis, MN, 1988).

The emergence of our understanding of mission is outlined in S. Cummings and J. Davies' 'Mission, Vision, Fusion' (*Long Range Planning*, 27: 147–150, 1994). The Ashridge Mission Model is developed in A. Campbell, D. Yeung and M. Devine's *A Sense of Mission* (FT/Pitman, London, 1993).

The Soul of the New Consumer by David Lewis and Darren Bridger is published by Nicholas Brearley (London, 2001).

The notion of ethos can be connected to emergent ideas relating to corporate identity, M. Schultz, M.J. Hatch and M.H. Larsen's *The Expressive Organization – Linking Identity, Reputation and the Corporate Brand* (Oxford University Press, Oxford, 2000) is an excellent collection of new thinking on this theme.

Direct references not attributable to the above chapter lists are as follows. The introductory quotation from Herbert Simon is from *Administrative Behavior: A Study of Decision-making Processes in Administration* (Macmillan, New York, 1957). Milton Friedman's views on business ethics have been widely stated and are backed up in Peter Drucker's *Management Tasks and Responsibilities* (Butterworth-Heinemann, London, 1973). The quotes about individual managers not being able to create morality are from Beauchamp and Bowie (details above) and J.W. Collins ('Is business ethics an oxymoron?' *Business Horizons*, September/October: 1–8, 1994) respectively. The commentary on the 'Tylenol capsule crisis' is from *Strategic Management: Strategy Formulation and Implementation* by J.A. Pearce and R.B. Robinson, Jr. (Irwin, Homewood IL, 1988). Scott Adams on mission statements is from *The Dilbert Principle* (London: Boxtree, 1996) and his adventures as management consultant, Ray Mebert, are reported in 'Dilbert creator slips into fake role' (*Austin American Statesman*, 16 November 1997). S.S. Mathur and A. Kenyon's *Creating Value: Shaping Tomorrow's Business* is published by Butterworth-Heinemann (London, 1997). For editorial commentary on BP becoming 'Beyond Petroleum' see *The Daily Telegraph* (6 August 2000) or New Zealand's *Otago Daily Times* (7 August 2000). On Body Shop's particular *telos* leading it to take a strong interest in its home town see 'Body Shop founders take a philanthropic approach to financial troubles at home' (*Financial Times*, 1 February 1999).

Chapter 6: ReConceiving Strategy

If this book is being used for teaching purposes, this chapter can easily be used as a springboard to incorporate more material on strategic management and spend more sessions looking at a variety of additional strategy frameworks. Hence, the list below pays specific attention to material that could be used as additional course reading and sources that provide more potentially useful strategy frameworks and ideas than space (and copyright requirements) allow here.

The Alps story at the head of this chapter is taken from a chapter by Karl Weick entitled 'Substitutes for strategy' in *The Competitive Challenge* edited by J. Teece (Balinger, Cambridge, MA, 1987). The 'despairing editorial' quoted is Milan Zeleny's 'The Fall of Strategic Planning' (*Human Systems Management*, Vol. 16, 1997).

To see how the shape and perspective of Modern scientific reasoning and bureaucracy influenced what are considered to be the origins of corporate strategy, read the introductions to A. Chandler's influential *Strategy and Structure* (MIT Press, Cambridge, MA, 1962) and *The Visible Hand* (Harvard University Press, Cambridge, MA, 1977). Also, look at I. Ansoff's *Corporate Strategy* (McGraw-Hill, New York, 1965) and his introductory chapter of *Business Strategy*, 'Toward a Strategic Theory of the Firm' (Penguin, Harmondsworth, 1969). K. Andrews' *Harvard Business Review* article 'Toward Professionalism in Business Management' (Mar./Apr., 1969) comments on how Chandlerian bureaucracy and the organization of business schools inform one another.

Michael Porter's 'Value Chain', 'Generic Strategy Matrix' and '5-Forces of Industry' are built up in *Competitive Strategy: Techniques for Analyzing Industries and Competitors* (Free Press, New York) and *Competitive Advantage* (Free Press, New York, 1985).

A good overview of the 'turf wars' between strategy's bottom-up emergence and top-down planning schools can be gained by reading the exchange between Henry Mintzberg and Igor Ansoff in Vols 11 and 12 (1990 and 1991) of the *Strategic Management Journal* (an edited version is reproduced in *Strategy: Process, Content, Context*, B. De Wit and R. Meyer (eds), ITP, London, 1994). Mintzberg's *The Rise and Fall of Strategic Planning* (Free Press, New York, 1994) develops the 'anti-establishment' argument further. Ralph Stacey's *Dynamic Strategic Management for the 1990s* (Kogan Page, London, 1990) and Gary Hamel's 'Strategy as Revolution' (*Harvard Business Review*, July/Aug., 69–82, 1996) are perhaps even more vitriolic. Michael Porter's *Harvard Business Review* article 'What is Strategy?' (Nov./Dec., 1996) shows the 'empire striking back'.

E.E. Chaffe's evolutionary view of strategy schools is presented in 'Three Models of Strategy' (*Academy of Management Review*, 10: 89–98, 1985). Mintzberg's bemoaning of strategy's ancient military heritage can be seen in 'Crafting Strategy' (*Harvard Business Review*, Jul-/Aug., 66–75, 1987). Ghemawat's quotation is taken from *Strategy and the Business Landscape* (Addison-Wesley, Reading, MA, 1999).

For a further discussion on how Premodern thinking influences the Greek's approach to strategy, see S. Cummings' 'Pericles of Athens – Drawing from the Essence of Strategy' (*Business Horizons*, Jan./Feb.: 22–27, 1995).

I am indebted to David Stewart at Victoria University of Wellington for the $C + M = SP$ equation (he claims to be indebted to Sebastian Green, now at the University of Cork, for it). *Mr. Beck's Underground Map* (K. Garland, Capital Transport Publishing, London, 1994) is a fascinating account of one man's vision and the uniquely memorable London Tube map. Taking this non-representative 'osteopathic' grids-plus-networks approach enables many more frameworks to be utilized than the ones covered here. Three good sources of further traditional strategy models are: S. Harding and T. Long's *MBA Management Models* (Gower, London, 1998) which provides one-page synopses of all the most referred to frameworks; J. Kay's *Foundations of Corporate Success* (Oxford University Press, Oxford, 1993), which has a particularly concise section on the history of the main strategy frames at the end; and B. De Wit and R. Meyer's *Strategy: Process, Content, Context – An International Perspective* (ITP, London, 1998), which is an excellent compilation of the key articles. Books that further develop the idea of using many perspectives to think strategy rather than seeking to identify the best or 'cutting edge' include H. Mintzberg, B. Awstrand and J. Lampel's *The Strategy Safari: A Guided Tour through the Jungles of Strategic Management* (Prentice-Hall, Englewood Cliffs, NJ, 1998) and S. Cummings and D. Wilson's (eds) *Images of Strategy* (Blackwell, Oxford, Forthcoming). For a more academic overview, try A. Pettigrew, H. Thomas and R. Whittington's (eds) *Handbook of Strategy and Management* (Sage, London, 2001).

Key works on resource-based theory include: B. Wernerfelt's 'A resource-based view of the firm' (*Strategic Management Journal*, 5: 171–80, 1984) and J.B. Barney's 'Organizational culture: Can it be a source of sustained competitive advantage?' (*Academy of Management Review*, 11: 656–65, 1986) and 'Firm resources and sustained competitive advantage' (*Journal of Management*, 17: 99–120, 1991).

It can be useful to flesh out how 'non-rational' forces like history, political networks and culture can steer strategy from the bottom-up by viewing one of the many fly-on-the-wall documentaries that have become popular lately and then analyse them using historical or political frameworks. The oldest, and in many ways still the best, is *Decision Steel* (still available on video from Granada Television). It focuses on the political machinations involved in deciding whether to purchase plants using a new form of steel-making in Scotland. Frameworks like those in J. Pfeffer's *Power in Organizations* (Pitman, London, 1981), R. Greene's *The 48 Laws of Power* (Penguin, Harmondsworth, 2000) and in G. Morgan's 'Interests, Conflict and Power: Organizations as Political Systems' (*Images of Organization*, Sage, Beverley Hills, CA, 1997); and ideas like the Icarus Paradox (that those that get very good at doing something gradually question the assumptions upon which that behaviour is based less and less, until their downfall), 'escalation' (that as more and more energy is invested into making a decision the possibility of 'doing nothing', even if this may be the best thing to do, decreases), and Foucault's seeing power in terms of networks seen and unseen, can all be gainfully employed to analyse cases like this. Given the lack of frameworks that have sprung directly from the emergence perspective, borrowing frameworks from other spheres such as these enables seeing how strategy can be influenced from places other than the top in ways that are not what we might call 'rational', for better and for worse.

With regard to the *Networks Shape Strategy* Case Box, William Foote Whyte or Foucault's original studies are worth reading. Whyte's groundbreaking ethnography is written up in *Street Corner Society* (Chicago University Press, Chicago, 1981). Foucault describes his relational understanding of power in a chapter entitled 'Method' in his *History of Sexuality: An Introduction* (Random House, New York, 1978). However, if these are unobtainable (or if you find them impenetrable), then a more recent *Harvard Business Review* article 'Informal networks: The company behind the chart' (in D. Krackhardt and J.R. Hanson, *Harvard Business Review*, July/Aug., 1993) addresses most of the ideas expressed here.

Continuing on the network theme, R. Norman and R. Ramirez's 'From value chain to value constellation' (*Harvard Business Review*, July–August, pp. 65–77, 1993) is a useful means of developing the themes touched on in the 'Modern Grids and Premodern Webs' section of this chapter; as are Rosabeth Moss Kanter's views on cooperation being just as important as competition (for example, *Rosabeth Moss Kanter on the Frontiers of Management*, Harvard Business School, Boston, MA, 1997) and a number of works that have been written on the pros and cons of strategic alliances (De Wit and Meyer, see above, contains a good sample).

David Knights' article critiquing Porter's models in particular and simple theories of management in general is 'Changing Spaces: The Disruptive Impact of a new Epistemological Location for the Study of Management' (*Academy of Management Review*, Vol. 17: 514–536, 1992). Nigella Lawson's words come from *How to Eat – The Pleasures and Principles of Good Food* (Random House, London, 1999).

P.A. Argenti and J. Forman's 'The Communication Advantage: A Constituency-focussed Approach to Formulating and Implementing Strategy' (in M. Schultz, M.J. Hatch and M.H. Larsen's *The Expressive Organization – Linking Identity, Reputation and the Corporate Brand*, Oxford University Press, Oxford, pp. 233–45, 2000) provides an interesting further point of connection between Aristotle's thinking and strategy formulation.

Direct references not attributable to the above chapter lists are as follows. Michael Foucault's introductory quotation is from *Power/knowledge, Selected Interviews and Other Writings 1972–77* (Harvester Press, Brighton, 1980). The quote from Michael Craig-Martin that follows is from *Building Tate Modern: Herzog & De Meuron Transforming Giles Gilbert Scott*, by Rowan Moore, Raymund Ryan, Adrian Hardwicke and Gavin Stamp (Tate Gallery Publishing, London, 2000). The 'despairing editorial' excerpt is from M. Zeleny, 'The fall of strategic planning' (*Human Systems Management*, 16: 77–9, 1997). Peter Drucker's 1959 'Long range planning' is published in *Management Science* (5: 238–49). The teaching text definition of strategy is from Pearce and Robinson's *Strategic Management* (details above). Hamel and Prahalad's ideas with regard to strategic intent can be found in G. Hamel and C.K. Prahalad 'Strategic intent' (*Harvard Business Review*, May/June: 63–76, 1989). R. Pascale's 'bottom-up' perspective is described in 'Perspectives on strategy: the real story behind Honda's success' (*California Management Review*, 26: 47–72, 1984). P. Ghemawat's *Strategy and the Business Landscape* is published by Addison-Wesley (Reading MA, 1999). Xenophon's description of a strategist is from *Memorabila*, 3.1, and Plato's introduction to section 3 is from *Phaedrus* (many translations of both are available). The Herzog & be Meuron quotation at the head of section 4 was part of an opening exhibition for the Tate Bankside Gallery in 2000 (further details can be found in *Building Tate Modern*, details above).

Chapter 7: ReGenerating Change

The inaugural special issue of *The Academy of Management Executive* was published in February 1987. The 'transformation process' featured at the bottom of Figure 7.1 is from this journal. The diagram above it is from D. Nadler and M. Tushman's 'A Model for Diagnosing Organizational Behavior' (*Organizational Dynamics*, Autumn: 35–51, 1980). J.P. Kotter's model is from 'Leading Change: Why Transformation Efforts Fail' (*Harvard Business Review*, Mar./Apr.: 59–67, 1995). A. Pettigrew and R. Whipp's ideas are from their book *Managing Change for Competitive Success* (Blackwell, Oxford, 1991) and L. Greiner's are taken from 'Evolution and Revolution as Organizations Grow' (*Harvard Business Review*, July/Aug.: 37–46). An alternative 'Postmodern' assessment of change can be found in R. Chia's 'A 'rhizomic' model of organizational change and transformation: perspective from a metaphysics of change' (*British Journal of Management* 10: 209–227, 1999). The other sources mentioned in this chapter are covered in more detail in 'Toward *Demokratia*: Myth and the Management of Change in Ancient Athens' (S. Cummings and J. Brocklesby, *Journal of Organizational Change Management*, 10: 71–95, 1997).

This last paper also provides a fuller assessment of Kleisthenes' reconfiguration of Athens. For further reading on this topic C. Fornara and L. Samons'

Athens from Cleisthenes to Pericles (University of California Press, Berkeley, CA, 1991) has some interesting stuff on Kleisthenes' 'vision'; D. Whitehead's *The Demes of Attica* (Princeton University Press, Princeton, NJ, 1986), is a good assessment of the structural configuration of Athens; and E. Kearn's 'Change and Continuity in Religious Structures After Cleisthenes' (P.A. Cartledge and F.D. Harvey (eds) *Crux*, Imprint, London, 1985) is very good on the 'mythological' configuration. F. Nietzsche's quotes are from *The Birth of Tragedy* (Doubleday, New York, 1956). M. Heidegger's notion of 'Throwness' is developed in *Being and Time* (Blackwell, Oxford, 1962). *Being-in-the-world: A Commentary on Heidegger's Being and Time, Division 1* (MIT Press, Cambridge, MA, 1991) by H.L. Dreyfus provides an excellent analysis of the idea.

The state of strategy and the 're-emergence' of 'strategic agility' is discussed by H. Mintzberg, R. Pascale, M. Goold and R. Rumelt in 'The "Honda Effect" Revisited' (*California Management Review*, vol. 38, 1996). Other works mentioned in the concluding part of this chapter are Mintzberg's *The Strategy Safari: A Guided Tour Through the Jungles of Strategic Management* (Prentice-Hall, Englewood Cliffs, NJ, 1998) and 'Organigraphs: Drawing how Companies Really Work' (*Harvard Business Review*, Sept./Oct., 1999); C. Bartlett and S. Ghoshal's *The Individualized Corporation* (HarperBusiness, New York, 1997); 'Best practice does not equal best strategy' by P.M. Nattermann (*McKinsey Quarterly*, Vol. 2, 2000); and S.W. Floyd and B. Wooldridge's *Building Strategy from the Middle* (Sage, Beverly Hills, CA, 2000). On the re-emergence of Aristotelian themes in management see H. Tsoukas and S. Cummings' 'Marginalization and Recovery: The Emergence of Aristotelian Themes in Organization Studies' (*Organization Studies*, 18: 655–83, 1997).

Direct references not attributable to the above chapter lists are as follows. M. Beer 'Revitalizing organizations: Change process and emergent model' (*Academy of Management Executive*, 1: 51–6, 1987). H.J. Johansson, P. McHugh, A.J. Pendlebury and W.A. Wheeler III *Business Process Reengineeing: Breakpoint Strategies for Market Dominance* (Wiley, New York, 1993). N. Tichy *Handbook for Revolutionaries* (Doubleday, New York, 1993). N. Tichy and S. Sherman *Control your Destiny or Someone Else Will* (Doubleday, New York, 1993). D. Stace and D. Dunphy *Beyond the Boundaries: Leading and Recreating the Successful Organization* (McGraw-Hill, Sydney, 1994). R.N. Beck 'Visions, values, and strategies: Changing attitudes and culture' (*Academy of Management Executive*, 1: 33–40, 1987). M. Chen 'Sun Tzu's thinking and contemporary business' (*Business Horizons*, Mar/April: 42–8, 1994). T.J. Larkin and S. Larkin 'Reaching and changing frontline employees' (*Harvard Business Review*, May/June: 95–104, 1996). R.D. Smither *The Psychology of Work and Human Performance* (Harper-Collins, New York, 1994). K. Lewin *Field Theory in Social Science* (Harper, New York, 1951). R.R. Blake and J.S. Mouton *How to Assess the Strengths and Weaknesses of a Business Enterprise*

(Scientific Methods Inc, Austin TE, 1972). *The Dynamics of Planned change* is by R. Lippet, J. Watson and B. Westley (Harcourt and Brace, New York, 1958). N.M. Tichy and M.A. Devanna's change ideas are from *The Transformational Leader* (Wiley, New York, 1990). *Better Change: Best Practices for Transforming your Organization* is by the Price Waterhouse Change Integration Team (Irwin, New York, 1995). (Plutarch's biography of Theseus is from *Parallel Lives* (details above). The Sophocles quotation that begins section 3 is from *Antigone* (many translations are available). Special thanks to Matt Hardisty and Stacy Arnold for their diagrams reproduced in Figure 7.5.

Index